Phyllis E. Anderson.

Rousseau: "We
were born free,
but everywhere
we are in
chains".

THE IMPORTANCE OF LIVING

WORKS BY LIN YUTANG

In English (except the last five titles, the following are published in Shanghai by the Commercial Press).

Letters of a Chinese Amazon
Readings in Modern Journalistic Prose
The Little Critic : First Series (1930-1932)
The Little Critic: Second Series (1933-1935)
Confucius Saw Nancy (*A Drama*) and Essays about Nothing
A Nun of Taishan and Other Translations
Kaiming English Books
Kaiming English Grammar Based on Notional Categories
A History of the Press and Public Opinion in China
My Country and My People
The Importance of Living

In Chinese

Philological Essays (*Yüyenhsüeh Lunts'ung*)
Skirmishes (*Chienfuchi*)
The Lone Wayfarer (*Tahuangchi*)
It Seems to Me (*Woti Hua*), 2 vols.

LIN YUTANG

THE IMPORTANCE OF LIVING

WILLIAM · HEINEMANN · LTD
LONDON   ::   TORONTO

FIRST PUBLISHED MAY 1938
REPRINTED JULY, SEPTEMBER, NOVEMBER, DECEMBER 1938
JANUARY, MAY 1939, MARCH, OCTOBER 1940

PRINTED IN GREAT BRITAIN AT THE WINDMILL PRESS
KINGSWOOD, SURREY

It is not truth that makes man great, but man that makes truth great.

CONFUCIUS

Only those who take leisurely what the people of the world are busy about can be busy about what the people of the world take leisurely.

CHANG CH'AO

From the gate-posts of a house in
Szechuan —
"In the evening mists, far removed from city
                                    clamour,
Under the bamboos of my planting, I play my
                                    lute,
In the quiet of my life's ending, duty
                                    completed,
With my sons and sons' children, rest,
                        and make poems."

————

" 'shua' means to play, to linger, to idle, to
neglect one's duty, to amuse neself. It expresses
that blessed philosophy of leisure; it is an
attitude of mind remaining from the old days
of indolence, when for those who had plenty
of money, and for sages and poets to whom
money was nothing, there was really nothing to
do from morning till evening but gaze at the
bamboos reflected in the tranquil river,

smoke the water-pipe, drink tea from covered teacups and wine from minute wine-cups, and lie in the shade exchanging gossip and composing balanced couplets with his friends."

————

PREFACE

THIS IS A PERSONAL TESTIMONY, *a testimony of my own experience of thought and life. It is not intended to be objective and makes no claim to establish eternal truths. In fact I rather despise claims to objectivity in philosophy; the point of view is the thing. I should have liked to call it "A Lyrical Philosophy," using the word "lyrical" in the sense of being a highly personal and individual outlook. But that would be too beautiful a name and I must forgo it, for fear of aiming too high and leading the reader to expect too much, and because the main ingredient of my thought is matter-of-fact prose, a level easier to maintain because more natural. Very much contented am I to lie low, to cling to the soil, to be of kin to the sod. My soul squirms comfortably in the soil and sand and is happy. Sometimes when one is drunk with this earth, one's spirit seems so light that he thinks he is in heaven. But actually he seldom rises six feet above the ground.*

I should have liked also to write the entire book in the form of a dialogue like Plato's. It is such a convenient form for personal, inadvertent disclosures, for bringing in the significant trivialities of our daily life, above all for idle rambling about the pastures of sweet, silent thought. But somehow I have not done so. I do not know why. A fear, perhaps, that this form of literature being so little in vogue to-day, no one probably would read it, and a writer after all wants to be read. And when I say dialogue, I do not mean answers and questions like newspaper interviews, or those leaders chopped up into short paragraphs; I mean really good, long, leisurely discourses extending several pages at a stretch, with many detours, and coming back to the original point of discussion by a short cut at the most unexpected spot, like a man returning home by climbing over a hedge, to the surprise of his walking companion. Oh, how I love to reach home by climbing over the back fence, and to travel on bypaths! At least my companion will grant that I am familiar with the way home and with the surrounding countryside . . . But I dare not.

[vii]

PREFACE

I am not original. The ideas expressed here have been thought and expressed by many thinkers of the East and West over and over again; those I borrow from the East are hackneyed truths there. They are, nevertheless, my ideas; they have become a part of my being. If they have taken root in my being, it is because they express something original in me, and when I first encountered them, my heart gave an instinctive assent. I like them as ideas and not because the person who expressed them is of any account. In fact, I have travelled the bypaths in my reading as well as in my writing. Many of the authors quoted are names obscure and may baffle a Chinese professor of literature. If some happen to be well known, I accept their ideas only as they compel my intuitive approval and not because the authors are well known. It is my habit to buy cheap editions of old, obscure books and see what I can discover there. If the professors of literature knew the sources of my ideas, they would be astounded at the Philistine. But there is a greater pleasure in picking up a small pearl in an ash-can than in looking at a large one in a jeweller's window.

I am not deep and not well-read. If one is too well-read, then one does not know right is right and wrong is wrong. I have not read Locke or Hume or Berkeley, and have not taken a college course in philosophy. Technically speaking, my method and my training are all wrong, because I do not read philosophy, but only read life at first hand. That is an unconventional way of studying philosophy—the incorrect way. Some of my sources are: Mrs. Huang, an amah in my family who has all the ideas that go into the breeding of a good woman in China; a Soochow boat-woman with her profuse use of expletives; a Shanghai street car conductor; my cook's wife; a lion cub in the zoo; a squirrel in Central Park in New York; a deck steward who made one good remark; that writer of a column on astronomy (dead for some ten years now); all news in boxes; and any writer who does not kill our sense of curiosity in life or who has not killed it in himself . . . how can I enumerate them all?

Thus deprived of academic training in philosophy, I am less scared to write a book about it. Everything seems clearer and simpler for it, if that is any compensation in the eyes of orthodox philosophy. I doubt it. I know there will be complaints that my words are not long enough, that I make things too easy to understand, and finally that I lack cautiousness, that I do not whisper low and trip with mincing steps in the sacred mansions of philosophy, looking properly sacred as I ought to do. Courage seems to be the rarest of all virtues in a modern philosopher. But I have always wandered outside the precincts of philosophy and that gives me courage. There is a method of appealing to one's own intuitive judgment, of thinking out one's own ideas and forming one's own independent judgments, and confessing them in public with a childish impudence, and sure enough, some kindred souls in another corner of the world will agree with you. A person forming his ideas in this manner will often be astounded to discover how another writer said exactly the same things and felt exactly the same way, but perhaps expressed the ideas more easily and more gracefully. It is then that he discovers the ancient author and the ancient author bears him witness, and they become for ever friends in spirit.

There is therefore the matter of my obligations to these authors, especially my Chinese friends in spirit. I have for my collaborators in writing this book a company of genial souls, who I hope like me as much as I like them. For in a very real sense, these spirits have been with me, in the only form of spiritual communion that I recognize as real—when two men separated by the ages think the same thoughts and sense the same feelings and each perfectly understands the other. In the preparation of this book, a few of my friends have been especially helpful with their contributions and advice: Po Chüyi of the eighth century, Su Tungp'o of the eleventh, and that great company of original spirits of the sixteenth and seventeenth centuries—the romantic and voluble T'u Ch'ihshui, the playful, original Yüan Chunglang, the deep, magnificent Li Chowu, the sensitive and sophisticated Chang Ch'ao, the epicure Li Liweng, the happy and gay old hedonist Yüan Tsets'ai, and the bubbling, joking, effervescent Chin Shengt'an—unconventional souls all, men with too much independent judgment and too much feeling for things to be liked by the orthodox critics, men too good to be "moral" and too moral to be "good" for the Confucianists. The smallness of the select company has made the enjoyment of their presence all the more valued and sincere. Some of these may happen not to be quoted, but they are here with me in this book all the same. Their coming back to their own in China is only a matter of time. . . . There have been others, names less well known, but

PREFACE

no less welcome for their apt remarks, because they express my sentiments so well. I call them my Chinese Amiels—people who don't talk much, but always talk sensibly, and I respect their good sense. There are others again who belong to the illustrious company of "Anons" of all countries and ages, who in an inspired moment said something wiser than they knew, like the unknown fathers of great men. Finally there are greater ones still, whom I look up to more as masters than as companions of the spirit, whose serenity of understanding is so human and yet so divine, and whose wisdom seems to have come entirely without effort because it has become completely natural. Such a one is Chuangtse, and such a one is T'ao Yüanming, whose simplicity of spirit is the despair of smaller men. I have sometimes let these souls speak directly to the reader, making proper acknowledgment, and at other times, I have spoken for them while I seem to be speaking for myself. The older my friendship with them, the more likely is my indebtedness to their ideas to be of the familiar, elusive and invisible type, like parental influence in a good family breeding. It is impossible to put one's finger on a definite point of resemblance. I have also chosen to speak as a modern, sharing the modern life, and not only as a Chinese; to give only what I have personally absorbed into my modern being, and not merely to act as a respectful translator of the ancients. Such a procedure has its drawbacks, but on the whole, one can do a more sincere job of it. The selections are therefore as highly personal as the rejections. No complete presentation of any one poet or philosopher is attempted here, and it is impossible to judge of them through the evidences on these pages. I must therefore conclude by saying as usual that the merits of this book, if any, are largely due to the helpful suggestions of my collaborators, while for the inaccuracies, deficiencies and immaturities of judgment, I alone am responsible.

Again I owe my thanks to Mr. and Mrs. Richard J. Walsh, first, for suggesting the idea of the book, and secondly, for their useful and frank criticism. I must also thank Mr. Hugh Wade for co-operating on preparing the manuscript for the press and on the proofs, and Miss Lillian Peffer for making the Index.

LIN YUTANG

New York City
July 30, 1937

CONTENTS

[xi]

CONTENTS

[xii]

CONTENTS

CONTENTS

THE IMPORTANCE OF LIVING

CHAPTER ONE

The Awakening

I. APPROACH TO LIFE

IN WHAT FOLLOWS I am presenting the Chinese point of view, because I cannot help myself. I am interested only in presenting a view of life and of things as the best and wisest Chinese minds have seen it and expressed it in their folk wisdom and their literature. It is an idle philosophy born of an idle life, evolved in a different age, I am quite aware. But I cannot help feeling that this view of life is essentially true, and since we are alike under the skin, what touches the human heart in one country touches all. I shall have to present a view of life as Chinese poets and scholars evaluated it with their common sense, their realism and their sense of poetry. I shall attempt to reveal some of the beauty of the pagan world, a sense of the pathos and beauty and terror and comedy of life, viewed by a people who have a strong feeling of the limitations of our existence, and yet somehow retain a sense of the dignity of human life.

The Chinese philosopher is one who dreams with one eye open, who views life with love and sweet irony, who mixes his cynicism with a kindly tolerance, and who alternately wakes up from life's dream and then nods again, feeling more alive when he is dreaming than when he is awake, thereby investing his waking life with a dream-world quality. He sees with one eye closed and with one eye opened the futility of much that goes on around him and of his own endeavours, but barely retains enough sense of reality to determine to go through with it. He is seldom disillusioned because he has no illusions, and seldom disappointed because he never had extravagant hopes. In this way his spirit is emancipated.

For, after surveying the field of Chinese literature and philosophy, I come to the conclusion that the highest ideal of Chinese culture has always been a man with a sense of *detachment* (*takuan*) toward life based on a sense of wise disenchantment. From this detachment comes *high-mindedness* (*k'uanghuai*), a high-mindedness which enables one to go through life with tolerant irony and escape the temptations of fame and wealth and achievement, and eventually makes him take what comes. And from this detachment arise also his sense of freedom, his love of vagabondage and his pride and nonchalance. It is only with this sense of freedom and nonchalance that one eventually arrives at the keen and intense joy of living.

It is useless for me to say whether my philosophy is valid or not for the Westerner. To understand Western life, one would have to look at it as a Westerner-born, with his own temperament, his bodily attitudes and his own set of nerves. I have no doubt that American nerves can stand a good many things that Chinese nerves cannot stand, and *vice versa*. It is good that it should be so —that we should all be born different. And yet it is all a question of relativity. I am quite sure that amidst the hustle and bustle of American life, there is a great deal of wistfulness, of the divine desire to lie on a plot of grass under tall beautiful trees of an idle afternoon and *just do nothing*. The necessity for such common cries as "Wake up and live" is to me a good sign that a wise portion of American humanity prefer to dream the hours away. The American is after all not as bad as all that. It is only a question whether he will have more or less of that sort of thing, and how he will arrange to make it possible. Perhaps the American is merely ashamed of the word "loafing" in a world where everybody is doing something, but somehow, as sure as I know he is also an animal, he likes sometimes to have his muscles relaxed, to stretch on the sand, or to lie still with one leg comfortably curled up and one arm placed below his head as his pillow. If so, he cannot be very different from Yen Huei, who had exactly that virtue and whom Confucius desperately admired among all his disciples. The only thing I desire to see is that he be honest about it, and that he proclaim to the world that he likes it when he likes it, that it is not when he is working in the office but when he is lying idly on the sand that his soul utters, "Life is beautiful."

We are, therefore, about to see a philosophy and art of living as the mind of the Chinese people as a whole has understood it. I am inclined to think that, in a good or bad sense, there is nothing like it in the world. For here we come to an entirely new way of looking at life by an entirely different type of mind. It is a truism to say that the culture of any nation is the product of its mind. Consequently, where there is a national mind so racially different and historically isolated from the Western cultural world, we have the right to expect new answers to the problems of life, or what is better, new methods of approach, or, still better, a new posing of the problems themselves. We know some of the virtues and deficiencies of that mind, at least as revealed to us in the historical past. It has a glorious art and a contemptible science, a magnificent common sense and an infantile logic, a fine womanish chatter about life and no scholastic philosophy. It is generally known that the Chinese mind is an intensely practical, hard-headed one, and it is also known to some lovers of Chinese art that it is a profoundly sensitive mind; by a still smaller proportion of people it is accepted as also a profoundly poetic and philosophical mind. At least the Chinese are noted for taking things philosophically, which is saying more than the statement that the Chinese have a great philosophy or have a few great philosophers. For a nation to have a few philosophers is not so unusual, but for a nation to take things philosophically is terrific. It is evident anyway that the Chinese as a nation are more philosophic than efficient, and that if it were otherwise, no nation could have survived the high blood-pressure of an efficient life for four thousand years. Four thousand years of efficient living would ruin any nation. An important consequence is that, while in the West the insane are so many that they are put in an asylum, in China the insane are so unusual that we worship them, as anybody who has a knowledge of Chinese literature will testify. And that, after all, is what I am driving at. Yes, the

Chinese have a light, an almost gay, philosophy, and the best proof of their philosophic temper is to be found in this wise and merry philosophy of living.

II. A PSEUDO-SCIENTIFIC FORMULA

Let us begin with an examination of the Chinese mental make-up which produced this philosophy of living: great realism, inadequate idealism, a high sense of humour, and a high poetic sensitivity to life and nature.

Mankind seems to be divided into idealists and realists, and idealism and realism are the two great forces moulding human progress. The clay of humanity is made soft and pliable by the water of idealism, but the stuff that holds it together is after all the clay itself, or we might all evaporate into Ariels. The forces of idealism and realism tug at each other in all human activities, personal, social and national, and real progress is made possible by the proper mixture of these two ingredients, so that the clay is kept in the ideal pliable, plastic condition, half moist and half dry, not hardened and unmanageable, nor dissolving into mud. The soundest nations, like the English, have realism and idealism mixed in proper porportions, like the clay which neither hardens and so gets past the stage for the artist's moulding, nor is so wishy-washy that it cannot retain its form. Some countries are thrown into perpetual revolutions because into their clay has been injected some liquid of foreign ideals which is not yet properly assimilated, and the clay is therefore not able to keep its shape.

A vague, uncritical idealism always lends itself to ridicule and too much of it might be a danger to mankind, leading it round in a futile wild-goose chase for imaginary ideals. If there were too many of these visionary idealists in any society or people, revolutions would be the order of the day. Human society would be like an idealistic couple for ever getting tired of one place and changing their residence regularly once every three months, for the simple reason that no one place is ideal and the place where one is not seems always better because one is not there. Very fortunately, man is also gifted with a sense of humour, whose function, as I conceive it, is to exercise criticism of man's dreams, and bring them in touch with the world of reality. It is important that man dreams, but it is perhaps equally important that he can laugh at his own dreams. That is a great gift, and the Chinese have plenty of it.

The sense of humour, which I shall discuss at more length in a later chapter, seems to be very closely related to the sense of reality, or realism. If the joker is often cruel in disillusioning the idealist, he nevertheless performs a very important function right there by not letting the idealist bump his head against the stone wall of reality and receive a ruder shock. He also gently eases the tension of the hot-headed enthusiast and makes him live longer. By preparing him for disillusion, there is probably less pain in the final impact, for a humorist is always like a man charged with the duty of breaking sad news gently to a dying patient. Sometimes the gentle warning from a humorist saves the dying patient's life. If idealism and disillusion must necessarily go together in this world, we must say that life is cruel, rather than the joker who reminds us of life's cruelty.

I have often thought of formulas by which the mechanism of human progress and historical change can be expressed. They seem to be as follows:

Reality   – Dreams = Animal Being
Reality   + Dreams = A Heart-ache (usually called Idealism)
Reality   + Humour = Realism (also called Conservatism)
Dreams – Humour = Fanaticism
Dreams + Humour = Fantasy
Reality   + Dreams + Humour = Wisdom

So then, wisdom, or the highest type of thinking, consists in toning down our dreams or idealism with a good sense of humour, supported by reality itself.

As pure ventures in pseudo-scientific formulations, we may proceed to analyse national characters in the following manner.

I say "pseudo-scientific" because I distrust all dead and mechanical formulas for expressing anything connected with human affairs or human personalities. Putting human affairs in exact formulas shows in itself a lack of the sense of humour and therefore a lack of wisdom. I do not mean that these things are not being done: they are. That is why we get so much pseudo-science to-day. When a psychologist can measure a man's I.Q. or P.Q.,[1] it is a pretty poor world, and specialists have risen to usurp humanized scholarship. But if we recognize that these formulas are no more than handy, graphic ways of expressing certain opinions, and so long as we don't drag in the sacred name of science to help advertise our goods, no harm is done. The following are my formulas for the characters of certain nations, entirely personal and completely incapable of proof or verification. Anyone is free to dispute them and change them or add his own, if he does not claim that he can prove his private opinions by a mass of statistical facts and figures. Let "R" stand for a sense of reality (or realism), "D" for dreams (or idealism), "H" for a sense of humour, and— adding one important ingredient—"S" for sensitivity.[2] And further let "4" stand for "abnormally high," "3" stand for "high," "2" for "fair," and "1" for "low," and we have the following pseudo-chemical formulas for the following national characters. Human beings and communities behave then differently according to their different compositions, as sulphates and sulphides or carbon monoxide and carbon dioxide behave differently from one another. For me, the interesting thing always is to watch how human communities or nations behave differently under identical conditions. As we cannot invent words like "humoride" and "humorate" after the fashion of chemistry, we may put it thus: "3 grains of Realism, 2 grains of Dreams, 2 grains of Humour and 1 grain of Sensitivity make an Englishman."[3]

[1] I am not objecting to the limited utility of intelligence tests but to their claims to mathematical accuracy or constant dependability as measures of human personality.

[2] In the sense of the French word *sensibilité*.

[3] Some might with good reason suggest the including of an "L" standing for logic or the rational faculty, as an important element in shaping human progress. This "L" will then often function or weigh against sensitivity, a direct perception of things. Such a formula might be attempted. For me personally, the role of the rational faculty in human affairs is rather low.

$$R_3D_2H_2S_1 = \text{The English}$$
$$R_2D_3H_3S_3 = \text{The French}$$
$$R_3D_3H_2S_2 = \text{The Americans}$$
$$R_3D_4H_1S_2 = \text{The Germans}$$
$$R_2D_4H_1S_1 = \text{The Russians}$$
$$R_2D_3H_1S_1 = \text{The Japanese}$$
$$R_4D_1H_3S_3 = \text{The Chinese}$$

I do not know the Italians, the Spanish, the Hindus and others well enough even to essay a formula on the subject, realizing that the above are shaky enough as they are, and in any case are enough to bring down a storm of criticism upon my head. Probably these formulas are more provocative than authoritative. I promise to modify them gradually for my own use as new facts are brought to my knowledge, or new impressions are formed. That is all they are worth to-day—a record of the progress of my knowledge and the gaps of my ignorance.

Some observations may be necessary. It is easy to see that I regard the Chinese as most closely allied to the French in their sense of humour and sensitivity, as is quite evident from the way the French write their books and eat their food, while the more volatile character of the French comes from their greater idealism, which takes the form of love of abstract ideas (recall the manifestos of their literary, artistic and political movements). "R_4" for Chinese realism makes the Chinese the most realistic people; "D_1" accounts for something of a drag in the changes in their pattern or ideal of life. The high figures for Chinese humour and sensitivity, as well as for their realism, are perhaps due to my too close association and the vividness of my impressions. For Chinese sensitivity, little justification is needed; the whole story of Chinese prose, poetry and painting proclaims it. . . . The Japanese and Germans are very much alike in their comparative lack of humour (such is the general impression of people), yet it is really impossible to give a "zero" for any one characteristic in any one nation, not even for idealism in the Chinese people. It is all a question of degree; such statements as a complete lack of this or that quality are not based on an intimate knowledge of the peoples. For this reason, I give the Japanese and the Germans "H_1" instead of "H_0," and I intuitively feel that I am right. But I do believe that the Japanese and the Germans suffer politically at present, and have suffered in the past, for lacking a better sense of humour. How a Prussian *Geheimrat* loves to be called a *Geheimrat*, and how he loves his buttons and metal pins! A certain belief in "logical necessity" (often "holy" or "sacred"), a tendency to fly too straight at a goal instead of circling around it, often carries one too far. It is not so much what you believe in that matters, as the way in which you believe it and proceed to translate that belief into action. By "D_3" for the Japanese I am referring to their fanatic loyalty to their emperor and to the state, made possible by a low mixture of humour. For idealism must stand for different things in different countries, as the so-called sense of humour really comprises a very wide variety of things. . . . There is an interesting tug between idealism and realism in America, both given high figures, and that produces the energy characteristic of the Americans. What American idealism is, I had better leave it to the Americans to find out; but they are always enthusiastic about something or other. A great deal of this idealism is noble, in the sense that the Americans are easily appealed to by noble ideals or noble words; but some of it is mere gullibility. The American sense of humour again means a different thing from the Continental sense of humour, but really I think that, such as it is (the love of fun and an innate, broad common sense), it is the greatest asset of the American nation. In the coming years of critical change, they will have great need of that broad common sense referred to by James Bryce, which I hope will tide them over these critical times. I give American sensitivity a low figure because of my impression that they can stand so many things. There is no use quarrelling about this, because we will be quarrelling about words. . . . The English seem to be on the whole the soundest race: contrast their "R_3D_2" with the French "R_2D_3." I am all for "R_3D_2." It bespeaks stability. The ideal formula for me would seem to be $R_3D_2H_3S_2$, for too much idealism or too much sensitivity is not a good thing, either. And if I give "S_1" for English sensitivity, and if that is too low, who is to blame for it except the English themselves? How can I tell whether the English ever feel anything—joy, happiness, anger, satisfaction—when they are determined to look so glum on all occasions?

We might apply the same formula to writers and poets. To take a few well-known types:

$$\begin{aligned}
\text{Shakespeare}[1] &= R_4D_4H_3S_4 \\
\text{Heine} &= R_3D_3H_4S_3 \\
\text{Shelley} &= R_1D_4H_1S_4 \\
\text{Poe} &= R_3D_4H_1S_4 \\
\text{Li Po} &= R_1D_3H_2S_4 \\
\text{Tu Fu} &= R_3D_3H_2S_4 \\
\text{Su Tungp'o} &= R_3D_2H_4S_3
\end{aligned}$$

These are no more than a few impromptu suggestions. But it is clear that all poets have a high sensitivity, or they wouldn't be poets at all. Poe, I feel, is a very sound genius, in spite of his weird, imaginative gift. Doesn't he love "ratiocination"?

So my formula for the Chinese national mind is:

$$R_4D_1H_3S_3$$

There we start with an "S_3," standing for high sensitivity, which guarantees a proper artistic approach to life and answers for the Chinese affirmation that this earthly life is beautiful and the consequent intense love of this life. But it signifies more than that; actually it stands for the artistic approach even to philosophy. It accounts for the fact that the Chinese philosopher's view of life is essentially the poet's view of life, and that, in China, philosophy is married to poetry rather than to science as it is in the West. It will become amply clear from what follows that this high sensitivity to the pleasures and pains and flux and change of the

---

[1] I have hesitated a long time between giving Shakespeare "S_4" and "S_3". Finally his "Sonnets" decided it. No school-teacher has experienced greater fear and trembling in grading a pupil than I in trying to grade Shakespeare.

colours of life is the very basis that makes a light philosophy possible. Man's sense of the tragedy of life comes from his sensitive perception of the tragedy of a departing spring, and a delicate tenderness toward life comes from a tenderness toward the withered blossoms that bloomed yesterday. First the sadness and sense of defeat, then the awakening and the laughter of the old rogue-philosopher.

On the other hand, we have "R_4" standing for intense realism, which means an attitude of accepting life as it is and of regarding a bird in the hand as better than two in the bush. This realism, therefore, both reinforces and supplements the artist's affirmation that this life is transiently beautiful, and it all but saves the artist and poet from escaping from life altogether. The Dreamer says "Life is but a dream," and the Realist replies, "Quite correct. And let us live this dream as beautifully as we can." But the realism of one awakened is the poet's realism and not that of the business man, and the laughter of the old rogue is no longer the laughter of the young go-getter singing his way to success with his head up and his chin out, but that of an old man running his finger through his flowing beard, and speaking in a soothingly low voice. Such a dreamer loves peace, for no one can fight hard for a dream. He will be more intent to live reasonably and well with his fellow-dreamers. Thus is the high tension of life lowered.

But the chief function of this sense of realism is the elimination of all non-essentials in the philosophy of life, holding life down by the neck, as it were, for fear that the wings of imagination may carry it away to an imaginary and possibly beautiful, but unreal, world. And after all, the wisdom of life consists in the elimination of non-essentials, in reducing the problems of philosophy to just a few—the enjoyment of the home (the relationship between man and woman and child), of living, of Nature and of culture—and in showing all the other irrelevant scientific disciplines and futile chases after knowledge to the door. The problems of life for the Chinese philosopher then become amazingly few and simple. It means also an impatience with metaphysics and with the pursuit of knowledge that does not lead to any practical bearing on life itself. And it also means that every human activity, whether the acquiring of knowledge or the acquiring of things, has to be submitted immediately to the test of life itself and of its subserviency to the end of living. Again—and here is a significant result—the end of living is not some metaphysical entity—but just living itself.

Gifted with this realism, and with a profound distrust of logic and of the intellect itself, philosophy for the Chinese becomes a matter of direct and intimate feeling of life itself, and refuses to be encased in any system. For there is a robust sense of reality, a sheer animal sense, a spirit of reasonableness which crushes reason itself and makes the rise of any hard-and-fast philosophic system impossible. There are the three religions of China, Confucianism, Taoism and Buddhism, all magnificent systems in themselves, and yet robust common sense dilutes them all and reduces them all into the common problem of the pursuit of a happy human life. The mature Chinese is always a person who refuses to think too hard or to believe in any single idea or faith or school of philosophy whole-heartedly. When a friend of Confucius told him that he always thought three times before he acted, Confucius wittily replied, "To think twice is quite enough." A follower of a school of philosophy is but a student of philosophy, but a man is a student, or perhaps a master, of life.

The final product of this culture and philosophy is this: in China, as compared with the West, man lives a life closer to nature and closer to childhood, a life in which the instincts and the emotions are given free play and emphasized against the life of the intellect, with a strange combination of devotion to the flesh and arrogance of the spirit, of profound wisdom and foolish gaiety, of high sophistication and childish naïveté. I would say, therefore, that this philosophy is characterized by: first, a gift for seeing life whole in art; secondly, a conscious return to simplicity in philosophy; and thirdly, an ideal of reasonableness in living. The end product is, strange to say, a worship of the poet, the peasant and the vagabond.

III. THE SCAMP AS IDEAL

To me, spiritually a child of the East and the West, man's dignity consists in the following facts which distinguish man from animals. First, that he has a playful curiosity and a natural genius for exploring knowledge; second, that he has dreams and a lofty idealism (often vague, or confused, or cocky, it is true, but nevertheless worthwhile); third, and still more important, that he is able to correct his dreams by a sense of humour, and thus restrain his idealism by a more robust and healthy realism; and finally, that he does not react to surroundings mechanically and uniformly as animals do, but possesses the ability and the freedom to determine his own reactions and to change surroundings at his will. This last is the same as saying that human personality is the last thing to be reduced to mechanical laws; somehow the human mind is for ever elusive, uncatchable and unpredictable, and manages to wriggle out of mechanistic laws or a materialistic dialectic that crazy psychologists and unmarried economists are trying to impose upon him. Man, therefore, is a curious, dreamy, humorous and wayward creature.

In short, my faith in human dignity consists in the belief that man is the greatest scamp on earth. Human dignity must be associated with the idea of a scamp and not with that of an obedient, disciplined and regimented soldier. The scamp is probably the most glorious type of human being, as the soldier is the lowest type, according to this conception. It seems in my last book, *My Country and My People*, the net impression of readers was that I was trying to glorify the "old rogue." It is my hope that the net impression of the present one will be that I am doing my best to glorify the scamp or vagabond. I hope I shall succeed. For things are not so simple as they sometimes seem. In this present age of threats to democracy and individual liberty, probably only the scamp and the spirit of the scamp alone will save us from becoming lost as serially numbered units in the masses of disciplined, obedient, regimented and uniformed coolies. The scamp will be the last and most formidable enemy of dictatorships. He will be the champion of human dignity and individual freedom, and will be the last to be conquered. All modern civilization depends entirely upon him.

Probably the Creator knew well that, when He created man upon this earth, He was producing a scamp, a brilliant scamp, it is true, but a scamp nonetheless. The scamp-like qualities of man are, after all, his most hopeful qualities. This scamp that the Creator has produced is undoubtedly a brilliant chap. He is still a very unruly and awkward adolescent, thinking himself greater and wiser than he really is, still full of mischief and naughtiness and love of a free-for-all. Nevertheless, there is so much good in him that the Creator might still be willing to pin on him His hopes, as a father sometimes pins his hopes on a brilliant but somewhat erratic son of twenty. Would He be willing some day to retire and turn over the management of this universe to this erratic son of His? I wonder. . . .

Speaking as a Chinese, I do not think that any civilization can be called complete until it has progressed from sophistication to unsophistication, and made a conscious return to simplicity of thinking and living, and I call no man wise until he has made the progress from the wisdom of knowledge to the wisdom of foolishness, and become a laughing philosopher, feeling first life's tragedy and then life's comedy. For we must weep before we can laugh. Out of sadness comes the awakening and out of the awakening comes the laughter of the philosopher, with kindliness and tolerance to boot.

The world, I believe, is far too serious, and being far too serious, it has need of a wise and merry philosophy. The philosophy of the Chinese art of living can certainly be called the "gay science," if anything can be called by that phrase used by Nietzsche. After all, only a gay philosophy is profound philosophy; the serious philosophies of the West haven't even begun to understand what life is. To me personally, the only function of philosophy is to teach us to take life more lightly and gaily than the average business man does, for no business man who does not retire at fifty, if he can, is in my eyes a philosopher. This is not merely a casual thought, but is a fundamental point of view with me. The world can be made a more peaceful and more reasonable place to live in only when men have imbued themselves in the light gaiety of this spirit. The modern man takes life far too seriously, and because he is too serious, the world is full of troubles. We ought, therefore, to take time to examine the origin of that attitude which will make possible a whole-hearted enjoyment of this life and a more reasonable, more peaceful and less hot-headed temperament.

I am perhaps entitled to call this the philosophy of the Chinese people rather than of any one school. It is a philosophy that is greater than Confucius and greater than Laotse, for it transcends these and other ancient philosophers; it draws from these fountain springs of thought and harmonizes them into a whole, and from the abstract outlines of their wisdom it has created an art of living in the flesh, visible, palpable and understandable by the common man. Surveying Chinese literature, art and philosophy as a whole, it has become quite clear to me that the philosophy of a wise disenchantment and a hearty enjoyment of life is their common message and teaching—the most constant, most characteristic and most persistent refrain of Chinese thought.

CHAPTER TWO

Views of Mankind

I. CHRISTIAN, GREEK AND CHINESE

THERE ARE SEVERAL VIEWS of mankind, the traditional
Christian theological view, the Greek pagan view, and the
Chinese Taoist-Confucianist view. (I do not include the
Buddhist view because it is too sad.) Deeper down in their
allegorical sense, these views after all do not differ so much from
one another, especially when the modern man with better biological and anthropological knowledge gives them a broader interpretation. But these differences in their original forms exist.

The traditional, orthodox Christian view was that man was
created perfect, innocent, foolish and happy, living naked in the
Garden of Eden. Then came knowledge and wisdom and the Fall
of Man, to which the sufferings of man are due, notably (1) work
by the sweat of one's brow for man, and (2) the pangs of labour
for women. In contrast with man's original innocence and perfection, a new element was introduced to explain his present imperfection, and that is of course the Devil, working chiefly through
the body, while his higher nature works through the soul. When
the "soul" was invented in the history of Christian theology I am
not aware, but this "soul" became a something rather than a function, an entity rather than a condition, and it sharply separated
man from the animals, which have no souls worth saving. Here
the logic halts, for the origin of the Devil had to be explained,
and when the medieval theologians proceeded with their usual
scholastic logic to deal with the problem, they got into a quandary.
They could not have very well admitted that the Devil, who was
Not-God, came from God Himself, nor could they quite agree

that in the original universe, the Devil, a Not-God, was co-eternal
with God. So in desperation they agreed that the Devil must
have been a fallen angel, which rather begs the question of the
origin of evil (for there still must have been another Devil to
tempt this fallen angel), and which is therefore unsatisfactory, but
they had to leave it at that. Nevertheless from all this followed
the curious dichotomy of the spirit and the flesh, a mythical conception which is still quite prevalent and powerful to-day in
affecting our philosophy of life and happiness.[1]

Then came the Redemption, still borrowing from the current
conception of the sacrificial lamb, which went still farther back
to the idea of a God Who desired the smell of roast meat and
could not forgive for nothing. From this Redemption, at one
stroke a means was found by which all sins could be forgiven,
and a way was found for perfection again. The most curious
aspect of Christian thought is the idea of perfection. As this
happened during the decay of the ancient worlds, a tendency grew
up to emphasize the after-life, and the question of salvation
supplanted the question of happiness or simple living itself. The
notion was how to get away from this world alive, a world which
was apparently sinking into corruption and chaos and doomed.
Hence the overwhelming importance attached to immortality.
This represents a contradiction of the original Genesis story that
God did not want man to live for ever. The Genesis story of the
reason why Adam and Eve were driven out of the Garden of Eden
was not that they had tasted of the Tree of Knowledge, as is
popularly conceived, but the fear lest they should disobey a second
time and eat of the Tree of Life and live for ever:

And the Lord God said, Behold, the man is become as one of
us, to know good and evil: and now, *lest he put forth his hand, and
take also of the tree of life, and eat, and live for ever*:

[1] It is a happy fact that with the progress of modern thought, the Devil is the first
to be thrown overboard, I believe that of a hundred *liberal* Christians to-day who
still believe in God in some form or other, not more than five believe in a real Devil,
except in a figurative sense. Also the belief in a real Hell is disappearing before the
belief in a real Heaven.

Therefore the Lord God sent him forth from the Garden of Eden, to till the ground from whence he was taken.

So he drove out the man; and he placed at the east of the Garden of Eden cherubim, and a flaming sword which turned every way, *to keep the way of the tree of life.*

The Tree of Knowledge seemed to be somewhere in the centre of the garden, but the Tree of Life was near the eastern entrance, where, for all we know, cherubim are still stationed to guard the approach by men.

All in all, there is still a belief in total depravity, that enjoyment of this life is sin and wickedness, that to be uncomfortable is to be virtuous, and that on the whole man cannot save himself except by a greater power outside. The doctrine of sin is still the basic assumption of Christianity as generally practised to-day, and Christian missionaries trying to make converts generally start out by impressing upon the party to be converted a consciousness of sin and of the wickedness of human nature (which is, of course, the *sine qua non* for the need of the ready-made remedy which the missionary has up his sleeve). All in all, you can't make a man a Christian unless you first make him believe he is a sinner. Someone has said rather cruelly, "Religion in our country has so narrowed down to the contemplation of sin that a respectable man does not any longer dare to show his face in the church."

The Greek pagan world was a different world by itself and therefore their conception of man was also quite different. What strikes me most is that the Greeks made their gods like men, while the Christians desired to make men like the gods. That Olympian company is certainly a jovial, amorous, loving, lying, quarrelling and vow-breaking, petulant lot; hunt-loving, chariot-riding and javelin-throwing like the Greeks themselves—a marrying lot, too, and having unbelievably many illegitimate children. So far as the difference between gods and men is concerned, the gods merely had divine powers of hurling thunderbolts in heaven and raising vegetation on earth, were immortal, and drank nectar instead of wine—the fruits were pretty much the same. One feels one can be intimate with this crowd, can go hunting with a knapsack on one's back with Apollo or Athene, or stop Mercury on the way and chat with him as with a Western Union messenger boy, and if the conversation gets too interesting, we can imagine Mercury saying, "Yeah. Okay. Sorry, but I'll have to run along and deliver this message at 72nd Street." The Greek men were not divine, but the Greek gods were human. How different from the perfect Christian God! And so the gods were merely another race of men, a race of giants, gifted with immortality, while men on earth were not. Out of this background came some of the most inexpressibly beautiful stories of Demeter and Proserpina and Orpheus. The belief in the gods was taken for granted, for even Socrates, when he was about to drink hemlock, proposed a libation to the gods to speed him on his journey from this world to the next. This was very much like the attitude of Confucius. It was necessarily so in that period; what attitude toward man and God the Greek spirit would take in the modern world there is unfortunately no chance of knowing. The Greek pagan world was not modern, and the modern Christian world is not Greek. That's the pity of it.

On the whole, it was accepted by the Greeks that man's was a mortal lot, subject sometimes to a cruel Fate. That once accepted, man was quite happy as he was, for the Greeks loved this life and this universe, and were interested in understanding the good, the true and the beautiful in life, besides being fully occupied in scientifically understanding the physical world. There was no mythical "Golden Period" in the sense of the Garden of Eden, and no allegory of the Fall of Man; the Hellenes themselves were but human creatures transformed from pebbles picked up and thrown over their shoulders by Deucalion and his wife Pyrrha, as they were coming down to the plain after the Great Flood. Diseases and cares were explained comically; they came through the uncontrollable desire of a young woman to open and see a box of jewels—Pandora's Box. The Greek fancy was beautiful. They took human nature largely as it was: the Christians might say they were "resigned" to the mortal lot. But it was so beautiful to be mortal: there was free room for the exercise of understanding and the free, speculative spirit. Some of the Sophists thought man's nature good, and some thought man's nature bad, but there wasn't the sharp contradiction of Hobbes and Rousseau. Finally, in Plato, man was seen to be a compound of desires, emotions, and thought, and ideal human life was the living together in harmony of these three parts of his being under the guidance of wisdom or true understanding. Plato thought "ideas" were immortal, but individual souls were either base or noble, according as they loved justice, learning, temperance and beauty or not. The soul also acquired an independent and immortal existence in Socrates; as we are told in "Phaedo," "When the soul exists in herself, and is released from the body, and the body is released from the soul, what is this but death?" Evidently the belief in immortality of the human soul is something which the Christian, Greek, Taoist and Confucianist views have in common. Of course this is nothing to be jumped at by modern believers in the immortality of the soul. Socrates' belief in immortality would probably mean nothing to a modern man, because many of his premises in support of it, like re-incarnation, cannot be accepted by the modern man.

The Chinese view of man also arrived at the idea that man is the Lord of the Creation ("Spirit of the Ten Thousand Things"), and in the Confucianist view, man ranks as the equal of heaven and earth in the "Trio of Geniuses." The background was animistic: everything was alive or inhabited by a spirit—mountains, rivers, and everything that reached a grand old age. The winds and thunder were spirits themselves; each of the great mountains and each river was ruled by a spirit who practically owned it; each kind of flower had a fairy in heaven attending to its seasons and its welfare, and there was a Queen of All Flowers whose birthday came on the twelfth day of the second moon; every willow tree, pine tree, cypress, fox or turtle that reached a grand old age, say over a few hundred years, acquired by that very fact immortality and became a "genius."

With this animistic background, it is natural that man is also considered a manifestation of the spirit. This spirit, like all life in the entire universe, is produced by the union of the male, active, positive or *yang* principle, and the female, passive, negative or *yin* principle—which is really no more than a lucky, shrewd guess at positive and negative electricity. When this spirit becomes incarnated in a human body, it is called *p'o;* when unattached to a body and floating about as spirit it is called *hwen*. (A man of forceful personality or "spirits" is spoken of as having a lot of *p'oli*, or *p'o*-energy.) After death, this *hwen* continues to wander about. Normally it does not bother people, but if no one buries and offers sacrifices to the deceased, the spirit becomes a "wandering ghost," for which reason an All Souls' Day is set apart on the fifteenth day of the seventh moon for a general sacrifice to those drowned in water or dead and unburied in a strange land. Also, if the deceased was murdered or died suffering a wrong, the sense of injustice in the ghost compels it to hang about and cause trouble until the wrong is avenged and the spirit is satisfied. Then all trouble is stopped.

While living, man, who is spirit taking shape in a body, necessarily has certain passions, desires, and a flow of "vital energy," or in more easily understood English, just "nervous energy." In and for themselves, these are neither good nor bad, but just something given and inseparable from the characteristically human life. All men and women have passions, natural desires and noble ambitions, and also a conscience; they have sex, hunger, fear, anger, and are subject to sickness, pain, suffering and death. Culture consists in bringing about the expression of these passions and desires in harmony. That is the Confucianist view, which believes that by living in harmony with this human nature given us, we can become the equals of heaven and earth, as quoted at the end of Chapter VI. The Buddhists, however, regard the mortal desires of the flesh essentially as the medieval Christians did—they are a nuisance to be done away with. Men and women who are too intelligent, or inclined to think too much, sometimes accept this view and become monks and nuns; but on the whole, Confucian good sense forbids it. Then also, with a Taoistic touch, beautiful and talented girls suffering a harsh fate are regarded as "fallen fairies," punished for having mortal thoughts or some neglect of duty in heaven and sent down to this earth to live through a predestined fate of mortal sufferings.

Man's intellect is considered as a flow of energy. Literally this intellect is "spirit of a genius" (*chingshen*), the word "genius" being essentially taken in the sense in which we speak of fox genii, rock genii and pine genii. The nearest English equivalent is, as I have suggested, "vitality" or "nervous energy," which ebbs and flows at different times of the day and of the person's life. Every man born into this world starts out with certain passions and desires and this vital energy, which run their course in different cycles through childhood, youth, maturity, old age and death. Confucius said, "When young, beware of fighting; when strong, beware of sex; and when old, beware of possession," which simply means that a boy loves fighting, a young man loves women, and an old man loves money.

Faced with this compound of physical, mental and moral assets, the Chinese takes an attitude toward man himself, as toward all other problems, which may be summed up in the phrase: "Let us be reasonable." This is an attitude of expecting neither too much nor too little. Man is, as it were, sandwiched between heaven and earth, between idealism and realism, between lofty thoughts and the baser passions. Being so sandwiched is the very essence of humanity; it is human to have thirst for knowledge and thirst for water, to love a good idea and a good dish of pork with bamboo shoots, and to admire a beautiful saying and a beautiful woman. This being the case, our world is necessarily an imperfect world. Of course there is a chance of taking human society in hand and making it better, but the Chinese do not expect either perfect peace or perfect happiness. There is a story illustrating this point of view. There was a man who was in Hell and about to be reincarnated, and he said to the King of Re-incarnation, "If you want me to return to the earth as a human being, I will go only on my own conditions." "And what are they?" asked the King. The man replied, "I must be born the son of a cabinet minister and father of a future 'Literary Wrangler' (the scholar who comes out first at the national examinations). I must have ten thousand acres of land surrounding my home and fish-ponds and fruits of every kind and a beautiful wife and pretty concubines, all good and loving to me, and rooms stocked to the ceiling with gold and pearls and cellars stocked full of grain and trunks chock-full of money, and I myself must be a Grand Councillor or a Duke of the First Rank and enjoy honour and prosperity and live until I am a hundred years old." And the King of Re-incarnation replied, "If there was such a lot on earth, I would go and be re-incarnated myself, and not give it to you!"

The reasonable attitude is, since we've got this human nature, let's start with it. Besides, there is no escaping from it anyway. Passions and instincts are originally good or originally bad, but there is not much use talking about them, is there? On the other hand, there is the danger of our being enslaved by them. Just stay in the middle of the road. This reasonable attitude creates such a *forgiving* kind of philosophy that, at least to a cultured, broad-minded scholar who lives according to the spirit of reasonableness, any human error or misbehaviour whatsoever, legal or moral or political, which can be labelled as "common human nature" (more literally, "man's normal passions"), is excusable. The Chinese go so far as to assume that Heaven or God Himself is quite a reasonable being, that if you live reasonably, according to your best lights, you have nothing to fear, that peace of conscience is the greatest of all gifts, and that a man with a clear conscience need not be afraid even of ghosts. With a reasonable God supervising the affairs of reasonable and some unreasonable beings, everything is quite all right in this world. Tyrants die; traitors commit suicide; the grasping fellow is seen selling his property; the sons of a powerful and rich collector of curios (about whom tales are told of grasping greed or extortion by power) are seen selling out the collection on which their father spent so much thought and trouble, and these same curios are now being dispersed among other families; murderers are found out and dead and wronged women are avenged. Sometimes, but quite seldom, an oppressed person cries out, "Heaven has no eyes!" (Justice is blind.) Eventually, both in Taoism and in Confucianism, the conclusion and highest goal of this philosophy is complete understanding of and harmony with nature, resulting in what I may call "reasonable naturalism," if we must have a term for classification. A reasonable naturalist then settles down to this life with a sort of animal satisfaction. As Chinese illiterate women put it, "Others gave birth to us and we give birth to others. What else are we to do?"

There is a terrible philosophy in this saying, "Others gave birth to us and we give birth to others." Life becomes a biological procession and the very question of immortality is side-tracked. For that is the exact feeling of a Chinese grandfather holding his grandchild by the hand and going to the shops to buy some candy, with the thought that in five or ten years he will be returning to his grave or to his ancestors. The best that we can hope for in this life is that we shall not have sons and grandsons of whom we need be ashamed. The whole pattern of Chinese life is organized according to this one idea.

II. EARTH-BOUND

The situation then is this: man wants to live, but he still must live upon this earth. All questions of living in heaven must be brushed aside. Let not the spirit take wings and soar to the abode of the gods and forget the earth. Are we not mortals, condemned to die? The span of life vouchsafed us, threescore and ten, is short enough, if the spirit gets too haughty and wants to live for ever, but on the other hand, it is also long enough, if the spirit is a little humble. One can learn such a lot and enjoy such a lot in seventy years, and three generations is a long, long time to see human follies and acquire human wisdom. Anyone who is wise and has lived long enough to witness the changes of fashion and morals and politics through the rise and fall of three generations should be perfectly satisfied to rise from his seat and go away saying, "It was a good show," when the curtain falls.

[25]

For we are of the earth, earth-born and earth-bound. There is nothing to be unhappy about the fact that we are, as it were, delivered upon this beautiful earth as its transient guests. Even if it were a dark dungeon, we still would have to make the best of it; it would be ungrateful of us not to do so when we have, instead of a dungeon, such a beautiful earth to live on for a good part of a century. Sometimes we get too ambitious and disdain the humble and yet generous earth. Yet a sentiment for this Mother Earth, a feeling of true affection and attachment, one must have for this temporary abode of our body and spirit, if we are to have a sense of spiritual harmony.

We have to have, therefore, a kind of animal scepticism as well as animal faith, taking this earthly life largely as it is. And we have to retain the wholeness of nature that we see in Thoreau who felt himself kin to the sod and partook largely of its dull patience, in winter expecting the sun of spring, who in his cheapest moments was apt to think that it was not his business to be "seeking the spirit," but as much the spirit's business to seek him, and whose happiness, as he described it, was a good deal like that of the woodchucks. The earth, after all, is real, as the heaven is unreal: how fortunate is man that he is born between the real earth and the unreal heaven!

Any good practical philosophy must start out with the recognition of our having a body. It is high time that some among us made the straight admission that we are animals, an admission which is inevitable since the establishment of the basic truth of the Darwinian theory and the great progress of biology, especially bio-chemistry. It was very unfortunate that our teachers and philosophers belonged to the so-called intellectual class, with a characteristic professional pride of intellect. The men of the spirit were as proud of the spirit as the shoemaker is proud of leather. Sometimes even the spirit was not sufficiently remote and abstract and they had to use the words "essence" or "soul" or "idea," writing them with capital letters to frighten us. The human body was distilled in this scholastic machine into a spirit, and the spirit was further concentrated into a kind of essence, forgetting that even alcoholic drinks must have a "body"—mixed with plain water—if they are to be palatable at all. And we poor laymen were supposed to drink that concentrated quintessence of spirit. This over-emphasis on the spirit was fatal. It made us war with our natural instincts, and my chief criticism is that it made a whole and rounded view of human nature impossible. It proceeded also from an inadequate knowledge of biology and psychology, and of the place of the senses, emotions and, above all, instincts in our life. Man is made of flesh and spirit both, and it should be philosophy's business to see that the mind and body live harmoniously together, that there be a reconciliation between the two.

III. SPIRIT AND FLESH

The most obvious fact which philosophers refuse to see is that we have got a body. Tired of seeing our mortal imperfections and our savage instincts and impulses, sometimes our preachers wish that we were made like angels, and yet we are at a total loss to imagine what the angels' life would be like. We either give the angels a body and a shape like our own—except for a pair of wings—or we don't. It is interesting that the general conception of an angel is still that of a human body with a pair of wings. I sometimes think that it is an advantage even for angels to have a body with the five senses. If I were to be an angel, I should like to have a schoolgirl complexion, but how am I going to have a schoolgirl complexion without a skin? I still should like to drink a glass of tomato juice or iced orange juice, but how am I going to appreciate iced orange juice without having thirst? And how am I going to enjoy food, when I am incapable of hunger? How would an angel paint without pigment, sing without the hearing of sounds, smell the fine morning air without a nose? How would he enjoy the immense satisfaction of scratching an itch, if his skin doesn't itch? And what a terrible loss in the capacity for happiness that would be! Either we have to have bodies and have all our bodily wants satisfied, or else we are pure spirits and have no satisfactions at all. All satisfactions imply want.

[27]

I sometimes think what a terrible punishment it would be for a ghost or an angel to have no body, to look at a stream of cool water and have no feet to plunge into it and get a delightful cooling sensation from it, to see a dish of Peking or Long Island duck and have no tongue to taste it, to see crumpets and have no teeth to chew them, to see the beloved faces of our dear ones and have no emotions to feel toward them. Terribly sad it would be if we should one day return to this earth as ghosts and move silently into our children's bedroom, to see a child lying there in bed and have no hands to fondle him and no arms to clasp him, no chest for his warmth to penetrate to, no round hollow between cheek and shoulder for him to nestle against, and no ears to hear his voice.

A defence of the angels-without-bodies theory will be found to be most vague and unsatisfying. Such a defender might say, "Ah, yes, but in the world of spirit, we don't need such satisfactions." "But what instead have you got?" Complete silence; or perhaps, "Void—Peace—Calm." "What then do you gain by it?" "Absence of work and pain and sorrow." I admit such a heaven has a tremendous attraction to galley slaves. Such a negative ideal and conception of happiness is dangerously near to Buddhism and is ultimately to be traced to Asia (Asia Minor, in this case) rather than Europe.

Such speculations are necessarily idle, but I may at least point out that the conception of a "senseless spirit" is quite unwarranted, since we are coming more and more to feel that the universe itself is a sentient being. Perhaps motion rather than standing still will be a characteristic of the spirit, and one of the pleasures of a bodiless angel will be to revolve like a proton around a nucleus at the speed of twenty or thirty thousand revolutions a second. There may be a keen delight in that, more fascinating than a ride on a Coney Island scenic railway. It will certainly be a kind of *sensation*. Or perhaps the bodiless angel will dart like light or cosmic rays in ethereal waves around curved space at the rate of 183,000 miles per second. There must still be spiritual pigments for the angels to paint and enjoy *some* form of creation, ethereal vibrations for the angels to feel as tone and sound and colour, and ethereal breeze to brush against the angels' cheeks. Otherwise spirit itself would stagnate like water in a cesspool, or feel like men on a hot, suffocating summer afternoon without a whiff of fresh air. There must still be motion and emotion (in whatever form) if there is to be life; certainly not complete rest and insensitiveness.

IV. A BIOLOGICAL VIEW

The better knowledge of our own bodily functions and mental processes gives us a truer and broader view of ourselves and takes away from the word "animal" some of its old bad flavour. The old proverb that "to understand is to forgive" is applicable to our own bodily and mental processes. It may seem strange, but it is true, that the very fact that we have a better understanding of our bodily functions makes it impossible for us to look down upon them with contempt. The important thing is not to say whether our digestive process is noble or ignoble; the important thing is just to understand it, and somehow it becomes extremely noble. This is true of every biological function or process in our body, from perspiration and the elimination of waste to the functions of the pancreatic juice, the gall, the endocrine glands and the finer emotive and cogitative processes. One no longer despises the kidney, one merely tries to understand it; and one no longer looks upon a bad tooth as symbolic of the final decay of our body and a reminder to attend to the welfare of our soul, but merely goes to a dentist, has it examined, explained and properly fixed up. Somehow a man coming out from a dentist's office no longer despises his teeth, but has an increased respect for them—because he is going to gnaw apples and chicken bones with increased delight. As for the superfine metaphysician who says that the teeth belong to the devil, and the Neo-Platonists who deny that individual teeth exist, I always get a satirical delight in seeing a philosopher suffering from a tooth-ache and an optimistic poet suffering from dyspepsia. Why doesn't he go on with his philosophic disquisitions, and why does he hold his hand against his cheek, just as you or I or the woman in the next house would do? And why does optimism seem so unconvincing to a dyspeptic poet? Why doesn't he sing any more? How ungrateful it is, of him, therefore, to forget the intestines and sing about the spirit when the intestines behave and give him no trouble!

Science, if anything, has taught us an increased respect for our body, by deepening a sense of the wonder and mystery of its workings. In the first place, genetically, we begin to understand how we came about, and see that, instead of being made out of clay, we are sitting on the top of the genealogical tree of the animal kingdom. That must be a fine sensation, sufficiently satisfying for any man who is not intoxicated with his own spirit. Not that I believe dinosaurs lived and died millions of years ago *in order that* we to-day might walk erect with our two legs upon this earth. Without such gratuitous assumptions, biology has not at all destroyed a whit of human dignity, or cast doubt upon the view that we are probably the most splendid animals ever evolved on this earth. So that is quite satisfying for any man who wants to insist on human dignity. In the second place, we are more impressed than ever with the mystery and beauty of the body. The workings of the internal parts of our body and the wonderful correlation between them compel in us a sense of the extreme difficulty with which these correlations are brought about and the extreme simplicity and finality with which they are nevertheless accomplished. Instead of simplifying these internal chemical processes by explaining them, science makes them all the more difficult to explain. These processes are incredibly more difficult than the layman without any knowledge of physiology usually imagines. The great mystery of the universe without is similar in quality to the mystery of the universe within.

The more a physiologist tries to analyse and study the biophysical and bio-chemical processes of human physiology, the more his wonder increases. That is so to the extent that sometimes it compels a physiologist with a broad spirit to accept the mystic's view of life, as in the case of Dr. Alexis Carrel. Whether we agree with him or not, as he states his opinions in *Man, the Unknown,* we must agree with him that the facts are there, unexplained and unexplainable. We begin to acquire a sense of the intelligence of matter itself:

> The organs are correlated by the organic fluids and the nervous system. Each element of the body adjusts itself to the others, and the others to it. This mode of adaptation is essentially teleological. If we attribute to tissues an intelligence of the same kind as ours, as mechanists and vitalists do, the physiological processes appear to associate together in view of the end to be attained. The existence of finality within the organism is undeniable. Each part seems to know the present and future needs of the whole, and acts accordingly. The significance of time and space is not the same for our tissues as for our mind. The body perceives the remote as well as the near, the future as well as the present.[1]

And we should wonder, for instance, and be extremely amazed that our intestines heal their own wounds, entirely without our voluntary effort:

> The wounded loop first becomes immobile. It is temporarily paralysed, and fecal matter is thus prevented from running into the abdomen. At the same time, some other intestinal loop, or the surface of the omentum, approaches the wound and, owing to a known property of peritoneum, adheres to it. Within four or five hours the opening is occluded. Even if the surgeon's needle has drawn the edges of the wound together, healing is due to spontaneous adhesion of the peritoneal surfaces.[2]

Why do we despise the body, when the flesh itself shows such intelligence? After all, we are endowed with a body, which is a self-nourishing, self-regulating, self-repairing, self-starting and

[1] *Man, the Unknown,* p. 197.
[2] *Ibid.,* p. 200.

self-reproducing machine, installed at birth and lasting like a good grandfather clock for three-quarters of a century, requiring very little attention. It is a machine provided with wireless vision and wireless hearing, with a more highly complicated system of nerves and lymphs than the most complicated telephone and telegraph system of the world. It has a system of filing reports done by a vast complexus of nerves, managed with such efficiency that some files, the less important ones, are kept in the attic and others are kept in a more convenient desk, but those kept in the attic, which may be thirty years old and rarely referred to, are nevertheless there and sometimes can be found with lightning speed and efficiency. Then it also manages to go about like a motor-car with perfect knee-action and absolute silence of engines, and if the motor-car has an accident and breaks its glass or its steering wheel, the car automatically exudes or manufactures a substance to replace the glass and does its best to grow a steering wheel, or at least manages to do the steering with a swollen end of the steering shaft; for we must remember that when one of our kidneys is cut out, the other kidney swells and increases its function to insure the passage of the normal volume of urine. Then it also keeps up a normal temperature within a tenth of a Fahrenheit degree, and manufactures its own chemicals for the processes of transforming food into living tissues.

Above all, it has a sense of the rhythm of life, and a sense of time, not only of hours and days, but also of decades; the body regulates its own childhood, puberty and maturity, stops growing when it should no longer grow, and brings forth a wisdom tooth at a time when no one of us ever thought of it. Our conscious wisdom has nothing to do with our wisdom tooth. It also manufactures specific antidotes against poison, on the whole with amazing success, and it does all these things with absolute silence, without the usual racket of a factory, so that our superfine metaphysician may not be disturbed and is free to think about his spirit or his essence.

V. HUMAN LIFE A POEM

I think that, from a biological standpoint, human life almost reads like a poem. It has its own rhythm and beat, its internal cycles of growth and decay. It begins with innocent childhood, followed by awkward adolescence trying awkwardly to adapt itself to mature society, with its young passions and follies, its ideals and ambitions; then it reaches a manhood of intense activities, profiting from experience and learning more about society and human nature; at middle age, there is a slight easing of tension, a mellowing of character like the ripening of fruit or the mellowing of good wine, and the gradual acquiring of a more tolerant, more cynical and at the same time a kindlier view of life; then in the sunset of our life, the endocrine glands decrease their activity, and if we have a true philosophy of old age and have ordered our life pattern according to it, it is for us the age of peace and security and leisure and contentment; finally, life flickers out and one goes into eternal sleep, never to wake up again. One should be able to sense the beauty of this rhythm of life, to appreciate, as we do in grand symphonies, its main theme, its strains of conflict and the final resolution. The movements of these cycles are very much the same in a normal life, but the music must be provided by the individual himself. In some souls, the discordant note becomes harsher and harsher and finally overwhelms or submerges the main melody. Sometimes the discordant note gains so much power that the music can no longer go on, and the individual shoots himself with a pistol or jumps into a river. But that is because his original *leit-motif* has been hopelessly overshadowed through the lack of a good self-education. Otherwise the normal human life runs to its normal end in a kind of dignified movement and procession. There are sometimes in many of us too many *staccatos* or *impetuosos*, and because the tempo is wrong, the music is not pleasing to the ear; we might have more of the grand rhythm and majestic tempo of the Ganges, flowing slowly and eternally into the sea.

No one can say that a life with childhood, manhood and old

age is not a beautiful arrangement; the day has its morning, noon and sunset, and the year has its seasons, and it is good that it is so. There is no good or bad in life, except what is good according to its own season. And if we take this biological view of life and try to live according to the seasons, no one but a conceited fool or an impossible idealist can deny that human life can be lived like a poem. Shakespeare has expressed this idea more graphically in his passage about the seven stages of life, and a good many Chinese writers have said about the same thing. It is curious that Shakespeare was never very religious, or very much concerned with religion. I think this was his greatness; he took human life largely as it was, and intruded himself as little upon the general scheme of things as he did upon the characters of his plays. Shakespeare was like Nature herself, and that is the greatest compliment we can pay to a writer or thinker. He merely lived, observed life and went away.

CHAPTER THREE

Our Animal Heritage

I. THE MONKEY EPIC

BUT IF THIS BIOLOGICAL VIEW helps us to appreciate the beauty and rhythm of life, it also shows our ludicrous limitations. By presenting to us a more correct picture of what we are as animals, it enables us to better understand ourselves and the progress of human affairs. A more generous sympathy, or even tolerant cynicism, comes with a truer and deeper understanding of human nature which has its roots in our animal ancestry. Gently reminding ourselves that we are children of the Neanderthal or the Peking man, and further back still of the anthropoid apes, we eventually achieve the capacity of laughing at our sins and limitations, as well as admiring our monkey cleverness, which we call a sense of human comedy. This is a beautiful thought suggested by the enlightening essay of Clarence Day, *This Simian World*. Reading that essay of Day's, we can forgive all our fellow-men, the censors, publicity chiefs, Fascist editors, Nazi radio announcers, senators and law-makers, dictators, economic experts, delegates to international conferences and all the busybodies who try to interfere with other people's lives. We can forgive them because we begin to understand them.

In this sense, I come more and more to appreciate the wisdom and insight of the great Chinese monkey epic, *Hsiyuchi*. The progress of human history can be better understood from this point of view; it is so similar to the pilgrimage of those imperfect, semi-human creatures to the Western Heaven—the Monkey Wuk'ung representing the human intellect, the Pig Pachieh representing our lower nature, Monk Sand representing common sense,

[35]

and the Abbot Hsüantsang representing wisdom and the Holy Way. The Abbot, protected by this curious escort, was engaged upon a journey from China to India to procure sacred Buddhist books. The story of human progress is essentially like the pilgrimage of this variegated company of highly imperfect creatures, continually landing in dangers and ludicrous situations through their own folly and mischief. How often the Abbot has to correct and chastise the mischievous Monkey and the sensuous Pig, for ever led by their sadly imperfect minds and their lower passions into all sorts of scrapes! The instincts of human frailty, of anger, revenge, impetuousness, sensuality, lack of forgiveness, above all self-conceit and lack of humility, for ever crop up during this pilgrimage of mankind toward sainthood. The increase of destructiveness goes side by side with the increase of human skill, for, like the Monkey with magical powers, we are able to-day to walk upon the clouds and turn somersaults in the air (which is called "looping-the-loop" in modern terms), to pull monkey hair out of our monkey legs and transform them into little monkeys to harass our enemy, to knock at the very gates of Heaven, brush the Heavenly Gate-keeper brusquely aside and demand a place in the company of the gods.

The Monkey was clever, but he was also conceited; he had enough monkey magic to push his way into Heaven, but he had not enough sanity and balance and temperance of spirit to live peacefully there. Too good perhaps for this earth and its mortal existence, he was yet not good enough for Heaven and the company of the immortals. There was something raw and mischievous and rebellious in him, some dregs unpurged in his gold, and that was why when he entered Heaven he created a terrific scare there, like a wild lion let loose from a menagerie cage in the streets of a city, in the preliminary episode before he joined the pilgrims' party. Through his inborn incorrigible mischief, he spoiled the Annual Dinner Party given by the Western Queen Mother of Heaven to all the gods, saints, and immortals of Heaven. Enraged that he was not invited to the party, he posed as a messenger of God and sent the Bare-footed Fairy on his way to the feast in a wrong direction by telling him that the place of the party had been changed, and then transformed himself into the shape of the Bare-footed Fairy and went to the feast himself. Quite a number of other fairies had been misled by him in this way. Then entering the courtyard, he saw he was the first arrival. Nobody was there except the servants guarding the jars of fairy wine in the corridor. He then transformed himself into a sleeping-sickness insect and stung the servants into sleep and drank the jars of wine. Half intoxicated, he tumbled into the hall and ate up the celestial peaches laid out at table. When the guests arrived and saw the despoiled dinner, he was already off for some other exploits at the home of Laotse, trying to eat his pills of immortality. Finally, still in disguise, he left Heaven, partly afraid of the consequences of his drunken exploits, but chiefly disgusted because he had not been invited to the Annual Dinner. He returned to his Monkey Kingdom where he was the king and told the little monkeys so, and set up a banner of rebellion against Heaven, writing on it the words "The Great Sage, Equal of Heaven." There followed then terrific combats between this Monkey and the heavenly warriors, in which the Monkey was not captured until the Goddess of Mercy knocked him down with a gentle sprig of flowers from the clouds.

So, like the Monkey, for ever we rebel and there will be no peace and humility in us until we are vanquished by the Goddess of Mercy, whose gentle flowers dropped from Heaven will knock us off our feet. And we shall not learn the lesson of true humility until science has explored the limits of the universe. For in the epic, the Monkey still rebelled even after his capture and demanded of the Jade Emperor in Heaven why he was not given a higher title among the gods, and he had to learn the lesson of humility by an ultimate bet with Buddha or God Himself. He made a bet that with his magical powers he could go as far as the end of the earth, and the stake was the title of "The Great Sage, Equal of Heaven," or else complete submission. Then he leaped into the air, and travelled with lightning speed across the continents until he came to a mountain with five peaks, which he thought must be as far as mortal beings had ever set foot. In order to leave a record of his having reached the place, he passed some monkey urine at the foot of the middle peak, and having satisfied himself with this feat, he came back and told Buddha about his journey. Buddha then opened one hand and asked him to smell his own urine at the base of the middle finger, and told him how all this time he had never left the palm. It was only then that the Monkey acquired humility, and after being chained to a rock for five hundred years, was freed by the Abbot and joined him in his pilgrimage.

After all, this Monkey, which is an image of ourselves, is an extremely lovable creature, in spite of his conceit and his mischief. So should we, too, be able to love humanity in spite of all its weaknesses and shortcomings.

II. IN THE IMAGE OF THE MONKEY

So then, instead of holding on to the Biblical view that we are made in the image of God, we come to realize that we are made in the image of the monkey, and that we are as far removed from the perfect God as, let us say, the ants are removed from ourselves. We are very clever, we are quite sure of that; we are often a little cocky about our cleverness, because we have a mind. But the biologist comes in to tell us that the mind after all is a very late development, as far as articulate thinking is concerned, and that among the things which go into the make-up of our moral fibre, we have besides the mind a set of animal or savage instincts, which are much more powerful and are in fact the explanation why we misbehave individually and in our group life. We are the better able to understand the nature of that human mind of which we are so proud. We see in the first place that, besides being a comparatively clever mind, it is also an inadequate mind. The evolution of the human skull shows us that it is nothing but an enlargement of one of the spinal vertebræ and that therefore its function, like that of the spinal cord, is essentially that of sensing danger, meeting the external environment and preserving life—not thinking. Thinking is generally very poorly done. Lord

Balfour ought to go down to posterity on the strength of his one saying that "the human brain is as much an organ for seeking food as the pig's snout." I do not call this real cynicism, I call it merely a generous understanding of ourselves.

We begin to understand genetically our human imperfections. Imperfect? Lord, yes, but the Lord never made us otherwise. But that is not the point. The whole point is, our remote ancestors swam and crawled and swung from one branch to another in the primeval forest in Tarzan fashion, or hung suspended from a tree like a spider monkey by an arm or a tail.[1] At each stage, considered by itself, it was rather marvellously perfect, to my way of thinking. But now we are called upon to do an infinitely more difficult job of readjustment.

When man creates a civilization of his own, he embarks upon a course of development that biologically might terrify the Creator Himself. So far as adaptation to nature is concerned, all nature's creatures are marvellously perfect, for those that are not perfectly adapted she kills off. But now we are no longer called upon to adapt ourselves to nature; we are called upon to adapt ourselves to ourselves, to this thing called civilization. All instincts were good, were healthy in nature; in society, however, we call all instincts savage. Every mouse steals—and he is not the less moral or more immoral for stealing—every dog barks, every cat doesn't come home at night and tears everything it can lay its paws upon, every lion kills, every horse runs away from the sight of danger, every tortoise sleeps the best hours of the day away, and every insect, reptile, bird and beast reproduces its kind in public. Now in terms of civilization, every mouse is a thief, every dog makes too much noise, every cat is an unfaithful husband, when he is not a savage little vandal, every lion or tiger is a murderer, every horse a coward, every tortoise a lazy louse, and finally, every insect, reptile, bird and beast is obscene when he performs his natural vital functions. What a wholesale transformation of

[1] Is this the reason why, when we are on a swing and about to swing forward after swinging backward, we get a tingle at the end of our spinal cord, where a tail formerly was? The reflex is still there and we are trying to catch on to something by a tail which has already disappeared.

values! And that is the reason why we sit back and wonder how the Lord made us so imperfect.

III. ON BEING MORTAL

There are grave consequences following upon our having this mortal body: first our being mortal, then our having a stomach, having strong muscles and having a curious mind. These facts, because of their basic character, profoundly influence the character of human civilization. Because this is so obvious, we never think about it. But we cannot understand ourselves and our civilization unless we see these consequences clearly.

I suspect that all democracy, all poetry, and all philosophy start out from this God-given fact that all of us, princes and paupers alike, are limited to a body of five or six feet and live a life of fifty or sixty years. On the whole, the arrangement is quite handy. We are neither too long nor too short. At least I am quite satisfied with five feet four. And fifty or sixty years seems to me such an awfully long time; it is, in fact, a matter of two or three generations. It is so arranged that when we are born, we see certain old grandfathers, who die in the course of time, and when we become grandfathers ourselves, we see other tiny tots being born. That seems to make it just perfect. The whole philosophy of the matter lies in the Chinese saying that "A man may own a thousand acres of land, and yet he still sleeps upon a bed of five feet" or sixty inches. It doesn't seem as if a king needed very much more than seven feet at the outside for his bed, and there he will have to go and stretch himself at night. I am therefore as good as a king. And no matter how rich a man is, few exceed the Biblical limit of threescore and ten. To live beyond seventy is to be called in Chinese "ancient-rare," because of the Chinese line that "it is rare for man to live over seventy since the ancient times."

And so in respect of wealth. Of this life, everybody has a share, but no one owns the mortgage. And so we are enabled to take this life more lightly; instead of being permanent tenants upon this earth, we become its transient guests, for guests we all are of this earth, the owners of the land no less than the share-croppers. It takes something out of the meaning of the word "landlord." No one really owns a house and no one really owns a field. As a Chinese poet says:

> What pretty, golden fields against a hill!
> Newcomers harvest crops that others till.
> Rejoice not, O newcomers, at your harvest;
> One waits behind—a new newcomer still!

The democracy of death is seldom appreciated. Without death, even St. Helena would have meant nothing to Napoleon, and I do not know what Europe would be like. There would be no biographies of heroes or conquerors, and even if there were, their biographers certainly would be less forgiving and sympathetic. We forgive the great of this world because they are dead. By their being dead, we feel that we have got even with them. Every funeral procession carries a banner upon which are written the words, "Equality of Mankind." What joy of life is seen in the following ballad that the oppressed people of China composed about the death of Ch'in Shih-huang, the builder of the Great Wall and the tyrant, who, while he lived, made "libellous thoughts in the belly" punishable by death, burned the Confucian books and buried hundreds of Confucian scholars alive:

> Ch'in Shih-huang is going to die! [1]
> He opened my door,
> And sat on my floor,
> He drank my gravy,
> And wanted some more.
> He sipped my wine,
> And couldn't tell what for;
> I'll bend my bow,
> And shoot him at the wall.
> When he arrives at Shach'iu,
> Then he is going to fall!

[1] By inversion, these ballads were reported by the Chinese historians as prophetic oracles, giving expression to the voice of God through the voice of the people. That explains the future tense. The Emperor did die at Shach'iu.

[41]

From this, then, a sense of human comedy and the very stuff of human poetry and philosophy take their rise. He who perceives death perceives a sense of the human comedy, and quickly becomes a poet. Shakespeare became a deep poet, when he had Hamlet trace the noble dust of Alexander, "till he find it stopping a bung-hole"; "Alexander died, Alexander was buried, Alexander returneth into dust; the dust is earth; of earth we make loam; and why of that loam, whereto he was converted, might they not stop a beer-barrel?" There is, after all, no more superb sense of comedy in Shakespeare than when he let King Richard II talk of graves, of worms and epitaphs and the antic that keeps court within the hollow crown that rounds the mortal temples of a king, or where he speaks of "a great buyer of land, with his statutes, his recognizances, his fines, his double vouchers, his recoveries," with all his fines ending in a "fine pate full of fine dirt." Omar Khayyàm and his Chinese counterpart, Chia Fuhsi (*alias* Mup'itse, an obscure Chinese poet), derived all their comic spirit and comic interpretation of history from the sense of death itself, by pointing to the foxes making their homes in the kings' graves. And Chinese philosophy first acquired depth and humour with Chuangtse, who based his entire philosophy, too, on a comment on the sight of a skull:

Chuangtse went to Ch'u and saw an empty skull with its empty and dried outline. He struck it with a horsewhip and asked it, "Hast thou come to this because thou loved pleasures and lived inordinately? Wert thou a refugee running away from the law? Didst thou do something wrong to bring shame upon thy parents and thy family? Or wert thou starved to death? Or didst thou come to thy old age and die a natural death?" Having said this, Chuangtse took the skull and slept upon it as a pillow. . . .

When Chuangtse's wife died, Hueitse went to express his condolence but found Chuangtse squatting on the ground and singing a song, beating time by striking an earthen basin. "Why, this woman has lived with you and borne you children. At the worst, you might refrain from weeping when her old body dies. Is it not rather too much that you should beat the basin and sing?"

And Chuangtse replied, "You are mistaken. When she first died, I could not also help feeling sad and moved, but I reflected that in the beginning she had no life, and not only no life, she had no bodily shape; and not only no bodily shape, she had no ghost. Caught in this everchanging flux of things, she became a ghost, the ghost became a body, and the body became alive. Now she has changed again and become dead, and by so doing she has joined the eternal procession of spring, summer, autumn and winter. Why should I make so much noise and wail and weep over her while her body lies quietly there in the big house? That would be a failure to understand the course of things. That is why I stopped crying."

Thus I see both poetry and philosophy began with the recognition of our mortality and a sense of the evanescence of time. This sense of life's evanescence is back of all Chinese poetry, as well as of a good part of Western poetry—the feeling that life is essentially but a dream, while we row, row our boat down the river in the sunset of a beautiful afternoon, that flowers cannot bloom for ever, the moon waxes and wanes, and human life itself joins the eternal procession of the plant and animal worlds in being born, growing to maturity and dying to make room for others. Man began to be philosophical only when he saw the vanity of this earthly existence. Chuangtse said that he once dreamed of being a butterfly, and while he was in the dream, he felt he could flutter his wings and everything was real, but that on waking up, he realized that he was Chuangtse and Chuangtse was real. Then he thought and wondered which was really real, whether he was really Chuangtse dreaming of being a butterfly, or really a butterfly dreaming of being Chuangtse. Life, then, is really a dream, and we human beings are like travellers floating down the eternal river of time, embarking at a certain point and disembarking again at another point in order to make room for others waiting below the river to come aboard. Half of the poetry of life would be gone, if we did not feel that life was either a dream, or a voyage with transient travellers, or merely a stage in which the actors seldom realized that they were playing their parts. So wrote a Chinese scholar, Liu Tasheng, to his friend:

Of all the things in the world, that in which we are most earnest is to be an official, and that which we call the most frivolous is to be an actor in a play. But I think this is all foolishness. I have often seen on the stage how the actors sing and weep and scold each other and crack jokes, believing that they are real people. But the real thing in a play is not the ancient characters thus being enacted, but rather these actors who enact them. They all have their parents, wives and children, all want to feed their parents, wives and children, and all do so by singing and weeping and laughing and scolding and cracking jokes. They are the real ancient characters that they try to portray. I have also seen how some of these actors, who wear an official cap and gown and by their own acting believe themselves to be real officials, so much so that they think no one in the world ever suspects they are acting. They do not realize that while they bow and kowtow to each other and sit and talk and look about, and even while they are the dignified officials before whom the prisoners tremble, they are only actors who by their singing and weeping and laughing and scolding and cracking jokes are trying to feed their parents, wives and children! Alas! that there are people who stick to a certain play, a certain role, a certain text and a certain accent or style of delivery, until the entire asset of their bowels and internal organs (i.e., instincts and emotions) are dominated by the play, without realizing once that they are really actors!

IV. ON HAVING A STOMACH

One of the most important consequences of our being animals is that we have got this bottomless pit called the stomach. This fact has coloured our entire civilization. The Chinese epicure Li Liweng wrote a complaint about our having this bottomless pit, in the prefatory note to the section on food in his book on the general art of living.

I see that the organs of the human body, the ear, the eye, the nose, the tongue, the hands, the feet and the body, have all a necessary function, but the two organs which are totally unnecessary but with which we are nevertheless endowed are the mouth and the stomach, which cause all the worry and trouble of mankind throughout the ages. With this mouth and this stomach, the matter of getting a living becomes complicated, and when the matter of getting a living becomes complicated, we have cunning and falsehood and dishonesty in human affairs. With the coming of cunning and falsehood and dishonesty in human affairs, comes the criminal law, so that the king is not able to protect with his mercy, the parents are not able to gratify their love, and even the kind Creator is forced to go against His will. All this comes of a little lack of forethought in His design for the human body at the time of the creation, and is the consequence of our having these two organs. The plants can live without a mouth and a stomach, and the rocks and the soil have their being without any nourishment. Why, then, must we be given a mouth and a stomach and endowed with these two extra organs? And even if we were to be endowed with these organs, He could have made it possible for us to derive our nourishment as the fish and shell fish derive theirs from water, or the cricket and the cicada from the dew, who all are able to obtain their growth and energy this way and swim or fly or jump or sing. Had it been like this, we should not have to struggle in this life and the sorrows of mankind would have disappeared. On the other hand, He has given us not only these two organs, but has also endowed us with manifold appetites or desires, besides making the pit bottomless, so that it is like a valley or a sea that can never be filled. The consequence is that we labour in our life with all

[45]

the energy of the other organs, in order to supply inadequately the needs of these two. I have thought over this matter over and over again, and cannot help blaming the Creator for it. I know, of course, that He must have repented of His mistake also, but simply feels that nothing can be done about it now, since the design or pattern is already fixed. How important it is for a man to be very careful at the time of the conception of a law or an institution!

There is certainly nothing to be done about it, now that we have got this bottomless pit to fill, and the fact of our having possessed a stomach has, to say the least, coloured the course of human history. With a generous understanding of human nature, Confucius reduced the great desires of human beings to two: alimentation and reproduction, or in simpler terms, food and drink and women. Many men have circumvented sex, but no saint has yet circumvented food and drink. There are ascetics who have learned to live a continent life, but even the most spiritual of men cannot forget about food for more than four or five hours. The most constant refrain of our thought occurring unfailingly every few hours is, "When do I eat?" This occurs at least three times a day, and in some cases four or five times. International conferences, in the midst of discussion of the most absorbing and most critical political situations, have to break up for the noon meal. Parliaments have to adjust their schedule of sessions to meal hours. A coronation ceremony that lasts more than five or six hours or conflicts with the midday meal, will be immediately denounced as a public nuisance. And stomach-gifted that we all are, the best arrangement we can think of when we gather to render public homage to a grandfather is to give him a birthday feast.

There is a reason for it. Friends that meet at meals meet at peace. A good birds'-nest soup or a delicious chow mein has the tendency to assuage the heat of our arguments and tone down the harshness of our conflicting points of view. Put two of the best friends together when they are hungry, and they will invariably end up in a quarrel. The effect of a good meal lasts not only a few hours, but for weeks and months. We rather hesitate to review unfavourably a book written by somebody who gave us a good dinner three or four months ago. It is for this reason that, with the Chinese deep insight into human nature, all quarrels and disputes are settled at dinner tables instead of at the court of justice. The pattern of Chinese life is such that we not only settle disputes at dinner, after they have arisen, but also forestall the arising of disputes by the same means. In China, we bribe our way into the good will of everybody by frequent dinners. It is, in fact, the only safe guide to success in politics. Should someone take the trouble of compiling statistical figures, he would be able to find an absolute correlation between the number of dinners a man gives to his friends and the rate or speed of his official promotion.

But, constituted as we all are, how can we react otherwise? I do not think this is peculiarly Chinese. How can an American postmaster-general or chief of department decline a private request for a personal favour from some friend at whose home he has eaten five or six good meals? I bet on the Americans being as human as the Chinese. The only difference is the Americans haven't got insight into human nature or haven't proceeded logically to organize their political life in accordance with it. I guess there is something similar to this Chinese way of life in the American political world, too, since I cannot but believe human nature is very much the same and we are all so much alike under the skin. Only I don't notice it practised so generally as in China. The only thing I have heard of is that candidates for public office give outings for the families in the districts, bribing the mothers by feeding their children with ice cream and soda pop. The inevitable conviction of the people after such a public feeding is that "He's a jolly good fellow," which usually bursts out in song. This is merely another form of the practice of the medieval lords and nobles in Europe who, on the occasion of a wedding or a noble's birthday, gave their tenants a generous feast with liberal meats and wine.

So basically influenced are we by this matter of food and drink that revolutions, peace, war, patriotism, international understanding, our daily life and the whole fabric of human social life are profoundly influenced by it. What was the cause of the French Revolution? Rousseau and Voltaire and Diderot? No, just food. What is the cause of the Russian Revolution and the Soviet experiment? Just food again. As for war, Napoleon showed the essential depth of his wisdom by saying that "an army fights on its stomach." And what is the use of saying, "Peace, Peace," when there is no peace below the diaphragm? This applies to nations as well as individuals. Empires have collapsed and the most powerful regimes and reigns of terror have broken down when the people were hungry. Men refuse to work, soldiers refuse to fight, prima donnas refuse to sing, senators refuse to debate, and even presidents refuse to rule the country when they are hungry. And what does a husband work and sweat in the office the whole day for, except the prospect of a good meal at home? Hence the proverb that the best way to a man's heart is through his stomach. When his flesh is satisfied, his spirit is calmer and more at ease, and he becomes more amorous and appreciative. Wives have complained that husbands don't notice their new dresses, new shoes, new eyebrows, or new covers for chairs. But have wives ever complained that husbands don't notice a good steak or a good omelette? . . . What is patriotism but love of the good things we ate in our childhood? I have said elsewhere that the loyalty to Uncle Sam is the loyalty to doughnuts and ham and sweet potatoes and the loyalty to the German *Vaterland* is the loyalty to *Pfannkuchen* and Christmas *Stollen*. As for international understanding, I feel that macaroni has done more for our appreciation of Italy than Mussolini. It is a pity that, in the minds of some people, at least, who are not in favour of the Mussolini regime, what macaroni has done Mussolini has undone in the cause of understanding between Italy and the outside world. That is because in food, as in death, we feel the essential brotherhood of mankind.

How a Chinese spirit glows over a good feast! How apt is he to cry out that life is beautiful when his stomach and his intestines

are well filled! From this well-filled stomach suffuses and radiates
a happiness that is spiritual. The Chinese relies upon instinct and
his instinct tells him that when the stomach is right, everything is
right. That is why I claim for the Chinese a life closer to instinct
and a philosophy that makes a more open acknowledgment of it
possible. The Chinese idea of happiness is, as I have noted elsewhere, being "warm, well filled, dark and sweet"—referring to
the condition of going to bed after a good supper. It is for this
reason that a Chinese poet says, "A well-filled stomach is indeed
a great thing; all else is luxury."

With this philosophy, therefore, the Chinese have no prudery
about food, or about eating it with gusto. When a Chinese drinks
a mouthful of good soup, he gives a hearty smack. Of course, that
would be bad table manners in the West. On the other hand, I
strongly suspect that Western table manners, compelling us to
sip our soup noiselessly and eat our food quietly with the least
expression of enjoyment, are the true reason for the arrested
development of the art of cuisine. Why do the Westerners talk
so softly and look so miserable and decent and respectable at their
meals? Most Americans haven't got the good sense to take a
chicken drumstick in their hand and chew it clean, but continue
to pretend to play at it with a knife and fork, feeling utterly
miserable and afraid to say a thing about it. This is criminal when
the chicken is really good. As for the so-called table manners,
I feel sure that the child gets his first initiation into the sorrows
of this life when his mother forbids him to smack his lips. Such
is human psychology that if we don't express our joy, we soon
cease to feel it even, and then follow dyspepsia, melancholia,
neurasthenia and all the mental ailments peculiar to the adult
life. One ought to imitate the French and sigh an "Ah!" when the
waiter brings a good veal cutlet, and makes a sheer animal grunt
like "Ummm!" after tasting the first mouthful. What shame is
there in enjoying one's food, what shame in having a normal,
healthy appetite? No, the Chinese are different. They have bad
table manners, but great enjoyment of a feast.

In fact, I believe the reason why the Chinese failed to develop

c

botany and zoology is that the Chinese scholar cannot stare coldly
and unemotionally at a fish without immediately thinking of how
it tastes in the mouth and wanting to eat it. The reason I don't
trust Chinese surgeons is that I am afraid that when a Chinese
surgeon cuts up my liver in search of a gall-stone, he may forget
about the stone and put my liver in a frying-pan. For I see a
Chinese cannot look at a porcupine without immediately thinking
of ways and means of cooking and eating its flesh without being
poisoned. Not to be poisoned is for the Chinese the only practical, important aspect of it. The taste of the porcupine meat is
supremely important, if it should add one more flavour known
to our palate. The bristles of the porcupine don't interest us.
How they arose, what is their function and how they are connected with the porcupine's skin and endowed with the power
of sticking up at the sight of an enemy are questions that seem to
the Chinese eminently idle. And so with all the animals and
plants, the proper point of view is how we humans can enjoy
them and not what they are in themselves. The song of the bird,
the colour of the flower, the petals of the orchid, the texture of
chicken meat are the things that concern us. The East has to
learn from the West the entire sciences of botany and zoology,
but the West has to learn from the East how to enjoy the trees, the
flowers, and the fishes, birds and animals, to get a full appreciation
of the contours and gestures of different species and associate them
with different moods or feelings.

Food, then, is one of the very few solid joys of human life. It
is a happy fact that this instinct of hunger is less hedged about with
taboos and a social code than the other instinct of sex, and that,
generally speaking, no question of morality arises in connection
with food. There is much less prudery about food than there is
about sex. It is a happy condition of affairs that philosophers,
poets, merchants and artists can join together at a dinner, and
without a blush perform the function of feeding themselves in
open public, although certain savage tribes are known to have
developed a sense of modesty about food and eat only when they
are individually alone. The problem of sex will come in for

consideration later, but here at least is an instinct which, because less hampered, produces fewer forms of perversion and insanity and criminal behaviour. This difference between the instinct of hunger and the instinct of sex in their social implications is quite natural. But the fact remains that here is one instinct which does not complicate our psychological life, but is a pure boon to humanity. The reason is because it is the one instinct about which humanity is pretty frank. Because there is no problem of modesty here, there is no psychosis, neurosis or perversion connected with it. There is many a slip between the cup and the lip, but once food gets inside the lips, there is comparatively little side-tracking. It is freely admitted that everybody must have food, which is not the case with the sexual instinct. And being gratified, it leads to no trouble. At the worst, some people eat their way into dyspepsia, or an ulcered stomach or a hardened liver, and a few dig their graves with their own teeth—there are cases of Chinese dignitaries among my contemporaries who do this—but even then, they are not ashamed of it.

For the same reason, fewer social crimes arise from food than from sex. The criminal code has comparatively little to do with the sins of illegal, immoral and faithless eating, while it has a large section on adultery, divorce, and assault on women. At the worst, husbands may ransack the ice-box, but we seldom hang a man for spiking a Frigidaire. Should such a case ever be brought up, the judge will be found to be full of compassion. The frank admission of the necessity of every man feeding himself makes this possible. Our hearts go out to people in famine, but not to the cloistered nuns.

This speculation is far from being idle because there is little public ignorance about the subject of food, as compared with public ignorance on the subject of sex, which is appalling. There are Manchu families which school their daughters in the art of love as well as in the art of cooking before their marriage, but how much of this is done elsewhere in the world? The subject of food enjoys the sunshine of knowledge, but sex is still surrounded with fairy tales, myths and superstitions. There is sunshine about the subject of food, but very little sunshine about the subject of sex.

On the other hand, it is highly unfortunate that we haven't got a gizzard or a crop or a maw. In that case, human society would be altered beyond recognition; in fact, we should have an altogether different race of men. A human race endowed with gullets or gizzards would be found to have the most peaceful, contented and sweet nature, like the chicken or the lamb. We might grow a beak, which would alter our sense of beauty, or we might have merely done with rodent teeth. Seeds and fruits might be sufficient, or we might pasture on the green hillsides, for Nature is so abundant. Because we should not have to fight for our food and dig our teeth into the flesh of our defeated enemy, we would not be the terrible warlike creatures that we are to-day.

There is a closer relation between food and temperament—in Nature's terms—than we thought. All herbivorous animals are peaceful by nature: the lamb, the horse, the cow, the elephant, the sparrow, etc.; all carnivorous animals are fighters: the wolf, the lion, the tiger, the hawk, etc. Had we been an herbivorous race, our nature would certainly be more elephantine. Nature does not produce a pugnacious temperament where no fighting is needed. Cocks still fight with each other, but they fight not about food, but about women. There would still be a little fighting of this sort among the males in human society, but it would be vastly different from this fighting for exported canned goods that we see in present-day Europe.

I do not know about monkeys eating monkeys, but I do know about men eating men, for certainly all evidences of anthropology point to a pretty universal practice of cannibalism. That was our carnivorous ancestry. Is it therefore any wonder that we are still eating each other in more senses than one—individually, socially and internationally? There is this much to be said for the cannibals: that they are sensible about this matter of killing. Conceding that killing is an undesirable but unavoidable evil, they proceed to get something out of it by eating the delicious sirloins, ribs and livers of their dead enemies. The difference between cannibals and civilized men seems to be that cannibals kill their enemies and eat them, while civilized men kill their foes and bury them, put a cross over their bodies and offer up prayers for their souls. Thus we add stupidity to conceit and a bad temper.

I quite realize that we are on the road to perfection, which means that we are excusably imperfect at present. That, I think, is what we are. Not until we develop a gizzard temper can we call ourselves truly civilized. I see in the present generation of men both carnivorous and herbivorous animals—those who have a sweet temper and those who have not. The herbivorous men go their way through life minding their own business, while the carnivorous men make their living by minding that of others. If I abjured politics ten years ago, after having a foretaste of it during four months, it was because I early made the discovery that I was not by nature a carnivorous animal, although I enjoy a good steak. Half of the world spends its time doing things, and half the world spends its time making others do things for them, or making it impossible for others to do anything. The characteristic of the carnivorous is a certain sheer delight in pugilism, log-rolling, wire-pulling, and in double-crossing, outwitting and forestalling the enemy, all done with a genuine interest and real ability, for which, however, I confess I fail to have the slightest appreciation. But it is all a matter of instinct; men born with this pugilistic instinct seem to enjoy and revel in it, while real creative ability, ability in doing their own jobs or knowing their own subjects, seems at the same time usually to be under-developed. How many good, quiet herbivorous professors are totally lacking in rapacity and the ability to get ahead in competition with others, and yet how truly I admire them! In fact I may essay the opinion that all the world's creative artists are vastly better at minding their own business than minding that of others, and are therefore of the herbivorous species. True evolution of mankind consists in the multiplication of the herbivorous *homo sapiens* over against the carnivorous variety. For the moment, however, the carnivorous must still be our rulers. That must be so in a world believing in strong muscles.

V. ON HAVING STRONG MUSCLES

Another important consequence of our being animals and of our having mortal bodies is that we are susceptible to murder, and the average man doesn't like murder. True, we have a divine desire for knowledge and wisdom, but with knowledge come also differences of points of view and therefore arguments. Now in a world of immortals, arguments would last for ever, for I can conceive of no way of settling a dispute, if neither of the disputing immortals is willing to admit that he is wrong. In a world of mortals, the situation is different. The disputing party generally gets so obnoxious in the eyes of his opponent—and the more obnoxious he will appear, the more embarrassingly right his arguments are—so that the latter just kills him, and that settles the argument. If "A" kills "B," "A" is right; and if "B" kills "A," "B" is right. This, we hardly need remind ourselves, is the old, old method of settling arguments among brutes. In the animal kingdom, the lion is always right.

This is basically so true of human society that it offers a good interpretation of human history, even down to the present time. After all, Galileo retracted as well as discovered certain ideas about the roundness of the earth and the solar system. He retracted because he had a mortal body, susceptible to murder or torture. It would have taken infinite trouble to have argued with Galileo, and if Galileo had had no mortal body, you could never have convinced him that he was wrong, and that would have been an eternal nuisance. As it was, however, a torture chamber or a prison cell, not to speak of the gallows or the stake, sufficed to show how wrong he was. The clergy and the gentlemen of the period were determined to have a showdown with Galileo. The fact that Galileo was convinced that he was wrong strengthened the belief of the clergy of that period that they were right. That settled the matter very neatly.

There is something convenient and handy and efficient about this method of settling quarrels. Wars of depredation, religious wars, the conflict of Saladin and the Christians, the Inquisition, the burning of witches, the more modern preaching of the Christian gospel and proselytizing of heathens by gun-boats, the bearing of the White Man's Burden by the same means, the spread of civilization to Ethiopia by Mussolini's tanks and aeroplanes—all these proceed upon this animal logic to which all mankind is heir. If the Italians have better guns and shoot straighter and kill more people, Mussolini carries civilization to Ethiopia, and if, on the other hand, the Ethiopians have better guns and shoot straighter and kill more people, then Haile Selassie carries civilization to Italy.

There is something of the noble lion in us that disdains arguments. Hence our glorification of the soldier because he makes short shrift with dissenters. The quickest way to shut up a man who believes he is right, and who shows the propensity to argue, is to hang him. Men resort to talking only when they haven't the power to enforce their convictions upon others. On the other hand, men who act and have the power to act seldom talk. They despise arguments. After all, we talk in order to influence people, and if we know we can influence people, or control them, where is the need for talking at all? In this connection, is it not somewhat disheartening that the League of Nations talked so much during the last Manchurian and Ethiopian wars? It was altogether pathetic. There is something ominous about this quality of the League of Nations. On the other hand, this method of settling arguments by force can sometimes be carried to absurdity, if there is no sense of humour, as when the Japanese actually believe they can stamp out anti-Japanese feeling among the Chinese by bombing and machine-gunning them. That is why I am always slow to admit that we are rational animals.

I have always thought that the League of Nations was an excellent School for Modern Languages, specializing in translation of the modern tongues, giving the hearers excellent practice by first making an accomplished orator deliver a perfect address in English, and after the audience is thus made acquainted with the gist and content of the speech, having it rendered into fluent, flawless, classical French by a professional translator, with intonation, accent and all. In fact, it is better than the Berlitz School; it is a school of modern languages and public speaking to boot. One of my friends, in fact, reported that, after a six months' stay at Geneva, his lisping habit which had bothered him for years was cured. But the amazing fact is that even in this League of Nations, consecrated to the exchange of opinions, in an institution that conceivably has no other purpose than talking, there should be a distinction between Big Talkers and Small Talkers, the Big Talkers being those having Big Fists and the Small Talkers being those having Small Fists, which shows the whole thing is quite silly, if not a fake. As if the nations with Small Fists couldn't talk as fluently as the others! That is to say, if we mean just talking. . . . I cannot but think that this inherent belief in the eloquence of the Big Fist belongs to that animal heritage we have spoken of. (I shouldn't like to use the word "brute" here, and yet it would seem most appropriate in this connection.)

Of course, the gist of the matter lies in the fact that mankind is endowed with a chattering instinct as well as the fighting instinct. The tongue is, historically speaking, as old as the fist or the strong arm. The ability to talk distinguishes man from animals, and the mixture of verbiage and barrage seems to be a peculiarly human trait. This would seem to point to the permanency of institutions like the League of Nations, or the American Senate, or a tradesmen's convention—anything that affords men an opportunity to talk. It seems we humans are destined to chatter in order to find out who is right. That is all right; chattering is a characteristic of the angels. The peculiarly human trait lies in the fact that we chatter to a certain point until one of the parties of the dispute who has a stronger arm feels so embarrassed or angered— "Embarrassment leads naturally to anger," the Chinese say—until that embarrassed and therefore angered party thinks that this chattering has gone far enough, bangs the table, takes his opponent by the neck, gives him a wallop, and then looks about and asks the audience, which is the jury, "Am I right or am I wrong?" And as we learn at every tea-house, the audience invariably replies, "You are right!" Only humans ever settle a thing like that. Angels settle arguments all by chatter; brutes settle arguments all by muscle and claws; human beings alone settle them by a strange confusion of muscle and chatter. Angels believe sheerly in right; brutes believe sheerly in might; and human beings alone believe that might is right. Of the two, the chattering instinct, or the effort to find out who is right, is of course the nobler instinct. Some day we must all just chatter. That will be the salvation of mankind. At present, we must be content with the tea-house method and tea-house psychology. It doesn't matter whether we settle an argument in a tea-house or at the League of Nations; at both places, we are consistently and characteristically human.

I have witnessed two such tea-house scenes, one in 1931–32 and one in 1936. And the most amusing thing is, there was an admixture of a third instinct, modesty, in these two squabbles. In the 1931 affair, we were at the tea-house and there was one party in dispute with another and we were supposed to be the jury in the matter. The charge was some sort of a theft or steal-ing of property. The fellow with the strong arm at first joined in the argument, made an address to justify himself, spoke of his infinite patience with his neighbour—what restraint, what magnanimity, what unselfishness of motive in his desire to culti-vate his neighbour's garden! The funny thing was, he encouraged us to go on with our chatter while he stole outside the room and completed the stealing by staking up a fence around the stolen property, and then came in to ask us to go and see for ourselves if he wasn't right. We all went, saw the new fence being steadily pushed farther and farther to the West, for even then the fence was being constantly shifted. "Now, then, am I right or wrong?" We returned the verdict of "You are wrong!"—a little impudent of us to have said that. Thereupon the fellow with the strong arm protested that he was publicly insulted, that *his sense of modesty was injured* and his honour besmirched. Angrily and proudly he walked out of the room, wiping the dust off his shoes with sneering contempt, thinking us not good company for him. Imagine a man like that feeling insulted! That is why I say the third instinct of modesty complicates the matter. Thereupon the tea-house lost a good bit of its reputation as a place for scientific settling of private quarrels.

Then in 1936 we were called upon to judge another dispute. Another fellow with a strong arm said he would lay the facts of the dispute before the table and ask for justice. I heard the word "justice" with a shudder. And we believed him—not without a premonition as to the awkwardness of the situation or our questionable capacity as a jury. Determined to justify our reputation as fair-minded and competent judges, we, almost to a man, told him to his face that he was wrong, that he was nothing but a bully. He, too, felt insulted; again his sense of modesty was injured and his honour was besmirched. Well, then, he took the opponent by the neck and went outside and killed him, and then he came back and asked us, "Now am I right or wrong?" And we echoed, "You are right!" with a profound bow. Still not satisfied, he asked us, "Am I good enough company for you now?" and we shouted like a regular tea-house crowd, "Of course you are!" But what modesty on the part of the killer!

That is human civilization in the year of Our Lord 1936. I think the evolution of law and justice must have passed through scenes like the above in its earliest dawn, when we were little better than savages. From that tea-house scene to the Supreme Court of Justice, where the convicted does not protest that he is insulted by the conviction, seems a long, long way of development. For some ten years, while we started the tea-house, we thought we were on the road to civilization, but a wiser God, knowing human beings and our essential human traits, might have predicted the set-back. He might have known how we must fail and falter at the beginning, being only half civilized as we are at present. For the present, the reputation of the tea-house is gone, and we are back to falling upon each other and tearing each other's hair out and digging our teeth into each other's flesh, in the true grand style of the jungle. . . . Still I am not in total despair. That thing called modesty or shame is after all a good thing, and the chattering instinct also. The way I look at it is we are quite devoid of real shame at present. But let us continue to pretend that we have a sense of shame, and continue to chatter. By chattering we shall one day attain the blessed state of the angels.

VI. ON HAVING A MIND

The human mind, you say, is probably the noblest product of the Creation. This is a proposition that most people will admit, particularly when it refers to a mind like Albert Einstein's that can prove curved space by a long mathematical equation, or Edison's that can invent the gramophone and the motion picture, or the minds of other physicists who can measure the rays of an advancing or receding star or deal with the constitution of the unseen atoms, or that of the inventor of natural-colour movie cameras. Compared with the aimless, shifting and fumbling curiosity of the monkeys, we must agree that we have a noble, a glorious intellect that can comprehend the universe in which we are born.

The average mind, however, is charming rather than noble. Had the average mind been noble, we should be completely rational beings without sins or weaknesses or misconduct, and what an insipid world that would be! We should be so much less charming as creatures. I am such a humanist that saints without sins don't interest me. But we are charming in our irrationality, our inconsistencies, our follies, our sprees and holiday gaieties, our prejudices, bigotry and forgetfulness. Had we all perfect brains, we shouldn't have to make new resolutions every New Year. The beauty of the human life consists in the fact that, as we review on New Year's Eve our last New Year resolutions, we find we have fulfilled a third of them, left unfulfilled another third, and can't remember what the other third was. A plan that is sure to be carried out down to its last detail already loses interest for me. A general who goes to battle and is completely sure of his victory beforehand, and can even predict the exact number of casualties, will lose all interest in the battle, and might just as well throw up the whole thing. No one would play chess if he knew his opponent's mind—good, bad or indifferent—was infallible. All novels would be unreadable did we know exactly how the mind of each character was going to work and were we able consequently to predict the exact outcome. The reading of a novel is but the chase of a wayward and unpredictable mind making its incalculable decisions at certain moments, through a maze of evolving circumstances. A stern, unforgiving father who does not at some moment relax ceases to impress us as human, and even a faithless husband who is for ever faithless soon forfeits the reader's interest. Imagine a renowned, proud composer, whom no one could induce to compose an opera for a certain beautiful woman, but who, on hearing that a hated rival composer is thinking of doing it, immediately snatches at the job; or a scientist who in his life has consistently refused to publish his writings in newspapers, but who, on seeing a rival scientist make a slip with one single letter, forgets his own rule and rushes into print. There we have laid our finger upon the singularly *human* quality of the mind.

The human mind is charming in its unreasonableness, its inveterate prejudices, and its waywardness and unpredictability. If we haven't learned this truth, we have learned nothing from the century of study of human psychology. In other words, our minds still retain the aimless, fumbling quality of simian intelligence.

Consider the evolution of the human mind. Our mind was originally an organ for sensing danger and preserving life. That this mind eventually came to appreciate logic and a correct mathematical equation I consider a mere accident. Certainly it was not created for that purpose. It was created for sniffing food, and if after sniffing food, it can also sniff an abstract mathematical formula, that's all to the good. My conception of the human brain, as of all animal brains, is that it is like an octopus or a starfish with tentacles, tentacles for feeling the truth and eating it. To-day we still speak of "feeling" the truth, rather than "thinking" it. The brain, together with other sensory organs, constitutes the feelers. How its tenacles feel the truth is still as great a mystery in physics as the sensitivity to light of the purple in the eye's retina. Every time the brain dissociates itself from the collaborating sensory apparatus and indulges in so-called "abstract thinking," every time it gets away from what William James calls the perceptual reality and escapes into the world of conceptual reality, it becomes devitalized, dehumanized and degenerate. We all labour under the misconception that the true function of the mind is thinking, a misconception that is bound to lead to serious mistakes in philosophy unless we revise our notion of the term "thinking" itself. It is a misconception that is apt to leave the philosopher disillusioned when he goes out of his studio and watches the crowd at the market. As if thinking had much to do with our everyday behaviour!

The late James Harvey Robinson has tried to show, in *The Mind in the Making*, how our mind gradually evolved from, and is still operating upon, four underlying layers: the animal mind, the savage mind, the childish mind and the traditional civilized mind, and has further shown us the necessity of developing a more critical mind if the present human civilization is to continue. In my scientific moments, I am inclined to agree with him, but in my wiser moments, I doubt the feasibility, or even the desirability, of such a step of general progress. I prefer to have our mind charmingly unreasonable as it is at present. I should hate to see a world in which we are all perfectly rational beings. Do I distrust scientific progress? No, I distrust sainthood. Am I anti-intellectualistic? Perhaps yes; perhaps no. I am merely in love with life, and being in love with life, I distrust the intellect profoundly. Imagine a world in which there are no stories of murder in newspapers, every one is so omniscient that no house ever catches fire, no aeroplane ever has an accident, no husband deserts his wife, no pastor elopes with a choir-girl, no king abdicates his throne for love, no man changes his mind and everyone proceeds to carry out with logical precision a career that he mapped out for himself at the age of ten—good-bye to this happy human world! All the excitement and uncertainty of life would be gone. There would be no literature because there would be no sin, no misbehaviour, no human weakness, no upsetting passion, no prejudices, no irregularities and, worst of all, no surprises. It would be like a horse-race in which every one of the forty or fifty thousand spectators knew the winner. Human fallibility is the very essence of the colour of life, as the upsets are the very colour and interest of a steeplechase. Imagine a Doctor Johnson without his bigoted prejudices! If we were all completely rational beings, we should then, instead of growing into perfect wisdom, degenerate into automatons, the human mind serving merely to register certain impulses as unfailingly as a gas meter. That would be inhuman, and anything inhuman is bad.

My readers may suspect that I am trying a desperate defence of human frailties and making virtues of their vices, and yet it is not so. What we gained in correctness of conduct through the development of a completely rational mind, we should lose in the fun and colour of life. And nothing is so uninteresting as to spend one's life with a paragon of virtue as a husband or wife. I have no doubt that a society of such perfectly rational beings would be perfectly fitted to survive, and yet I wonder whether survival on such terms is worth having. Have a society that is well-ordered, by all means—but not too well-ordered! I recall the ants, who, to my mind, are probably the most perfectly rational creatures on earth. No doubt ants have evolved such a perfect socialist state that they have been able to live on this pattern for probably the last million years. So far as complete rationality of conduct is concerned, I think we have to hand it to the ants, and let the human beings come second (I doubt very much whether they deserve that). The ants are a hard-working, sane, saving and thrifty lot. They are the socially regimented and individually disciplined beings that we are not. They don't mind working fourteen hours a day for the state or the community; they have a sense of duty and almost no sense of rights; they have persistence, order, courtesy and courage, and above all, self-discipline. We are poor specimens of self-discipline, not even good enough for museum pieces.

Run across any hall of honour, with statues of the great men of history lining the corridor, and you will perceive that rationality of conduct is probably the last thing to be recalled from their lives. This Julius Cæsar, who fell in love with Cleopatra—noble Julius Cæsar, who was so completely irrational that he almost forgot (as Antony did entirely forget) an empire for a woman. That Moses, who in a fit of rage shattered the sacred stone tablets which had taken him forty days on Mount Sinai to inscribe in company with God, and in that he was no more rational than the Israelites who forsook God and took to worshipping the Golden Calf during his absence. That King David, who was alternately cruel and generous, alternately religious and impious, who worshipped God and sinned and wrote psalms of repentance and worshipped God again. King Solomon, the very image of wisdom, who couldn't do a thing about his son . . . Confucius, who told a visitor he was not at home and then, as the visitor was just outside the door, sang upstairs in order to let him know that he was at home . . . Jesus, with his tears at Gethsemane and his doubts on the cross . . . Shakespeare, who bequeathed his "second-best bed" to his wife . . . Milton, who couldn't get along with his seventeen-year-old wife and therefore wrote a treatise on divorce and, being attacked, then burst forth into a defence of the liberty of speech in *Areopagitica* . . . Goethe, who went through the Church's wedding ceremony with his wife, their nineteen-year-old son standing by their side . . . Jonathan Swift and Stella . . . Ibsen and Emilie Bardach (he kept rational—good for him). . . .

Is it not plain that passion rather than reason rules the world? And that what made these great men lovable, what made them human, was not their rationality, but their lack of rationality? Chinese obituary notices and biographical sketches of men and women written by their children are so unreadable, so uninteresting and so untrue, because they make all their ancestors appear abnormally and wholly virtuous beings. . . . The great criticism of my book on China by my countrymen is that I make the Chinese too human, that I have painted their weaknesses as well as their strength. My countrymen (at least the little bureaucrats) believe that if I had painted China as a paradise inhabited by Confucianist saints only, living in a millennium of peace and reason, I could have done more effective propaganda for my country! There is really no limit to the stupidity of bureaucrats. . . . But the very charm of biography, its very readability, depends on showing the human side of a great character which is so similar to ours. Every touch of irrational behaviour in a biography is a stroke in convincing reality. On that alone, the success of Lytton Strachey's portraits depends.

An excellent illustration of a perfectly sound mind is provided by the English. The English have got bad logic, but very good tentacles in their brains for sensing danger and preserving life. I have not been able to discover anything logical in their national behaviour or their rational history. Their universities, their constitution, their Anglican Church are all pieces of patchwork, being the steady accretions of a process of historical growth. The very strength of the British Empire consists in the English lack of cerebration, in their total inability to see the other man's point of view, and in their strong conviction that the English way is the only right way and English food is the only good food. The moment the Englishmen learn to reason and lose their strong confidence in themselves, the British Empire will collapse. For no one can go about conquering the world if he has doubts about himself. You can make absolutely nothing out of the English attitude toward their king, their loyalty to, and their quite genuine affection for, a king who is deprived by them of the liberty of speech and is summarily told to behave or quit the throne. . . . When Elizabethan England needed pirates to protect the Empire, she was able to produce enough pirates to meet the situation and glorified them. In every period, England was able to fight the right war, against the right enemy, with the right ally, on the right side, at the right time, and call it by a wrong name. They didn't do it by logic, did they? They did it by their tentacles.

The English have a ruddy complexion, developed no doubt by the London fog and by cricket. A skin that is so healthy cannot help playing an important part in their thinking, that is, in the process of feeling their way through life. And as the English think with their healthy skin, so the Chinese think with their profound intestines. That is a pretty generally established matter in China. We Chinese know that we do think with our intestines; scholars are said to have "a bellyful of ideas," or "of scholarship," "of poetry and literature," or "a bellyful of sorrow," or "of anger," "remorse," "chagrin," or "longing." Chinese lovers separated from each other write letters to say that "their sorrowful intestines are tied into a hundred knots," or that at their last parting "their intestines were broken." Chinese scholars who have arranged their ideas for an essay or a speech, but have not written them down on paper, are said to have their "belly manuscript" ready. They have got their ideas all arranged down there. I'm quite sure they have. This is, of course, all strictly scientific and capable of proof, especially when modern psychologists come to understand better the emotional quality and texture of our thought. But the Chinese don't need any scientific proof. They just feel it down there. Only by appreciating the fact that the emotional quality of Chinese melodies all starts from below the diaphragm of the singers, can one understand Chinese music with its profound emotional colour.

One must never deprecate the capacity of the human mind when dealing with the natural universe or anything except human relationships. Optimistic about the conquests of science, I am less hopeful about the general development of a critical mind in dealing with human affairs, or about mankind reaching a calm and understanding far above the sway of passions. Mankind as individuals may have reached austere heights, but mankind as social groups are still subject to primitive passions, occasional back-slidings and outcroppings of the savage instincts, and occasional waves of fanaticism and mass hysteria.

Knowing then our human frailties, we have the more reason to hate the despicable wretch who in demagogue fashion makes use of our human foibles to hound us into another world war; who inculcates hatred, of which we already have too much; who glorifies self-aggrandizement and self-interest, of which there is no lack; who appeals to our animal bigotry and racial prejudice; who deletes the fifth commandment in the training of youth and encourages killing and war as noble, as if we were not already warlike enough creatures; and who whips up and stirs our mortal passions, as if we were not already very near the beast. This wretch's mind, no matter how cunning, how sagacious, how worldly-wise, is itself a manifestation of the beast. The gracious spirit of wisdom is tied down to a beast or a demon in us, which by this time we have come to understand is nothing but our animal heritage, or rather it ties this demon down by an old and worn leash and holds it but in temporary submission. At any time the leash may snap, and the demon be unleashed, and amidst hosannas the car of Juggernaut will ride roughshod over us, just to remind us once more how terribly near the savage we have been all this time, and how superficial is our civilization. Civilization will then be turned into a magnificent stage, on which Moors will kill Christians and Christians will kill Moors and Negroes fall upon whites and whites stab Negroes and field-mice emerge from sewers to eat human corpses and hawks circle in the air over an abundant human feast—all just to remind ourselves of the brotherhood of animals. Nature is quite capable of such experiments.

Psycho-analysts often cure mental patients by making them review their past and see their life objectively. Perhaps if mankind will think more of their past, they will also have a better mastery over themselves. The knowledge that we have an animal heritage and that we are very near the beasts might help to check our behaving like beasts. This animal heritage of ours makes it easier to see ourselves as we are in animal fables and satires, as in *Æsop's Fables,* Chaucer's *Parliament of Fowles,* Swift's *Gulliver's Travels* and Anatole France's *Penguin Island.* These animal fables were good in Æsop's day and will still be good in the year A.D. 4000.

How can we remedy the situation? The critical mind is too thin and cold, thinking itself will help little and reason will be of small avail; only the spirit of reasonableness, a sort of warm, glowing, emotional and intuitive thinking, joined with compassion, will insure us against a reversion to our ancestral type. Only the development of our life to bring it into harmony with our instincts can save us. I consider the education of our senses and our emotions rather more important than the education of our ideas.

CHAPTER FOUR

On Being Human

I. ON HUMAN DIGNITY

IN THE PRECEDING CHAPTER we have seen man's mortal heritage, the part he shares with the animal world, and its consequences on the character of human civilization. But still we find the picture is not complete. There is still something missing for a well-rounded view of human nature and human dignity. Ah, human dignity—that is the word! There is a need of emphasizing that and there is a need of knowing what that dignity consists of, lest we confuse the issue and lose it. For there is a very evident danger of our losing that dignity in the twentieth century and especially in the present and immediate following decades.

"Don't you think a man is the most amazing of animals, if you insist that we are animals?" I quite agree. Man alone has invented a civilization, and this is not something to be lightly dismissed. There are perhaps finer animals with better forms and nobler structures, like the horse; with finer muscles, like the lion; with a finer sense of smell and greater docility and loyalty, like the dog; or better vision, like the eagle; or a better sense of direction, like the homing pigeon; with greater thrift and discipline and capacity for hard work, like the ant; with a sweeter temper like the dove or the deer; more patience and contentment like the cow; better singers, like the lark; and better-dressed beings, like the parrot and the peacock. Still there is something in a monkey that makes me prefer the monkey to all these animals, and something of the monkey curiosity and monkey cleverness in man that makes me prefer to be a man. Granted that ants are more rational and better-disciplined beings than ourselves, as I have pointed out, and granted that they have a more stable form of government than present-day Spain, still they haven't got a library or a museum, have they? Any time ants or elephants can invent a giant telescope or discover a new variable star or predict a solar eclipse, or seals can discover the science of calculus or beavers can cut the Panama Canal, I will hand them the championship as masters of the world and Lords of Creation. Yes, we can be proud of ourselves, but we had better find out what it is that we have got to be proud of, what is the essence of human dignity.

This human dignity, as I have already hinted at the beginning of this book, consists of four characteristics of the scamp, who has been glorified by Chinese literature. They are: a playful curiosity, a capacity for dreams, a sense of humour to correct those dreams, and finally a certain waywardness and incalculability of behaviour. Together they represent the Chinese version of the American doctrine of the individual. It is impossible to paint a more glowing portrait of the individualist than has been done for the scamp in Chinese literature, and it is certainly no accident that Walt Whitman, the greatest literary champion of American individualism, is himself called the "Magnificent Idler."

II. ON PLAYFUL CURIOSITY: THE RISE OF HUMAN CIVILIZATION

How did the human scamp begin his ascent to civilization? What were the first signs of promise in him, or of his developing intelligence? The answer is undoubtedly to be found in man's playful curiosity, in his first efforts to fumble about with his hands and turn everything inside out to examine it, as a monkey in his idle moments turns the eyelid or the ear-lobe of a fellow-monkey, looking for lice or for nothing at all—just turning about for turning about's sake. Go to the zoo and watch a pair of monkeys picking each other's ears, and there you have the promise of an Isaac Newton or an Albert Einstein.

This figure of the playful, fumbling activities of the exploring human hand is more than a figure. It is a scientific truth. The very basis of human civilization started with the emancipation of the hands consequent upon man's assuming an erect stature and becoming a biped. Such playful curiosity we see even in cats, the moment their front paws are relieved from the duty of walking and supporting the body. It might have been quite as possible for a civilization to be developed from cats as well as from monkeys, except for the fact that in the case of the monkeys, the fingers were already well developed through the clasping of branches, whereas the cat's paws were still paws—merely lumps of flesh and cartilage.

Let me for a moment forget that I am not a qualified biologist and speculate about the rise of human civilization from this emancipation of the hands, because I have a few things to say here, which may or may not have been observed by others. The assumption of an erect stature and the consequent emancipation of the hand had extremely far-reaching results. It brought about the use of tools, the sense of modesty, the subjection of women, and in this connection probably also the development of language, and finally a prodigious increase in playful curiosity and the instinct of exploration. It is pretty well known that human civilization began with the discovery of tools and that this came from the development of the human hands. When the big anthropoid ape descended partially from the tree, probably because his body was too heavy, he had two roads to follow, either that of a baboon, going on all fours, or that of the orang-outang, learning to walk on its hind legs. Human ancestry could not possibly have come from the baboon, a quadruped (or quadrumanum), because the baboon's front paws were too much occupied. On the other hand, with an erect posture more or less successfully acquired by the orang-outang, the hands acquired freedom, and how significant was this freedom for all civilization! By that time, the anthropoid ape certainly had learned already to pick fruit with his hands, instead of with his big jaws. It was but a simple step, when he took to living in a cave on a high cliff, to pick stones and pebbles and roll them down from the cliff on his enemies. That was the first tool man ever used. There we must picture a constant fumbling and manipulating activity of his hands, grasping at things for some purpose or for no purpose. There would be sharp flints or jagged pieces of rocks which through his aimless fumbling were accidentally discovered to be more useful for killing than round pieces of stone. The mere act of turning things about, for instance, of looking at the back as well as the front of an ear-lobe, must have already increased his power for conceiving things in their totality and therefore also the number of images he carried in his brain, thus stimulating the growth of the frontal lobes of the brain.

I believe the mystery of the origin of sexual modesty in man, which is totally absent in animals, is also due to this erect posture. For by this new posture, which Father Nature in his scheme of things probably never intended, certain posterior parts of the body at one stroke came to occupy the centre of the body, and what was naturally behind came in front. Allied to this terrible new situation were other maladjustments chiefly affecting women, causing frequent abortions and menstrual troubles. Anatomically, our muscles were designed and developed for the quadruped position. The mother pig, for instance, carries its litter of pig embryos logically suspended from its horizontal spine, like wash hung on a line with its weight properly distributed. Asking the human pregnant mother to stand erect is like tipping the wash-line vertically and expecting the clothes to remain in position. Our peritoneal muscles are badly designed for that: if we were originally bipeds, such muscles should be nicely attached to the shoulder, and the whole thing would be a more pleasant job. Anybody with a knowledge of the anatomy of the human womb and ovaries should be surprised that they keep in position and function at all, and that there are not more dislocations and menstrual troubles. The whole mystery of menstruation has never yet been satisfactorily explained, but I am quite sure that, even granted that a periodical renewal of ova is necessary, we must admit that the function is carried out in a most inefficient, unnecessarily long and needlessly painful manner, and I have no doubt that this inefficiency is due to the biped position.

This, then, led to the subjection of women and probably also to the development of human society with its present characteristics.

I do not think that if the human mother could walk on all fours, she would have been subjected by her husband at all. Two forces came into play simultaneously. On the one hand, men and women were already by that time idle, curious and playful creatures. The amorous instinct developed new expressions. Kissing was still not entirely pleasant, or wholly successful, as we can see it between two chimpanzees kissing each other with hard, clapping, protruding jaws. But the hand developed new, more sensitive and softer movements, the movements of patting, pawing, tickling and embracing, all as incidental results of chasing lice on each other's body. I have no doubt that lyrical poetry would not have developed if our hairy human ancestors had had no lice on their bodies. This, then, must have helped considerably to develop the amorous instinct.

On the other hand, the biped human pregnant mother was now for a considerably longer period subjected to a state of grievous helplessness. During the earlier period of imperfect adjustment to the erect position, I can see that it was even more difficult for the pregnant mother to carry her load and go about, especially before the legs and heels were properly modified, and the pelvis was properly projected backwards to counter-balance the burden in front. At the earliest stages, the biped position was so awkward that a Pleistocene mother must have shamefacedly gone on all fours when nobody was looking, to relieve her aching spine. What with these inconveniences and other women's troubles, the human mother began to use other tactics and play for love, thereby losing some of her spirit of independence. Good Lord, she had need of being patted and pawed during those times of confinement! The erect posture prolonged, too, the period of infancy by making it difficult for the human baby to learn to walk. While the baby calf or baby elephant can trot about practically as soon as it is born, the human baby took two or three years to learn the job, and who was the most natural person to look after him except the mother? [1]

[1] This parental care gradually became more and more lengthened in period, so that while a savage child of six or seven is practically independent, the child in civilization takes a quarter of a century to learn to make his living, and even then has to learn it all over again.

Man then went off into a completely new path of development. Human society developed from the single fact that sex, in the broadest sense of the word, began to colour human daily life. The human female was more consciously and constantly a female than a female animal—the negress more than the tigress, and the countess more than the lioness. Specialization between men and women in the civilized sense began to develop, and the female, instead of the traditional male, began to decorate herself, probably by picking hair out of her face and her breast. It was all a matter of tactics for survival. We see these tactics clearly in animals. The tiger attacks, the tortoise hides, and the horse runs away— all for survival. Love or beauty and the gentle cunning of womanhood had then a survival value. The man probably had a stronger arm, and there was no use fighting him; why not, therefore, bribe and flatter and please him? That is the very character of our civilization even to-day. Instead of learning to repel and attack, woman learned to attract, and instead of trying to achieve her goal by force, she tried her best to achieve it by softer means. And after all, softness is civilization. I rather think therefore that human civilization began with woman rather than with man.

And then I also cannot help but think that woman played a greater role than man in the development of chattering, which we call language to-day. The instinct for chatter is so deep in women that I firmly believe they must have helped to create human language in a more important manner than men. Early men, I imagine, were quite morose, silent creatures. I suppose human language began when the first male anthropoids were away from their cave dwellings hunting, and two women neighbours were discussing before their caves whether William was a better fellow than Harold or Harold was a better fellow than William, and how Harold was disgustingly amorous last night, and how easily he could be offended. In some such form, human language must have begun. It cannot be otherwise. Of course the taking of food by hands, thus relieving the original double duty of the jaw in both taking and eating food, eventually made it possible also for the jaw gradually to recede and diminish in size, and

[73]

thus also helped toward the development of human language.

But, as I have suggested, the most important consequence of this new posture was the emancipation of the hands for turning things about and examining them inside out, as symbolized in the pastime of chasing lice by monkeys. From this chasing of lice, the development of the spirit of free inquiry into knowledge had its start. To-day human progress still consists very largely in chasing after some form or other of lice that is bothering human society. An instinct for curiosity has been developed which compels the human mind to explore freely and playfully into all kinds of subjects and social diseases. This mental activity has nothing to do with seeking food; it is an exercise of the human spirit pure and simple. The monkeys do not chase after lice in order to eat them, but for the sheer fun of it. And this is the characteristic of all worth-while human learning and human scholarship, an interest in things in themselves and a playful, idle desire to know them as they are, and not because that knowledge directly or immediately helps in feeding our stomach. (If I contradict myself here as a Chinese, I am happy as a Chinese that I contradict myself.) This I regard as characteristically human and contributing very largely to human dignity. Knowledge, or the process of seeking knowledge, is a form of play; it is certainly so with all scientists and inventors who are worth anything and who truly accomplish worth-while results. Good medical research doctors are more interested in microbes than in human beings, and astronomers will try to record or register the movements of a distant star hundreds of millions of miles away from us, although the star cannot possibly have any direct bearing on human life on this planet. Almost all animals, especially the young, have also the play instinct, but it is in man alone that playful curiosity has been developed to an important extent.

It is for this reason that I hate censors and all agencies and forms of government that try to control our thought. I cannot but believe that such a censor or such a ruler is wilfully or unintentionally insulting human intelligence. If the liberty of thought is the highest activity of the human mind, then the suppression of that liberty must be the most degrading to us as human beings. Euripides defined the slave as a man who has lost his liberty of thought or opinion. Every autocracy is a factory for turning out gorgeous Euripidean slaves. Don't we have fine examples of them, East and West, in the twentieth century and at the very home of culture? Every autocratic government, no matter in what form, therefore, is intellectually retrograde. We have seen it in the Middle Ages in general, and in the Spanish Inquisition in particular. Short-sighted politicians or clergymen may think that uniformity of belief and thought contributes toward peace and order, but historically the consequence is always depressing and degrading to the human character. Such autocrats must have a great contempt for the people in general when they do not confine themselves to ordering a nation's external conduct, but proceed also to regiment the people's inner thoughts and beliefs. They have a naïve assurance that human minds will put up with this uniformity and that they will like or dislike a book or a concerto or a moving picture exactly as the official propagandist or chief of publicity bureau tells them to. Every autocratic government has tried to confuse literature with propaganda, art with politics, anthropology with patriotism, and religion with worship of the living ruler.

It simply can't be done, and if the controllers of thought go too far in running against human nature itself, they are thereby sowing the seeds of their downfall. As Mencius put it, "If the ruler considers the people as blades of grass, then the people will consider their ruler as a robber or enemy." There is no greater robber in this world than he who robs us of our liberty of thought. Deprived of that, we might as well go down on all fours, call the whole biped experiment of walking on two legs a mistake, and revert to our earlier posture of at least some 30,000 years ago. In Mencian terms, therefore, the people will resent this robber as much as the latter despises the people, and exactly in the same proportion. The more the robber takes away, the more the people hate him. And as nothing is so precious and personal and intimate as our intellectual, moral or religious beliefs, no greater hatred can be aroused in us than by the man who deprives us of the right to believe what we believe. But such short-sighted stupidity is natural in an autocrat, because I believe such autocrats are always intellectually retrograde. And the resilience of human character and unconquerable liberty of the human conscience always spring back and hit the autocratic ruler with a vengeance.

III. ON DREAMS

Discontent, they say, is divine; I am quite sure, anyway, that discontent is human. The monkey was the first morose animal, for I have never seen a truly sad face in animals except in the chimpanzee. And I have often thought such a one a philosopher, because sadness and thoughtfulness are so akin. There is something in such a face which tells me that he is thinking. Cows don't seem to think, at least they don't seem to philosophize, because they look always so contented, and while elephants may store up a terrific anger, the eternal swinging of their trunks seems to take the place of thinking and banish all brooding discontent. Only a monkey can look thoroughly bored with life. Great indeed is the monkey!

Perhaps after all philosophy began with the sense of boredom. Anyway it is characteristic of humans to have a sad, vague and wistful longing for an ideal. Living in a real world, man has yet the capacity and tendency to dream of another world. Probably the difference between man and the monkeys is that the monkeys are merely bored, while man has boredom plus imagination. All of us have the desire to get out of an old rut, and all of us wish to be something else, and all of us dream. The private dreams of being a corporal, the corporal dreams of being a captain, and the captain dreams of being a major or colonel. A colonel, if he is worth his salt, thinks nothing of being a colonel. In more graceful phraseology, he calls it merely an opportunity to serve his fellow-men. And really there is very little else to it. The plain fact is, Joan Crawford thinks less of Joan Crawford and Janet Gaynor thinks less of Janet Gaynor than the world thinks of them. "Aren't you remarkable?" the world says to all the great, and the great, if they are truly great, always reply, "What is remarkable?" The world is therefore pretty much like an *à la carte* restaurant where everybody thinks the food the next table has ordered is so much more inviting and delicious than his own. A contemporary Chinese professor has made the witticism that in the matter of desirability, "Wives are always better if they are others', while writing is always better if it is one's own." In this sense, therefore, there is no one completely satisfied in this world. Everyone wants to be somebody so long as that somebody is not himself.

This human trait is undoubtedly due to our power of imagination and our capacity for dreaming. The greater the imaginative power of a man, the more perpetually he is dissatisfied. That is why an imaginative child is always a more difficult child; he is more often sad and morose like a monkey than happy and contented like a cow. Also divorce must necessarily be more common among the idealists and the more imaginative people than among the unimaginative. The vision of a desirable ideal life companion has an irresistible force which the less imaginative and less idealistic never feel. On the whole, humanity is as much led astray as led upwards by this capacity for idealism, but human progress without this imaginative gift is itself unthinkable.

Man, we are told, has aspirations. They are very laudable things to have, for aspirations are generally classified as noble. And why not? Whether as individuals or as nations, we all dream and act more or less in accordance with our dreams. Some dream a little more than others, as there is a child in every family who dreams more and perhaps one who dreams less. And I must confess to a secret partiality for the one who dreams. Generally he is the sadder one, but no matter; he is also capable of greater joys and thrills and heights of ecstasy. For I think we are constituted like a receiving set for ideas, as radio sets are equipped for receiving music from the air. Some sets with a finer response pick up the finer short waves which are lost to the other sets, and why, of course, that finer, more distant music is all the more precious if only because it is less easily perceivable.

[77]

And those dreams of our childhood, they are not so unreal as we might think. Somehow they stay with us throughout our life. That is why, if I had my choice of being any one author in the world, I would be Hans Christian Andersen rather than anybody else. To write the story of *The Mermaid,* or to be the Mermaid ourselves, thinking the Mermaid's thoughts and aspiring to be old enough to come up to the surface of the water, is to have felt one of the keenest and most beautiful delights that humanity is capable of.

And so, out in an alley, up in an attic, or down in the barn or lying along the waterside, a child always dreams, and the dreams are real. So Thomas Edison dreamed. So Robert Louis Stevenson dreamed. So Sir Walter Scott dreamed. All three dreamed in their childhood. And out of the stuff of such magic dreams are woven some of the finest and most beautiful fabrics we have ever seen. But these dreams are also partaken of by lesser children. The delights they get are as great, if the visions or contents of their dreams are different. Every child has a soul which yearns, and carries a longing on his lap and goes to sleep with it, hoping to find his dream come true when he wakes up with the morn. He tells no one of these dreams, for these dreams are his own, and for that reason they are a part of his innermost growing self. Some of these children's dreams are clearer than others, and they have a force which compels their own realization; on the other hand, with growing age, those less clear dreams are forgotten, and we all live through life trying to tell those dreams of our childhood, and "sometimes we die ere we find the language."

And so with nations, too. Nations have their dreams and the memories of such dreams persist through generations and centuries. Some of these are noble dreams, and others wicked and ignoble. The dreams of conquest and of being bigger and stronger than all the others are always bad dreams, and such nations always have more to worry about than others who have more peaceful dreams. But there are other and better dreams, dreams of a better world, dreams of peace and of nations living at peace with one another, and dreams of less cruelty, injustice, and poverty and suffering. The bad dreams tend to destroy the good dreams of humanity, and there is a struggle and a fight between these good and bad dreams. People fight for their dreams as much as they fight for their earthly possessions. And so dreams descend from the world of idle visions and enter the world of reality, and become a real force in our life. However vague they are, dreams have a way of concealing themselves and leave us no peace until they are translated into reality, like seeds germinating under ground, sure to sprout in their search for the sunlight. Dreams are very real things.

There is also a danger of our having confused dreams and dreams that do not correspond to reality. For dreams are escapes also, and a dreamer often dreams to escape from the present world, hardly knowing where. The Blue Bird always attracts the romanticist's fancy. There is such a human desire to be different from what we are, to get out of the present ruts, that anything which offers a change always has a tremendous appeal to average humanity. A war is always attractive because it offers a city clerk the chance of donning a uniform and wearing puttees and a chance for travel *gratis,* while an armistice or peace is always desirable after three or four years in the trenches because it offers the soldier a chance to come back home and wear civilian dress and a scarlet necktie once more. Some such excitement humanity evidently needs, and if war is to be avoided, governments may just as well recruit people between twenty and forty-five under a conscript system and send them on European tours to see some exposition or other, once every ten years. The British Government is spending five billion pounds on its Rearmament Programme, a sum sufficient to send every Englishman on a trip to the Riviera. The argument is, of course, that expenditures on war are a necessity while travel is a luxury. I feel inclined to disagree: travel is a necessity, while war is a luxury.

There are other dreams too. Dreams of Utopia and dreams of immortality. The dream of immortality is entirely human—note its universality—although it is vague like the rest, and few people know what they are going to do when they find eternity hanging on their hands. After all, the desire for immortality is very much akin to the psychology of suicide, its exact opposite. Both presume that the present world is not good enough for us. Why is the present world not good enough for us? We should be more surprised at the question than at any answer to the question if we were out on a visit to the country on a spring day.

And so with dreams of Utopia also. Idealism is merely that state of mind which believes in another world order, no matter what kind of an order, so long as it is different from the present one. The idealistic liberal is always one who thinks his own country the worst possible country and the society in which he lives the worst of all possible forms of society. He is still the fellow in the *à la carte* restaurant who believes that the next table's order of dishes is better than his own. As the *New York Times's* "Topics" writer says, only the Russian Dnieper Dam is a real dam in the eyes of these liberals and democracies have never built any dams. And of course only the Soviets have built a subway. On the other hand, the Fascist press tells their people that only in their country have mankind discovered the only sensible, right and working form of government. Therein lies the danger of Utopian liberals as well as of Fascist propaganda chiefs, and as a very necessary corrective, they can have nothing better than a sense of humour.

IV. ON THE SENSE OF HUMOUR

I doubt whether the importance of humour has been fully appreciated, or the possibility of its use in changing the quality and character of our entire cultural life—the place of humour in politics, humour in scholarship, and humour in life. Because its function is chemical, rather than physical, it alters the basic texture of our thought and experience. Its importance in national life we can take for granted. The inability to laugh cost the former Kaiser Wilhelm an empire, or as an American might say, cost the German people billions of dollars. Wilhelm Hohenzollern probably could laugh in his private life, but he always looked so terribly impressive with his upturned moustache in public, as if he was always angry with somebody. And then the quality of his laughter and the things he laughed at—laughter at victory, at success, at getting on top of others—were just as important factors in determining his life fortune. Germany lost the war because Wilhelm Hohenzollern did not know when to laugh, or what to laugh at. His dreams were not restrained by laughter.

It seems to me the worst comment on dictatorships is that presidents of democracies can laugh while dictators always look so serious—with a protruding jaw, a determined chin, and a pouched lower lip, as if they were doing something terribly important and the world could not be saved, except by them. Franklin D. Roosevelt often smiles in public—good for him, and good for the American people who like to see their president smile. But where are the smiles of the European dictators? Or don't their people want to see them smile? Or must they indeed look either frightened, or dignified, or angry, or in any case look frightfully serious in order to keep themselves in the saddle? The best thing I have ever read about Hitler is that he is completely natural in private. It somehow restores my confidence in him. But something must be wrong with dictatorships if dictators have to look either angry or else vainglorious. The whole temper is wrong.

We are not indulging in idle fooling now, discussing the smiles of dictators; it is terribly serious when our rulers do not smile, because they have got all the guns. On the other hand, the tremendous importance of humour in politics can be realized only when we picture for ourselves (by that faculty for dreaming known as "D") a world of joking rulers. Send, for instance, five or six of the world's best humorists to an international conference, and give them the plenipotentiary powers of autocrats, and the world will be saved. As humour necessarily goes with good sense and the reasonable spirit, plus some exceptionally subtle powers of the mind in detecting inconsistencies and follies and bad logic, and as this is the highest form of human intelligence, we may be sure that each nation will thus be represented at the conference by its sanest and soundest mind. Let Shaw represent Ireland, Stephen Leacock represent Canada; G. K. Chesterton is dead, but P. G. Wodehouse or Aldous Huxley may represent England. Will Rogers is dead, otherwise he would make a fine diplomat representing the U.S.; we can have in his stead Robert Benchley or Heywood Broun. There will be others from Italy and France and Germany and Russia. Send these people to a conference on the eve of a great war, and see if they can start a European war, no matter how hard they try. Can you imagine this bunch of international diplomats starting a war or even plotting for one? The sense of humour forbids it. All people are too serious and half-insane when they declare a war against another people. They are so sure that they are right and that God is on their side. The humorists, gifted with better horse-sense, don't think so. You will find George Bernard Shaw shouting that Ireland is wrong, and a Berlin cartoonist protesting that the mistake is all theirs, and Heywood Broun claiming the largest share of bungling for America, while Stephen Leacock in the chair makes a general apology for mankind, gently reminding us that in the matter of stupidity and sheer foolishness no nation can claim itself to be the superior of others. How in the name of humour are we going to start a war under these conditions?

For who have started wars for us? The ambitious, the able, the clever, the scheming, the cautious, the sagacious, the haughty, the over-patriotic, the people inspired with the desire to "serve" mankind, people who have a "career" to carve and an "impression" to make on the world, who expect and hope to look down the ages from the eyes of a bronze figure sitting on a bronze horse in some square. Curiously, the able, the clever, and the ambitious and haughty are at the same time the most cowardly and muddle-headed, lacking in the courage and depth and subtlety of the humorists. They are for ever dealing with trivialities, while the humorists with their greater sweep of mind can envisage larger things. As it is, a diplomat who does not whisper in a low voice and look properly scared and intimidated and correct and cautious is no diplomat at all. . . . But we don't even have to have a conference of international humorists to save the world. There is a sufficient stock of this desirable commodity called a sense of humour in all of us. When Europe seems to be on the brink of a catastrophic war, we may still send to the conferences our worst diplomats, the most "experienced" and self-assured, the most ambitious, the most whispering, most intimidated and correct and properly scared, even the most anxious to "serve" mankind. If it be required that, at the opening of every morning and afternoon session, ten minutes be devoted to the showing of a Mickey Mouse picture, at which all the diplomats are compelled to be present, any war can still be averted.

This I conceive to be the chemical function of humour: to change the character of our thought. I rather think that it goes to the very root of culture, and opens a way to the coming of the Reasonable Age in the future human world. For humanity I can visualize no greater ideal than that of the Reasonable Age. For that, after all, is the only important thing, the arrival of a race of men imbued with a greater reasonable spirit, with greater prevalence of good sense, simple thinking, a peaceable temper and a cultured outlook. The ideal world for mankind will not be a rational world, nor a perfect world in any sense, but a world in which imperfections are readily perceived and quarrels reasonably settled. For mankind, that is frankly the best we can hope for and the noblest dream that we can reasonably expect to come true. This seems to imply several things: a simplicity of thinking, a gaiety in philosophy and a subtle common sense, which will make this reasonable culture possible. Now it happens that subtle common sense, gaiety of philosophy and simplicity of thinking are characteristic of humour and must arise from it.

It is difficult to imagine this kind of a new world because our present world is so different. On the whole, our life is too complex, our scholarship too serious, our philosophy too sombre, and our thoughts too involved. This seriousness and this involved complexity of our thought and scholarship make the present world such an unhappy one to-day.

Now it must be taken for granted that simplicity of life and thought is the highest and sanest ideal for civilization and culture, that when a civilization loses simplicity and the sophisticated do not return to unsophistication, civilization becomes increasingly full of troubles and degenerates. Man then becomes the slave of the ideas, thoughts, ambitions and social systems that are his own product. Mankind, overburdened with this load of ideas and ambitions and social systems, seems unable to rise above them. Luckily, however, there is a power of the human mind which can transcend all these ideas, thoughts and ambitions and treat them with a smile, and this power is the subtlety of the humorist. Humorists handle thoughts and ideas as golf or billiard champions handle their balls, or as cowboy champions handle their lariats. There is an ease, a sureness, a lightness of touch, that comes from mastery. After all, only he who handles his ideas lightly is master of his ideas, and only he who is master of his ideas is not enslaved by them. Seriousness, after all, is only a sign of effort, and effort is a sign of imperfect mastery. A serious writer is awkward and ill at ease in the realm of ideas as a *nouveau riche* is awkward, ill at ease and self-conscious in society. He is serious because he has not come to feel at home with his ideas.

Simplicity, then, paradoxically is the outward sign and symbol of depth of thought. It seems to me simplicity is about the most difficult thing to achieve in scholarship and writing. How difficult is clarity of thought, and yet it is only as thought becomes clear that simplicity is possible. When we see a writer belabouring an idea we may be sure that the idea is belabouring him. This is proved by the general fact that the lectures of a young college assistant instructor, freshly graduated with high honours, are generally abstruse and involved, and true simplicity of thought and ease of expression are to be found only in the words of the older professors. When a young professor does not talk in pedantic language, he is then positively brilliant, and much may be expected of him. What is involved in the progress from technicality to simplicity, from the specialist to the thinker, is essentially a process of digestion of knowledge, a process that I compare strictly to metabolism. No learned scholar can present to us his specialized knowledge in simple human terms until he has digested that knowledge himself and brought it into relation with his observations of life. Between the hours of his arduous pursuit of knowledge (let us say the psychological knowledge of William James), I feel there is many a "pause that refreshes," like a cool drink after a long fatiguing journey. In that pause many a truly human specialist will ask himself the all-important question, "What on earth am I talking about?" Simplicity presupposes digestion and also maturity: as we grow older, our thoughts become clearer, insignificant and perhaps false aspects of a question are lopped off and cease to disturb us, ideas take on more definite shapes and long trains of thought gradually shape themselves into a convenient formula which suggests itself to us one fine morning, and we arrive at that true luminosity of knowledge which is called wisdom. There is no longer a sense of effort, and truth becomes simple to understand because it becomes clear, and the reader gets that supreme pleasure of feeling that truth itself is simple and its formulation natural. This naturalness of thought and style, which is so much admired by Chinese poets and critics, is often spoken of as a process of gradually maturing development. As we speak of the growing maturity of Su Tungp'o's prose, we say that he has "gradually approached naturalness"—a style that has shed off its youthful love of pomposity, pedantry, virtuosity and literary showmanship.

Now it is natural that the sense of humour nourishes this simplicity of thinking. Generally, a humorist keeps closer touch with facts, while a theorist dwells more on ideas, and it is only when one is dealing with ideas in themselves that his thoughts get incredibly complex. The humorist, on the other hand, indulges in flashes of common sense or wit, which show up the contradictions of our ideas with reality with lightning speed, thus greatly simplifying matters. Constant contact with reality gives the humorist a bounce, and also a lightness and subtlety. All forms of pose, sham, learned nonsense, academic stupidity and social humbug are politely but effectively shown the door. Man becomes wise because man becomes subtle and witty. All is simple. All is clear.

[85]

It is for this reason that I believe a sane and reasonable spirit, characterized by simplicity of living and thinking, can be achieved only when there is a very much greater prevalence of humorous thinking.

V. ON BEING WAYWARD AND INCALCULABLE

It seems that to-day the scamp is being displaced by the soldier as the highest ideal of a human being. Instead of wayward, incalculable, unpredictable free individuals, we are going to have rationalized, disciplined, regimented and uniformed, patriotic coolies, so efficiently controlled and organized that a nation of fifty or sixty millions can believe in the same creed, think the same thoughts and like the same food. Clearly two opposite views of human dignity are possible: the one regarding the scamp, and the other regarding the soldier, as the ideal; the one believing that a person who retains his freedom and individuality is the noblest type, and the other believing that a person who has completely lost independent judgment and surrendered all rights to private beliefs and opinions to the ruler or the state is the best and noblest being. Both views are defensible, one by common sense, and the other by logic. It should not be difficult to defend by logic the ideal of the patriotic automaton as a model citizen, useful as a means to serve another external goal, which is the strength of the state, which exists again for another goal, the crushing of other states. All that can be easily demonstrated by logic—a logic so simple and naïve that all idiots fall for it. Incredible as it may seem, such a view has been upheld and is still being upheld in many "civilized" and "enlightened" European countries. The ideal citizen is the soldier who thought he was being transported to Ethiopia and found himself in Guadalajara. Among such ideal citizens two classes, "A" and "B," may again be distinguished. The "A" class, consisting of the better citizens from the point of view of the state or its ruler, are those who, on discovering that they have been landed in Spain, are still extremely sweet and amiable and offer up thanks to God directly or through the army chaplain for sending them, by a kind of providential miracle, to the thick of the battle to die for the state. Class "B" would be those insufficiently civilized beings who feel an inner resentment at the discovery. Now for myself, that inner resentment, that *human recalcitrancy*, is the only sign of human dignity, the only spark of hope illuminating for me the otherwise sombre and dismal picture, the only hope for a restoration of human decency in some future more civilized world.

It is clear, then, that, in spite of all logic, I am still for the scamp. I am all for the scamp, or the tramp, and for "Mary, Mary, quite contrary." Our contrary-mindedness is our only hope for civilization. My reason is simple: that we are descended from the monkeys and not from the cows, and that therefore we are better monkeys, nobler monkeys, for being contrary-minded. I am selfish enough as a human being to desire a sweet and contented temper for the cows, who can be led to the pasture or to the slaughter-house at human behest with equal magnanimity and nobility of mind, motivated by the sole desire to sacrifice themselves for their master. At the same time, I am such a lover of humanity as not to desire that we become cows ourselves. The moment cows rebel and feel our recalcitrancy, or begin to act waywardly and less mechanically, I call them human. The reason I think all dictatorships are wrong is a biological reason. Dictators and cows go well together, but dictators and monkeys don't.

In fact, my respect for Western civilization has been considerably lowered since the nineteen-twenties. I had been ashamed of Chinese civilization, and I had honoured the West, for I regarded it as a stain upon Chinese civilization that we had not developed a constitution and the idea of civil rights, and I decidedly thought that a constitutional government, republican or monarchical, was an advance in human culture. Now in the very home of Western civilization, I have the pleasure and satisfaction of seeing that human rights and individual liberty, even the common-sense rights of individual freedom of belief that we in China enjoy and have always enjoyed, can be trampled upon, that a constitutional government is no longer thought of as the highest form of government, that there are more Euripidean slaves in Central Europe than in feudalistic China, and that some Western nations have more logic and less common sense than we Chinese. What more easy than for me to play the trump card from my sleeve by producing the Chinese ideal of the happy-go-lucky, carefree scamp, tramp and vagabond, which is the highest cultural ideal of a human being according to the Chinese conception? Has the West a trump card to match, something to show that its doctrine of individual liberty and civil rights is a serious and deep-rooted belief or instinct, with enough vitality to stage a come-back and swing the pendulum of thought in the other direction, after the present fashion for glorified, uniformed coolies is gone? I am waiting to see it.

It is easy to see how the European tradition of individual liberty and freedom has been forgotten, and why the pendulum is swinging in the wrong direction to-day. The reasons are two: first, the consequences of the present economic movement toward collectivism, and second, a heritage from the mechanistic outlook of mid-Victorian times. It seems that in the present age of rising collectivism of all sorts—social, economic and political—mankind is naturally forgetting and forfeiting its right to human recalcitrancy and losing sight of the dignity of the individual. With the predominance of economic problems and economic thinking, which is overshadowing all other forms of human thinking, we remain completely ignorant of, and indifferent to, a more humanized knowledge and a more humanized philosophy, a philosophy that deals with the problems of the individual life. This is natural. As a man who has an ulcered stomach spends all his thought on his stomach, so a society with a sick and aching economics is for ever preoccupied with thoughts of economics. Nevertheless, the result is that we remain totally indifferent to the individual and have almost forgotten that he exists. A man used to be a man for a' that. To-day he is generally conceived as an automaton blindly obeying material or economic laws. We no longer think of a man as a man, but as a cog in a wheel, a member of a union or a class, an alien to be imported by quotas, a *petit bourgeois* to be referred to with contempt, or a capitalist to be denounced, or a worker to be regarded as a comrade because he is a worker. It seems that to label a man as a *petit bourgeois* or a "capitalist" or a "worker" is already to understand him completely, and he can be conveniently hated or hailed as a comrade accordingly. We are no longer individuals, no longer men, but only classes. May I suggest that this is an over-simplification of things? The scamp has completely disappeared as an ideal, and so has the man with his gloriously scamp-like qualities of reacting freely and incalculably to his external surroundings. Instead of men, we have members of a class; instead of ideas and personal prejudices and idiosyncrasies, we have ideologies, or class thoughts; instead of personalities, we have blind forces; and instead of individuals, we have a Marxian dialectic controlling and foreshadowing all human activities with unfailing precision. We are all progressing happily and enthusiastically toward the model of the ants.

Of course I realize that I am talking nothing but old-fashioned democratic individualism. But may I also remind the Marxists that Karl Marx was himself a product of the Hegelian logic of a century ago and of the English classical school of economics of the mid-Victorian period? And nothing is so old-fashioned to-day as Hegelian logic or the mid-Victorian precision school of economic thought—nothing so unconvincing and untrue and so totally devoid of common sense, from the Chinese humanist point of view. But we can understand how this mechanistic view of man came about at a time when mechanistic science was proud of its achievements and its conquests over nature. This science was pilfered, its mechanistic logic transferred to apply to human society, and the always imposing name of "natural laws" was very much sought after by the students of human affairs. Hence the prevalent theory that the surroundings are greater than the man and that human personalities can be almost reduced to equations. That may be good economics, but bad biology. Good biology recognizes the individual's power of reaction as just as important a factor in the development of life as the physical environment, as any wise doctor will admit that the patient's temperament and individual reactions are an all-important factor in the fight against a disease. Medical doctors to-day recognize more and more the incalculable factor of the individual. Many patients, who by all logic and precedents ought to die, simply refuse to do so and shock the doctor by their recovery. A doctor who prescribes an identical treatment for an identical disease in two individuals and expects an identical development may be properly classified as a social menace. No less a social menace are the social philosophers who forget the individual, his capacity for reacting in a different manner from others, and his generally wayward and incalculable behaviour.

Perhaps I don't understand economics, but economics does not understand me, either. That is why economics is still floundering to-day and hardly dares pop up its head as a science. The sad thing about economics is that it is no science, if it stops at commodities and does not go beyond to human motives, and if it does go beyond to human motives, it is still no science, or at best a pseudo-science, if it tries to reach human motives by statistical averages. It hasn't developed even a technique suitable to the examination of the human mind, and if it carries over to the realm of human activities its mathematical approach and its love of drawing statistical averages, it stands in still greater danger of floundering in ignorance. That is why every time an important economic measure is about to be adopted, two economic experts or authorities will come out exactly on opposite sides. Economics, after all, goes back to the idiosyncrasies of the human mind, and of these idiosyncrasies the experts have no ghost of an idea. One believed that, should England go off the gold standard, there would be a catastrophe, while another believed, with equal cock-sureness, that England's going off the gold standard would be the only salvation. When people begin to buy and when people begin to sell are problems that the best experts cannot reasonably fore-tell. It is entirely due to this fact that speculations on the stock exchange are possible. It remains true that the stock exchange cannot, with the best assemblage of world economic data, scientifically predict the rise and fall of gold or silver or commodities, as the weather bureau can forecast the weather. The reason clearly lies in the fact that there is a human element in it, that when too many people are selling out, some will start buying in, and when too many people are buying in, a few people will start selling out. Thus is introduced the element of human resilience and human uncertainty. It is to be presumed, of course, that every person who is selling out regards as a fool the other person who is buying in what he is selling out, and *vice versa*. Who are the fools only future events can prove. This is merely an illustration of the incalculableness and waywardness of human behaviour, which is true not only in the hard and matter-of-fact dealings of business, but also in the shaping of the course of history by human psychology, and in all human reactions toward morals, customs, and social reforms.

VI. THE DOCTRINE OF THE INDIVIDUAL

Man to-day may be living in a democratic country to a greater or lesser extent threatened by great social changes, or he may be living in a communist country tending more and more to approach and come back to the democratic ideal, or he may be living under a dictatorship which may survive him or which more probably he will survive. In any case, his individual life remains an integrated whole, shaped by the currents of the times, but still retaining its individuality.

Philosophy not only begins with the individual, but also ends with the individual. For an individual is the final fact of life. He is an end in himself, and not a means to other creations of the human mind. The greatest empire of the world, like the British Empire, exists in order that an Englishman in Sussex may live a fairly happy and reasonable life; a false philosophy would assume that the Englishman in Sussex lives in order that there may be the great British Empire. The best social philosophies do not claim any greater objective than that the individual human beings living under such a regime shall have happy individual lives. If there are social philosophies which deny the happiness of the individual life as the final goal and aim of civilization, those philosophies are the product of a sick and unbalanced mind.

As far as culture is concerned, I am inclined to think that the final judgment of any particular type of culture is what type of men and women it turns out. It is in this sense that Walt Whitman, one of the wisest and most far-seeing of Americans, struggles in his essay *Democratic Vistas* to bring forth the principle of individuality or "personalism," as the end of all civilization:

> And, if we think of it, what does civilization itself rest upon —and what object has it, with its religions, arts, schools, etc., but rich, luxuriant, varied personalism? To that all bends; and it is because toward such result democracy alone, on anything like Nature's scale, breaks up the limitless fallows of humankind, and plants the seed, and gives fair play, that its claims now precede the rest. The literature, songs, æsthetics, etc., of a country are of importance principally because they furnish the materials and suggestions of personality for the women and men of that country, and enforce them in a thousand effective ways.

Speaking of the individuality as a final fact, Whitman says:

> There is, in sanest hours, a consciousness, a thought that rises, independent, lifted out from all else, calm, like the stars, shining eternal. This is the thought of identity—yours for you, whoever you are, as mine for me. Miracle of miracles, beyond statement, most spiritual and vaguest of earth's dreams, yet hardest basic fact, and only entrance to all facts. In such devout hours, in the midst of the significant wonders of heaven and earth (significant only because of the Me in the centre), creeds, conventions, fall away and become of no account before this simple idea. Under the luminousness of real vision, it alone takes possession, takes value. Like the shadowy dwarf in the fable, once liberated and look'd upon, it expands over the whole earth, and spreads to the roof of heaven.

The temptation is strong to quote more from this typically

American philosopher's most eloquent glorification of the individual, summed up in the following manner:

> . . . and, as an eventual conclusion and summing up (or else the entire scheme of things is aimless, a cheat, a crash), the simple idea that the last, best dependence is to be upon humanity itself, and its own inherent, normal, full-grown qualities, without any superstitious support whatever.
>
> The purpose of democracy . . . is, through many transmigrations, and amid endless ridicules, arguments and ostensible failures, to illustrate, at all hazards, this doctrine or theory that man, properly train'd in sanest, highest freedom, may and must become a law, and series of laws, unto himself. . . .

After all, it is not our surroundings, but our reactions toward them that count. France, Germany, England and America are all living in the same machine civilization, yet their patterns and flavours of life are all different, and all solve their political problems in different ways. It is foolish to assume that man must be swamped by the machine in a uniform, helpless manner, when we realize there is such room for variety of life, when we see that two drivers on the same truck will take a joke differently. A father of two sons who gives them the same education and the same start in life, will see how they gradually shape their lives according to the inner laws of their own being. Even if both turn out to be presidents of banks with exactly the same capitalization, yet in all things that matter, in all things that make for happiness, they are different, different in their address, accent and temperament; in their policies and ways of handling problems; in the way they get on with their staff, whether they are feared or loved, harsh and exacting or pleasant and easy-going; in the way they save and spend their money; and different in their personal lives as coloured by their hobbies, their friends, their clubs, their reading and their wives. Such is the rich variety possible in identical surroundings that no one can take up the obituary page of a newspaper, without wondering how persons living in the same generation and dying on the same day have led entirely different lives, how some plodded on in a chosen vocation with a singular devotion and found happiness in it, how others had a checkered and varied career, how some invented, some explored, some cracked jokes, some were morose and without a sense of humour, some sky-rocketed to fame and wealth and died in the cold, dark cinders of the rocket, and some sold ice and coal and were stabbed to death in their cellar homes with a hoard of twenty thousand dollars in gold. Yes, human life is wondrous strange still, even in an industrial age. So long as man is man, variety will still be the flavour of life.

There is no such thing as determinism in human affairs, whether politics or social revolution. The human factor is what upsets the calculations of the propounders of new theories and systems, and what defeats the originators of laws, institutions and social panaceas, whether it be the Oneida Community, or the American Federation of Labour, or Judge Lindsay's companionate marriage. The quality of the bride and bridegroom is more important than the conventions of marriage and divorce, and the men administering or upholding the laws are more important than the laws themselves.

But the importance of the individual comes not only from the fact that the individual life is the end of all civilization, but also from the fact that the improvement of our social and political life and international relationships comes from the aggregate action and temper of the individuals which compose a nation and is eventually based on the temper and quality of the individual. In national politics and the evolution of a country from one stage to another, the determining factor is the temperament of the people. For above the laws of industrial development, there is the more important factor of a nation's way of doing things and solving problems. Rousseau as little foresaw the course of the French Revolution and the appearance of Napoleon, as Karl Marx foresaw the actual development of his socialistic theories and the appearance of Stalin. The course of the French Revolution was not determined by the slogan of Liberty, Equality and Fraternity, but by certain traits in human nature in general and in the French temperament in particular. Karl Marx's predictions about the course of the socialist revolution have failed miserably, despite his rigorous dialectic. By all the laws of logic, as he predicted, a revolution of the proletariat should have come where the industrial civilization was most advanced and where there was a strong class of proletarian workers—first in England, perhaps in the United States and possibly in Germany. Instead, Communism had first a chance to be put on trial in an agricultural country like Russia where there was no important proletarian class at all. What Karl Marx forgot to calculate was the human factor in England and in the United States and the Englishman's or American's *way of doing things* and of solving problems. The great omission in all immature economics is the neglect to provide for a *je ne sais quoi* factor in national affairs. The English distrust of theories and slogans, the Englishman's way of slowly bungling, if necessary, but in any case slowly finding his way, the Anglo-Saxon's love of individual liberty, self-respect, good sense and love of order, are things which are more powerful in shaping the course of events in England and America than all the logic of the German dialectician.

And so the conduct of a nation's affairs and the course of its social and political development are eventually based on the ideas which govern the individuals. This racial temperament, the thing we abstractly call "the genius of the people," is after all an aggregate of the individuals who comprise that nation, for it is nothing but the character of a nation in action, as it faces certain problems or crises. There is nothing more false than the notion that this "genius" is a mythological entity like the "soul" in medieval theology, as if it were something more than a figure of speech. The genius of a nation is nothing but the character of its conduct and its way of doing things. So far from being an abstract entity with an independent existence of its own, as we sometimes think of the "destiny" of a nation, this genius can be seen only in action; it is a matter of choice, of certain selections and rejections, preferences and prejudices, which determine the nation's final course of action in a given crisis or situation. Historians of the old school would like to think with Hegel that the history of a nation is but the development of an idea, proceeding by a kind of mechanical necessity, whereas a more subtle and realistic view of history is that it was very largely a matter of chance. At every critical period, the nation made a choice, and in the choice we see a struggle of opposing forces and conflicting passions, and a little more of this kind of sentiment or a little less of that kind might have tipped the scale in the other direction. The so-called genius of a nation, as expressed in such a given crisis, was a decision by the nation that they would like to have a little more of one thing, or had had enough of it. For after all every nation went ahead with what it liked, or what appealed to its sentiments, and rejected what it would not tolerate. Such a choice was based on a current of ideas and a set of moral sentiments and social prejudices.

In the last constitutional crisis of England, eventually compelling the abdication of a king, we see most clearly this thing called the character of a people in action, revealed by its approvals and disapprovals, its tide of changing emotions, in a conflict among many working motives of assumed validity. Such motives were personal loyalty to a popular prince, the Church of England's prejudice against a divorcée, the Englishman's traditional conception of a king, the question whether a king's private affair was or could be a private affair, and whether a king should be more than a figurehead, or whether he should have definite Labourite sympathies. A little more of any one of these conflicting sentiments might have brought about a different solution of the crisis.

And so throughout current history, whether Zenoviev, Kamenev and Piatakoff might have been killed and Radek imprisoned, whether "counter-revolutionary" plots and rebellion against the Stalin regime might or might not be so extensive, whether the German Catholic and Protestant churches might or might not hold their integrity in their resistance against the Nazi regime (that is, how much human resilience there is in Germany), whether England might turn truly Labourite, and whether the American Communist party might grow or lose in public favour, are things which eventually are determined by the ideas, sentiments and character of the individual members of the states concerned. In all this moving panorama of human history, I see only flux and change, determined by man's own wayward and incalculable and unpredictable choice.

In this sense, Confucianism connected the question of world peace with the cultivation of our personal lives. The very first lesson that Confucian scholars since the Sung Dynasty have decided should be learned by the child at school contains this passage:

The ancient people who desired to have a clear moral harmony in the world would first order their national life; those who desired to order their national life would first regulate their home life; those who desired to regulate their home life would first cultivate their personal lives; those who desired to cultivate their personal lives would first set their hearts right; those who desired to set their hearts right, would first make their wills sincere; those who desired to make their wills sincere would first arrive at understanding; understanding comes from the exploration of knowledge of things. When the knowledge of things is gained, then understanding is reached; when understanding is reached, then the will is sincere; when the will is sincere, then the heart is set right; when the heart is set right, then the personal life is cultivated; when the personal life is cultivated, then the home life is regulated; when the home life is regulated, then the national life is orderly; and when the national life is orderly: then the world is at peace. From the Emperor down to the common man, the cultivation of the personal life is the foundation for all. It is impossible that when the foundation is disorderly, the superstructure can be orderly. There has never been a tree whose trunk is slender and whose top branches are heavy and strong. There is a cause and a sequence in things, and a beginning and end in human affairs. To know the order of precedence is to have the beginning of wisdom.

CHAPTER FIVE

Who Can Best Enjoy Life?

I. FIND THYSELF: CHUANGTSE

IN MODERN LIFE, a philosopher is about the most honoured and most unnoticed person in the world, if indeed such a person exists. "Philosopher" has become merely a term of social compliment. Anyone who is abstruse and unintelligible is called "a philosopher." Anyone who is unconcerned with the present is also called "a philosopher." And yet there is some truth in the latter meaning. When Shakespeare made Touchstone say in *As You Like It*, "Hast any philosophy in thee, shepherd?" he was using it in the second meaning. In this sense, philosophy is but a common, rough-and-ready outlook on things or on life in general, and every person has more or less of it. Anyone who refuses to take the entire panorama of reality on its surface value, or refuses to believe every word that appears in a newspaper, is more or less a philosopher. He is the fellow who refuses to be taken in.

There is always a flavour of disenchantment about philosophy. The philosopher looks at life as an artist looks at a landscape— through a veil or a haze. The raw details of reality are softened a little to permit us to see its meaning. At least that is what a Chinese artist or a Chinese philosopher thinks. The philosopher is therefore the direct opposite of the complete realist who, busily occupied in his daily business, believes that his successes and failures, his losses and gains, are absolute and real. There is nothing to be done about such a person because he does not even doubt and there is nothing in him to start with. Confucius said: "If a person does not say to himself 'What to do? What to do?' indeed I do not know what to do with such a person!"

—one of the few conscious witticisms I have found in Confucius.

I hope to present in this chapter some opinions of Chinese philosophers on a design for living. The more these philosophers differ, the more they agree—that man must be wise and unafraid to live a happy life. The more positive Mencian outlook and the more roguishly pacifist Laotsean outlook merge together in the Philosophy of the Half-and-Half, which I may describe as the average Chinaman's religion. The conflict between action and inaction ends in a compromise, or contentment with a very imperfect heaven on earth. This gives rise to a wise and merry philosophy of living, eventually typified in the life of T'ao Yüanming—in my opinion China's greatest poet and most harmonious personality.

The only problem unconsciously assumed by all Chinese philosophers to be of any importance is: how shall we enjoy life, and who can best enjoy life? No perfectionism, no straining after the unattainable, no postulating of the unknowable; but taking poor, mortal human nature as it is, how shall we organize our life that we can work peacefully, endure nobly and live happily?

Who are we? That is the first question. It is a question almost impossible to answer. But we all agree that the busy self occupied in our daily activities is not quite the real self. We are quite sure we have lost something in the mere pursuit of living. When we watch a person running about looking for something in a field, the wise man can set a puzzle for all the spectators to solve: what has that person lost? Someone thinks it is a watch; another thinks it is a diamond brooch; and others will essay other guesses. After all these guesses have failed, the wise man who really doesn't know what the person is seeking after tells the company: "I'll tell you. He has lost some breath." And no one can deny that he is right. So we often forget our true self in the pursuit of living, like a bird forgetting its own danger in pursuit of a mantis, which again forgets its own danger in pursuit of another prey, as is so beautifully expressed in a parable by Chuangtse:

When Chuangtse was wandering in the park at Tiao-ling, he

saw a strange bird which came from the south. Its wings were seven feet across. Its eyes were an inch in circumference. And it flew close past Chuangtse's head to alight in a chestnut grove.

"What manner of bird is this?" cried Chuangtse. "With strong wings it does not fly away. With large eyes it does not see."

So he picked up his skirts and strode towards it with his cross-bow, anxious to get a shot. Just then he saw a cicada enjoying itself in the shade, forgetful of all else. And he saw a mantis spring and seize it, forgetting in the act its own body, which the strange bird immediately pounced upon and made its prey. And this it was which had caused the bird to forget its own nature.

"Alas!" cried Chuangtse with a sigh, "how creatures injure one another. Loss follows the pursuit of gain."

So he laid aside his bow and went home, driven away by the park-keeper who wanted to know what business he had there.

For three months after this, Chuangtse did not leave the house; and at length Lin Chü asked him, saying, "Master, how is it that you have not been out for so long?"

"While keeping my physical frame," replied Chuangtse, "I lost sight of my real self. Gazing at muddy water, I lost sight of the clear abyss. Besides, I have learnt from the Master as follows:—'When you go into the world, follow its customs.' Now when I strolled into the park at Tiao-ling, I forgot my real self. That strange bird which flew close past me to the chestnut grove, forgot its nature. The keeper of the chestnut grove took me for a thief. Consequently I have not been out."[1]

Chuangtse was the eloquent follower of Laotse, as Mencius was the eloquent follower of Confucius, both separated from their masters by about a century. Chuangtse was a contemporary of Mencius, as Laotse was probably a contemporary of Confucius. But Mencius agreed with Chuangtse that we have lost something and the business of philosophy is to discover and recover that which is lost—in this case, "a child's heart," according to Mencius.

[1] From Professor H A. Giles's translation, *Chuang Tzu* (Quatrich, London), which is a complete translation of Chuangtse's works.

"A great man is he who has not lost the heart of a child," says this philosopher. Mencius regards the effect of the artificial life of civilization upon the youthful heart born in man as similar to the deafforestation of our hills:

There was once a time when the forests of the Niu Mountain were beautiful. But can the mountain any longer be regarded as beautiful, since being situated near a big city, the woodsmen have hewed the trees down? The days and nights gave it rest, and the rains and the dew continued to nourish it, and a new life was continually springing up from the soil, but then the cattle and the sheep began to pasture upon it. That is why the Niu Mountain looks so bald, and when people see its baldness, they imagine that there was never any timber on the mountain. Is this the true nature of the mountain? And is there not a heart of love and righteousness in man, too? But how can that nature remain beautiful when it is hacked down every day, as the woodsman chops down the trees with his axe? To be sure, the nights and days do the healing and there is the nourishing air of the early dawn, which tends to keep him sound and normal, but this morning air is thin and is soon destroyed by what he does in the day. With this continuous hacking of the human spirit, the rest and recuperation obtained during the night are not sufficient to maintain its level, and when the night's recuperation does not suffice to maintain its level, then the man degrades himself to a state not far from the beast's. People see that he acts like a beast and imagine that there was never any true character in him. But is this the true nature of man?

II. PASSION, WISDOM AND COURAGE: MENCIUS

The ideal character best able to enjoy life is a warm, carefree and unafraid soul. Mencius enumerated the three "mature virtues" of his "great man" as "wisdom, compassion and courage." I should like to lop off one syllable and regard as the qualities of a great soul passion, wisdom and courage. Luckily, we have in the English language the word "passion" which in its usage very nearly corresponds to the Chinese word *ch'ing*. Both words start out with the narrower meaning of sexual passion, but both have a much wider significance. As Chang Ch'ao says, "A passionate nature always loves women, but one who loves women is not necessarily a passionate nature." And again, "Passion holds up the bottom of the world, while genius paints its roof." For unless we have passion, we have nothing to start out in life with at all. It is passion that is the soul of life, the light in the stars, the lilt in music and song, the joy in flowers, the plumage in birds, the charm in woman, and the life in scholarship. It is as impossible to speak of a soul without passion as to speak of music without expression. It is that which gives us inward warmth and the rich vitality which enables us to face life cheerily.

Or perhaps I am wrong in choosing the word "passion" when I speak of what the Chinese writers refer to as *ch'ing*. Should I translate it by the word "sentiment," which is gentler and suggests less of the tumultuous qualities of stormy passion? Or perhaps we mean by it something very similar to what the early Romanticists call "sensibility," which we find in a warm, generous and artistic soul. It is strange that among the Western philosophers so few, except Emerson, Amiel, Joubert and Voltaire, have a good word to say for passion. Perhaps we are arguing about words merely, while we mean the same thing. But then, if passion is different from sentiment and means something tumultuous and upsetting, then we haven't got a Chinese word for it, and we still have to go back to the old word *ch'ing*. Is this an index of a difference in racial temperament, of the absence among the Chinese people of grand and compelling passions, which eat up one's soul and form the stuff of tragedy in Western literature? Is this the reason why Chinese literature has not developed tragedy in the Greek sense; why Chinese tragic characters at the critical moment, weep, give up their sweethearts to their enemy, or as in the case of Ch'u Pawang, stab their sweethearts and then plunge the knife into their own breasts? It is a sort of ending that will be found unsatisfying to a Western audience, but as Chinese life is, so is Chinese literature. Man struggles with fate, gives up the battle, and the tragedy comes *in the aftermath,* in a flood of reminiscences, of vain regret and longing, such as we see in the tragedy of Emperor T'ang Minghuang, who after granting the suicide of his beloved queen to placate a rebellious army, lives in a dream world in memory of her. The tragic sense is shown in the remaining part of the Chinese play long after the dénouement, in a swelling crescendo of sorrow. As he travels in his exile, he hears the distant music of cowbells in the hills on a rainy day and he composes the "Song of Rain on Cowbells" in her honour; everything he sees or touches, a little perfumed scarf that still retains its old scent, or an old maidservant of hers, reminds him of his beloved queen, and the play ends with him searching for her soul with the help of Taoist priests in the abode of the Immortals. So then, we have here a romantic sensibility, if we are not allowed to speak of it as passion. But it is passion mellowed down to a gentle glow. So it is characteristic of Chinese philosophers that while they disparage the human "desires" (in the sense of the "seven passions"), they have never disparaged passion or sentiment itself, but made it the very basis of a normal human life, so much so that they regard "the passion between husband and wife as the very foundation of all normal human life."

It is unfortunately true that this matter of passion, or still better, sentiment, is something born in us, and that as we cannot choose our parents, we are born with a given cold or warm nature. On the other hand, no child is born with a really cold heart, and it is only in proportion as we lose that youthful heart that we lose the inner warmth in ourselves. Somewhere in our adult life, our sentimental nature is killed, strangled, chilled or atrophied by an unkind surrounding, largely through our own fault in neglecting to keep it alive, or our failure to keep clear of such surroundings. In the process of learning "world experience," there is many a violence done to our original nature, when we learn to harden ourselves, to be artificial, and often to be cold-hearted and cruel, so that as one prides oneself upon gaining more and more worldly

experience, his nerves become more and more sensitive and benumbed—especially in the world of politics and commerce. As a
result, we get the great "go-getter" pushing himself forward to
the top and brushing everybody aside; we get the man of iron will
and strong determination, with the last embers of sentiment,
which he calls foolish idealism or sentimentality gradually dying
out in his breast. It is that sort of person who is beneath my
contempt. The world has too many cold-hearted people. If
sterilization of the unfit should be carried out as a state policy,
it should begin with sterilizing the morally insensible, the artistically stale, the heavy of heart, the ruthlessly successful, the cold-
heartedly determined and all those people who have lost the
sense of fun in life—rather than the insane and the victims of
tuberculosis. For it seems to me that while a man with passion
and sentiment may do many foolish and precipitate things, a man
without passion or sentiment is a joke and a caricature. Compared
with Daudet's Sappho, he is a worm, a machine, an automaton,
a blot upon this earth. Many a prostitute lives a nobler life than
a successful business man. What if Sappho sinned? For although
she sinned, she also loved, and to those who love much, much
will be forgiven. Anyway, she emerged out of an equally harsh
business environment with more of the youthful heart than many
of our millionaires. The worship of Mary Magdalene is right. It
is unavoidable that passion and sentiment should lead us into
mistakes for which we are duly punished, yet there is many an
indulgent mother who by her indulgence often let her love get
the better of her judgment, and yet who, we feel sure, in her old
age felt that she had had a more happy life with her family than
many rigorous and austere souls. A friend told me the story of
an old lady of seventy-eight who said to him, "As I look back
upon my seventy-eight years, it still makes me happy to think of
when I sinned; but when I think I was stupid, I cannot forgive
myself even at this late day."

But life is harsh, and a man with a warm, generous and sentimental nature may be easily taken in by his cleverer fellow-man.
The generous in nature often make mistakes by their generosity,

by their too generous regard of their enemies and faith in their friends. Sometimes the generous man comes home disillusioned to write a poem of bitterness. That is the case of many a poet and scholar in China, as for instance that great tea-drinker, Chang Tai, who generously squandered his fortune, was betrayed by his own closest friends and relatives, and set down in twelve poems some of the bitterest verses I have ever read. But I have a suspicion that he kept on being generous to the end of his days, even when he was quite poor and destitute, being many times on the verge of starvation, and I have no doubt that those bitter sentiments passed away like a cloud and he was still quite happy.

Nevertheless this warm generosity of soul has to be protected against life by a philosophy, because life is harsh, warmth of soul is not enough, and passion must be joined to wisdom and courage. To me wisdom and courage are the same thing, for courage is born of an understanding of life; he who completely understands life is always brave. Anyway, that type of wisdom which does not give us courage is not worth having at all. Wisdom leads to courage by exercising a veto against our foolish ambitions and emancipating us from the fashionable humbug of this world, whether humbug of thought or humbug of life.

There is a wealth of humbug in this life, but the multitudinous little humbugs have been classified by Chinese Buddhists under two big humbugs: fame and wealth. There is a story that Emperor Ch'ienlung once went up a hill overlooking the sea during his trip to South China and saw a great number of sailing ships busily plying the China Sea to and fro. He asked his minister what the people in those hundreds of ships were doing, and his minister replied that he saw only two ships, and their names were "Fame" and "Wealth." Many cultured persons were able to escape the lure of wealth, but only the very greatest could escape the lure of fame. Once a monk was discoursing with his pupil on these two sources of worldly cares, and said: "It is easier to get rid of the desire for money than to get rid of the desire for fame. Even retired scholars and monks still want to be distinguished and well known among their company. They want to give public discourses to a large audience, and not retire to a small monastery talking to one pupil, like you and me now." The pupil replied: "Indeed, Master, you are the only man in the world who has conquered the desire for fame!" And the Master smiled.

From my own observation of life, this Buddhist classification of life's humbugs is not complete, and the great humbugs of life are three, instead of two: Fame, Wealth and Power. There is a convenient American word which again combines these three humbugs into the One Great Humbug: Success. But many wise men know that the desires for success, fame and wealth are euphemistic names for the fears of failure, poverty and obscurity, and that these fears dominate our lives. There are many people who have already attained both fame and wealth, but who still insist on ruling others. They are the people who have consecrated their lives to the service of their country. The price is often very heavy. Ask a wise man to wave his silk hat to a crowd and make seven speeches a day and give him a presidency, and he will refuse to serve his country. James Bryce thinks the system of democratic government in America is such that it is hardly calculated to attract the best men of the country into politics. I think the strenuousness of a presidential campaign alone is enough to frighten off all the wise souls of America. A public office often demands that a man attend six dinners a week in the name of consecrating his life to the service of mankind. Why does he not consecrate himself to a simple supper at home and to his bed and his pyjamas? Under the spell of that humbug of fame or power, a man is soon prey to other incidental humbugs. There will be no end to it. He soon begins to want to reform society, to uplift others' morality, to defend the church, to crush vice, to map programmes for others to carry out, to block programmes that other people have mapped out, to read before a convention a statistical report of what other people have done for him under his administration, to sit on committees examining blue-prints of an exposition, even to open an insane asylum (what cheek!)—in general, to interfere in other people's lives. He soon forgets that these gratuitous assumptions of responsibility, these problems of reforming people and doing this and preventing one's rivals from doing that, never existed for him before, perhaps had not even entered his mind. How completely the great problems of labour, unemployment and tariffs leave the mind of a defeated presidential candidate even two weeks after an election! Who is he that he should want to reform other people and uplift their morals and send other people into an insane asylum? But these primary and secondary humbugs keep him happily busy, if he is successful, and give him the illusion that he is really doing something and is therefore "somebody."

Yet there is a secondary social humbug, quite as powerful and universal, the humbug of fashion. The courage to be one's own natural self is quite a rare thing. The Greek philosopher Democritus thought he was doing a great service to mankind by liberating it from the oppression of two great fears: the fear of God and the fear of death. But even that does not liberate us from another equally universal fear: the fear of one's neighbours. Few men who have liberated themselves from the fear of God and the fear of death are yet able to liberate themselves from the fear of man. Consciously or unconsciously, we are all actors in this life playing to the audience in a part and style approved by them.

This histrionic talent, together with the related talent for imitation, which is a part of it, are the most outstanding traits of our simian inheritance. There are undoubted advantages to be derived from this showmanship, the most obvious being the plaudits of the audience. But then the greater the plaudits, the greater also are the flutterings of heart back-stage. And it also helps one to make a living, so that no one is quite to blame for playing his part in a fashion approved by the gallery.

The only objection is that the actor may replace the man and take entire possession of him. There are a few select souls who can wear their reputation and a high position with a smile and remain their natural selves; they are the ones who know they are acting when they are acting, who do not share the artificial illusions of rank, title, property and wealth, and who accept these things with a tolerant smile when they come their way, but refuse to believe that they themselves are thereby different from ordinary human beings. It is this class of men, the truly great in spirit, who remain essentially simple in their personal lives. It is because they do not entertain these illusions that simplicity is always the mark of the truly great. Nothing shows more conclusively a small mind than a little government bureaucrat suffering from illusions of his own grandeur, or a social upstart displaying her jewels, or a half-baked writer imagining himself to belong to the company of the immortals and immediately becoming a less simple and less natural human being.

So deep is our histrionic instinct that we often forget that we have real lives to live off-stage. And so we sweat and labour and go through life, living not for ourselves in accordance with our true instincts, but for the approval of society, like "old spinsters working with their needles to make wedding dresses for other women," as the Chinese saying goes.

III. CYNICISM, FOLLY AND CAMOUFLAGE: LAOTSE

Paradoxically, Laotse's most wicked philosophy of "the old rogue" has been responsible for the highest ideal of peace, tolerance, simplicity and contentment. Such teachings include the wisdom of the foolish, the advantage of camouflage, the strength of weakness, and the simplicity of the truly sophisticated. Chinese art itself, with its poetic illusion and its glorification of the simple life of the wood-cutter and the fisherman, cannot exist apart from this philosophy. And at the bottom of Chinese pacificism is the willingness to put up with temporary losses and bide one's time, the belief that, in the scheme of things, with nature operating by the law of action and reaction, no one has a permanent advantage over the others and no one is a "damn fool" all the time.

> The greatest wisdom seems like stupidity.
> The greatest eloquence like stuttering.

Movement overcomes cold,
But staying overcomes heat.
So he by his limpid calm
Puts everything right under heaven.[1]

Knowing, then, that in Nature's ways no man has a permanent advantage over others and no man is a damn fool all the time, the natural conclusion is that there is no use for contention. In Laotse's words, the wise man "does not contend, and for that very reason no one under Heaven can contend with him." Again he says, "Show me a man of violence that came to a good end, and I will take him for my teacher." A modern writer might add, "Show me a dictator that can dispense with the services of a secret police, and I will be his follower." For this reason, Laotse says, "When the Tao prevails not, horses are trained for battle; when the Tao prevails, horses are trained to pull dung-carts."

The best charioteers do not rush ahead;
The best fighters do not make displays of wrath.
The greatest conqueror wins without joining issue;
The best user of men acts as though he were their inferior.
This is called the power that comes of not contending,
Is called the capacity to use men,
The secret of being mated to heaven, to what was of old.

The law of action and reaction brings about violence rebounding to violence:

He who by Tao purposes to help a ruler of men
Will oppose all conquest by force of arms;
For such things are wont to rebound.
Where armies are, thorns and brambles grow.
The raising of a great host
Is followed by a year of dearth.
Therefore a good general effects his purpose and then stops;
he does not take further advantage of his victory.

[1] This and the following quotations from Laotse's *Taotehching* are from Arthur Waley's excellent translation, *The Way and Its Power* (Allen & Unwin, London).

Fulfils his purpose and does not glory in what he has done;
Fulfils his purpose and does not boast of what he has done;
Fulfils his purpose, but takes no pride in what he has done;
Fulfils his purpose, but only as a step that could not be
   avoided.
Fulfils his purpose, but without violence;
For what has a time of vigour also has a time of decay.
This is against Tao,
And what is against Tao will soon perish.

My feeling is that, if Laotse had been invited to take the chair at
the Versailles Conference, there would not be a Hitler to-day.
Hitler claims that he and his work must have been "blessed by
God," on the evidence of his miraculous rise to power. I am
inclined to think that the matter is simpler than that, that he was
blessed by the spirit of Clemenceau. Chinese pacificism is not that
of the humanitarian, but that of the old rogue—based not upon
universal love, but upon a convincing type of subtle wisdom.

What is in the end to be shrunk
Must first be stretched.
Whatever is to be weakened
Must begin by being made strong.
What is to be overthrown
Must begin by being set up.
He who would be a taker
Must begin as a giver.
This is called "dimming" one's light.
It is thus that the soft overcomes the hard
And the weak, the strong.
"It is best to leave the fish down in his pool;
Best to leave the State's sharpest weapons
   where none can see them."

There has never been a more effective sermon more effectively
preached on the strength of weakness, the victory of the peace-
loving and the advantage of lying low than by Laotse. For water

remains for Laotse forever as the symbol of the strength of the weak—water that gently drips and makes a hole in a rock, and water which has the great Taoistic wisdom of seeking the lowest level:

> How did the great rivers and seas get their kingship over
>   the hundred lesser streams?
> Through the merit of being lower than they; that was
>   how they got their kingship.

An equally common symbol is that of "the Valley," representing the hollow, the womb and mother of all things, the *yin* or the Female.

> The Valley Spirit never dies.
> It is named the Mysterious Female.
> And the Doorway of the Mysterious Female
> Is the base from which Heaven and Earth sprang.
> It is there within us all the while;
> Draw upon it as you will, it never runs dry.

It would not be at all far-fetched to say that Oriental civilization represents the female principle, while the Occidental civilization represents the male principle. Anyway, there is something terribly resembling the womb or valley in China's passive strength that, in Laotsean language, "receives into it all things under heaven, and being a valley, has all the time a power that suffices."

Against the desire of Julius Cæsar to be the first man in a village Laotse gives the opposite counsel of "Never be the first in the world." This thought of the danger of being eminent is expressed by Chuangtse in the form of a satire against Confucius and his display of knowledge. There were many such libels against Confucius in the books of Chuangtse, for Confucius was dead when Chuangtse wrote, and there was no libel law in China.

> When Confucius was hemmed in between Ch'en and Ts'ai,
> he passed seven days without food.
> The minister Jen went to condole with him, and said, "You
> were near, Sir, to death."

"I was indeed," replied Confucius.

"Do you fear death, Sir?" inquired Jen.

"I do," said Confucius.

"Then I will try to teach you," said Jen, "the way not to die.

"In the eastern sea there are certain birds, called the *i-erh*. They behave themselves in a modest and unassuming manner, as though unpossessed of ability. They fly simultaneously; they roost in a body. In advancing, none strives to be first; in retreating, none venture to be last. In eating, none will be the first to begin; it is considered proper to take the leavings of others. Therefore, in their own ranks they are at peace, and the outside world is unable to harm them. And thus they escape trouble.

"Straight trees are the first felled. Sweet wells are soonest exhausted. And you, you make a show of your knowledge in order to startle fools. You cultivate yourself in contrast to the degradation of others. And you blaze along as though the sun and moon were under your arms; consequently, you cannot avoid trouble. . . ."

"Good indeed!" replied Confucius; and forthwith he took leave of his friends and dismissed his disciples and retired to the wilds, where he dressed himself in skins and serge and fed on acorns and chestnuts. He passed among the beasts and birds and they took no heed of him.[1]

I have made a poem which sums up for me the message of Taoistic thought:

> There is the wisdom of the foolish,
> The gracefulness of the slow,
> The subtlety of stupidity,
> The advantage of lying low.

This must sound to Christian readers like the Sermon on the Mount, and perhaps seem equally ineffective to them. Laotse gave the Beatitudes a cunning touch when he added: "Blessed are

[1] Giles's translation.

the idiots, for they are the happiest people on earth." Following Laotse's famous dictum that "The greatest wisdom is like stupidity; the greatest eloquence like stuttering," Chuangtse says: "Spit forth intelligence." Liu Chungyüan in the eighth century called his neighbourhood hill "the Stupid Hill" and the nearby river "the Stupid River." Cheng Panch'iao in the eighteenth century made the famous remark: "It is difficult to be muddle-headed. It is difficult to be clever, but still more difficult to graduate from cleverness into muddle-headedness." The praise of folly has never been interrupted in Chinese literature. The wisdom of this attitude can at once be understood through the American slang expression: "Don't be too smart." The wisest man is often one who pretends to be a "damn fool."

In the Chinese culture, therefore, we see the curious pheno-menon of a high intellect growing suspicious of itself and developing, so far as I know, the only gospel of ignorance and the earliest theory of camouflage as the best weapon in the battle of life. From Chuangtse's advice to "spit forth intelligence" it is but a short step to the glorification of the idiot, which we see constantly reflected in Chinese paintings and literary sketches of the beggar, or the disguised immortal, or the crazy monk, or the extraordinary recluse, as seen in *The Travels of Mingliaotse* (Chapter XI). The wise disenchantment with life receives a romantic or religious touch and enters the realm of poetic fantasy, when the poor, ragged and half-crazy monk becomes for us the symbol of highest wisdom and nobility of character.

The popularity of fools is an undeniable fact. I have no doubt that, East or West, the world hates a man who is too smart in his dealings with his fellow-men. Yüan Chunglang wrote an essay showing why he and his brothers chose to keep four extremely stupid and extremely loyal servants. Anyone can run over the names of his friends and associates in his mind and verify this fact for himself, that those we like are not those we respect for distinguished ability and those we respect for distinguished ability are not those we like, and that we like a stupid servant because he is more reliable, and because in his company we can better relax and do not have to set up a condition of defence against his presence. Most wise men choose to marry a not too smart wife, and most wise girls choose a not too smart husband as a life companion.

There have been a number of famous fools in Chinese history, all extremely popular and beloved for their real or affected craziness. Among these, for instance, is the famous Sung painter, Mi Fei, styled "Mi Tien" (or "Mi the Crazy One"), who got this title because he once appeared in a ceremonial robe to worship a piece of jagged rock that he called his "father-in-law." Both Mi Fei and the famous Yüan painter, Ni Yünlin, had a mild form of dirt-phobia or fastidious cleanliness. There was the famous crazy poet-monk Hanshan, who went about with dishevelled hair and bare feet, doing odd kitchen jobs at different monasteries, eating the left-overs, and scribbling immortal poetry on the temple and kitchen walls. The greatest crazy monk who has captured the imagination of the Chinese people is undoubtedly Chi Tien ("Chi the Crazy One"), or Chi Kung ("Master Chi"), who is the hero of a popular romance steadily being lengthened and added to until it is about three times the size of *Don Quixote*, and still seems endless. For he lives in a world of magic, medicine, roguery, and drunkenness, and possesses the gift of appearing at different cities several hundred miles apart on the same day. The temple to his honour still stands at Hupao near the West Lake of Hangchow to-day. To a lesser degree, the great romantic geniuses of the sixteenth and seventeenth centuries, while decidedly as normal as we, tended through their unconventionalities of appearance and conduct to give people an impression of being crazy, such as Hsü Wench'ang, Li Chowu and Chin Shengt'an (literally, "the Sigh of the Sage," a name he gave himself because he said that when he was born, a mysterious sigh was heard in the village temple of Confucius).

IV. "PHILOSOPHY OF HALF-AND-HALF": TSESSE

I have no doubt that a philosophy which enjoins the carefree and conscience-free life has a strong tendency to warn us away from a too busy life and from too great responsibilities, and therefore tends to decrease the desire for action. On the other hand, the modern man needs this refreshing wind of cynicism which cannot but do him some good. Probably more harm is done by a forward-looking philosophy delivering man over to a life of futile wasteful activities than is ever done by all the cynicism of the ancient and modern philosophies combined. There are too many physiological impulses for action in every man, ready to counteract this philosophy, and in spite of the popularity of this great Philosophy of the Scamp, the Chinese people are still one of the most industrious on earth. The majority of men cannot be cynics, simply because the majority of men are not philosophers.

As far as I can see, therefore, there is very little danger of cynicism being transformed into a general vogue followed by the herd. Even in China, where the Taoist philosophy finds an instinctive response in the Chinese breast, and where that philosophy has been at work for several thousand years, staring at us from every poem and every scroll of landscape painting, life still goes on merrily with lots of people believing in wealth and fame and power, quite determined and anxious to serve their country. Were it not so, human life would not be able to get along at all. No, the Chinese are cynics and poets only when they have failed; most of my countrymen are still very good showmen. The effect of Taoistic cynicism has been only to slow down the tempo of life, and in the case of natural calamities and human misrule, to promote trust in the law of action and reaction, which brings about justice in the end.

And yet there is an opposite influence in Chinese thought in general which counteracts this carefree philosophy, the philosophy of the natural vagabond. Opposed to the philosophy of nature's gentlemen, there is the philosophy of society's gentlemen; opposed to Taoism, there is Confucianism. Insofar as

Taoism and Confucianism mean merely the negative and positive outlooks on life, I do not think they are Chinese, but are inherent in all human nature. We are all born half Taoists and half Confucianists. The logical conclusion of a thorough-going Taoist would be to go to the mountains and live as a hermit or a recluse, to imitate as far as possible the simple carefree life of the woodcutter and the fisherman, the woodcutter who is lord of the green hills and the fisherman who is the owner of the blue waters. The Taoist recluse, half-hidden in the clouds on top of the mountain, looks down at the woodcutter and the fisherman holding an idle conversation, remarking that the hills go on being green and the waters go on flowing just to please themselves, entirely oblivious of the two tiny conversationalists. From this reflection, he gets a sense of perfect peace. And yet it is poor philosophy that teaches us to escape from human society altogether.

There is still a greater philosophy than this naturalism, namely, the philosophy of humanism. The highest ideal of Chinese thought is therefore a man who does not have to escape from human society and human life in order to preserve his original, happy nature. He is only a second-rate recluse, still slave to his environment, who has to escape from the cities and live away in the mountains in solitude. "The Great Recluse is the city recluse," because he has sufficient mastery over himself not to be afraid of his surroundings. He is therefore the Great Monk (the *kaoseng*) who returns to human society and eats pork and drinks wine and mixes with women, without detriment to his own soul. There is, therefore, the possibility of the merging of the two philosophies. The contrast between Confucianism and Taoism is relative, the two doctrines setting forth only two great extremes, and between them there are many intermediate stages.

Those are the best cynics who are half-cynics. The highest type of life after all is the life of sweet reasonableness as taught by Confucius' grandson, Tsesse, author of *The Golden Mean*. No philosophy, ancient or modern, dealing with the problems of human life has yet discovered a more profound truth than this doctrine of a well-ordered life lying somewhere between the two extremes—the Doctrine of the Half-and-Half. It is that spirit of sweet reasonableness, arriving at a perfect balance between action and inaction, shown in the ideal of a man living in half-fame and semi-obscurity; half-lazily active and half-actively lazy; not so poor that he cannot pay his rent, and not so rich that he doesn't have to work a little or couldn't wish to have slightly more to help his friends; who plays the piano, but only well enough for his most intimate friends to hear, and chiefly to please himself; who collects, but just enough to load his mantelpiece; who reads, but not too hard; learns a lot but does not become a specialist; writes, but has his correspondence to *The Times* half of the time rejected and half of the time published—in short, it is that ideal of middle-class life which I believe to be the sanest ideal of life ever discovered by the Chinese. This is the ideal so well expressed in Li Mi-an's "The Half-and-Half Song":

> By far the greater half have I seen through
> This floating life—ah, there's a magic word—
> This "half"—so rich in implications.
> It bids us taste the joy of more than we
> Can ever own. Half-way in life is man's
> Best state, when slackened pace allows him ease;
> A wide world lies half-way 'twixt heaven and earth;
> To live half-way between the town and land,
> Have farms half-way between the streams and hills;
> Be half-a-scholar, and half-a-squire, and half
> In business; half as gentry live,
> And half related to the common folk;
> And have a house that's half genteel, half plain,
> Half elegantly furnished and half bare;
> Dresses and gowns that are half old, half new,
> And food half epicure's, half simple fare;
> Have servants not too clever, not too dull;
> A wife who's not too simple, nor too smart—
> So then, at heart, I feel I'm half a Buddha,

And almost half a Taoist fairy blest.
One half myself to Father Heaven I
Return; the other half to children leave—
Half thinking how for my posterity
To plan and provide, and yet half minding how
To answer God when the body's laid at rest.[1]
He is most wisely drunk who is half drunk;
And flowers in half-bloom look their prettiest;
As boats at half-sail sail the steadiest,
And horses held at half-slack reins trot best.
Who half too much has, adds anxiety,
But half too little, adds possession's zest.
Since life's of sweet and bitter compounded,
Who tastes but half is wise and cleverest.

We have here, then, a compounding of Taoistic cynicism with the Confucian positive outlook into a philosophy of the half-and-half. And because man is born between the real earth and the unreal heaven, I believe that, however unsatisfactory it may seem on the first look to a Westerner, with his incredibly forward-looking point of view, it is still the best philosophy, because it is the most human. After all, a half Lindbergh would be better, because more happy, than a complete Lindbergh. I am quite sure Lindbergh would be much happier if he had flown only half-way across the Atlantic. After all allowances are made for the necessity of having a few supermen in our midst—explorers, conquerors, great inventors, great presidents, heroes who change the course of history—the happiest man is still the man of the middle class who has earned a slight means of economic independence, who has done a little, but just a little, for mankind, and who is slightly distinguished in his community, but not too distinguished. It is only in this milieu of well-known obscurity and financial competence with a pinch, when life is fairly carefree and yet not altogether carefree, that the human spirit is happiest and succeeds best. After all, we have to get on in this life, and so we must bring philosophy down from heaven to earth.

[1] Literally, "Half thinking how to face King Yenlo of Hell."

V. A LOVER OF LIFE: T'AO YÜANMING

It has been shown, therefore, that with the proper merging of the positive and the negative outlooks on life, it is possible to achieve a harmonious philosophy of the "half-and-half" lying somewhere between action and inaction, between being led by the nose into a world of futile *busy-ness* and complete flight from a life of responsibilities, and that so far as we can discover with the help of all the philosophies of the world, this is the sanest and happiest ideal for man's life on earth. What is still more important, the mixture of these two different outlooks makes a harmonious personality possible, that harmonious personality which is the acknowledged aim of all culture and education. And significantly, out of this harmonious personality, we see a joy and love of life.

It is difficult for me to describe the qualities of this love of life; it is easier to speak in a parable or tell the story of a true lover of life, as he really lived. And the picture of T'ao Yüanming, the greatest poet and most harmonious product of Chinese culture, inevitably comes to my mind.[1] There will be no one in China to object when I say that T'ao represents to us the most perfectly harmonious and well-rounded character in the entire Chinese literary tradition. Without leading an illustrious official career, without power and outward achievements and without leaving us a greater literary heritage than a thin volume of poems and three or four essays in prose, he remains to-day a beacon shining through the ages, for ever a symbol to lesser poets and writers of what the highest human character should be. There is a simplicity in his life, as well as in his style, which is awe-inspiring and a constant reproach to more brilliant and more sophisticated natures. And he stands, to-day, as a perfect example of the true lover of life, because in him the rebellion against worldly desires did not lead him to attempt a total escape, but has reached a harmony with the life of the senses. About two centuries of literary romanticism and the Taoistic cult of the idle life and

[1] T'ao Ch'ien (*alias* "Yüanming"), A.D. 372-427.

rebellion against Confucianism had been working in China and joined forces with the Confucian philosophy of the previous centuries to make the emergence of this harmonious personality possible. In T'ao we find the positive outlook had lost its foolish complacency and the cynic philosophy had lost its bitter rebelliousness (a trait we see still in Thoreau—a sign of immaturity), and human wisdom first reaching full maturity in a spirit of tolerant irony.

T'ao represents to me that strange characteristic of Chinese culture, a curious combination of devotion to the flesh and arrogance of the spirit, of spirituality without asceticism and materialism without sensuality, in which the senses and the spirit have come to live together in harmony. For the ideal philosopher is one who understands the charm of women without being coarse, who loves life heartily but loves it with restraint, and who sees the unreality of the successes and failures of the active world, and stands somewhat aloof and detached, without being hostile to it. Because T'ao reached that true harmony of spiritual development, we see a total absence of inner conflict and his life was as natural and effortless as his poetry.

T'ao was born toward the end of the fourth century of our era, the great grandson of a distinguished scholar and official, who in order to keep himself from being idle, moved a pile of bricks from one place to another in the morning, and moved them back in the afternoon. In his youth he accepted a minor official job in order to support his old parents, but soon resigned and returned to the farm, tilling the field himself as a farmer, from which he developed a kind of bodily ailment. One day he asked his relatives and friends, "Would it be all right for me to go out as a minstrel singer in order to pay for the upkeep of my garden?" On hearing this, certain of his friends got him a position as a magistrate of P'engcheh, near Kiukiang. Being very fond of wine, he commanded that all the fields belonging to the local government should be planted with glutinous rice, from which wine could be made, and only on the protestations of his wife did he allow one-sixth to be planted with another kind of rice. When a government delegate came and his secretary told him that he should receive the little fellow with his gown properly girdled, T'ao sighed and said, "I cannot bend and bow for the sake of five bushels of rice." And he immediately resigned and wrote that famous poem, "Ah, Homeward Bound I Go!" From then on, he lived the life of a farmer and repeatedly refused later calls to office. Poor himself, he lived in communion with the poor, and he expressed a certain paternal regret in a letter to his sons that they should be so poorly clad and do the work of a common labourer. But when he managed to send a peasant boy to his sons when he was away, to help them do the work of carrying water and gathering fuel, he said to them, "Treat him well, for he is also someone's son."[1]

His only weakness was a fondness for wine. Living very much to himself, he seldom saw guests, but whenever there was wine, he would sit down with the company, even though he might not be acquainted with the host. At other times, when he was the host himself and got drunk first, he would say to his guests, "I am drunk and thinking of sleep; you can all go." He had a stringed instrument, the *ch'in*, without any strings left. It was an ancient instrument that could be played only in an extremely slow manner and only in a state of perfect mental calm. After a feast, or when feeling in a musical mood, he would express his musical feelings by fondling and fingering this stringless instrument. "I appreciate the flavour of music; what need have I for the sounds from the strings?"

Humble and simple and independent, he was extremely chary of company. A magistrate, one Wang, who was his great admirer, wanted to cultivate his friendship, but found it very difficult to see him. With his perfect naturalness he said, "I'm keeping to myself because by nature I'm not made for the life of society, and I am staying in the house because of an ailment. Far be it from me to act in this manner in order to acquire a reputation for being high and aloof." Wang therefore had to plot with a friend in order to see him; this friend had to induce him to leave

1 Considered one of his greatest sayings by the Chinese.

his home, by inviting him to a feast and an accidental meeting. When he was half-way and stopped at a pavilion, wine was presented. T'ao's eyes brightened and he gladly sat down to drink, when Wang, who had been hiding nearby, came out to meet him. And he was so happy that he remained there talking with him the whole afternoon, and forgot to go on to his friend's place. Wang saw that he had no shoes on his feet and ordered his subordinates to make a pair for him. When these minor officials asked for the measurements, he stretched forth his feet and asked them to take the measure. And thereafter, whenever Wang wanted to see him, he had to wait in the forest or around the lake, so that perchance he might meet the poet. Once when his friends were brewing wine, they took his linen turban to use it as a strainer, and after the wine had been strained, he wound the turban again around his head.

There was then in the great Lushan Mountains, at whose foot he lived, a great society of illustrious *Zen* Buddhists, and the leader, a great scholar, tried to get him to join the Lotus Society. One day he was invited to come to a party, and his condition was that he should be allowed to drink. This breaking of the Buddhist rule was granted him and he went. But when it came to putting his name down as a member, he "knitted his brows and stole away." This was a society that so great a poet as Hsieh Lingyün had been very anxious to join, but could not get in. But still the abbot courted his friendship and one day he invited him to drink, together with another great Taoist friend. They were then a company of three; the abbot, representing Buddhism, T'ao representing Confucianism, and the other friend representing Taoism. It had been the abbot's life vow never to go beyond a certain bridge in his daily walks, but one day when he and the other friend were sending T'ao home, they were so pleasurably occupied in their conversation that the abbot went past the bridge without knowing it. When it was pointed out to him, the company of three laughed. This incident of the three laughing old men became the subject of popular Chinese paintings, because it symbolized the happiness and gaiety of three carefree, wise souls, representing three religions united by the sense of humour.

And so he lived and died, a carefree and conscience-free, humble peasant-poet, and a wise and merry old man. But something in his small volume of poems on drinking and the pastoral life, his three or four casual essays, one letter to his sons, three sacrificial prayers (including one to himself), and some of his remarks handed down to posterity shows a sentiment and a genius for harmonious living that reached perfect naturalness and never has yet been surpassed. It was this great love of life that was expressed in the poem which he wrote one day in November, A.D. 405, when he decided to lay down the burdens of the magistrate's office.[1]

Ah, homeward bound I go! why not go home, seeing that my field and garden with weeds are overgrown? Myself have made my soul serf to my body: why have vain regrets and mourn alone?

Fret not over bygones and the forward journey take. Only a short distance have I gone astray, and I know to-day I am right, if yesterday was a complete mistake.

Lightly floats and drifts the boat, and gently flows and flaps my gown. I inquire the road of a wayfarer, and sulk at the dimness of the dawn.

Then when I catch sight of my old roofs, joy will my steps quicken. Servants will be there to bid me welcome, and waiting at the door are the greeting children.

Gone to seed, perhaps, are my garden paths, but there will still be the chrysanthemums and the pine! I shall lead the youngest boy in by the hand, and on the table there stands a cup full of wine!

Holding the pot and cup I give myself a drink, happy to see in the courtyard the hanging bough. I lean upon the

---

[1] This poem is in the form of a *fu*, progressing in parallel constructions, like the *Psalms*, and sometimes rhymed.

southern window with an immense satisfaction, and note that the little place is cosy enough to walk around.

The garden grows more familiar and interesting with the daily walks. What if no one ever knocks at the always closed door! Carrying a cane I wander at peace, and now and then look aloft to gaze at the blue above.

There the clouds idle away from their mountain recesses without any intent or purpose, and birds, when tired of their wandering flights, will think of home. Darkly then fall the shadows and, ready to come home, I yet fondle the lonely pines and loiter around.

Ah, homeward bound I go! Let me from now on learn to live alone! The world and I are not made for one another, and why drive round like one looking for what he has not found?

Content shall I be with conversations with my own kin, and there will be music and books to while away the hours. The farmers will come and tell me that spring is here and there will be work to do at the western farm.

Some order covered wagons; some row in small boats. Sometimes we explore quiet, unknown ponds, and sometimes we climb over steep, rugged mounds.

There the trees, happy of heart, grow marvellously green, and spring water gushes forth with a gurgling sound. I admire how things grow and prosper according to their seasons, and feel that thus, too, shall my life go its round.

Enough! How long yet shall I this mortal shape keep? Why not take life as it comes, and why hustle and bustle like one on an errand bound?

Wealth and power are not my ambitions, and unattainable is the abode of the gods! I would go forth alone on a bright morning, or perhaps, planting my cane, begin to pluck the weeds and till the ground.

[124]

Or I would compose a poem beside a clear stream, or perhaps go up Tungkao and make a long-drawn call on the top of the hill. So would I be content to live and die, and without questionings of the heart, gladly accept Heaven's will.

T'ao might be taken as an "escapist," and yet it was not so. What he tried to escape from was politics and not life itself. If he had been a logician, he might have decided to escape from life altogether by becoming a Buddhist monk. With T'ao's great love of life, he could not have been willing to escape from it altogether. His wife and children were too real for him, his garden and the bough stretching across his courtyard and the lonely pines which he fondled were altogether too attractive, and being a reasonable man, instead of a logician, he stuck to them. That was his love of life and his jealousy over it, and it was from this positive, but reasonable, attitude toward life that he arrived at the feeling of harmony with life which was characteristic of his culture. From that harmony with life welled forth the greatest poetry in China. Of the earth and earth-born, his conclusion was not to escape from it but "to go forth alone on a bright morning, or perhaps, *planting his cane, begin to pluck the weeds and till the ground.*" T'ao merely returned to the farm and to his family. The end was harmony and not rebellion.

CHAPTER SIX

The Feast Of Life

I. THE PROBLEM OF HAPPINESS

THE ENJOYMENT OF LIFE covers many things: the enjoyment of ourselves, of home life, of trees, flowers, clouds, winding rivers and falling cataracts and the myriad things in Nature, and then the enjoyment of poetry, art, contemplation, friendship, conversation, and reading, which are all some form or other of the communion of spirits. There are obvious things like the enjoyment of food, a gay party or family reunion, an outing on a beautiful spring day; and less obvious things like the enjoyment of poetry, art and contemplation. I have found it impossible to call these two classes of enjoyment material and spiritual, first because I do not believe in this distinction, and secondly because I am puzzled whenever I proceed to make this classification. How can I say, when I see a gay picnic party of men and women and old people and children, what part of their pleasures is material and what part spiritual? I see a child romping about on the grass plot, another child making daisy chains, their mother holding a piece of sandwich, the uncle of the family biting a juicy, red apple, the father sprawling on the ground looking at the sailing clouds, and the grandfather holding a pipe in his mouth. Probably somebody is playing a gramophone, and from the distance there come the sound of music and the distant roar of the waves. Which of these pleasures is material and which spiritual? Is it so easy to draw a distinction between the enjoyment of a sandwich and the enjoyment of the surrounding landscape, which we call poetry? Is it possible to regard the enjoyment of music which we call art, as decidedly a higher type of pleasure than the smoking of a pipe, which we call material? This classification between material and spiritual pleasures is therefore confusing, unintelligible and untrue for me. It proceeds, I suspect, from a false philosophy, sharply dividing the spirit from the flesh, and not supported by a closer direct scrutiny of our real pleasures.

Or have I perhaps assumed too much and begged the question of the proper end of human life? I have always assumed that the end of living is the true enjoyment of it. It is so simply because it is so. I rather hesitate at the word "end" or "purpose." Such an end or purpose of life, consisting in its true enjoyment, is not so much a conscious purpose as a natural attitude toward human life. The word "purpose" suggests too much contriving and endeavour. The question that faces every man born into this world is not what should be his purpose, which he should set about to achieve, but just what to do with life, a life which is given him for a period of, on the average, fifty or sixty years? The answer that he should order his life so that he can find the greatest happiness in it is more a practical question, similar to that of how a man should spend his week-end, than a metaphysical proposition as to what is the mystic purpose of his life in the scheme of the universe.

On the contrary, I rather think that philosophers who start out to solve the problem of the purpose of life beg the question by assuming that life must have a purpose. This question, so much pushed to the fore among Western thinkers, is undoubtedly given that importance through the influence of theology. I think we assume too much design and purpose altogether. And the very fact that people try to answer this question and quarrel over it and are puzzled by it serves to show it up as quite vain and uncalled for. Had there been a purpose or design in life, it should not have been so puzzling and vague and difficult to find out.

The question may be divided into two: either that of a divine purpose, which God has set for humanity, or that of a human purpose, a purpose that mankind should set for itself. As far as the first is concerned, I do not propose to enter into the question, because everything that we think God has in mind necessarily proceeds from our own mind; it is what we imagine to be in God's mind, and it is really difficult for human intelligence to guess at a divine intelligence. What we usually end up with by this sort of reasoning is to make God the colour-sergeant of our army and to make Him as chauvinistic as ourselves; He cannot, so we conceive, possibly have a "divine purpose" and "destiny" for the world, or for Europe, but only for our beloved Fatherland. I am quite sure the Nazis can't conceive of God without a swastika arm-band. This *Gott* is always *mit uns* and cannot possibly be *mit ihnen*. But the Germans are not the only people who think this way.

As far as the second question is concerned, the point of dispute is not what *is*, but what *should be*, the purpose of human life, and it is therefore a practical, and not a metaphysical question. Into this question of what should be the purpose of human life, every man projects his own conceptions and his own scale of values. It is for this reason that we quarrel over the question, because our scales of values differ from one another. For myself, I am content to be less philosophical and more practical. I should not presume that there must be necessarily a purpose, a meaning of human existence. As Walt Whitman says, "I am sufficient as I am." It is sufficient that I live—and am probably going to live for another few decades—and that human life exists. Viewed that way, the problem becomes amazingly simple and admits of no two answers. What can be the end of human life except the enjoyment of it?

It is strange that this problem of happiness, which is the great question occupying the minds of all pagan philosophers, has been entirely neglected by Christian thinkers. The great question that bothers theological minds is not human happiness, but human "salvation"—a tragic word. The word has a bad flavour for me, because in China I hear every day someone talking about our "national salvation." Everybody is trying to "save" China. It suggests the feeling of people on a sinking ship, a feeling of ultimate doom and the best method of getting away alive. Christianity, which has been described as "the last sigh of two expiring worlds" (Greek and Roman), still retains something of that characteristic to-day in its preoccupation with the question of salvation. The question of living is forgotten in the question of getting away alive from this world. Why should man bother himself so much about salvation, unless he has a feeling of being doomed? Theological minds are so much occupied with salvation, and so little with happiness, that all they can tell us about the future is that there will be a vague heaven, and when questioned about what we are going to do there and how we are going to be happy in heaven, they have only ideas of the vaguest sort, such as singing hymns and wearing white robes. Mohammed at least painted a picture of future happiness with rich wine and juicy fruits and black-haired, big-eyed, passionate maidens that we laymen can understand. Unless heaven is made much more vivid and convincing for us, there is no reason why one should strive to go there, at the cost of neglecting this earthly existence. As someone says, "An egg to-day is better than a hen to-morrow." At least, when we're planning a summer vacation, we take the trouble to find out some details about the place we are going to. If the tourist bureau is entirely vague on the question, I am not interested; I remain where I am. Are we going to strive and endeavour in heaven, as I am quite sure the believers in progress and endeavour must assume? But how can we strive and make progress when we are already perfect? Or are we going merely to loaf and do nothing and not worry? In that case, would it not be better for us to learn to loaf while on this earth as a preparation for our eternal life?

If we must have a view of the universe, let us forget ourselves and not confine it to human life. Let us stretch it a little and include in our view the purpose of the entire creation—the rocks, the trees and the animals. There is a scheme of things (although "scheme" is another word, like "end" and "purpose," which I strongly distrust)—I mean there is a pattern of things in the creation, and we can arrive at some sort of opinion, however lacking in finality, about this entire universe, and then take our place in it. This view of nature and our place in it must be natural, since we are a vital part of it in our life and go back to it when we die. Astronomy, geology, biology and history all provide pretty good material to help us form a fairly good view if we don't attempt too much and jump at conclusions. It doesn't matter if, in this bigger view of the purpose of the creation, man's place recedes a little in importance. It is enough that he has a place, and by living in harmony with nature around him, he will be able to form a workable and reasonable outlook on human life itself.

II. HUMAN HAPPINESS IS SENSUOUS

All human happiness is biological happiness. That is strictly scientific. At the risk of being misunderstood, I must make it clearer: all human happiness is sensuous happiness. The spiritualists will misunderstand me, I am sure; the spiritualists and materialists must for ever misunderstand each other, because they don't talk the same language, or mean by the same word different things. Are we, too, in this problem of securing happiness to be deluded by the spiritualists, and admit that true happiness is only happiness of the spirit? Let us admit it at once and immediately proceed to qualify it by saying that the spirit is a condition of the perfect functioning of the endocrine glands. Happiness for me is largely a matter of digestion. I have to take cover under an American college president to ensure my reputation and respectability when I say that happiness is largely a matter of the movement of the bowels. The American college president in question used to say with great wisdom in his address to each class of freshmen, "There are only two things I want you to keep in mind: read the Bible and keep your bowels open." What a wise, genial old soul he was to have said that! If one's bowels move, one is happy, and if they don't move, one is unhappy. That is all there is to it.

Let us not lose ourselves in the abstract when we talk of happiness, but get down to facts and analyse for ourselves what are the truly happy moments of our life. In this world of ours, happiness is very often negative, the complete absence of sorrow or mortification or bodily ailment. But happiness can also be positive, and then we call it joy. To me, for instance, the truly happy moments are: when I get up in the morning after a night of perfect sleep and sniff the morning air and there is an expansiveness in the lungs, when I feel inclined to inhale deeply and there is a fine sensation of movement around the skin and muscles of the chest, and when, therefore, I am fit for work; or when I hold a pipe in my hand and rest my legs on a chair, and the tobacco burns slowly and evenly; or when I am travelling on a summer day, my throat parched with thirst, and I see a beautiful clear spring, whose very sound makes me happy, and I take off my socks and shoes and dip my feet in the delightful, cool water; or when after a perfect dinner I lounge in an arm-chair, when there is no one I hate to look at in the company and conversation rambles off at a light pace to an unknown destination, and I am spiritually and physically at peace with the world; or when on a summer afternoon I see black clouds gathering on the horizon and know for certain a July shower is coming in a quarter of an hour, but being ashamed to be seen going out into the rain without an umbrella, I hastily set out to meet the shower half-way across the fields and come home drenched through and through and tell my family that I was simply caught by the rain.

Just as it is impossible for me to say whether I love my children physically or spiritually when I hear their chattering voices or when I see their plump legs, so I am totally unable to distinguish between the joys of the mind and the joys of the flesh. Does anybody ever love a woman spiritually without loving her physically? And is it so easy a matter for a man to analyse and separate the charms of the woman he loves—things like laughter, smiles, a way of tossing one's head, a certain attitude toward things? And after all every girl feels happier when she is well-dressed. There is a soul-uplifting quality about lipstick and rouge and a spiritual calm and poise that comes from the knowledge of being well-dressed, which is real and definite for the girl herself and of which the spiritualist has no inkling of an idea. Being made of this mortal flesh, the partition separating our flesh from our spirit is extremely thin, and the world of spirit, with its finest emotions and greatest appreciations of spiritual beauty, cannot be reached except with our senses. There is no such thing as morality and immorality in the sense of touch, of hearing and vision. There is a great probability that our loss of capacity for enjoying the positive joys of life is largely due to the decreased sensibility of our senses and our lack of full use of them.

Why argue about it? Let us take concrete instances and cull examples from all the great lovers of life, Eastern and Western, and see what they describe as their own happy moments, and how intimately they are connected with the very senses of hearing and smelling and seeing. Here is a description of the high æsthetic pleasure that Thoreau[1] got from hearing the sound of crickets:

First observe the creak of crickets. It is quite general amid these rocks. The song of only one is more interesting to me. It suggests lateness, but only as we come to a knowledge of eternity after some acquaintance with time. It is only late for all trivial and hurried pursuits. It suggests a wisdom mature, never late, being above all temporal considerations, which possesses the coolness and maturity of autumn amidst the aspiration of spring and the heats of summer. To the birds they say: "Ah! you speak like children from impulse; Nature speaks through you; but with us it is ripe knowledge. The seasons do not revolve for us; we sing their lullaby." So they chant, eternal, at the roots of the grass. It is heaven where they are, and their dwelling need not be heaved up. For ever the same, in May and in November [?]. Serenely wise, their song has the security of prose. They have drunk no wine but the dew. It is no transient love-strain hushed when the incubating season is past, but a glorifying of God and enjoying of him for ever. They sit aside from the revolution of the seasons. Their strain is unvaried as Truth. Only in their saner moments do men hear the crickets.

[1] Thoreau is the most Chinese of all American authors in his entire view of life, and being a Chinese, I feel much akin to him in spirit. I discovered him only a few months ago, and the delight of the discovery is still fresh in my mind. I could translate passages of Thoreau into my own language and pass them off as original writing by a Chinese poet without raising any suspicion.

And see how Walt Whitman's senses of smell and sight and sound contribute to his spirituality and what great importance he places upon them:

> A snowstorm in the morning, and continuing most of the day. But I took a walk over two hours, the same woods and paths, amid the falling flakes. No wind, yet the musical low murmur through the pines, quite pronounced, curious, like waterfalls, now still'd, now pouring again. All the senses, sight, sound, smell, delicately gratified. Every snowflake lay where it fell on the evergreens, holly-trees, laurels, etc., the multitudinous leaves and branches piled, bulging-white, defined by edgelines of emerald—the tall straight columns of the plentiful bronze-topt pines—a slight resinous odour blending with that of the snow. (For there is a scent to every-thing, even the snow, if you can only detect it—no two places, hardly any two hours, anywhere, exactly alike. How different the odour of noon from midnight, or winter from summer, or a windy spell from a still one!)

How many of us are able to distinguish between the odours of noon and midnight, or of winter and summer, or of a windy spell and a still one? If man is so generally less happy in the cities than in the country, it is because all these variations and nuances of sight and smell and sound are less clearly marked and lost in the general monotony of grey walls and cement pavements.

The Chinese and the Americans are alike when it comes to the true limits and capacities and qualities of the happy moments. Before I translate the thirty-three happy moments given by a Chinese scholar, I want to quote by way of comparison another passage from Whitman, which will show the identity of our senses:

> A clear, crispy day—dry and breezy air, full of oxygen. Out of the sane, silent, beauteous miracles that envelop and fuse me —trees, water, grass, sunlight, and early frost—the one I am looking at most to-day is the sky. It has that delicate,

transparent blue peculiar to autumn, and the only clouds are little or larger white ones, giving their still and spiritual motion to the great concave. All through the earlier day (say from 7 to 11) it keeps a pure, yet vivid blue. But as noon approaches the colour gets lighter, quite grey for two or three hours—then still paler for a spell, till sun-down—which last I watch dazzling through the interstices of a knoll of big trees—darts of fire and a gorgeous show of light-yellow, liver-colour and red, with a vast silver glaze askant on the water—the transparent shadows, shafts, sparkle, and vivid colours beyond all the paintings ever made.

I don't know what or how, but it seems to me mostly owing to these skies (every now and then I think, while I have of course seen them every day of my life, I never really saw the skies before), I have had this autumn some wondrously contented hours—may I not say perfectly happy ones? As I've read, Byron just before his death told a friend that he had known but three happy hours during his whole existence. Then there is the old German legend of the king's bell, to the same point. While I was out there by the wood, that beautiful sunset through the trees, I thought of Byron's and the bell story, and the notion started in me that I was having a happy hour. (Though perhaps my best moments I never jot down; when they come I cannot afford to break the charm by inditing memoranda. I just abandon myself to the mood, and let it float on, carrying me in its placid ecstasy).

What is happiness, anyhow? Is this one of its hours, or the like of it?—so impalpable—a mere breath, an evanescent tinge? I am not sure—so let me give myself the benefit of the doubt. Hast Thou, pellucid, in Thy azure depths, medicine for case like mine? (Ah, the physical shatter and troubled spirit of me the last three years.) And dost Thou subtly mystically now drip it through the air invisibly upon me?

III. CHIN'S THIRTY-THREE HAPPY MOMENTS

We are now better prepared to examine and appreciate the happy moments of a Chinese, as he describes them. Chin Shengt'an, that great impressionistic critic of the seventeenth century, has given us, between his commentaries on the play *Western Chamber*, an enumeration of the happy moments which he once counted together with his friend, when they were shut up in a temple for ten days on account of rainy weather. These, then, are what he considers the truly happy moments of human life, moments in which the spirit is inextricably tied up with the senses:

1[1]: It is a hot day in June when the sun hangs still in the sky and there is not a whiff of wind or air, nor a trace of clouds; the front and back yards are hot like an oven and not a single bird dares to fly about. Perspiration flows down my whole body in little rivulets. There is the noonday meal before me, but I cannot take it for the sheer heat. I ask for a mat to spread on the ground and lie down, but the mat is wet with moisture and flies swarm about to rest on my nose and refuse to be driven away. Just at this moment when I am completely helpless, suddenly there is a rumbling of thunder and big sheets of black clouds overcast the sky and come majestically on like a great army advancing to battle. Rain-water begins to pour down from the eaves like a cataract. The perspiration stops. The clamminess of the ground is gone. All flies disappear to hide themselves and I can eat my rice. Ah, is this not happiness?

1: A friend, one I have not seen for ten years, suddenly arrives at sunset. I open the door to receive him, and without asking whether he came by boat or by land, and without bidding him to sit down on the bed or the couch, I go to the inner chamber and humbly ask my wife: "Have you got a gallon of wine like Su Tungp'o's wife?" My wife gladly

---

[1] When a Chinese draws up a set of seventeen or eighteen regulations, it is his custom (the idiom of our language) to set them down as "Articles 1, 1, 1, 1, 1, 1," etc.

takes out her gold hairpin to sell it. I calculate it will last us three days. Ah, is this not happiness?

1 : I am sitting alone in an empty room and I am just getting annoyed at a mouse at the head of my bed, and wondering what that little rustling sound signifies—what article of mine he is biting or what volume of my books he is eating up. While I am in this state of mind, and don't know what to do, I suddenly see a ferocious-looking cat, wagging its tail and staring with its wide-open eyes, as if it were looking at something. I hold my breath and wait a moment, keeping perfectly still, and suddenly with a little sound the mouse disappears like a whiff of wind. Ah, is this not happiness?

1 : I have pulled out the *hait'ang* and *chihching*[1] in front of my studio, and have just planted ten or twenty green banana trees there. Ah, is this not happiness?

1 : I am drinking with some romantic friends on a spring night and am just half intoxicated, finding it difficult to stop drinking and equally difficult to go on. An understanding boy servant at the side suddenly brings in a package of big fire-crackers, about a dozen in number, and I rise from the table and go and fire them off. The smell of sulphur assails my nostrils and enters my brain and I feel comfortable all over my body. Ah, is this not happiness?

1 : I am walking in the street and see two poor rascals engaged in a hot argument of words with their faces flushed and their eyes staring with anger as if they were mortal enemies, and yet they still pretend to be ceremonious to each other, raising their arms and bending their waists in salute, and still using the most polished language of *thou* and *thee* and *wherefore* and *is it not so?* The flow of words is interminable. Suddenly there appears a big husky fellow swinging his arms and coming up to them, and with a shout tells them to disperse. Ah, is this not happiness?

1 : To hear our children recite the classics so fluently, like

[1] *Hait'ang* is of the pyrus family, bearing fruits like crab-apples, and *chihching* blossoms in spring, with small violet flowers growing directly on the trunks and branches.

the sound of pouring water from a vase. Ah, is this not happiness?

1 : Having nothing to do after a meal I go to the shops and take a fancy to a little thing. After bargaining for some time, we still haggle about a small difference, but the shop-boy still refuses to sell it. Then I take out a little thing from my sleeve, which is worth about the same thing as the difference and throw it at the boy. The boy suddenly smiles and bows courteously saying, "Oh, you are too generous!" Ah, is this not happiness?

1 : I have nothing to do after a meal and try to go through the things in some old trunks. I see there are dozens or hundreds of I O Us from people who owe my family money. Some of them are dead and some still living, but in any case there is no hope of their returning the money. Behind people's backs I put them together in a pile and make a bonfire of them, and I look up to the sky and see the last trace of smoke disappear. Ah, is this not happiness?

1 : It is a summer day. I go bareheaded and barefooted, holding a parasol to watch young people singing Soochow folk-songs while treading the water-wheel. The water comes up over the wheel in a gushing torrent like molten silver or melting snow. Ah, is this not happiness?

1 : I wake up in the morning and seem to hear someone in the house sighing and saying that last night someone died. I immediately ask to find out who it is, and learn that it is the sharpest, most calculating fellow in town. Ah, is this not happiness?

1 : I get up early on a summer morning and see people sawing a large bamboo pole under a mat-shed, to be used as a water-pipe. Ah, is this not happiness?

1 : It has been raining for a whole month and I lie in bed in the morning like one drunk or ill, refusing to get up. Suddenly I hear a chorus of birds announcing a clear day. Quickly I pull aside the curtain, push open the window and see the beautiful sun shining and glistening and the forest

looks like having a bath. Ah, is this not happiness?

1: At night I seem to hear someone thinking of me in the distance. The next day I go to call on him. I enter his door and look about his room and see that this person is sitting at his desk, facing south, reading a document. He sees me, nods quietly and pulls me by the sleeve to make me sit down, saying, "Since you are here, come and look at this." And we laugh and enjoy ourselves until the shadows on the walls have disappeared. He is feeling hungry himself and slowly asks me, "Are you hungry, too?" Ah, is this not happiness?

1: Without any serious intention to build a house of my own, I happened, nevertheless, to start building one because a little sum had unexpectedly come my way. From that day on, every morning and every night I was told that I needed to buy timber and stone and tiles and bricks and mortar and nails. And I explored and exhausted every avenue of getting some money, all on account of this house, without, however, being able to live in it all this time, until I got sort of resigned to this state of things. One day, finally, the house is completed, the walls have been whitewashed and the floors swept clean; the paper windows have been pasted and scrolls of paintings are hung up on the walls. All the workmen have left, and my friends have arrived, sitting on different couches in order. Ah, is this not happiness?

1: I am drinking on a winter's night, and suddenly note that the night has turned extremely cold. I push open the window and see that snowflakes come down the size of a palm and there are already three or four inches of snow on the ground. Ah, is this not happiness?

1: To cut with a sharp knife a bright green water-melon on a big scarlet plate of a summer afternoon. Ah, is this not happiness?

1: I have long wanted to become a monk, but was worried because I would not be permitted to eat meat. If, then, I could be permitted to become a monk and yet eat meat publicly, why, then I would heat a basin of hot water, and with the help of a sharp razor shave my head clean in a summer month! Ah, is this not happiness?

1: To keep three or four spots of eczema in a private part of my body and now and then to scald or bathe it with hot water behind closed doors. Ah, is this not happiness?

1: To find accidentally a handwritten letter of some old friend in a trunk. Ah, is this not happiness?

1: A poor scholar comes to borrow money from me, but is shy about mentioning the topic, and so he allows the conversation to drift along on other topics. I see his uncomfortable situation, pull him aside to a place where we are alone and ask him how much he needs. Then I go inside and give him the sum and after having done this, I ask him: "Must you go immediately to settle this matter or can you stay a while and have a drink with me?" Ah, is this not happiness?

1: I am sitting in a small boat. There is a beautiful wind in our favour, but our boat has no sails. Suddenly there appears a big lorcha, coming along as fast as the wind. I try to hook on to the lorcha in the hope of catching on to it, and unexpectedly the hook does catch. Then I throw over a rope and we are towed along and I begin to sing the lines of Tu Fu: "The green makes me feel tender toward the peaks, and the red tells me there are oranges." And we break out in joyous laughter. Ah, is this not happiness?

1: I have been long looking for a house to share with a friend but have not been able to find a suitable one. Suddenly someone brings the news that there is a house somewhere, not too big, but with only about a dozen rooms, and that it faces a big river with beautiful green trees around. I ask this man to stay for supper, and after the supper we go over together to have a look, having no idea what the house is like. Entering the gate, I see that there is a large vacant lot about six or seven *mow*, and I say to myself, "I shall not have to worry about the supply of vegetables and melons henceforth." Ah, is this not happiness?

1: A traveller returns home after a long journey, and he sees the old city gate and hears the women and children on both banks of the river talking his own dialect. Ah, is this not happiness?

1: When a good piece of old porcelain is broken, you know there is no hope of repairing it. The more you turn it about and look at it, the more you are exasperated. I then hand it to the cook, asking him to use it as any old vessel, and give orders that he shall never let that broken porcelain bowl come within my sight again. Ah, is this not happiness?

1: I am not a saint, and am therefore not without sin. In the night I did something wrong and I get up in the morning and feel extremely ill at ease about it. Suddenly I remember what is taught by Buddhism, that not to cover one's sins is the same as repentance. So then I begin to tell my sin to the entire company around, whether they are strangers or my old friends. Ah, is this not happiness?

1: To watch someone writing big characters a foot high. Ah, is this not happiness?

1: To open the window and let a wasp out of the room. Ah, is this not happiness?

1: A magistrate orders the beating of the drum and calls it a day. Ah, is this not happiness?

1: To see someone's kite-line broken. Ah, is this not happiness?

1: To see a wild prairie fire. Ah, is this not happiness?

1: To have just finished repaying all one's debts. Ah, is this not happiness?

1: To read the Story of Curly-Beard.[1] Ah, is this not happiness?

Poor Byron, who had only three happy hours in his life! He was either of a morbid and enormously unbalanced spirit, or else

[1] The hero, known as "Curly-Beard," aided the escape of a pair of eloping lovers, and after giving them his home in a distant city, then disappeared.

he was affecting merely the fashionable *Weltschmerz* of his decade. Were the feeling of *Weltschmerz* not so fashionable, I feel bound to suspect that he must have confessed to at least thirty happy hours instead of three. Is it not plain from the above that the world is truly a feast of life spread out for us to enjoy—merely through the senses, and a type of culture which recognizes these sensual pleasures therefore makes it possible for us frankly to admit them? My suspicion is, the reason why we shut our eyes wilfully to this gorgeous world, vibrating with its own sensuality, is that the spiritualists have made us plain scared of them. A nobler type of philosophy should re-establish our confidence in this fine receptive organ of ours, which we call the body, and drive away first the contempt and then the fear of our senses. Unless these philosophers can actually sublimate matter and etherealize our body into a soul without nerves, without taste, without smell, and without sense of colour and motion and touch, and unless we are ready to go the whole way with the Hindu mortifiers of the flesh, let us face ourselves bravely as we are. For only a philosophy that recognizes reality can lead us into true happiness, and only that kind of philosophy is sound and healthy.

IV. MISUNDERSTANDINGS OF MATERIALISM

Chin's description of the happy moments of his life must have already convinced us that in real human life, the mental and the physical pleasures are inextricably tied up together. Mental pleasures are real only when they are felt through the body. I would include even the moral pleasures, too. He who preaches any kind of doctrine must be prepared to be misunderstood, as the Epicureans and Stoics were. How often people fail to see the essential kindness of spirit of a Stoic, like Marcus Aurelius, and how often the Epicurean doctrine of wisdom and restraint has been popularly construed as the doctrine of the man of pleasure! It will at once be brought up against this somewhat materialistic view of things, that it is selfish, that it lacks totally a sense of social responsibility, that it teaches one to enjoy one's self merely. This type of argument proceeds from ignorance; those who use it know not what they are talking about. They know not the kindness of the cynic, not the gentleness of temper of such a lover of life. Love of one's fellow-men should not be a doctrine, an article of faith, a matter of intellectual conviction, or a thesis supported by arguments. The love of mankind which requires reasons is no true love. This love should be perfectly natural, as natural for man as for the birds to flap their wings. It should be a direct feeling, springing naturally from a healthy soul, living in touch with Nature. No man who loves the trees truly can be cruel to animals or to his fellow-men. In a perfectly healthy spirit, gaining a vision of life and of one's fellow-men and a true and deep knowledge of Nature, kindness is the natural thing. That soul does not require any philosophy or man-made religion to tell him to be kind. It is because his spirit has been properly nourished through his senses, somewhat detached from the artificial life and the still more artificial learning of human society, that he is able to retain a true mental and moral health. We cannot, therefore, be accused of teaching unselfishness when we are scratching off the earth and enlarging the opening from which this spring of kindness will naturally flow.

Materialism has been misunderstood, grievously misunderstood. In this matter I must let George Santayana speak for us, who describes himself as "a materialist—perhaps the only one living," and who, nevertheless, as we all know, is probably one of the sweetest spirits of the present generation. He tells us that our prejudice against the materialistic philosophy is a prejudice of one looking at it from the outside. One gets a feeling of shock from certain deficiencies which are only apparent by comparison with one's old creed. But one can truly understand any foreign creed or religion or country only when one enters to live in spirit in that new world. There is a bounce and a joy, a wholesomeness of feeling in this so-called "materialism" which we usually fail to see entirely. As Santayana tells us, the true materialist is always like Democritus, the laughing philosopher. It is we, the "unwilling materialists," who aspire to spiritualism but nevertheless live a selfish materialistic life, "that have generally been awkwardly intellectual and incapable of laughter."

But a thorough materialist, one born to the faith and not half plunged into it by an unexpected christening in cold water, will be like the superb Democritus, a laughing philosopher. His delight in a mechanism that can fall into so many marvellous and beautiful shapes, and can generate so many exciting passions, should be of the same intellectual quality as that which the visitor feels in a museum of natural history, where he views the myriad butterflies in their cases, the flamingos and shell-fish, the mammoths and gorillas. Doubtless there were pangs in that incalculable life, but they were soon over; and how splendid meantime was the pageant, how infinitely interesting the universal interplay, and how foolish and inevitable those absolute little passions. Somewhat of that sort might be the sentiment that materialism would arouse in a vigorous mind, *active, joyful, impersonal, and in respect to private illusions not without a touch of scorn.*

To the genuine sufferings of living creatures the ethics that accompanies materialism has never been insensible; on the contrary, like other merciful systems, it has trembled too much at pain and tended to withdraw the will ascetically, lest the will should be defeated. *Contempt for mortal sorrows is reserved for those who drive with hosannas the Juggernaut car of absolute optimism. But against evils born of pure vanity and self-deception, against the verbiage by which man persuades himself that he is the goal and acme of the universe, laughter is the proper defence.* Laughter also has this subtle advantage, that it need not remain without an over-tone of sympathy and brotherly understanding; as the laughter that greets Don Quixote's absurdities and misadventures does not mock the hero's intent. His ardour was admirable, but the world must be known before it can be reformed pertinently, and happiness, to be attained, must be placed in reason.[1]

---

[1] From the essay on "Emotions of the Materialist," in *Little Essays of Santayana,* edited by Logan Pearsall Smith. (The italics are mine.)

What, then, is this mental life, or this spiritual life, of which we have been always so proud, and which we always place above the life of the senses? Unfortunately modern biology has a tendency to track the spirit down to its lair, finding it to be a set of fibres, liquids and nerves. I almost believe that optimism is a fluid, or at least it is a condition of the nerves made possible by certain circulating fluids. Whence does the mental life arise, and from what does it take its being and derive its nourishment? Philosophers have long pointed out that all human knowledge comes from sensuous experience. We can no more attain knowledge of any kind without the senses of vision and touch and smell than a camera can take pictures without a lens and a sensitive plate. The difference between a clever man and a dull fellow is that the former has a set of finer lenses and perceiving apparatus by which he gets a sharper image of things and retains it longer. And to proceed from the knowledge of books to the knowledge of life, mere thinking or cogitation is not enough; one has to feel one's way about—to sense things as they are and to get a correct impression of the myriad things in human life and human nature not as unrelated parts, but as a whole. In this matter of feeling about life and of gaining experience, all our senses co-operate, and it is through the co-operation of the senses, and of the heart with the head, that we can have intellectual warmth. Intellectual warmth, after all, is the thing, for it is the sign of life, like the colour of green in a plant. We detect life in one's thought by its presence or absence of warmth, as we detect life in a half dried-up tree struggling after some unfortunate accident, by noting the greenness of its leaves and the moisture and healthy texture of its fibre.

V. HOW ABOUT MENTAL PLEASURES?

Let us take the supposedly higher pleasures of the mind and the spirit, and see to what extent they are vitally connected with our senses, rather than with our intellect. What are those higher spiritual pleasures that we distinguish from those of the lower senses? Are they not parts of the same thing, taking root and ending up in the senses, and inseparable from them? As we go over these higher pleasures of the mind—literature, art, music, religion and philosophy—we see what a minor role the intellect plays in comparison with the senses and feelings. What does a painting do except to give us a landscape or a portrait and recall in us the sensuous pleasures of seeing a real landscape or a beautiful face? And what does literature do except to re-create a picture of life, to give us the atmosphere and colour, the fragrant smell of the pastures or the stench of city gutters? We all say that a novel approaches the standard of true literature in proportion as it gives us real people and real emotions. The book which takes us away from this human life, or merely coldly dissects it, is not literature and the more humanly true a book is, the better literature we consider it. What novel ever appeals to a reader if it contains only a cold analysis, if it fails to give us the salt and tang and flavour of life?

As for the other things, poetry is but truth coloured with emotion, music is sentiment without words, and religion is but wisdom expressed in fancy. As painting is based on the sense of colour and vision, so poetry is based on the sense of sound and tone and rhythm, in addition to its emotional truth. Music is pure sentiment itself, dispensing entirely with the language of words with which alone the intellect can operate. Music can portray for us the sounds of cowbells and fish-markets and the battlefield; it can portray for us even the delicacy of the flowers, the undulating motion of the waves, or the sweet serenity of the moonlight; but the moment it steps outside the limit of the senses and tries to portray for us a philosophic idea, it must be considered decadent and the product of a decadent world.

And did not the degeneration of religion begin with reason itself? As Santayana says, the process of degeneration of religion was due to too much reasoning: "This religion unhappily long ago ceased to be wisdom expressed in fancy in order to become superstition overlaid with reasoning." The decay of religion is due to the pedantic spirit, in the invention of creeds, formulas, articles of faith, doctrines and apologies. We become increasingly less pious as we increasingly justify and rationalize our beliefs and become so sure that we are right. That is why every religion becomes a narrow sect, which believes itself to have discovered the only truth. The consequence is that the more we justify our beliefs, the more narrow-minded we become, as is evident in all religious sects. This has made it possible for religion to be associated with the worst forms of bigotry, narrow-mindedness and even pure selfishness in personal life. Such a religion nourishes a man's selfishness not only by making it impossible for him to be broad-minded toward other sects, but also by turning the practice of religion into a private bargain between God and himself, in which the party of the first part is glorified by the party of the second part, singing hymns and calling upon His name on every conceivable occasion, and in return the party of the first part is to bless the party of the second part, bless particularly himself more than any other person and his own family more than any other family. That is why we find selfishness of nature goes so well with some of the most "religious" and regularly church-going old women. In the end, the sense of self-justification, of having discovered the only truth, displaces all the finer emotions from which religion took its rise.

I can see no other reason for the existence of art and poetry and religion except as they tend to restore in us a freshness of vision and a more emotional glamour and more vital sense of life. For as we grow older in life, our senses become gradually benumbed, our emotions become more callous to suffering and injustice and cruelty, and our vision of life is warped by too much preoccupation with cold, trivial realities. Fortunately, we have a few poets and artists who have not lost that sharpened sensibility, that fine emotional response and that freshness of vision, and whose duties are therefore to be our moral conscience, to hold up a mirror to our blunted vision, to tone up our withered nerves. Art should be a satire and a warning against our paralysed emotions, our devitalized thinking and our denaturalized living. It teaches us unsophistication in a sophisticated world. It should restore to us health and sanity of living and enable us to recover from the fever and delirium caused by too much mental activity. It should sharpen our senses, re-establish the connection between our reason and our human nature, and assemble the ruined parts of a dislocated life again into a whole, by restoring our original nature. Miserable indeed is a world in which we have knowledge without understanding, criticism without appreciation, beauty without love, truth without passion, righteousness without mercy, and courtesy without a warm heart!

As for philosophy, which is the exercise of the spirit *par excellence,* the danger is even greater that we lose the feeling of life itself. I can understand that such mental delights include the solution of a long mathematical equation, or the perception of a grand order in the universe. This perception of order is probably the purest of all our mental pleasures and yet I would exchange it for a well-prepared meal. In the first place, it is in itself almost a freak, a by-product of our mental occupations, enjoyable because it is gratuitous, but not in any case as imperative for us as other vital processes. That intellectual delight is, after all, similar to the delight of solving a crossword puzzle successfully. In the second place, the philosopher at this moment more often than not is likely to cheat himself, to fall in love with this abstract perfection, and to conceive a greater logical perfection in the world than is really warranted by reality itself. It is as much a false picture of things as when we paint a star with five points— a reduction to formula, an artificial stylizing, an over-simpli- fication. So long as we do not overdo it, this delight in perfection is good, but let us remind ourselves that millions of people can be happy without discovering this simple unity of design. We really can afford to live without it. I prefer talking with a coloured maid to talking with a mathematician; her words are more concrete, her laughter is more energetic, and I generally gain more in knowledge of human nature by talking with her. I am such a materialist that at any time I would prefer pork to poetry, and would waive a piece of philosophy for a piece of fillet, brown and crisp and garnished with good sauce.

Only by placing living above thinking can we get away from this heat and the rebreathed air of philosophy and recapture some of the freshness and naturalness of true insight of the child. Any true philosopher ought to be ashamed of himself when he sees a child, or even a lion cub in a cage. How perfectly nature has fashioned him with his paws, his muscles, his beautiful coat of fur, his pricking ears, his bright round eyes, his agility and his sense of fun! The philosopher ought to be ashamed that God-made perfection has sometimes become man-made imperfection, ashamed that he wears spectacles, has no appetite, is often distressed in mind and heart, and is entirely unconscious of the fun in life. From this type of philosopher nothing is to be gained, for nothing that he says can be of importance to us. That philosophy alone can be of use to us which joins hands merrily with poetry and establishes for us a truer vision, first of nature and then of human nature.

Any adequate philosophy of life must be based on the harmony of our given instincts. The philosopher who is too idealistic is soon tripped up by nature herself. The highest conception of human dignity, according to the Chinese Confucianists, is when man reaches ultimately his greatest height, an equal of heaven and earth, by living in accordance with nature. This is the doctrine given in *The Golden Mean*, written by the grandson of Confucius.

What is God-given is called nature; to follow nature is called *Tao*[1] (the Way); to cultivate the Way is called culture. Before joy, anger, sadness and happiness are expressed, they are called the inner self; when they are expressed to the proper degree, they are called harmony. The inner self is the correct foundation of the world, and harmony is the illustrious Way. When a man has achieved the inner self and harmony, the heaven and earth are orderly and the myriad things are nourished and grow thereby.

---

[1] There is a strong element of Taoism in Confucianism, perhaps due to the influence of Taoistic thought, a fact which is not usually noticed. Anyway, here this passage stands in one of the Confucian *Four Books*, and similar passages in the *Analects* can be quoted.

HOW ABOUT MENTAL PLEASURES?

To arrive at understanding from being one's true self is called nature, and to arrive at being one's true self from understanding is called culture; he who is his true self has thereby understanding, and he who has understanding finds thereby his true self. Only those who are their absolute selves in the world can fulfil their own nature; only those who fulfil their own nature can fulfil the nature of others; only those who fulfil the nature of others can fulfil the nature of things; those who fulfil the nature of things are worthy to help Mother Nature in growing and sustaining life; and those who are worthy to help Mother Nature in growing and sustaining life are the equals of heaven and earth.

CHAPTER SEVEN

The Importance Of Loafing

I. MAN THE ONLY WORKING ANIMAL

THE FEAST OF LIFE IS, therefore, before us, and the only question is what appetite we have for it. The appetite is the thing, and not the feast. After all, the most bewildering thing about man is his idea of work and the amount of work he imposes upon himself, or civilization has imposed upon him. All nature loafs, while man alone works for a living. He works because he has to, because with the progress of civilization life gets incredibly more complex, with duties, responsibilities, fears, inhibitions and ambitions, born not of nature, but of human society. While I am sitting here before my desk, a pigeon is flying about a church steeple before my window, not worrying what it is going to have for lunch. I know that my lunch is a more complicated affair than the pigeon's, and that the few articles of food I take involve thousands of people at work and a highly complicated system of cultivation, merchandising, transportation, delivery and preparation. That is why it is harder for man to get food than for animals. Nevertheless, if a jungle beast were let loose in a city and gained some apprehension of what busy human life was all about, he would feel a good deal of scepticism and bewilderment about this human society.

The first thought that the jungle beast would have is that man is the only working animal. With the exception of a few draught-horses or buffaloes made to work a mill, even domestic pets don't have to work. Police dogs are but rarely called upon to do their duty; a house-dog supposed to watch a house plays most of the time, and takes a good nap in the morning whenever there is good, warm sunshine; the aristocratic cat certainly never works for a living, and gifted with a bodily agility which enables it to disregard a neighbour's fence, it is even unconscious of its captivity —it just goes wherever it likes to go. So, then, we have this toiling humanity alone, caged and domesticated, *but not fed,* forced by this civilization and complex society to work and worry about the matter of feeding itself. Humanity has its own advantages, I am quite aware—the delights of knowledge, the pleasures of conversation and the joys of the imagination, as for instance in watching a stage play. But the essential fact remains that human life has got too complicated and the matter of merely feeding ourselves, directly or indirectly, is occupying well over ninety per cent of our human activities. Civilization is largely a matter of seeking food, while progress is that development which makes food more and more difficult to get. If it had not been made so difficult for man to obtain his food, there would be absolutely no reason why humanity should work so hard. The danger is that we get over-civilized and that we come to a point, as indeed we have already done, when the work of getting food is so strenuous that we lose our appetite for food in the process of getting it. This doesn't seem to make very much sense, from the point of view either of the jungle beast or the philosopher.

Every time I see a city skyline or look over a stretch of roofs, I get frightened. It is positively amazing. Two or three water towers, the backs of two or three steel frames for billboards, perhaps a spire or two, and a stretch of asphalt roofing material and bricks going up in square, sharp, vertical outlines without any form or order, sprinkled with some dirty, discoloured chimneys and a few wash-lines and criss-cross lines of radio aerials. And looking down into a street, I see again a stretch of grey or discoloured red-brick walls, with tiny, dark, uniform windows in uniform rows, half open and half hidden by shades, with perhaps a bottle of milk standing on a window-sill and a few pots of tiny, sickly flowers on some others. A child comes up to the roof with her dog and sits on the roof-stairs every morning to get a bit of sunshine. And as I lift my eyes again, I see rows upon rows of roofs, miles of them, stretching in ugly square outlines to the distance. More water towers, more brick houses. And humanity live here. How do they live, each family behind one or two of these dark windows? What do they do for a living? It is staggering. Behind every two or three windows, a couple go to bed every night like pigeons returning to their pigeon-holes; then they wake up and have their morning coffee and the husband emerges into the street, going somewhere to find bread for the family, while the wife tries persistently and desperately to drive out the dust and keep the little place clean. By four or five o'clock they come out on their doorsteps to chat with and look at their neighbours and get a sniff of fresh air. Then night falls, they are dead tired and go to sleep again. And so they live!

There are others, more well-to-do people, living in better apartments. More "arty" rooms and lampshades. Still more orderly and more clean! They have a little more space, but only a little more. To rent a seven-room flat, not to speak of owning it, is considered a luxury! But it does not imply more happiness. Less financial worry and fewer debts to think about, it is true. But also more emotional complications, more divorce, more cat-husbands that don't come home at night, or the couple go prowling together at night, seeking some form of dissipation. *Diversion* is the word. Good Lord, they need to be diverted from these monotonous, uniform brick walls and shining wooden floors! Of course they go to look at naked women. Consequently more neurasthenia, more aspirin, more expensive illnesses, more colitis, appendicitis and dyspepsia, more softened brains and hardened livers, more ulcerated duodenums and lacerated intestines, overworked stomachs and overtaxed kidneys, inflamed bladders and outraged spleens, dilated hearts and shattered nerves, more flat chests and high blood-pressure, more diabetes, Bright's disease, beri-beri, rheumatism, insomnia, arterio-sclerosis, piles, fistulas, chronic dysentery, chronic constipation, loss of appetite and weariness of life. To make the picture perfect, more dogs and fewer children. The matter of happiness depends entirely upon the quality and temper of the men and women living in these elegant apartments.

Some indeed have a jolly life, others simply don't. But on the whole, perhaps they are less happy than the hard-working people; they have more *ennui* and more boredom. But they have a car, and perhaps a country home. Ah, the country home, that is their salvation! So then, people work hard in the country so that they can come to the city so that they can earn sufficient money and go back to the country again.

And as you take a stroll through the city, you see that back of the main avenue with beauty parlours and flower shops and shipping firms is another street with drug stores, grocery stores, hardware shops, barber shops, laundries, cheap eating places, news-stands. You wander along for an hour, and if it is a big city, you are still there; you see only more streets, more drug stores, grocery stores, hardware shops, barber shops, laundries, cheap eating places and news-stands. How do these people make their living? And why do they come here? Very simple. The laundry-men wash the clothes of the barbers and restaurant waiters, the restaurant waiters wait upon the laundrymen and barbers while they eat, and the barbers cut the hair of the laundrymen and waiters. That is civilization. Isn't it amazing? I bet some of the laundrymen, barbers and waiters never wander beyond ten blocks from their place of work in their entire life. Thank God they have at least the movies, where they can see birds singing on the screen, trees growing and swaying. Turkey, Egypt, the Himalayas, the Andes, storms, shipwrecks, coronation ceremonies, ants, caterpillars, musk-rats, a fight between lizards and scorpions, hills, waves, sands, clouds, and even a moon—all on the screen!

O wise humanity, terribly wise humanity! Of thee I sing. How inscrutable is the civilization where men toil and work and worry their hair grey to get a living and forget to play!

II. THE CHINESE THEORY OF LEISURE

The American is known as a great hustler, as the Chinese is known as a great loafer. And as all opposites admire each other, I suspect that the American hustler admires the Chinese loafer as much as the Chinese loafer admires the American hustler. Such things are called the charms of national traits. I do not know if eventually the West and the East will meet; the plain fact is that they are meeting now, and are going to meet more and more closely as modern civilization spreads, with the increase of communication facilities. At least, in China, we are not going to defy this machine civilization, and there the problem will have to be worked out as to how we are going to merge these two cultures, the ancient Chinese philosophy of life and the modern technological civilization, and integrate them into a sort of working way of life. The question is very much more problematical as to Occidental life ever being invaded by Oriental philosophy, although no one would dare to prophesy.

After all, the machine culture is rapidly bringing us nearer to the age of leisure, and man will be compelled to play more and work less. It is all a matter of environment, and when man finds leisure hanging on his hand, he will be forced to think more about the ways and means of wisely enjoying his leisure, conferred upon him, against his will, by rapidly improving methods of quick production. After all, no one can predict anything about the next century. He would be a brave man who dared even to predict about life thirty years from now. The constant rush for progress must certainly one day reach a point when man will be pretty tired of it all, and will begin to take stock of his conquests in the material world. I cannot believe that, with the coming of better material conditions of life, when diseases are eliminated, poverty is decreased and man's expectation of life is prolonged and food is plentiful, man will care to be as busy as he is to-day. I'm not so sure that a more lazy temperament will not arise as a result of this new environment.

Apart from all this, the subjective factor is always as important as the objective. Philosophy comes in as a way of changing man's outlook and also changing his character. How man is going to react toward this machine civilization depends on what kind of a man he is. In the realm of biology, there are such things as sensibility to stimulus, slowness or quickness of reaction, and

[154]

different behaviours of different animals in the same medium or environment. Some animals react more slowly than others. Even in this machine civilization, which I understand includes the United States, England, France, Germany, Italy and Russia, we see that different reactions toward the mechanical age arise from different racial temperaments. The chances of peculiar individual reactions to the same environment are not eliminated. For China, I feel the type of life resulting from it will be very much like that in modern France, because the Chinese and the French temperaments are so akin.

America to-day is most advanced in machine civilization, and it has always been assumed that the future of a world dominated by the machine will tend toward the present American type and pattern of life. I feel inclined to dispute this thesis, because no one knows yet what the American temperament is going to be. At best we can only describe it as a changing temperament. I do not think it at all impossible that there may be a revival of that period of New England culture so well described in Van Wyck Brooks's new book. No one can say that that flowering of New England culture was not typically American culture, and certainly no one can say that that ideal Walt Whitman envisaged in his *Democratic Vistas*, pointing to the development of free men and perfect mothers, is not the ideal of democratic progress. America needs only to be given a little respite, and there may be—I am quite sure there will be—new Whitmans, new Thoreaus and new Lowells, when that old American culture, cut short literally and figuratively by the gold rush, may blossom forth again. Will not, then, American temperament be something quite different from that of the present day, and very near to the temperament of Emerson and Thoreau?

Culture, as I understand it, is essentially a product of leisure. The art of culture is therefore essentially the art of loafing. From the Chinese point of view, the man who is wisely idle is the most cultured man. For there seems to be a philosophic contradiction between being busy and being wise. Those who are wise won't be busy, and those who are too busy can't be wise. The wisest man is therefore he who loafs most gracefully. Here I shall try to explain, not the technique and varieties of loafing as practised in China, but rather the philosophy which nourishes this divine desire for loafing in China and gives rise to that carefree, idle, happy-go-lucky—and often poetic—temperament in the Chinese scholars, and to a lesser extent, in the Chinese people in general. How did that Chinese temperament—that distrust of achievement and success and that intense love of living as such—arise?

In the first place, the Chinese theory of leisure, as expressed by a comparatively unknown author of the eighteenth century, Shu Paihsiang, who happily achieved oblivion, is as follows: time is useful because it is not being used. "Leisure in time is like unoccupied floor space in a room." Every working girl who rents a small room where every inch of space is fully utilized feels highly uncomfortable because she has no room to move about, and the moment she gets a rise in salary, she moves into a bigger room where there is a little more unused floor space, besides those strictly useful spaces occupied by her single bed, her dressing table and her two-burner gas range. It is that unoccupied space which makes a room habitable, as it is our leisure hours which make life endurable. I understand there is a rich woman living on Park Avenue who bought up a neighbouring lot to prevent anybody from erecting a skyscraper next to her house. She is paying a big sum of money in order to have space fully and perfectly made useless, and it seems to me she never spent her money more wisely.

In this connection, I might mention a personal experience. I could never see the beauty of skyscrapers in New York, and it was not until I went to Chicago that I realized that a skyscraper could be very imposing and very beautiful to look at, if it had a good frontage and at least half a mile of unused space around it. Chicago is fortunate in this respect, because it has more space than Manhattan. The tall buildings are better spaced, and there is the possibility of obtaining an unobstructed view of them from a long distance. Figuratively speaking, we, too, are so cramped in our life that we cannot enjoy a free perspective of the beauties of our spiritual life. We lack spiritual frontage.

[156]

III. THE CULT OF THE IDLE LIFE

The Chinese love of leisure arises from a combination of causes. It came from a temperament, was erected into a literary cult, and found its justification in a philosophy. It grew out of an intense love of life, was actively sustained by an underlying current of literary romanticism throughout the dynasties, and was eventually pronounced right and sensible by a philosophy of life, which we may, in the main, describe as Taoistic. The rather general acceptance of this Taoistic view of life is only proof that there is Taoistic blood in the Chinese temperament.

And here we must first clarify one point. The romantic cult of the idle life, which we have defined as a product of leisure, was decidedly not for the wealthy class, as we usually understand it to be. That would be an unmitigated error in the approach to the problem. It was a cult for the poor and unsuccessful and humble scholar who either had chosen the idle life or had idleness enforced upon him. As I read Chinese literary masterpieces, and as I imagine the poor schoolmaster teaching the poor scholars these poems and essays glorifying the simple and idle life, I cannot help thinking that they must have derived an immense personal satisfaction and spiritual consolation from them. Disquisitions on the handicaps of fame and advantages of obscurity sounded pleasing to those who had failed in the civil examinations, and such sayings as "Eating late (with appetite whetted) is eating meat" tended to make the bad provider less apologetic to his family. No greater misjudgment of literary history is made than when the young Chinese proletarian writers accuse the poets Su Tungp'o and T'ao Yüanming and others of belonging to the hated leisure-class intelligentsia—Su who sang about "the clear breeze over the stream and bright moon over the hills," and T'ao who sang about "the dew making wet his skirt" and "a hen roosting on the top of a mulberry tree." As if the river breeze and the moon over the hills and the hen roosting on a mulberry tree were owned only by the capitalist class! These great men of the past went beyond the stage of talking about peasant conditions, and

[157]

lived the life of the poor peasant themselves and found peace and harmony in it.

In this sense I regard this romantic cult of the idle life as essentially democratic. We can better understand this romantic cult when we picture for ourselves Laurence Sterne on his sentimental journey, or Wordsworth and Coleridge hiking through Europe on foot with a great sense of beauty in their breast but very little money in their purse. There was a time when one didn't have to be rich in order to travel, and even to-day travel doesn't have to be a luxury of the rich. On the whole, the enjoyment of leisure is something which decidedly costs less than the enjoyment of luxury. All it requires is an artistic temperament which is bent on seeking a perfectly useless afternoon spent in a perfectly useless manner. The idle life really costs so very little, as Thoreau took the trouble to point out in *Walden*.

The Chinese romanticists were, on the whole, men gifted with a high sensibility and a vagabond nature, poor in their worldly possessions, but rich in sentiment. They had an intense love of life which showed itself in their abhorrence of all official life and a stern refusal to make the soul serf to the body. The idle life, so far from being the prerogative of the rich and powerful and successful (how busy the successful American men are!), was in China an achievement of *high-mindedness*, a high-mindedness very near to the Western conception of the dignity of the tramp who is too proud to ask favours, too independent to go to work, and too wise to take the world's successes too seriously. This high-mindedness came from, and was inevitably associated with, a certain sense of *detachment* toward the drama of life; it came from the quality of being able to see through life's ambitions and follies and the temptations of fame and wealth. Somehow the high-minded scholar who valued his character more than his achievements, his soul more than fame or wealth, became by common consent the highest ideal of Chinese literature. Inevitably he was a man with great simplicity of living and a proud contempt for worldly success as the world understands it.

Great men of letters of this class—T'ao Yüanming, Su Tungp'o,

Po Chüyi, Yüan Chunglang, Yüan Tsets'ai—were generally enticed into a short term of official life, did a wonderful job of it, and then got exasperated with its eternal kowtowing and receiving and sending off of fellow-officials, and gladly laying down the burdens of an official life, returned wisely to the life of retirement. Yüan Chunglang wrote seven successive petitions to his superior, when he was magistrate of Soochow, complaining of these eternal kow-towings, and begging to be allowed to return to the life of the free and careless individual.

A rather extravagant example of the praise of idleness is found in the inscription of another poet, Po Yüchien, written for his studio, which he called "The Hall of Idleness":

I'm too lazy to read the Taoist classics, for *Tao* doesn't reside
    in the books;
Too lazy to look over the sutras, for they go no deeper in *Tao*
    than its looks.
The essence of Tao consists in a void, clear, and cool,
But what is this void except being the whole day like a
    fool?
Too lazy am I to read poetry, for when I stop, the poetry will
    be gone;
Too lazy to play on the *ch'in,* for music does on the string where
    it's born;
Too lazy to drink wine, for beyond the drunkard's dream there
    are rivers and lakes;
Too lazy to play chess, for besides the pawns there are other
    stakes;
Too lazy to look at the hills and streams, for there is a painting
    within my heart's portals;
Too lazy to face the wind and the moon, for within me is the
    Isle of the Immortals;
Too lazy to attend to worldly affairs, for inside me are my hut
    and my possessions;
Too lazy to watch the changing of the seasons, for within me
    are heavenly processions.

THE IMPORTANCE OF LOAFING

Pine trees may decay and rocks may rot; but I shall always remain what I am.

Is it not fitting that I call this the Hall of Idleness?

This cult of idleness was therefore always bound up with a life of inner calm, a sense of carefree irresponsibility and an intense whole-hearted enjoyment of the life of nature. Poets and scholars have always given themselves quaint names, like "The Guest of Rivers and Lakes" (Tu Fu); "The Recluse of the Eastern Hillside" (Su Tungp'o); the "Carefree Man of a Misty Lake"; and "The Old Man of the Haze-girdled Tower," etc.

No, the enjoyment of an idle life doesn't cost any money. The capacity for true enjoyment of idleness is lost in the moneyed class and can be found only among people who have a supreme contempt for wealth. It must come from an inner richness of the soul in a man who loves the simple ways of life and who is somewhat impatient with the business of making money. There is always plenty of life to enjoy for a man who is determined to enjoy it. If men fail to enjoy this earthly existence we have, it is because they do not love life sufficiently and allow it to be turned into a humdrum routine existence. Laotse has been wrongly accused of being hostile to life; on the other hand, I think he taught the renunciation of the life of the world exactly because he loved life all too tenderly, to allow the art of living to degenerate into a mere business of living.

For where there is love, there is jealousy; a man who loves life intensely must be always jealous of the few exquisite moments of leisure that he has. And he must retain the dignity and pride always characteristic of a vagabond. His hours of fishing must be as sacred as his hours of business, erected into a kind of religion as the English have done with sport. He must be as impatient at having people talk to him about the stock market at the golf club, as the scientist is at having anybody disturb him in his laboratory. And he must count the days of departing spring with a sense of sad regret for not having made more trips or excursions, as a business man feels when he has not sold so many wares in the day.

IV. THIS EARTH THE ONLY HEAVEN

A sad, poetic touch is added to this intense love of life by the realization that this life we have is essentially mortal. Strange to say, this sad awareness of our mortality makes the Chinese scholar's enjoyment of life all the more keen and intense. For if this earthly existence is all we have, we must try the harder to enjoy it while it lasts. A vague hope of immortality detracts from our whole-hearted enjoyment of this earthly existence. As Sir Arthur Keith puts it with a typically Chinese feeling, "For if men believe, as I do, that this present earth is the only heaven, they will strive all the more to make heaven of it." Su Tungp'o says, "Life passes like a spring dream without a trace," and that is why he clung to it so fondly and tenaciously. It is this sentiment of our mortal existence that we run across again and again in Chinese literature. It is this feeling of the impermanence of existence and the evanescence of life, this touch of sadness, which overtakes the Chinese poet and scholar always at the moment of his greatest feasting and merry-making, a sadness that is expressed in the regret that "the moon cannot always be so round and the flowers cannot for ever look so fair" when we are watching the full moon in the company of beautiful flowers. It was in that poem commemorating a gorgeous feast on "A Spring Night amidst Peach Blossoms" that Li Po penned the favourite line: "Our floating life is like a dream; how many times can one enjoy one's self?" And it was in the midst of a gay reunion of his happy and illustrious friends that Wang Hsichih wrote that immortal little essay, "The Orchid Pavilion," which gives, better than anything else, this typical feeling about the evanescence of life:

In the ninth year of the reign Yungho (A.D. 353) in the beginning of late spring we met at the Orchid Pavilion in Shanyin of Kweich'i for the Water Festival, to wash away the evil spirits. Here are gathered all the illustrious persons and assembled both the old and the young. Here are tall mountains and majestic peaks, trees with thick foliage and tall bamboos. Here are also clear streams and gurgling rapids, catching one's eye from the right and left. We group ourselves in order, sitting by the waterside, and drink in succession from a cup floating down the curving stream; and although there is no music from string and wood-wind instruments, yet with alternate singing and drinking, we are well disposed to thoroughly enjoy a quiet intimate conversation. To-day the sky is clear, the air is fresh and the kind breeze is mild. Truly enjoyable it is to watch the immense universe above and the myriad things below, travelling over the entire landscape with our eyes and allowing our sentiments to roam about at will, thus exhausting the pleasures of the eye and the ear.

Now when people gather together to surmise life itself, some sit and talk and unburden their thoughts in the intimacy of a room, and some, overcome by a sentiment, soar forth into a world beyond bodily realities. Although we select our pleasures according to our inclinations—some noisy and rowdy, and others quiet and sedate—yet when we have found that which pleases us, we are all happy and contented, to the extent of forgetting that we are growing old. And then, when satiety follows satisfaction, and with the change of circumstances, change also our whims and desires, there then arises a feeling of poignant regret. In the twinkling of an eye, the objects of our former pleasures have become things of the past, still compelling in us moods of regretful memory. Furthermore, although our lives may be long or short, eventually we all end in nothingness. "Great indeed are life and death" said the ancients. Ah! what sadness!

I often study the joys and regrets of the ancient people, and as I lean over their writings and see that they were moved exactly as ourselves, I am often overcome by a feeling of sadness and compassion, and would like to make those things clear to myself. Well I know it is a lie to say that life and death are the same thing, and that longevity and early death make no difference! Alas! as we of the present look upon those of the past, so will posterity look upon our present selves. Therefore have I put down a sketch of these contemporaries and their sayings at this feast, and although time and circumstances may change, the way they will evoke our moods of happiness and regret will remain the same. What will future readers feel when they cast their eyes upon this writing![1]

Belief in our mortality, the sense that we are eventually going to crack up and be extinguished like the flame of a candle, I say, is a gloriously fine thing. It makes us sober; it makes us a little sad; and many of us it makes poetic. But above all, it makes it possible for us to make up our mind and arrange to live sensibly, truthfully and always with a sense of our own limitations. It gives peace also, because true peace of mind comes from accepting the worst. Psychologically, I think, it means a release of energy.

When Chinese poets and common people enjoy themselves, there is always a subconscious feeling that the joy is not going to last for ever, as the Chinese often say at the end of a happy re-union, "Even the most gorgeous fair, with mat-sheds stretching over a thousand miles, must sooner or later come to an end." The feast of life is the feast of Nebuchadnezzar. This feeling of the dreamlike quality of our existence invests the pagan with a kind of spirituality. He sees life essentially as a Sung landscape artist sees mountain scenery, enveloped in a haze of mystery, sometimes with the air dripping with moisture.

Deprived of immortality, the proposition of living becomes a simple proposition. It is this: that we human beings have a limited span of life to live on this earth, rarely more than seventy years, and that therefore we have to arrange our lives so that we may live as happily as we can under a given set of circumstances. Here we are on Confucian ground. There is something mundane, something terribly earth-bound about it, and man proceeds to work with a dogged common sense, very much in the spirit of

[1] Incidentally, the manuscript of this essay, or rather its early rubbings, are to-day the most highly valued examples of Chinese calligraphy, because the writer and author, Wang Hsichih, is the acknowledged Prince of Calligraphy. For three times he failed to improve upon his original handwriting, and so to-day the script is preserved to us in rubbings, with all the deletions and additions as they stood in the first draft.

what George Santayana calls "animal faith." With this animal faith, taking life as it is, we made a shrewd guess, without Darwin's aid as to our essential kinship with animals. It made us, therefore, cling to life—the life of the instinct and the life of the senses—on the belief that, as we are all animals, we can be truly happy only when all our normal instincts are satisfied normally. This applies to the enjoyment of life in all its aspects.

Are we therefore materialistic? A Chinese would hardly know how to answer this question. For with his spirituality based on a kind of material, earth-bound existence, he fails to see the distinction between the spirit and the flesh. Undoubtedly he loves creature comforts, but then creature comforts are matters of the senses. It is only through the intellect that man attains the distinction between the spirit and the flesh, while our senses provide the portals to both, as we have already seen in the preceding chapter. Music, undoubtedly the most spiritual of our arts, lifting man to a world of spirit, is based on the sense of hearing. And the Chinese fails to see why a sympathy of tastes in the enjoyment of food is less spiritual than a symphony of sounds. Only in this realistic sense can we feel about the woman we love. A distinction between her soul and her body is impossible. For if we love a woman, we do not love her geometrical precision of features but rather her ways and gestures in motion, her looks and smiles. But are a woman's looks and smiles physical or spiritual? No one can say.

This feeling of the reality and spirituality of life is helped by Chinese humanism, in fact by the whole Chinese way of thinking and living. Chinese philosophy may be briefly defined as a pre-occupation with the knowledge of life rather than the knowledge of truth. Brushing aside all metaphysical speculations as irrelevant to the business of living, and as pale reflections engendered in our intellect, the Chinese philosophers clutch at life itself and ask themselves the one and only eternal question: "How are we to live?" Philosophy in the Western sense seems to the Chinese eminently idle. In its preoccupation with logic, which concerns itself with the method of arrival at knowledge, and epistemology, which poses the question of the possibility of knowledge, it has forgotten to deal with the knowledge of life itself. That is so much tomfoolery and a kind of frivolity, like wooing and court-ship without coming to marriage and the producing of children, which is as bad as having red-coated regiments marching in military parades without going to battle. The German philoso-phers are the most frivolous of all; they court truth like ardent lovers, but seldom propose to marry her.

V. WHAT IS LUCK?

The peculiar contribution of Taoism to the creation of the idle temperament lies in the recognition that there are no such things as luck and adversity. The great Taoist teaching is the emphasis on being over doing, character over achievement, and calm over action. But inner calm is possible only when man is not disturbed by the vicissitudes of fortune. The great Taoist philosopher Liehtse gave the famous parable of the *Old Man at the Fort*:

> An Old Man was living with his Son at an abandoned fort on the top of a hill, and one day he lost a horse. The neighbours came to express their sympathy for this misfortune, and the Old Man asked, "How do you know this is bad luck?" A few days afterwards, his horse returned with a number of wild horses, and his neighbours came again to congratulate him on this stroke of fortune, and the Old Man replied, "How do you know this is good luck?" With so many horses around, his son began to take to riding, and one day he broke his leg. Again the neighbours came around to express their sympathy, and the Old Man replied, "How do you know this is bad luck?" The next year, there was a war, and because the Old Man's son was crippled, he did not have to go to the front.

Evidently this kind of philosophy enables a man to stand a few hard knocks in life in the belief that there are no such things as hard knocks without advantages. Like medals, they always have a reverse side. The possibility of calm, the distaste for mere action

[165]

and bustle, and the running away from success and achievement are possible with this kind of philosophy, a philosophy which says: *Nothing matters to a man who says nothing matters.* The desire for success is killed by the shrewd hunch that the desire for success means very much the same thing as the fear of failure. The greater success a man has made, the more he fears a climb-down. The illusive rewards of fame are pitched against the tremendous advantages of obscurity. From the Taoist point of view, an educated man is one who believes he has not succeeded when he has, but is not so sure he has failed when he fails, while the mark of the half-educated man is his assumptions that his outward successes and failures are absolute and real.

Hence, the distinction between Buddhism and Taoism is this: the goal of the Buddhist is that he shall not want anything, while the goal of the Taoist is that he shall not be wanted at all. Only he who is not wanted by the public can be a carefree individual, and only he who is a carefree individual can be a happy human being. In this spirit Chuangtse, the greatest and most gifted among the Taoist philosophers, continually warns us against being too prominent, too useful and too serviceable. Pigs are killed and offered on the sacrificial altar when they become too fat, and beautiful birds are the first to be shot by the hunter for their beautiful plumage. In this sense, he told the parable of two men going to desecrate a tomb and robbing the corpse. They hammer the corpse's forehead, break his cheek-bones and smash his jaws, all because the dead man was foolish enough to be buried with a pearl in his mouth.

The inevitable conclusion of all this philosophizing is: why not loaf?

VI. THREE AMERICAN VICES

To the Chinese, therefore, with the fine philosophy that "Nothing matters to a man who says nothing matters," Americans offer a strange contrast. Is life really worth all the bother, to the extent of making our soul a slave to the body? The high spirituality of the philosophy of loafing forbids it. The most characteristic advertisement I ever saw was one by an engineering firm with the big words: "Nearly Right Is Not Enough." The desire for one hundred per cent efficiency seems almost obscene. The trouble with Americans is that when a thing is nearly right, they want to make it still better, while for a Chinese, nearly right is good enough.

The three great American vices seem to be efficiency, punctuality and the desire for achievement and success. They are the things that make the Americans so unhappy and so nervous. They steal from them their inalienable right of loafing and cheat them of many a good, idle and beautiful afternoon. One must start out with a belief that there are no catastrophes in this world, and that, besides the noble art of getting things done, there is a nobler art of leaving things undone. On the whole, if one answers letters promptly, the result is about as good or as bad as if he had never answered them at all. After all, nothing happens, and while one may have missed a few good appointments, one may have also avoided a few unpleasant ones. Most of the letters are not worth answering, if you keep them in your drawer for three months; reading them three months afterwards, one might realize how utterly futile and what a waste of time it would have been to answer them all. Writing letters really can become a vice. It turns our writers into fine promotion salesmen and our college professors into good efficient business executives. In this sense, I can understand Thoreau's contempt for the American who always goes to the post office.

Our quarrel is not that efficiency gets things done and very well done, too. I always rely on American water-taps, rather than on those made in China, because American water-taps do not leak. That is a consolation. Against the old contention, however, that we must all be useful, be efficient, become officials and have power, the old reply is that there are always enough fools in the world who are willing to be useful, be busy and enjoy power, and so somehow the business of life can and will be carried on. The only point is who are the wise, the loafers or the hustlers?

THE IMPORTANCE OF LOAFING

Our quarrel with efficiency is not that it gets things done, but that it is a thief of time when it leaves us no leisure to enjoy ourselves and that it frays our nerves in trying to get things done perfectly. An American editor worries his hair grey to see that no typographical mistakes appear on the pages of his magazine. The Chinese editor is wiser than that. He wants to leave his readers the supreme satisfaction of discovering a few typographical mistakes for themselves. More than that, a Chinese magazine can begin printing serial fiction and forget about it half-way. In America it might bring the roof down on the editors, but in China *it doesn't matter, simply because it doesn't matter.* American engineers in building bridges calculate so finely and exactly as to make the two ends come together within one-tenth of an inch. But when two Chinese begin to dig a tunnel from both sides of a mountain, both come out on the other side. The Chinese's firm conviction is that it doesn't matter so long as a tunnel is dug through, and if we have two instead of one, why, we have a double track to boot. Provided you are not in a hurry, two tunnels are as good as one, dug somehow, finished somehow and if the train can get through somehow. And the Chinese are extremely punctual, provided you give them plenty of time to do a thing. They always finish a thing on schedule, provided the schedule is long enough.

The tempo of modern industrial life forbids this kind of glorious and magnificent idling. But worse than that, it imposes upon us a different conception of time as measured by the clock, and eventually turns the human being into a clock himself. This sort of thing is bound to come to China, as is evident, for instance, in a factory of twenty thousand workers. The luxurious prospect of twenty thousand workers coming in at their own sweet pleasure at all hours is, of course, somewhat terrifying. Nevertheless, this is what makes life so hard and hectic. A man who has to be punctually at a certain place at five o'clock has the whole after-noon from one to five ruined for him already. Every American adult is arranging his time on the pattern of the schoolboy—three o'clock for this, five o'clock for that, six-thirty for change of dress; six-fifty for entering the taxi and seven o'clock for emerging into a hotel room. It just makes life not worth living.

And Americans have now come to such a sad state that they are booked up not only for the following day, or the following week, but even for the following month. An appointment three weeks ahead of time is a thing unknown in China. And when a Chinese receives an invitation card, happily he never has to say whether he is going to be present or not. He can put down on the invitation list "Coming" if he accepts, or "Thanks" if he declines, but in the majority of cases the invited party merely writes the word "Know," which is a statement of fact that he knows of the invitation and not a statement of intention. An American or a European leaving Shanghai can tell me that he is going to attend a committee meeting in Paris on April 19, 1938, at three o'clock and that he will be arriving in Vienna on May 21st by the seven o'clock train. If an afternoon is to be condemned and executed, must we announce its execution so early? Cannot a fellow travel and be lord of himself, arriving when he likes and taking departure when he likes?

But above all, the American's inability to loaf comes directly from his desire for doing things and in his placing action above being. We should demand that there be character in our lives as we demand there be character in all great art worthy of the name. Unfortunately, character is not a thing which can be manufactured overnight. Like the quality of mellowness in wine, it is acquired by standing still and by the passage of time. The desire of American old men and women for action, trying in this way to gain their self-respect and the respect of the younger generation, is what makes them look so ridiculous to an Oriental. Too much action in an old man is like a broadcast of jazz music from a megaphone on top of an old cathedral. Is it not sufficient that the old people *are* something? Is it necessary that they must be for ever *doing* something? The loss of the capacity for loafing is bad enough in men of middle age, but the same loss in old age is a crime committed against human nature.

Character is always associated with something old and takes time to grow, like the beautiful facial lines of a man in middle age, lines that are the steady imprint of the man's evolving character. It is somewhat difficult to see character in a type of life where every man is throwing away his last year's car and trading it in for the new model. As are the things we make, so are we ourselves. In 1937 every man and woman look 1937, and in 1938 every man and woman will look 1938. We love old cathedrals, old furniture, old silver, old dictionaries and old prints, but we have entirely forgotten about the beauty of old men. I think an appreciation of that kind of beauty is essential to our life, for beauty, it seems to me, is what is old and mellow and well-smoked.

Sometimes a prophetic vision comes to me, a beautiful vision of a millennium when Manhattan will go slow, and when the American "go-getter" will become an Oriental loafer. American gentlemen will float in skirts and slippers and amble on the sidewalks of Broadway with their hands in their pockets, if not with both hands stuck in their sleeves in the Chinese fashion. Policemen will exchange a word of greeting with the slow-devil at the crossings, and the drivers themselves will stop and accost each other and inquire after their grandmothers' health in the midst of traffic. Someone will be brushing his teeth outside his shopfront, talking the while placidly with his neighbours, and once in a while, an absent-minded scholar will sail by with a limp volume rolled up and tucked away in his sleeve. Lunch counters will be abolished, and people will be lolling and lounging in soft, low arm-chairs in an Automat, while others will have learned the art of killing a whole afternoon in some café. A glass of orange juice will last half an hour, and people will learn to sip wine by slow mouthfuls, punctuated by delightful, chatty remarks, instead of swallowing it at a gulp. Registration in a hospital will be abolished, "emergency wards" will be unknown, and patients will exchange their philosophy with their doctors. Fire engines will proceed at a snail's pace, their staff stopping on the way to gaze at and dispute over the number of passing wild geese in the sky. It is too bad that there is no hope of this kind of a millennium on Manhattan ever being realized. There might be so many more perfect idle afternoons.

CHAPTER EIGHT

The Enjoyment Of The Home

I. ON GETTING BIOLOGICAL

IT HAS SEEMED TO ME that the final test of any civilization is, what type of husbands and wives and fathers and mothers does it turn out? Besides the austere simplicity of such a question, every other achievement of civilization—art, philosophy, literature and material living—pales into insignificance.

This is a dose of soothing medicine that I have always given to my countrymen engaged in the head-racking task of comparing Chinese and Western civilizations, and it has become a trick with me, for the medicine always works. It is natural that the Chinese student of Western life and learning, whether in China or studying abroad, is dazzled by the brilliant achievements of the West, from medicine, geology, astronomy to tall skyscrapers, beautiful motor highways and natural-colour cameras. He is either enthusiastic about such achievements, or ashamed of China for not having made such achievements, or both. An inferiority complex sets in, and in the next moment you may find him the most arrogant, chauvinistic defender of the Oriental civilization, without knowing what he is talking about. Probably as a gesture, he will condemn the tall skyscrapers and the beautiful motor highways, although I haven't yet found one that condemns a good camera. His plight is somewhat pathetic, for that disqualifies him for judging the East and the West sanely and dispassionately. Perplexed and dazzled and harassed by such thoughts of inferiority, he has great need of what the Chinese call a medicine for "calming the heart" to allay his fever.

The suggestion of such a test as I propose has the strange effect of levelling all mankind by brushing aside all the non-essentials of civilization and culture and bringing all under a simple and clear equation. All the other achievements of civilization are then seen as merely means toward the end of turning out better husbands and wives and fathers and mothers. In so far as ninety per cent of mankind are husbands or wives and one hundred per cent have parents, and in so far as marriage and the home constitute the most intimate side of a man's life, it is clear that that civilization which produces better wives and husbands and fathers and mothers makes for a happier human life, and is therefore a higher type of civilization. The quality of men and women we live with is much more important than the work they achieve, and every girl ought to be grateful for any civilization that can present her with a better husband. Such things are relative, and ideal husbands and wives and fathers and mothers are to be found in every age and country. Probably the best way to get good husbands and wives is by eugenics, which saves us a great deal of trouble in educating wives and husbands. On the other hand, a civilization which ignores the home or relegates it to a minor position is apt to turn out poorer products.

I realize that I am getting biological. I *am* biological, and so is every man and woman. There is no use saying, "Let's get biological," because we are so whether we like it or not. Every man is happy biologically, angry biologically, or ambitious biologically, or religious or peace-loving biologically, although he may not be aware of it. As biological beings, there is no getting around the fact that we are all born as babies, suck at mothers' breasts and marry and give birth to other babies. Every man is born of a woman, and almost every man lives with a woman through life and is the father of boys and girls, and every woman is also born of a woman, and almost every woman lives with a man for life and gives birth to other children. Some have refused to become parents, like trees and flowers that refuse to produce seeds to perpetuate their own species, but no man can refuse to have parents, as no tree can refuse to grow from a seed. So then we come to the basic fact that the most primary relationship in

[172]

life is the relationship between man and woman and the child, and no philosophy of life can be called adequate or even called philosophy at all unless it deals with this essential relationship.

But the mere relationship between man and woman is not sufficient; the relationship must result in babies, or it is incomplete. No civilization has any excuse for depriving a man or woman of his or her right to have babies. I understand that this is a very real problem at present, that there are many men and women to-day who don't get married, and many others who, after getting married, refuse to have babies for one reason or another. My point of view is, whatever the reason may be, the fact of a man or woman leaving this world without children is the greatest crime he or she can commit against himself or herself. If sterility is due to the body, then the body is degenerate and wrong; if it is due to the high cost of living, then the high cost of living is wrong; if it is due to a too high standard of marriage, then the too high standard of marriage is wrong; if it is due to a false philosophy of individualism, then the philosophy of individualism is wrong; and if it is due to the entire fabric of social system, then the entire fabric of social system is wrong. Perhaps men and women of the twenty-first century will come to see this truth when we have made better progress in the science of biology and there is a better understanding of ourselves as biological beings. I am quite convinced that the twentieth century will be the century of biology, as the nineteenth century was the century of comparative natural science. When man comes to understand himself better and realizes the futility of warring against his own instincts, with which nature has endowed him, man will appreciate more such simple wisdom. We see already signs of this growing biological and medical wisdom, when we hear the Swiss psychologist Jung advise his rich women patients to go back to the country and raise chickens, children and carrots. The trouble with rich women patients is that they are not functioning biologically, or their biological functioning is disgracefully low-grade.

Man has not learned to live with woman, since history began. The strange thing is that no man has lived without a woman, in spite of that fact. No man can speak disparagingly of woman if he realizes that no one has come into this world without a mother. From birth to death, he is surrounded by women, as mother, wife and daughters, and even if he does not marry, he has still to depend on his sister, like William Wordsworth, or depend on his housekeeper, like Herbert Spencer. No fine philosophy is going to save his soul if he cannot establish a proper relationship with his mother or his sister, and if he cannot establish a proper relationship even with his housekeeper, may God have pity on him!

There is a certain pathos in a man who has not arrived at a proper relationship with woman and who has led a warped moral life, like Oscar Wilde, who still exclaims, "Man cannot live with a woman, nor can he live without her!" So that it seems human wisdom has not progressed an inch farther between the writer of a Hindu tale and Oscar Wilde at the beginning of the twentieth century, for that writer of the Hindu tale of the Creation expressed essentially the same thought four thousand years ago. According to this story of the Creation, in creating woman, God took of the beauty of the flowers, the song of the birds, the colours of the rainbow, the kiss of the breeze, the laughter of the waves, the gentleness of the lamb, the cunning of the fox, the waywardness of the clouds and the fickleness of the shower, and wove them into a female being and presented her to man as his wife. And the Hindu Adam was happy and he and his wife roved about on the beautiful earth. After a few days, Adam came to God and said, "Take this woman away from me, for I cannot live with her." And God listened to his request and took Eve away. Adam then became lonely and was still unhappy, and after a few days he came to God again and said, "Give me back my woman, for I cannot live without her." Again God listened to his request and returned him Eve. After a few days again, Adam came to God and asked, "Please take back this Eve that Thou hast created, for I swear I cannot live with her." In His infinite wisdom God again consented. When finally Adam came a fourth time and complained that he could not live without his female companion, God made him promise that he was not going to change his mind again and that he was going to throw in his lot with her, for better and for worse, and live together on this earth as best they knew how. I do not think the picture has essentially changed much, even to-day.

II. CELIBACY A FREAK OF CIVILIZATION

The taking of such a simple and natural biological viewpoint implies two conflicts: first, the conflict between individualism and the family, and second, a deeper conflict between the sterile philosophy of the intellect and the warmer philosophy of the instinct. For individualism and worship of the intellect are likely to blind a man to the beauties of home life, and of the two, I think the first is not so wicked as the second. A man believing in individualism and carrying it to its logical consequences can still be a very intelligent being, but a man believing in the cold head as against the warm heart is a fool. For the collectivism of the family as a social unit, there can be substitutes, but for the loss of the mating and paternal-maternal instincts, there can be none.

We have to start with the assumption that man cannot live alone in this world and be happy, but must associate himself with a group around him, and greater than himself. Man's self is not limited by his bodily proportions, for there is a greater self which extends as far as his mental and social activities go. In whatever age and country and under whatever form of government, the real life that means anything to a man is never co-extensive with his country or his age, but consists in that smaller circle of his acquaintances and activities which we call the "greater self." In this social unit he lives and moves and has his being. Such a social unit may be a parish, or a school, or a prison, or a business firm, or a secret society or a philanthropic organization. These may take the place of the home as a social unit, and sometimes entirely displace it. Religion itself or sometimes a big political movement may consume a man's whole being. But of all such groups, the home remains the only natural and biologically real, satisfying and meaningful unit of our existence. It is natural because every man finds himself already in a home when he is born, and also because it remains with one for life; and it is biologically real because the blood relationship lends the notion of such a greater self a visible reality. One who does not make a success of this natural group life cannot be expected to make a success of life in other groups. Confucius says, "The young should learn to be filial in the home and respectful in society; they should be conscientious and honest, and love all people and associate with the kindly gentlemen. *If after acting on these precepts, they still have energy left, let them read books."* Apart from the importance of this group life, man expresses and fulfils himself fully and reaches the highest development of his personality only in the harmonious complementing of a suitable member of the other sex.

Woman, who has a deeper biological sense than man, knows this. Subconsciously all Chinese girls dream of the red wedding petticoat and the wedding sedan, and all Western girls dream of the wedding veil and wedding bells. Nature has endowed women with too powerful a maternal instinct for it to be easily put out of the way by an artificial civilization. I have no doubt that nature conceives of woman chiefly as a mother, even more than as a mate, and has endowed her with mental and moral characteristics which are conducive to her role as mother, and which find their true explanation and unity in the maternal instinct—realism, judgment, patience with details, love of the small and helpless, desire to take care of somebody, strong animal love and hatred, great personal and emotional bias and a generally personal outlook on things. Philosophy, therefore, has gone far astray when it departs from nature's own conception and tries to make women happy without taking into account this maternal instinct which is the dominant trait and central explanation of her entire being. Thus with all uneducated and sanely educated women, the maternal instinct is never suppressed, comes to light in childhood and grows stronger and stronger through adolescence to maturity, while with man, the paternal instinct seldom becomes conscious until after thirty-five, or in any case until he has a son or daughter five years old. I do not think that a man of twenty-five ever thinks about becoming a father. He merely falls in love with a girl and accidentally produces a baby and forgets all about it, while his wife's thoughts are occupied with nothing else, until one day in his thirties he suddenly becomes aware that he has a son or daughter whom he can take to the market and parade before his friends, and only then does he begin to feel paternal. Few men of twenty or twenty-five are not *amused* at the idea of their becoming a father, and beyond amusement, there is little thought spent on it, whereas having a baby, even anticipating one, is probably the most serious thing that ever comes to a woman's life and changes her entire being to the point of effecting a transformation of her character and habits. The world becomes a different world for her when a woman becomes an expectant mother. Thenceforth she has no doubt whatever in her mind as to her mission in life or the purpose of her existence. She is wanted. She is needed. And she functions. I have seen the most pampered and petted only daughter of a rich Chinese family growing to heroic stature and losing sleep for months when her child was ill. In nature's scheme, no such paternal instinct is necessary and none is provided for, for man, like the drake or the gander, has little concern over his offspring otherwise than contributing his part. *Women, therefore, suffer most psychologically when this central motive power of their being is not expressed and does not function.* No one need tell me how kind American civilization is to women, when it permits so many nice women to go unmarried through no fault of their own.

I have no doubt that the maladjustment in American marriages is very largely due to this discrepancy between the maternal instinct of women and the paternal instinct of men. The so-called "emotional immaturity" of American young men can find no other explanation than in this biological fact; the men being brought up under a social system of over-pampering of youth do not possess the natural check of responsible thinking which the girls have through their greater maternal instinct. It would be ruinous if nature did not provide women with sufficient soberness when they are physiologically ready to become mothers, so nature just does it. Sons of poor families have responsible thinking

[177]   G

drilled into their system by harder circumstances, thus leaving only the pampered sons of rich families, in a nation which worships and pampers youth, in an ideal condition for developing into emotional and social incompetents.

After all, we are concerned only with the question: "How to live a happy life?" and no one's life can be happy unless beyond the superficial attainments of the external life, the deeper springs of his or her character are touched and find a normal outlet. Celibacy as an ideal in the form of "personal career" carries with it not only an individualistic, but also a foolishly intellectualistic taint, and is for the latter reason to be condemned. I always suspect the confirmed bachelor or unmarried woman who remains so by choice of being an ineffectual intellectualist, too much engrossed with his or her own external achievements, believing that he or she can, as a human being, find happiness in an effective substitute for the home life, or find an intellectual, artistic or professional interest which is deeply satisfying.

I deny this. This spectacle of individualism, unmarried and childless, trying to find a substitute for a full and satisfying life in "careers" and personal achievements and preventing cruelty to animals has struck me always as somewhat foolish and comical. It is psychologically symptomatic in the case of old maiden ladies trying to sue a circus manager for cruelty to tigers because their suspicion has been aroused by whipmarks on the animals' backs. Their protests seem to come out of a misplaced maternal instinct, applied to a wrong species, as if true tigers ever thought anything of a little whipping. These women are vaguely groping for a place in life and trying very hard to make it sound convincing to themselves and to others.

The rewards of political, literary and artistic achievement produce in their authors only a pale, intellectual chuckle, while the rewards of seeing one's own children grow up big and strong are wordless and immensely real. How many authors and artists are satisfied with their accomplishments in their old age, and how many regard them as more than mere products of their pastime, justifiable chiefly as means of earning a living? It is said that a few days before his death, Herbert Spencer had the eighteen volumes of *The Synthetic Philosophy* piled on his lap and, as he felt their cold weight, wondered if he would not have done better could he have a grandchild in their stead. Would not wise Elia have exchanged the whole lot of his essays for one of his "dream children"? It is bad enough to have *Ersatz*-sugar, *Ersatz*-butter and *Ersatz*-cotton, but it must be deplorable to have *Ersatz*-children! I do not question that there was a moral and æsthetic satisfaction to John D. Rockefeller in the feeling that he had contributed so much to human happiness over such a wide area. At the same time, I do not doubt that such a moral or æsthetic satisfaction was extremely thin and pale, easily upset by a stupid stroke on the golf course, and that his real, lasting satisfaction was John D., Jr.

To look at it from another aspect, happiness is largely a matter of finding one's life work, the work that one loves. I question whether ninety per cent of the men and women occupied in a profession have found the work that they really love. The much vaunted statement, "I love my work," I suspect, must always be taken with a grain of salt. One never says, "I love my home," because it is taken for granted. The average business man goes to his office in very much the same mood as Chinese women produce babies: everybody is doing it, and what else can I do? "I love my work," so says everybody. Such a statement is a lie in the case of lift-men and telephone girls and dentists, and a gross exaggeration in the case of editors, real estate agents and stockbrokers. Except for the Arctic explorer or the scientist in his laboratory, engaged in the work of discovery, I think, to *like* one's work, finding it congenial, is the best we can hope for. But even allowing for the figure of speech, there is no comparison between one's love of his work and the mother's love of her children. Many men have doubts about their true vocation, and shift from one to another, but there is never a doubt in a mother's mind concerning her life work, which is the taking care and guiding of the little ones. Successful politicians have thrown up politics, successful editors have thrown up magazine work, successful aviators have given up flying, successful boxers have given up the ring, and successful actors and actresses have given up the stage, but imagine mothers, successful or unsuccessful, giving up motherhood! It is unheard of. The mother has a feeling that she is wanted; she has found a place in life, and has the deep conviction that no one in the world can take her place, a conviction more profound than Hitler's that he must save Germany. And what can give man or woman a greater, deeper happiness than the satisfaction of knowing he or she has a definite place in life? Is it not common sense to say that whereas less than five per cent are lucky enough to find and be engaged in the work they love, a hundred per cent of parents find the work of looking after their children the most deep and engrossing of their life motives? Is it not true, therefore, that the chance of finding real happiness is surer and greater for a woman if she is engaged as a mother rather than as an architect, since nature never fails? Is it not true that marriage is the best profession for women?

My feminist readers must have sensed this all along, and bit by bit have begun trembling with rage as I grew more and more enthusiastic about the home, knowing that the cross of the home eventually must be borne by women. Such is exactly my intention and my thesis. It remains to be seen who is kinder to women, for it is with women's happiness alone that we are concerned, happiness not in terms of social achievements, but in terms of the depths of personal being. Even from the point of view of fitness or competency, I have no doubt that there are fewer bank presidents really fit for their jobs than women fit for motherhood. We have incompetent department chiefs, incompetent business managers, incompetent bankers, and incompetent presidents, but we rarely have incompetent mothers. So then women are fit for motherhood, they want it and they know it. I understand that there has been a swing in the right direction away from the feminist ideal among the American college girls of to-day, that the majority of them are able to look at life sanely enough to say openly that they want to get married. The ideal woman for me is one who loves her cosmetics along with her mathematics, and who is more feminine than feminist. Let them have their cosmetics, and *if they still have energy left,* as Confucius would say, let them play with mathematics also.

It is to be understood that we are talking of the average ideal of the average man and woman. There are distinguished and talented women as there are distinguished and talented men, whose creative ability accounts for the world's real progress. If I ask the average woman to regard marriage as the ideal profession and to bear babies and perhaps also wash dishes, I also ask the average man to forget the arts and just earn the family bread, by cutting hair or shining shoes or catching thieves or tinkering pots or waiting at tables. Since someone has to bear the babies and take care of them and see them safely through measles and raise them to be good and wise citizens, and since men are entirely ineffectual in bearing babies and frightfully awkward in holding and bathing them, naturally I look to the women to do the job. I'm not so sure which is the nobler work—comparing the averages—raising babies or cutting people's hair or shining people's shoes or opening doors at department stores. I don't see why women have to complain about washing dishes if their husbands have to open doors for strangers at department stores. Men used to stand behind counters and now girls have rushed in to take their place behind counters while the men open the doors, and they are welcome to it, if they think it is a nobler kind of work. Considered as a means of living, no work is noble and no work is ignoble. And I am not so sure that checking men's hats is necessarily more romantic than mending husbands' socks. The difference between the hat-check girl and the sock-darner at home is that the sock-darner has got a man over whose destiny it is her privilege to preside, while the hat-check girl hasn't. It is to be hoped, of course, that the wearer of the socks is worth the woman's labour, but it would be also unwarranted pessimism to lay down as a general rule that his socks are not worth her mending. Men are not all quite as worthless as that. The important point is that the general assumption that home life, with its important and sacred task of raising and influencing the young of the race, is too low, for women can hardly be called a sane social attitude, and it is possible only in a culture where woman and the home and motherhood are not sufficiently respected.

III. ON SEX APPEAL

Behind the façade of woman's rights and increased social privileges for women, I always think woman is not given her due even in modern America. Let us hope that my impression is incorrect, and that with the increase of woman's rights, chivalry has not decreased. For the two things do not necessarily go together, chivalry or true respect for women and allowing women to spend money, to go where they please, to hold executive jobs and to vote. It has seemed to me (a citizen of the Old World with the Old World outlook) that there are things which matter and things which don't, and that American women are far ahead of their Old World sisters in all things that don't matter, and remain very much in the same situation in all things that do. Anyway, there is no clear index of a greater chivalry in America than in Europe. What real authority the American woman does exercise is still from her traditional old throne—the hearth—over which she presides as the happy ministering angel. I have seen such angels, but only in the sanctity of a private home, where a woman glides along in the kitchen or in the parlour, true mistress of a home consecrated to family love. Somehow she suffuses a radiance which would be unthinkable or out of place in an office.

Is it merely because woman is more charming and more graceful in a chiffon dress than in a business jacket, or is it merely my imagination? The gist of the matter seems to lie in the fact that women at home are like fish in water. Clothe women in business jackets and men will regard them as co-workers with the right to criticize, but let them float about in georgette or chiffon one out of the seven office hours in the day and men will give up any idea of competing with them, and will merely sit back and wonder and gasp. Submitted to business routine, women are disciplined quite easily and make better routine workers than men, but the moment the office atmosphere is changed, as when a business staff meet at a wedding tea, and you will find that women immediately come into their own by advising their men colleagues or their boss to get a haircut, or where to get the best lotion for curing dandruff. In the office, women talk with civility; outside the office, they talk with authority.

Frankly speaking from a man's point of view—there is no use in pretending to speak otherwise—I think that the appearance of women in public has added greatly to the charm and amenities of life, life in the office and in the street, for the benefit of men; that voices in the offices are softer, colours gayer and the desks neater. I think also that not a whit of the sexual attraction or desire for sexual attraction provided by nature has changed, but that in America, men are having a greater time because American women are trying harder to please the men than, for instance, Chinese women, so far as attention to sex appeal is concerned. And my conclusion is that in the West, people think too much of sex and too little of women.

Western women spend almost as much time fixing their hair as Chinese women used to do; attend to their make-up more openly, constantly and ubiquitously; diet, exercise, massage and read advertisements for keeping the figure more assiduously; kick their legs up and down in bed to reduce their waistline more religiously; lift their faces and dye their hair, at an age at which no Chinese women ever think of doing such a thing. They are spending more money, not less, on lotions and perfumes, and there is a bigger business in beauty aids and day creams, night creams, vanishing creams, foundation creams, face creams, hand creams, pore creams, lemon creams, sun-tan oils, wrinkle oils, turtle oils, and every conceivable variety of perfumed oil. Perhaps it is simply because American women have more time and more money to spend. Perhaps they dress to please men and undress to please themselves, or the other way round, or both. Perhaps the reason is merely that Chinese women have fewer available modern beauty aids, for I hesitate very much to draw a distinction between races when it comes to woman's desire to attract men.

Chinese women were trying hard enough to please men by binding their own feet half a century ago, and now they have gaily capered their way from their "bow shoes" into high heels. I am not usually a prophet, but I can say with prophetic conviction that in the immediate future, Chinese women will be having their morning ten minutes of kicking their legs up and down in order to please their husbands or themselves. Yet the obvious fact is there: American women at present seem to be trying harder to please the men by spending more thought on their bodily sex appeal and dress with better understanding of sex appeal. The net result is that women as a whole, as seen in the parks and in the streets, have better figures and are better dressed, thanks to the continuous tremendous daily efforts of women to keep their figure—to the great delight of men. But I imagine how it must wear on their nerves. And when I speak of sex appeal, I mean it in contrast to motherhood appeal, or woman's appeal as a whole. I suspect this phase of modern civilization has stamped its character on modern love and marriage.

Art has made the modern man sex conscious. I have no doubt about it. First art and then commercial exploitation of the woman's body, down to its last curve and muscular undulation and the last painted toe-nail. I have never seen every part of a woman's body so completely exploited commercially, and find it hard to understand how American women have submitted so sweetly to this exploitation of their bodies. To an Oriental, it is hard to square this commercial exploitation of the female body with respect for women. Artists call it beauty, theatre-goers call it art, only producers and managers honestly call it sex appeal, and men generally have a good time. It is typical of a man-made and man-ruled society that women are stripped for commercial exploitation and men almost never, outside a few acrobats. On the stage, one sees women nearly undressed, while the men still keep their morning coats and black ties; in a woman-ruled world, one would certainly see the men half undressed while the women kept their skirts. Artists study male and female anatomy equally, but somehow find it difficult to turn their study of the male body beautiful to commercial account. The theatre strips to tease, but generally strips the women to tease the men, and does not strip the men to tease the women. Even in the higher-class shows, where they try to be both artistic and moral, people allow the women to be artistic and the men to be moral, but never insist on the women being moral and the men artistic. (All men actors in vaudeville shows merely try to be funny, even in dancing, which is supposed to be "artistic.") The commercial advertisements pick up the theme and play it up in endless variations, so that to-day all a man needs to do when he wants to be "artistic" is to take a copy of a magazine and run through the advertising section. The result is, the women themselves are so impressed with the duty of being artistic that they unconsciously accept the doctrine and starve themselves or submit to massage and rigorous discipline, in order to contribute toward a more beautiful world. The less clear-minded are almost led to think that their only way of getting a man and holding him is by sex appeal.

I consider that this over-emphasis on sex appeal involves an adolescent and inadequate view of the entire nature of woman, with certain consequences upon the character of love and marriage, whose conception becomes also false or inadequate. Woman is thus more thought of as a mating possibility than as a presiding spirit over the hearth. Woman is wife and mother both, but with the emphasis on sex as such, the notion of a mate displaces the notion of the mother, and I insist that woman reaches her noblest status only as mother, and that a wife who by choice refuses to become a mother immediately loses a great part of her dignity and seriousness and stands in danger of becoming a plaything. To me, any wife without children is a mistress, and any mistress with children is a wife, no matter what their legal standing is. The children ennoble and sanctify the mistress, and the absence of children degrades the wife. It is a truism that many modern women refuse to have babies because pregnancy would spoil their figures.

The amorous instinct has its proper contribution to make to the enrichment of life, yet it can be overdone to the detriment of woman herself. The strain of keeping up sex appeal necessarily falls upon the nerves of women and not of men. It is also unfair, for by placing a premium upon beauty and youth, middle-aged women are confronted with the hopeless task of fighting their grey hair and time's course. A Chinese poet has already warned us that the fountain of youth is a hoax, that no man can yet "tie a string to the sun" and hold back its course. Middle-aged woman's effort to keep up sex appeal thus becomes an arduous race with the years, which is quite senseless. Only humour can save the situation. If there is no use carrying on a hopeless fight against old age and white hair, why then not call the white hair beautiful? So sings Chu Tu:

> I've gained white hairs, some hundreds, on my head.
> As often as they're plucked, still more grow in their stead.
> Why not stop plucking, then, and let the white alone?
> Who has the time to fight against the silvery thread?

The whole thing is unnatural and unfair. It is unfair to the mother and older women, because as surely as a heavyweight champion must hand over his title in a few years to a younger challenger and an old champion horse must yield in a few years to a younger horse, so must the old women fight a losing battle against the younger women, and after all they are all fighting against their own sex. It is foolish, dangerous, and hopeless for middle-aged women to meet younger women on the issue of sex appeal. It is also foolish because there is more to a woman than her sex, and while wooing and courtship are necessarily largely based on physical attraction, maturer men and women should have out-grown it.

Man, we know, is the most amorous animal in the zoological kingdom. Besides this amorous instinct, however, there is an equally strong parental instinct, resulting in the human family life. The amorous and paternal instincts we share in common with most of the animals, but the beginnings of a human family life seem to be found among the gibbons. There is a danger, however, of the amorous instinct subjugating the family instinct in an over-sophisticated culture surrounding man with constant sexual stimuli in art, the movies and the theatre. In such a culture, the necessity of the family ideal can be easily forgotten, especially when in addition there is a current of individualistic ideas. In such a society, therefore, we get a strange view of marriage, as consisting of eternal kissing, generally ending with the wedding bells, and a strange view of woman, chiefly as man's mate and not as mother. The ideal woman, then, becomes a young woman with perfect physical proportions and physical charm, whereas for me, woman is never more beautiful than when she is standing over a cradle, never more serious and dignified than when she is holding a baby in her breast and leading a child of four or five years by the hand, and never more happy than, as I have seen in a Western painting, when she is lying in bed against a pillow and playing with a baby at her breast. Perhaps I have got a motherhood complex, but that is all right because psychological complexes never do a Chinese any harm. Any suggestion of an Œdipus complex or father-and-daughter complex, or of a son-and-mother complex, in a Chinese always seems to me ridiculous and unconvincing. I suggest that my view of woman is not due to a motherhood complex, but is due to the influence of the Chinese family ideal.

IV. THE CHINESE FAMILY IDEAL

I rather think that the Genesis story of the Creation needs to be rewritten all over again. In the Chinese novel *Red Chamber Dream*, the boy hero, a sentimental molly-coddle very fond of female company and admiring his beautiful female cousins intensely and all but sorry for himself for being a boy, says that "Woman is made of water and man is made of clay," the reason being that he thinks his female cousins are sweet and pure and clever, while he himself and his boy companions are ugly and muddle-headed and bad-tempered. If the writer of the Genesis story had been a Paoyü and knew what he was talking about, he would have written a different story. God took a handful of mud, moulded it into

[187]

human shape and breathed into its nostrils a breath, and there was Adam. But Adam began to crack and fall to pieces, and so He took some water, and with the water He moulded the clay, and this water which entered into Adam's being was called Eve, and only in having Eve in his being was Adam's life complete. At least that seems to me to be the symbolic significance of marriage. Woman is water and man is clay, and water permeates and moulds the clay, and the clay holds the water and gives its substance, in which water moves and lives and has its full being.

The analogy of clay and water in human marriage was long ago expressed by Madame Kuan, wife of the great Yüan painter Chao Mengfu and herself a painter and teacher at the Imperial Court. When in their middle age Chao's ardour was cooling, or anyway when he was thinking of taking a mistress, Madame Kuan wrote the following poem, which touched his heart and changed his mind:

'Twixt you and me
There's too much emotion.
That's the reason why
There's such a commotion!
Take a lump of clay,
Wet it, pat it,
And make an image of me,
And an image of you.
Then smash them, crash them,
And add a little water.
Break them and re-make them
Into an image of you,
And an image of me.
Then in my clay, there's a little of you.
And in your clay, there's a little of me.
And nothing ever shall us sever;
Living, we'll sleep in the same quilt,
And dead, we'll be buried together.

It is a well-known fact that Chinese society and Chinese life are organized on the basis of the family system. This system determines and colours the entire Chinese pattern of life. Whence came this family ideal of life? It is a question that has seldom been asked, for the Chinese seem to take it for granted, while foreign students do not feel competent to enter into the question. Confucius is reputed to have provided the philosophical foundation for the family system as the basis of all social and political life, with its tremendous emphasis on the husband-wife relationship as the foundation of all human relationships, on filial piety toward parents, annual visits to ancestral graves, ancestor worship, and the institution of the ancestral hall.

Chinese ancestor worship has already been called a religion by certain writers, and I believe this to a very great extent is correct. Its non-religious aspect is the exclusion or the much less significant place of the supernatural element. The supernatural is left almost untouched, and ancestor worship can go side by side with belief in a Christian, a Buddhist, or a Mohammedan god. The rituals of ancestor worship provide a form of religion and are both natural and justifiable because all beliefs must have an outward symbol and form. As it is, I do not think the respect paid to square wooden tablets about fifteen inches long, inscribed with the names of ancestors, is more religious or less so than the use of the picture of the King on a British postage stamp. In the first place, these ancestral spirits are conceived less as gods than as human beings, continuing to be served as they were in their old age by their descendants. There is no prayer for gifts and no prayer for cure of sickness, and none of the usual bargaining between the worshipper and the worshipped. In the second place, this ceremony of worship is no more than an occasion for pious remembrance of one's departed ancestors, on a day consecrated to family reunion and reflections of gratitude on what the ancestor has done for the family. At best, it is only a poor substitute for celebrating the ancestor's birthday when he was alive, but in spirit it differs in no way from the celebration of a parent's birthday, or of Mothers' Day in America.

The only objection which led Christian missionaries to forbid

Chinese converts to participate in the ceremonies and communal feasting and merry-making of ancestor worship is that the worshippers are required to kneel down before the ancestral tablets, thus infringing upon the first of the Ten Commandments. This is about the most flagrant instance of lack of understanding on the part of the Christian missionaries. Chinese knees are not quite as precious as Western knees, for we kneel down before emperors, magistrates and before our own parents on New Year's Day, when they are living. Consequently Chinese knees are naturally more flexible, and one doesn't become a heathen more or less by kneeling before an inscribed wooden tablet, resembling a calendar block. On the other hand, Chinese Christians in the villages and towns are forced to cut themselves off from the general community life by being forbidden to participate in the general feasting and merry-making, or even to contribute money toward the theatrical performances usual on such an occasion. The Chinese Christians, therefore, practically excommunicate themselves from their own clan.

There is hardly a question that, in many cases, this feeling of piety and of mystic obligation toward one's own family actually amounted to a deeply religious attitude. We have, for instance, the case of Yen Yüan, one of the greatest Confucianist leaders in the seventeenth century, who in his old age started out on a pathetic journey of search for his brother, in the hope that his brother might be found to have a son, since he himself had none. This follower of Confucianism, who believed in conduct more than in knowledge, was living in Szechuen. His brother had been missing for years. Tired of teaching the doctrines of Confucius, one day he felt what among missionaries would be regarded as a "divine call" to search for this lost brother. The situation was practically hopeless. He had no idea where his brother might be, or even if he were living. Travel was a highly perilous undertaking in those days, and the country was in disorder because of the collapse of the Ming regime. Still this old man set out on this truly religious journey, with no better means of locating his brother than pasting placards on city gates and inns wherever he went. Thus he travelled from Western China to the north-eastern provinces, covering over a thousand miles, and only after years of desperate search was he brought to the home of his brother through the latter's son recognizing his name on an umbrella left standing against a wall while he was in a public privy. His brother was then dead, but he achieved his goal, which was to find a male descendant for his ancestor's family.

Why Confucius laid such emphasis on filial piety nobody knows, but it has been suggested by Dr. John C. H. Wu in an illuminating essay[1] that the reason was that Confucius was born without a father. The psychological reason is therefore similar to that of the writer of *Home, Sweet Home*, who never knew a home in his entire life. Had Confucius' father been living when he was a child, the idea of fatherhood could not have been invested with such romantic glamour, and if his father had been living after he grew up, the result might have been still more disastrous. He would have been able to see his father's foibles, and he might have found the precept of absolute piety somewhat difficult to live up to. Anyway, his father was dead when he was born, and not only that, but Confucius did not even know where his father's grave was. He had been born out of wedlock, and his mother refused to tell him who his father was. When his mother died, he buried her (cynically, I suppose) at the "Road of the Five Fathers," and only after he had found out the location of his father's grave from an old woman, did he provide for the burial of his parents together at another place.

We have to let this ingenious theory stand for what it is worth. But for the necessity of the family ideal, there is no lack of reasons in Chinese literature. It starts out with a view of man not as an individual, but as a member of a family unit, is backed by the view of life which I may call the "stream-of-life" theory, and justified by a philosophy which regards the fulfilment of man's natural instincts as the ultimate goal of morals and politics.

The ideal of the family system is necessarily dead set against the ideal of personal individualism. No man, after all, lives as an

[1] "The Real Confucius," *T'ien Hsia Monthly* (Shanghai), Vol. I, No. 1.

individual completely alone, and the idea of such an individual has no reality to it. If we think of an individual and regard him as neither a son, nor a brother, nor a father, nor a friend, then what is he? Such an individual becomes a metaphysical abstraction. And being biologically-minded as the Chinese are, they naturally think of a man's biological relationships first. The family then becomes the natural biological unit of our existence, and marriage itself becomes a family affair, and not an individual affair.

In *My Country and My People* I have pointed out the evils of this all-engrossing family system, which can become a form of magnified selfishness, to the detriment of the state. But such evils are inherent in all human systems, in the family system as well as in the individualism and nationalism of the West, because of defects in human nature. In China, man is always thought of as greater and more important than the state, but he is never thought of as greater and more important than the family, because, apart from the family, he has no real existence. The evils of nationalism are just as apparent in modern Europe. The state can be easily transformed into a monster, as it already is in some countries, swallowing up the individual's liberty of speech, his freedom of religious conscience and belief, his personal honour, and even the last and final goal of individual happiness. The theoretical consequences of such a collectivistic view are quite apparent in both Fascism and Communism, and in fact have been already logically worked out by Karl Marx. A total annihilation of the parental instinct seems to be aimed at by the Marxian state, in which family affection and loyalty are openly denounced as bourgeois sentiments, sure to become extinct in a different material surrounding.[1] How Karl Marx was quite so cocksure about this point in biology I do not know. Wise in his economics, perhaps he was a moron in common sense. An American schoolboy would have guessed that five thousand years were too short for the atrophy of an instinct which had the momentum of a million years of development behind it. But such an argument, strange as it may seem, could appeal to a Western intellect as strictly logical.

[1] *The Communist Manifesto.*

It is, in the words of the writer of the *New York Times's* "Topics," "consistency gone mad." The conception of man waging a class war in obedience to certain mechanistic laws naturally deprives man of individual freedom of belief and action. According to such an extreme view, therefore, we have even less individualism than under the family system.

In place of this individualism and nationalism of the West, there is then the family ideal in which man is not regarded as an individual but as a member of a family and an essential part of the great stream of family life. That is what I mean by the "stream-of-life" theory. Human life as a whole may be regarded as consisting of different racial streams of life, but it is the stream of life in the family that a man feels and sees directly. In accordance with both a Chinese and Western analogy, we speak of the "family tree," and every man's life is but a section or a branch of that tree, growing upon the trunk and contributing by its very existence to its further growth and continuation. Human life, therefore, is inevitably seen as a growth or a continuance, in which every man plays a part or a chapter in the family history, with its obligations toward the family as a whole, bringing upon itself and upon the family life shame or glory.

This sense of family consciousness and family honour is probably the only form of team spirit or group consciousness in Chinese life. In order to play this game of life as well as, or better than, another team, every member of the family must be careful not to spoil the game, or to let his team down by making a false move. He should, if possible, try to bring the ball further down the field. A derelict son is a shame to himself and to his family in exactly the same sense as a quarter-back who makes a fumble and loses the ball. And he who comes out on top in the civil examinations is like a player who makes a touch-down. The glory is his own and at the same time that of his family. The benefits of one's becoming a *chuangyüan* ("No. 1" in the Imperial examinations), or even a third-class *chinshih*, are both sentimentally and materially shared by members of his immediate family, his relatives, his clan, and even his town. For a hundred or two hundred years afterwards, the townspeople will still boast that they produced a *chuangyüan* in such and such a reign. In comparison with the family and town rejoicing when a man got a *chuangyüan* or *chinshih* and came home to place a golden-painted tablet of honour high upon his ancestral hall, with his mother probably shedding tears and the entire clan feeling themselves honoured by the great occasion, the getting of a college diploma to-day is a pretty dull and tame affair.

In this picture of the family life there is room for the greatest variety and colour. Man himself passes through the stages of childhood, youth, maturity and old age: first being taken care of by others, then taking care of others, and in old age again being taken care of by others; first obeying and respecting others, and later being obeyed and respected in turn in proportion as he grows older. Above all, colour is lent to this picture by the presence of women. Into this picture of the continuous family life comes woman, not as a decoration or a plaything, nor even essentially as a wife, but as a vital and essential part of the family tree—the very thing which makes continuity possible. For the strength of any particular branch of a family depends so much upon the woman married into the home and the blood she contributes to the family heritage. A wise patriarch is pretty careful to select women of sound heritage, as a gardener is careful to select the proper strain for grafting a branch. It is pretty well suspected that a man's life, particularly his home life, is made or unmade by the wife he marries, and the entire character of the future family is determined by her. The health of one's grandchildren and the type of family breeding that they are going to receive (upon which great emphasis is laid) depend entirely upon the breeding of the daughter-in-law herself. Thus there is a kind of amorphous and ill-defined eugenic system, based on belief in heredity and often placing great emphasis on *menti* (literally, "door and home" or lineage or family standing), but in any case based on standards of desirability in the health, beauty and breeding of the bride as seen by the eyes of the parents or grandparents of the family. In general, the emphasis is upon family breeding (in the same sense that a Westerner would choose a girl from a "good home"), representing the fine old traditions of thrift, hard work, good manners and civility. And when sometimes a parent discovers, to his sorrow, that his son has married a worthless daughter-in-law with no manners, he always secretly curses the other family for not training their daughter better. Hence upon the mother and father devolves the duty of training their daughters so that they shall not be ashamed of them when they marry into another household—as, for instance, when they do not know how to cook or how to make a good New Year pudding.

According to the stream-of-life theory as seen in the family system, immortality is almost visible and touchable. Every grandfather seeing his grandchild going to school with a satchel feels that truly he is living over again in the life of the child, and when he touches the child's hand or pinches his cheeks, he knows it is flesh of his own flesh and blood of his own blood. His own life is nothing but a section of the family tree, or of the great family stream of life flowing on for ever, and therefore he is happy to die. That is why a Chinese parent's greatest concern is to see that his sons and daughters are properly married before he dies, for that is an even more important concern than the site of his own grave or the selection of a good coffin. For he cannot know what kind of life his children are going to have until he sees with his own eyes what type of girls and men his sons and daughters marry, and if the daughters-in-law and sons-in-law look pretty satisfactory, he is quite willing to "close his eyes without regret" on his deathbed.

The net result of such a conception of life is that one gets a lengthened outlook on everything, for life is no more regarded as beginning and ending with that of the individual. The game is continued by the team after the centre or the quarter-back is put out of action. Success and failure begin to take on a different complexion. The Chinese ideal of life is to live so as not to be a shame to one's ancestors and to have sons of whom one need not be ashamed. A Chinese official when resigning office often quotes the line:

> Having sons, I am content with life;
> Without office, my body is light.

The worst thing that can happen to a man, probably, is to have unworthy sons who cannot "maintain the family glory" or even the family fortune. The millionaire father of a gambling son sees his fortune dispersed already, the fortune that he has taken a lifetime to build up. When the son fails, the failure is absolute. On the other hand, a far-sighted widow is able to endure years of misery and ignominy and even persecution, if she has a good boy of five. Chinese history and literature are full of such widows who endured all kinds of hardships and persecutions, but who lived for the day when their sons should do well and prosper, and perhaps even become prominent citizens. The latest case is Chiang Kai-shek himself, who as a boy was persecuted with his widowed mother by their neighbours. The widow did not fail so long as there was hope in her son. The success of widows in giving their children a perfect education of character and morals, through woman's generally more realistic sense, has often led me to think that fathers are totally unnecessary, so far as the upbringing of children is concerned. The widow always laughs the loudest because she laughs last.

Such an arrangement of life in the family, then, is *satisfying* because a man's life in all its biological aspects is well taken care of. That, after all, was Confucius' chief concern. The final ideal of government, as Confucius conceived it, was curiously biological: "The old shall be made to live in peace and security, the young shall learn to love and be loyal, that inside the chamber there may be no unmarried maids, and outside the chamber there may be no unmarried males." This is all the more remarkable because it is not merely a statement of a side issue, but of the *final goal of government*. This is the humanist philosophy known as *tach'ing*, or "fulfilment of instincts." Confucius wanted to be pretty sure that all our human instincts are satisfied, because only thus can we have moral peace through a satisfying life, and because only moral peace is true peace. It is a kind of political ideal which aims at making politics unnecessary, because it will be a peace that is stable and based upon the human heart.

[196]

V. ON GROWING OLD GRACEFULLY

The Chinese family system, as I conceive it, is largely an arrangement of particular provision for the young and the old, for since childhood and youth and old age occupy half of our life, it is important that the young and the old live a satisfactory life. It is true that the young are more helpless and can take less care of themselves, but on the other hand, they can get along better without material comforts than the old people. A child is often scarcely aware of material hardships, with the result that a poor child is often as happy as, if not happier than, a rich child. He may go barefooted, but that is a comfort, rather than a hardship to him, whereas going barefooted is often an intolerable hardship for old people. This comes from the child's greater vitality, the bounce of youth. He may have his temporary sorrows, but how easily he forgets them! He has no idea of money and no millionaire complex, as the old man has. At the worst, he collects only cigar coupons for buying a pop-gun, whereas the dowager collects Liberty Bonds. Between the fun of these two kinds of collection there is no comparison. The reason is the child is not yet intimidated by life as all grown-ups are. His personal habits are as yet unformed and he is not a slave to a particular brand of coffee, and he takes whatever comes along. He has very little racial prejudice and absolutely no religious prejudice. His thoughts and ideas have not fallen into certain ruts. Therefore, strange as it may seem, old people are even more dependent than the young because their fears are more definite and their desires are more delimited.

Something of this tenderness toward old age existed already in the primeval consciousness of the Chinese people, a feeling that I can compare only to the Western chivalry and feeling of tenderness toward women. If the early Chinese people had any chivalry, it was manifested not toward women and children, but toward the old people. That feeling of chivalry found clear expression in Mencius in some such saying as, "The people with grey hair should not be seen carrying burdens on the street," which was expressed as the final goal of a good government. Mencius also described the four classes of the world's most helpless people as: "The widows, widowers, orphans and old people without children." Of these four classes the first two were to be taken care of by a political economy which should be so arranged that there would be no unmarried men and women. What was to be done about the orphans Mencius did not say, so far as we know, although orphanages have always existed throughout the ages, as well as pensions for old people. Every one realizes, however, that orphanages and old age pensions are poor substitutes for the home. The feeling is that the home alone can provide anything resembling a satisfactory arrangement for the old and the young. But for the young, it is to be taken for granted that not much need be said, since there is natural paternal affection. "Water flows downwards and not upwards," the Chinese always say, and therefore the affection for parents and grandparents is something that stands more in need of being taught by culture. A natural man loves his children, but a cultured man loves his parents. In the end, the teaching of love and respect for old people became a generally accepted principle, and if we are to believe some of the writers the desire to have the privilege of serving their parents in their old age actually became a consuming passion. The greatest regret a Chinese gentleman could have was the eternally lost opportunity of serving his old parents with medicine and soup on their death-bed, or not to be present when they died. For a high official in his fifties or sixties not to be able to invite his parents to come from their native village and stay with his family at the capital, "seeing them to bed every night and greeting them every morning," was to commit a moral sin of which he should be ashamed and for which he had constantly to offer excuses and explanations to his friends and colleagues. This regret was expressed in two lines by a man who returned too late to his home, when his parents had already died:

The tree desires repose, but the wind will not stop;
The son desires to serve, but his parents are already gone.

It is to be assumed that if man were to live this life like a poem, he would be able to look upon the sunset of his life as his happiest period, and instead of trying to postpone the much feared old age, be able actually to look forward to it, and gradually build up to it as the best and happiest period of his existence. In my efforts to compare and contrast Eastern and Western life, I have found no differences that are absolute except in this matter of the attitude towards age, which is sharp and clear-cut and permits of no intermediate positions. The differences in our attitude towards sex, toward women, and toward work, play and achievement are all relative. The relationship between husband and wife in China is not essentially different from that in the West, nor even the relationship between parent and child. Not even the ideas of individual liberty and democracy and the relationship between the people and their ruler are, after all, so very different. But in the matter of our attitude toward age, the difference is absolute, and the East and the West take exactly opposite points of view. This is clearest in the matter of asking about a person's age or telling one's own. In China, the first question a person asks the other on an official call, after asking about his name and surname, is, "What is your glorious age?" If the person replies apologetically that he is twenty-three or twenty-eight, the other party generally comforts him by saying that he has still a glorious future, and that one day he may become old. But if the person replies that he is thirty-five or thirty-eight, the other party immediately exclaims with deep respect, "Good luck!"; enthusiasm grows in proportion as the gentleman is able to report a higher and higher age, and if the person is anywhere over fifty, the inquirer immediately drops his voice in humility and respect. That is why all old people, if they can, should go and live in China, where even a beggar with a white beard is treated with extra kindness. People in middle age actually look forward to the time when they can celebrate their fifty-first birthday, and in the case of successful merchants or officials, they would celebrate even their forty-first birthday with great pomp and glory. But the fifty-first birthday, or the half-century mark, is an occasion of rejoicing for people of all classes. The sixty-first is a happier and grander occasion than the fifty-first and the seventy-first is still happier and grander, while a man able to celebrate his eighty-first birthday is actually looked upon as one specially favoured by Heaven. The wearing of a beard becomes the special prerogative of those who have become grandparents, and a man doing so without the necessary qualifications, either of being a grandfather or being on the other side of fifty, stands in danger of being sneered at behind his back. The result is that young men try to pass themselves off as older than they are by imitating the pose and dignity and points of view of the old people, and I have known young Chinese writers graduated from the middle schools, anywhere between twenty-one and twenty-five, writing articles in the magazines to advise what "the young men ought and ought not to read," and discussing the pitfalls of youth with a fatherly condescension.

This desire to grow old and in any case to appear old is understandable when one understands the premium generally placed upon old age in China. In the first place, it is a privilege of the old people to talk, while the young must listen and hold their tongue. "A young man is supposed to have ears and no mouth," as a Chinese saying goes. Men of twenty are supposed to listen when people of thirty are talking, and these in turn are supposed to listen when men of forty are talking. As the desire to talk and to be listened to is almost universal, it is evident that the further along one gets in years, the better chance he has to talk and to be listened to when he goes about in society. It is a game of life in which no one is favoured, for everyone has a chance of becoming old in his time. Thus a father lecturing his son is obliged to stop suddenly and change his demeanour the moment the grandmother opens her mouth. Of course he wishes to be in the grandmother's place. And it is quite fair, for what right have the young to open their mouths when the old men can say, "I have crossed more bridges than you have crossed streets"? What right have the young got to talk?

In spite of my acquaintance with Western life and the Western attitude toward age, I am still continually shocked by certain expressions for which I am totally unprepared. Fresh illustrations of this attitude come up on every side. I have heard an old lady remarking that she has had several grandchildren, but, "It was the first one that *hurt*." With the full knowledge that American people hate to be thought of as old, one still doesn't quite expect to have it put that way. I have made allowance for people in middle age this side of fifty who, I can understand, wish to leave the impression that they are still active and vigorous, but I am not quite prepared to meet an old lady with grey hair facetiously switching the topic of conversation to the weather, when the conversation without any fault of mine naturally drifted toward her age. One continually forgets it when allowing an old man to enter a lift or a car first; the habitual expression "after age" comes up to my lips, then I restrain myself and am at a loss for what to say in its place. One day, being forgetful, I blurted out the usual phrase in deference to an extremely dignified and charming old man, and the old man seated in the car turned to his wife and remarked jokingly to her, "This young man has the cheek to think that he is younger than myself!"

The whole thing is as senseless as can be. I just don't see the point. I can understand young and middle-aged unmarried women refusing to tell their age, because there the premium upon youth is entirely natural. Chinese girls, too, get a little scared when they reach twenty-two and are unmarried or not engaged. The years are slipping by mercilessly. There is a feeling of fear of being left out, what the Germans call a *Torschlusspanik*, the fear of being left in the park when the gates close at night. Hence it has been said that the longest year of a woman's life is when she is twenty-nine: she remains twenty-nine for three or four or five years. But apart from this, the fear of letting people know one's age is nonsensical. How can one be thought wise unless one is thought to be old? And what do the young really know about life, about marriage and about the true values? Again I can understand that the whole pattern of Western life places a premium on youth and therefore makes men and women shrink from telling people their age. A perfectly efficient and vigorous woman secretary of forty-five is, by a curious twist of reasoning, immediately thought of as worthless when her age becomes known. What wonder that she wants to hide her age in order to keep her job? But then the pattern of life itself and this premium placed upon youth are nonsensical. There is absolutely no meaning to it, so far as I can see. This sort of thing is undoubtedly brought about by business life, for I have no doubt there must be more respect for old age in the home than in the office. I see no way out of it until the American people begin somewhat to despise work and efficiency and achievement. I suspect when an American father looks upon the home and not the office as his ideal place in life, and can openly tell people, as Chinese parents do, with absolute equanimity that now he has a good son taking his place and is honoured to be fed by him, he will be anxiously looking forward to that happy time, and will count the years impatiently before he reaches fifty.

It seems a linguistic misfortune that hale and hearty old men in America tell people that they are "young," or are told that they are "young" when really what is meant is that they are healthy. To enjoy health in old age, or to be old and healthy, is the greatest of human luck, but to call it "healthy and young" is but to detract from that glamour and impute imperfection to what is really perfect. After all, there is nothing more beautiful in this world than a healthy wise old man, with "ruddy cheeks and white hair," talking in a soothing voice about life as one who knows it. The Chinese realize this, and have always pictured an old man with "ruddy cheeks and white hair" as *the symbol of ultimate earthly happiness*. Many Americans must have seen Chinese pictures of the God of Longevity, with his high forehead, his ruddy face, his white beard—and how he smiles! The picture is so vivid. He runs his fingers through the thin flowing beard coming down to the breast and gently strokes it in peace and contentment, dignified because he is surrounded with respect, self-assured because no one ever questions his wisdom, and kind because he has seen so much of human sorrow. To persons of great vitality we also pay the compliment of saying that "the older they grow, the more vigorous they are," and a person like David Lloyd George would be referred to as "Old Ginger," because he gains in pungency with age.

On the whole, I find grand old men with white beards missing in the American picture. I know that they exist, but they are perhaps in a conspiracy to hide themselves from me. Only once, in New Jersey, did I meet an old man with anything like a respectable beard. Perhaps it is the safety razor that has done it, a process as deplorable and ignorant and stupid as the deafforestation of the Chinese hills by ignorant farmers, who have deprived North China of its beautiful forests and left the hills as bald and ugly as the American old men's chins. There is yet a mine to be discovered in America, a mine of beauty and wisdom that is pleasing to the eye and thrilling to the soul, when the American has opened his eyes to it and starts a general programme of reclamation and reafforestation. Gone are the grand old men of America! Gone is Uncle Sam with his goatee, for he has taken a safety razor and shaved it off, to make himself look like a frivolous young fool with his chin sticking out instead of being drawn in gracefully, and a hard glint shining behind horn-rimmed spectacles. What a poor substitute that is for the grand old figure! My attitude on the Supreme Court question (although it is none of my business) is purely determined by my love for the face of Charles Evans Hughes. Is he the only grand old man left in America, or are there more of them? He should retire, of course, for that is only being kind to him, but any accusation of senility seems to me an intolerable insult. He has a face that we would call "a sculptor's dream."

I have no doubt that the fact that the old men of America still insist on being so busy and active can be directly traced to individualism carried to a foolish extent. It is their pride and their love of independence and their shame of being dependent upon their children. But among the many human rights the American people have provided for in their Constitution, they have strangely forgotten about the right to be fed by their children, for it is a right and an obligation growing out of service. How can anyone deny that parents who have toiled for their children in their youth, have lost many a good night's sleep when they were ill, have washed their diapers long before they could talk and have spent about a quarter of a century bringing them up and fitting them for life, have the right to be fed by them and loved and respected when they are old? Can one not forget the individual and his pride of self in a general scheme of home life in which men are justly taken care of by their parents and, having in turn taken care of their children, are also justly taken care of by the latter? The Chinese have not got the sense of individual independence because the whole conception of life is based upon mutual help within the home; hence there is no shame attached to the circumstance of one's being served by his children in the sunset of one's life. Rather it is considered good luck to have children who can take care of one. One lives for nothing else in China.

In the West, the old people efface themselves and prefer to live alone in some hotel with a restaurant on the ground floor, out of consideration for their children and an entirely unselfish desire not to interfere in their home life. But the old people *have* the right to interfere, and if interference is unpleasant, it is nevertheless natural, for all life, particularly the domestic life, is a lesson in restraint. Parents interfere with their children, anyway, when they are young, and the logic of non-interference is already seen in the results of the Behaviourists, who think that all children should be taken away from their parents. If one cannot tolerate one's own parents when they are old and comparatively helpless, parents who have done so much for us, whom else can one tolerate in the home? One has to learn self-restraint, anyway, or even marriage will go on the rocks. And how can the personal service and devotion and adoration of loving children ever be replaced by the best hotel waiters?

The Chinese idea supporting this personal service to old parents is expressly defended on the sole ground of gratitude. The debts to one's friends may be numbered, but the debts to one's parents are beyond number. Again and again, Chinese essays on filial piety mention the fact of washing diapers, which takes on significance when one becomes a parent himself. In return, therefore, is it not right that, in their old age, the parents should be served with the best food and have their favourite

[204]

dishes placed before them? The duties of a son serving his parents are pretty hard, but it is sacrilege to make a comparison between nursing one's own parents and nursing a stranger in a hospital. For instance, the following are some of the duties of the junior at home, as prescribed by T'u Hsishih and incorporated in a book of moral instruction very popular as a text in the old schools:

In the summer months, one should, while attending to his parents, stand by their side and fan them, to drive away the heat and the flies and mosquitoes. In winter, he should see that the bed quilts are warm enough and the stove fire is hot enough, and see that it is just right by attending to it constantly. He should also see if there are holes or crevices in the doors and windows, that there may be no draught, to the end that his parents are comfortable and happy.

A child above ten should get up before his parents in the morning, and after the toilet go to their bed and ask if they have had a good night. If his parents have already got up, he should first curtsy to them before inquiring after their health, and should retire with another curtsy after the question. Before going to bed at night, he should prepare the bed, when the parents are going to sleep, and stand by until he sees that they have fallen off to sleep and then pull down the bed curtain and retire himself.

Who, therefore, wouldn't want to be an old man or an old father or grandfather in China?

This sort of thing is being very much laughed at by the proletarian writers of China as "feudalistic," but there is a charm to it which makes any old gentleman inland cling to it and think that modern China is going to the dogs. The important point is that *every man grows old in time,* if he lives long enough, as he certainly desires to. If one forgets this foolish individualism which seems to assume that an individual can exist in the abstract and be literally independent, one must admit that we must so plan our pattern of life that the golden period lies ahead in old age and not behind us in youth and innocence. For if we take the reverse attitude, we are committed without our knowing to a race with the merciless course of time, forever afraid of what lies ahead of us—a race, it is hardly necessary to point out, which is quite hopeless and in which we are eventually all defeated. No one can really stop growing old; he can only cheat himself by not admitting that he is growing old. And since there is no use fighting against nature, one might just as well grow old gracefully. The symphony of life should end with a grand finale of peace and serenity and material comfort and spiritual contentment, and not with the crash of a broken drum or cracked cymbals.

CHAPTER NINE

The Enjoyment Of Living

I. ON LYING IN BED

IT SEEMS I AM destined to become a market philosopher, but it can't be helped. Philosophy generally seems to be the science of making simple things difficult to understand, but I can conceive of a philosophy which is the science of making difficult things simple. In spite of names like "materialism," "humanism," "transcendentalism," "pluralism," and all the other long-winded "isms," I contend that these systems are no deeper than my own philosophy. Life, after all, is made up of eating and sleeping, of meeting and saying good-bye to friends, of reunions and farewell parties, of tears and laughter, of having a haircut once in two weeks, of watering a potted flower and watching one's neighbour fall off his roof, and the dressing up of our notions concerning these simple phenomena of life in a kind of academic jargon is nothing but a trick to conceal either an extreme paucity or an extreme vagueness of ideas on the part of the university professors. Philosophy therefore has become a science by means of which we begin more and more to understand less and less about ourselves. What the philosophers have succeeded in is this: the more they talk about it, the more confused we become.

It is amazing how few people are conscious of the importance of the art of lying in bed, although actually, in my opinion, nine-tenths of the world's most important discoveries, both scientific and philosophical, are come upon when the scientist or philosopher is curled up in bed at two or five o'clock in the morning.

Some people lie in the daytime and others lie at night. Now by "lying" I mean at the same time physical and moral lying, for the two happen to coincide. I find that those people who agree with me in believing in lying in bed as one of the greatest pleasures of life are the honest men, while those who do not believe in lying in bed are liars and actually lie a lot in the daytime, morally and physically. Those who lie in the daytime are the moral uplifters, kindergarten teachers and readers of *Æsop's Fables*, while those who frankly admit with me that a man ought to consciously cultivate the art of lying in bed are the honest men who prefer to read stories without a moral like *Alice in Wonderland*.

Now what is the significance of lying in bed, physically and spiritually? Physically, it means a retreat to oneself, shut up from the outside world, when one assumes the physical posture most conducive to rest and peace and contemplation. There is a certain proper and luxurious way of lying in bed. Confucius, that great artist of life, "never lay straight" in bed "like a corpse," but always curled up on one side.[1] I believe one of the greatest pleasures of life is to curl up one's legs in bed. The posture of the arms is also very important, in order to reach the greatest degree of æsthetic pleasure and mental power. I believe the best posture is not lying flat on the bed, but being upholstered with big soft pillows at an angle of thirty degrees with either one arm or both arms placed behind the back of one's head. In this posture any poet can write immortal poetry, any philosopher can revolutionize human thought, and any scientist can make epoch-making discoveries.

It is amazing how few people are aware of the value of solitude and contemplation. The art of lying in bed means more than physical rest for you, after you have gone through a strenuous day, and complete relaxation, after all the people you have met and interviewed, all the friends who have tried to crack silly jokes, and all your brothers and sisters who have tried to rectify your behaviour and sponsor you into heaven have thoroughly got on your nerves. It is all that, I admit. But it is something more. If properly cultivated, it should mean a mental house-cleaning. Actually, many business men who pride themselves on rushing

[1] *Analects*, Chapter X.

about in the morning and afternoon and keeping three desk telephones busy all the time on their desk, never realize that they could make twice the amount of money if they would give themselves one hour's solitude awake in bed, at one o'clock in the morning or even at seven. What does it matter even if one stays in bed at eight o'clock? A thousand times better that he should provide himself with a good tin of cigarettes on his bedside table and take plenty of time to get up from bed and solve all his problems of the day before he brushes his teeth. There, comfortably stretched or curled up in his pyjamas, free from the irksome woollen underwear or the irritating belt or suspenders and suffocating collars and heavy leather boots, when his toes are emancipated and have recovered the freedom which they inevitably lose in the daytime, the real business head can *think*, for only when one's toes are free is his head free, and only when one's head is free is real thinking possible. Thus in that comfortable position, he can ponder over his achievements and mistakes of yesterday and single out the important from the trivial in the day's programme ahead of him. Better that he arrived at ten o'clock in his office master of himself than that he should come punctually at nine or even a quarter before to watch over his subordinates like a slave-driver and then "hustle about nothing," as the Chinese say.

But for the thinker, the inventor and the man of ideas, lying quietly for an hour in bed accomplishes even more. A writer could get more ideas for his articles or his novel in this posture than he could by sitting doggedly before his desk morning and afternoon. For there, free from telephone calls and well-meaning visitors and the common trivialities of everyday life, he sees life through a glass or a beaded screen, as it were, and a halo of poetic fancy is cast around the world of realities and informs it with a magic beauty. There he sees life, not in its rawness but suddenly transformed into a picture more real than life itself, like the great paintings of Ni Yünlin or Mi Fei.

Now what actually happens in bed is this: When one is in bed the muscles are at rest, the circulation becomes smoother and more regular, respiration becomes steadier, and all the optical, auditory and vaso-motor nerves are more or less completely at rest, bringing about a more or less complete physical quietude, and *therefore making mental concentration, whether on ideas or on sensations, more absolute*. Even in respect to sensations, those of smell or hearing for example, our senses are the keenest in that moment. All good music should be listened to in the lying condition. Li Liweng said in his essay on "Willows" that one should learn to listen to the birds at dawn *when lying in bed*. What a world of beauty is waiting for us, if we learn to wake up at dawn and listen to the heavenly concert of the birds ! Actually there is a profusion of bird music in most towns, although I am sure many residents are not aware of it. For instance, this was what I recorded of the sounds I heard in Shanghai one morning :

This morning I woke up at five after a very sound sleep and listened to a most gorgeous feast of sounds. What woke me up were the factory whistles of a great variety of pitch and force. After a while, I heard a distant clatter of horses' hoofs; it must have been cavalry passing down Yuyuen Road ; and in that quiet dawn it gave me more æsthetic delight than a Brahms symphony. Then came a few early chirps from some kind of birds. I am sorry I am not proficient in bird lore, but I enjoyed them all the same.

There were other sounds, of course—some foreigner's "boy," presumably after a night of dissipation outside, appeared at about half-past five and began to knock at someone's back door. A scavenger was then heard sweeping a neighbouring alleyway with the swish-swash of his bamboo broom. All of a sudden, a wild duck, I suppose, would sail by in the sky, leaving echoes of his *kung-ting* in the air. At twenty-five past six I heard the distant rumble of the engine of the Shanghai-Hangchow train arriving at the Jessfield Station. There were one or two sounds coming from the children in their sleep in the next room. Life then began to stir and a distant hum of human activities in the near and distant neighbourhood gradually increased in volume and intensity. Downstairs in the house itself, the servants had got up, too. Windows were being opened. A hook was being placed in position. A slight cough. A soft tread of footsteps. A clanging of cups and saucers. And suddenly the baby cried, "Mamma!"

This was the natural concert I heard that morning in Shanghai. Throughout the whole spring that year my greatest delight was to listen to a kind of bird probably called a quail or partridge in English. Its love-call consists of four notes (*do. mi : re* | — :—. *ti,*) the *re* lasting two or three beats and ending in the middle of a beat, followed by an abrupt, staccato *ti* in the lower octave. It is the song I used to hear in the mountains in the south. The most beautiful part of it was that a male bird would start the call on top of a tree about twenty yards from my place early at dawn, and a female bird would counterpoint it at a distance of about a hundred yards. Then once in a while there would be a slight variation, a quickening as it were of tempo and of the bird's heart, and the last staccato note would be left out. This bird-song stands out pre-eminently among those of others, of which there is a great profusion. I am at a loss to describe these songs except by resort to musical notation, but I know they include the songs of orioles and magpies and woodpeckers, and the cooing of pigeons. The sparrows seem to wake up later, and the reason, I suppose, must be as our great epicure-poet Li Liweng gave it. The other birds have to sing early because they are continually afraid of men's guns and children's stones during the day. These birds, therefore, can sing at ease only before this insufferable human species wake up from their sleep. As soon as men wake up, the birds can never finish their song at ease. But the sparrows can, because they are not afraid, and therefore they can sleep longer.

II. ON SITTING IN CHAIRS

I want to write about the philosophy of sitting in chairs because I have a reputation for lolling. Now there are many lollers among my friends and acquaintances, but somehow I have acquired a special reputation for lolling, at least in the Chinese literary world. I contend that I am not the only loller in this modern world and that my reputation has been greatly exaggerated. It happened like this: I started a magazine called the *Analects Fortnightly,* in which I consistently tried to disprove the myth of the harmfulness of smoking. In spite of the fact that we did not have cigarette advertisements in our magazine, I wrote and published essay after essay praising the virtues of Lady Nicotine. Somehow, therefore, a legend developed that I was a man doing nothing the whole day but lolling idly on a sofa smoking a cigar, and in spite of my disclaimers and my protests that I am one of the hardest-working men in China, the legend had got about and was constantly used as an evidence of my belonging to the hateful leisure-class intelligentsia. Two years after, the situation was aggravated by the fact that I started another magazine devoted to the familiar essay. Bored stiff by the dilatory, hypocritical and pompous style of Chinese editorials, which is the result of the method of teaching school composition a generation ago, making young boys of twelve or thirteen write essays on "The Salvation of the Country" and "The Virtue of Persistence," I saw that the introduction of a more familiar style of writing was the means of emancipating Chinese prose from the strait-jacket of Confucian platitudes. It happened, however, that I translated the phrase "familiar style" by a Chinese phrase meaning "leisurely style." This was a signal for attack from the Communist camp, and now I have the indisputable reputation of being the most leisurely of all leisurely writers in China and therefore the most unforgivable, "while we are living in this period of national humiliation."

I admit that I do loll about in my friends' drawing-rooms, but so do the others. What are arm-chairs for, anyway, except for people to loll in? If gentlemen and ladies of the twentieth century were supposed to sit upright all the time with absolute dignity, there should be no arm-chairs at all in the modern drawing-room, but we should all be sitting on stiff redwood furniture, with most ladies' feet dangling about a foot from the ground.

In other words, there is a philosophy about lolling in chairs. The mention of the word "dignity" explains exactly the origin of the difference in the styles of sitting between the ancient and the modern people. The ancient people sat in order to look dignified, while modern people sit in order to be comfortable. There is a philosophic conflict between the two, for, according to ancient notions only half a century ago, comfort was a sin, and to be comfortable was to be disrespectful. Aldous Huxley has made this sufficiently plain in his essay on "Comfort." The feudalistic society which made the rise of the arm-chair impossible until modern days, as described by Huxley, was exactly the same as that which existed in China up to a generation ago. To-day any man who calls himself another's friend must not be afraid to put his legs on top of a desk in his friend's room, and we take that as a sign of familiarity instead of disrespect, although to put one's legs on top of a desk in the presence of a member of the older generation would be a different matter.

There is a closer relationship between morals and architecture and interior decoration than we suspect. Huxley has pointed out that Western ladies did not take frequent baths because they were afraid to see their own naked bodies, and this moral concept delayed the rise of the modern white-enamelled bath-tub for centuries. One can understand why in the design of old Chinese furniture there was so little consideration for human comfort only when we realize the Confucian atmosphere in which people moved about. Chinese redwood furniture was designed for people to sit upright in, because that was the only posture approved by society. Even Chinese emperors had to sit on a throne on which I would not think of remaining for more than five minutes, and for that matter the English kings were just as badly off. Cleopatra went about inclining on a couch carried by servants, because apparently she had never heard of Confucius. If Confucius should have seen her doing that, he would certainly have "struck her shin with a stick," as he did to one of his old disciples, Yüan Jang, when the latter was found sitting in an incorrect posture. In the Confucian society in which we lived, gentlemen and ladies had to hold themselves perfectly erect, at least on formal occasions, and any sign of putting one's leg up would be at once construed as a sign of vulgarity and lack of culture. In fact, to show extra respect, as when seeing official superiors, one had to sit gingerly on the edge of a chair at an oblique angle, which was a sign of respect and of the height of culture. There is also a close connection between the Confucian tradition and the discomforts of Chinese architecture, but we will not go into that now.

Thanks to the romantic movement in the later eighteenth and earlier nineteenth centuries, this tradition of classical decorum has broken down, and to be comfortable is no longer a sin. On the other hand, a more truthful attitude towards life has taken its place, due as much to the romantic movement as to a better understanding of human psychology. The same change of attitude which has ceased to regard theatrical amusements as immoral and Shakespeare as a "barbarian" has also made possible the evolution of ladies' bathing costumes, clean bath-tubs and comfortable arm-chairs and divans, and of a more truthful and at the same time intimate style of living and writing. In this sense there is a true connection between my habit of lolling on a sofa and my attempt to introduce a more intimate and free-and-easy writing into modern Chinese journalism.

If we admit that comfort is not a sin, then we must also admit that the more comfortably a man arranges himself in an arm-chair in a friend's drawing-room, the greater respect he is showing to his host. After all, to make oneself at home and look restful is only to help one's host or hostess succeed in the difficult art of hospitality. How many hostesses have feared and trembled for an evening party in which the guests are not willing to loosen up and just be themselves! I have always helped my hosts and hostesses by putting a leg up on top of a tea-table or whatever happens to be the nearest object, and in that way forced everybody else to throw away the cloak of false dignity.

Now I have discovered a formula regarding the comparative comfort of furniture. This formula may be stated in very simple terms: the lower a chair is, the more comfortable it becomes. Many people have sat down on a certain chair in a friend's home and wondered why it is so cosy. Before the discovery of this formula, I used to think that students of interior decoration probably had a mathematical formula for the proportion between height and width and angle of inclination of chairs which conduced to the maximum comfort of sitters. Since the discovery of this formula, I have found that it is simpler than that. Take any Chinese redwood furniture and saw off its legs a few inches, and it immediately becomes more comfortable; and if you saw off another few inches, then it becomes still more comfortable. The logical conclusion of this is, of course, that one is most comfortable when one is lying perfectly flat on a bed. The matter is as simple as that.

From this fundamental principle, we may derive the corollary that when we find ourselves sitting in a chair that is too high and can't saw its legs off, all we have to do is seek some object in the foreground on which we can rest our legs and therefore theoretically decrease the difference between the levels of our hips and our feet. One of the commonest devices that I use is to pull out a drawer in my desk and put my feet on it. But the intelligent application of this corollary I can leave to everybody's common sense.

To correct any misunderstanding that I am lolling all the time for sixteen waking hours of the day, I must hasten to explain that I am capable of sitting doggedly at a desk or in front of a typewriter for three hours. Just because I wish to make it clear that relaxation of our muscles is not necessarily a crime, I do not mean that we should keep our muscles relaxed all the time, or that this is the most hygienic posture to be assumed all the time. That is far from my intention. After all, human life goes in cycles of work and play, of tension and relaxation. The male brain energy and capacity for work goes in monthly cycles just like women's bodies. William James said that when the chains of a bicycle are kept too tight, they are not conducive to the easiest running, and so with the human mind. Everything, after all, is a matter of habit. There is an infinite capacity in the human body for adjustments. Japanese who have the habit of sitting with crossed legs on the floor are liable to get cramps, I suspect, when they are made to sit on chairs. Only by alternating between the absolutely erect working posture of office hours and the posture of stretching ourselves on a sofa after a hard day's work can we achieve that highest wisdom of living.

A word to the ladies: when there is nothing in the immediate foreground on which you can rest your feet, you can always curl up your legs on a sofa. You never look more charming than when you are in that attitude.

III. ON CONVERSATION

"Talking with you for one night is better than studying books for ten years,"—this was the comment of an old Chinese scholar after he had had a conversation with another friend. There is much truth in that statement, and to-day the phrase "a night's talk" has become a current expression for a happy conversation with a friend at night, either past or anticipated. There are two or three books which resemble an English "week-end omnibus," bearing the title *A Night's Talk,* or *A Night's Talk in the Mountains.* Such a supreme pleasure as a perfect conversation with a friend at night is necessarily rare, for as Li Liweng has pointed out, those who are wise seldom know how to talk, and those who talk are seldom wise. The discovery of a man up in a mountain temple, who really understands life and at the same time understands the art of conversation, must therefore be one of the keenest pleasures, like the discovery of a new planet by an astronomer or of a new variety of plant by a botanist.

People to-day are complaining that the art of conversation around a fire-place or on cracker barrels is becoming lost, owing to the tempo of business life to-day. I am quite sure that this tempo has something to do with it, but believe also that the distortion of the home into an apartment without a log fire began the destruction of the art of conversation, and the influence of the motor car completed it. The tempo is entirely wrong, for conversation exists only in a society of men imbued in the spirit of leisure, with its ease, its humour, and its appreciation of light nuances. For there is an evident distinction between mere talking and conversation as such. This distinction is made in the Chinese language between *shuohua* (speaking) and *t'anhua* (conversation), which implies the discourse is more chatty and leisurely and the topics of conversation are more trivial and less business-like. A similar difference may be noted between business correspondence and the letters of literary friends. We can speak or discuss business with almost any person, but there are very few people with whom we can truly hold a night's conversation. Hence, when we do find a true conversationalist, the pleasure is equal to, if not above, that of reading a delightful author, with the additional pleasure of hearing his voice and seeing his gestures. Sometimes we find it at the happy reunion of old friends, or among acquaintances indulging in reminiscences, sometimes in the smoking-room of a night train, and sometimes at an inn on a distant journey. There will be chats about ghosts and fox-spirits, mixed with amusing tales or impassioned comments on dictators and traitors, and sometimes before we know it, light is shown by a wise observer and conversationalist on things taking place in a certain country which are a premonition of the impending collapse or change in a regime. Such conversations remain among the memories that we cherish for life.

Of course, night is the best time for conversation, because there is a certain lack of glamour in conversations during the daytime. The place of conversation seems to me entirely unimportant. One can enjoy a good conversation on literature and philosophy in an eighteenth-century salon, or sitting on barrels at a plantation of an afternoon. Or it may be on a windy or rainy night when we are travelling in a river boat and the lantern lights from boats anchoring on the opposite bank of the river cast their reflections into the water and we hear the boatmen tell us stories about the girlhood of the Queen. In fact, the charm of conversation lies in the fact that the circumstances in which it takes place the place, the time and the persons engaged in it, vary from occasion to occasion. Sometimes we remember it in connection with a breezy moonlight night, when the cassia flowers are in bloom, and sometimes we associate it in memory with a dark and stormy night when a log fire is glowing on the hearth, and sometimes we remember we were sitting on top of a pavilion watching boats coming down the river, and perhaps a boat was overturned by the swift current, or again, we were sitting in the waiting-room of a railway station in the small hours of the morning. These pictures associate themselves indelibly with our memory of those particular conversations. There were perhaps two or three persons in the room, or perhaps five or six; maybe old Chen was slightly drunk that night, or old Chin had a cold in the nose and spoke with a slight twang, adding to the particular flavour of that evening. Such is human life that "the moon cannot always be round, the flowers cannot always look so fine and good friends cannot always meet together," and I do not think the gods will be jealous of us when we engage in such simple pastimes.

As a rule, a good conversation is always like a good familiar essay. Both its style and its contents are similar to that of the essay. Such topics as fox-spirits, flies, the strange ways of Englishmen, the difference between Oriental and Occidental culture, the bookstalls along the Seine, a nymphomaniac apprentice in a tailor shop, anecdotes of our rulers, statesmen and generals, the method of preserving "Buddha's Fingers" (a variety of citron)—these are all good and legitimate topics of conversation. The point it has most in common with the essay is its leisurely style. However weighty and important the topic may be, involving reflections on the sad change or state of chaos of one's own country, or the sinking of civilization itself under a current of mad political ideas, depriving man of liberty, human dignity and even the goal of human happiness, or even involving moving questions of truth and justice, still such ideas are expressed in a casual, leisurely and intimate manner. For in civilization, however a man chafes and is angry at the robbers of our liberty, we are allowed only to express our sentiments by a light smile around our lips or at the tip of our pen. Our really impassioned tirades, in which we give full rein to our sentiments, may be heard only by a few of our most intimate friends. Hence the requisite condition of a true conversation is that we are able to air our views at leisure in the intimacy of a room with a few good friends and with no people around whom we hate to look at.

It is easy to see this contrast between the true *genre* of conversation and other kinds of polite exchange of opinion by referring to the similar contrast between a good familiar essay and the statements of politicians. Although there are a good deal more noble sentiments expressed in politicians' statements, sentiments of democracy, desire for service, interest in the welfare of the poor, devotion to the country, lofty idealism, love of peace and assurances of unfailing international friendship, and absolutely no suggestions of greed for power or money or fame, yet there is a smell about it which puts one off at a distance, like an over-dressed and over-painted lady. On the other hand, when we hear a true conversation or read a good familiar essay, we feel that we have seen a plainly dressed country maiden washing clothes by the river-bank, with perhaps her hair a little dishevelled and one button loose, but withal charming and intimate and likeable. That is the familiar charm and studied negligence aimed at in a Western woman's négligé. Some of this familiar charm of intimacy must be a part of all good conversations and all good essays.

The proper style of conversation is, therefore, a style of intimacy and nonchalance, in which the parties engaged have lost their self-consciousness and are entirely oblivious of how they dress, how they speak, how they sneeze, and where they put their hands, and are equally indifferent as to which way the conversation is drifting. We can engage in a true conversation only when we meet our intimate friends and are prepared to unburden our hearts to each other. One of them has put his feet on a neighbouring table, another is sitting on a window-sill, and still another is sitting on the floor, upholstered by a cushion which he has snatched from the sofa, thus leaving one-third of the sofa seat uncovered. For it is only when your hands and feet are relaxed and the position of your body is at ease that your heart can be at ease also. It is then that:

> Before my face are friends who know my heart,
> And at my side are none who hurt my eyes.

This is the absolutely necessary condition of all conversation worthy of the name of an art. And since we do not care what we are talking about, the conversation will drift farther and farther, without order and without method, and the company break up, happy of heart.

Such is the connection between leisure and conversation and the connection between conversation and the rise of prose that I believe the truly cultured prose of a nation was born at a time when conversation had already developed as a fine art. This we see most clearly in the development of Chinese and Greek prose. I cannot otherwise imagine an explanation for the vitality of Chinese thought in the centuries following Confucius, giving birth to the so-called "Nine Schools of Thought," than the development of a cultured background, in which there was a class of scholars whose business was only to talk. For confirmation of my theory, we find there were five great rich noblemen, noted for their generosity, chivalry and fondness for guests. All of them had thousands of scholarly guests at their homes, as for instance Mengch'ang of Ch'i Kingdom who was reputed to have three thousand scholars, or "guests" wearing "pearled shoes," being "fed" at his home. One can imagine the conversational hubbub that was going on in those houses. The content of the conversation of scholars of those days is to-day reflected in the books of *Liehtse, Huainantse, Chankuots'eh* and *Lülan*. It is noteworthy that with respect to the last one, which was a book admittedly written by Lü's guests but published in his name (in a sense similar to the "patrons" of English sixteenth-century and seventeenth-century authors), there was already developed the idea of the art of living well, in the formula that it would be better to live well or not at all. There was besides a class of brilliant sophists or professional talkers, who were engaged by the different warring states and sent out as diplomats to avert a crisis or persuade a hostile army to retreat from the walls of a besieged city, or to bring about an alliance, as so many did. Such professional sophists were always distinguished by their wit, their clever parables and their general persuasive power. The conversations or clever arguments of such sophists are preserved for us in the book *Chankuots'eh*. From such an atmosphere of free and playful discussion arose some of the greatest names in philosophy: Yang Chu, noted for his cynicism; Hanfeitse, noted for his realism (similar to Machiavelli's, but more tempered), and the great diplomat, Yentse, noted for his wit.

An example of the cultured social life existing in the third century B.C., toward the end of this period, may be seen in the record of how a certain scholar by the name of Li Yüan succeeded in presenting his accomplished sister to the court of a rich patron in the Kingdom of Ch'u. The patron in turn secured the favour of the King for this girl, which was eventually responsible for the destruction of the Kingdom of Ch'u by the conquering army of the First Emperor of Ch'in, who united the Chinese Empire.

Formerly there was Li Yüan, serving as a subordinate of Prince Ch'unshen, the Prime Minister of the King of Ch'u. Li had a sister by the name of Nühuan who spoke to him one day, "I hear that the King is without an heir. If you will present me to the Prime Minister, through him I will be able to see the King." "But the Prime Minister is a high official," replied her brother. "How dare I mention it to him?" "You just go and see him," said his sister, "and then tell him that you have to come home because a noble guest has arrived. He will then ask you who is the noble guest and you can reply that you have a sister, that the Prime Minister of the Kingdom of Lu has heard of her reputation and has sent a delegate to ask for her from you, and that a messenger from home has just brought the news. He will then ask, what can your sister do? And you will reply that I can play on the *ch'in*, can read and write, and have mastered one of the classics. He is certain to send for me that way."

Li then promised to do as she said, and the next morning, after seeing the Prime Minister, he said, "A messenger from home told me that there is a guest from a distant country, and I must return to receive him." The Prime Minister Ch'unshen then actually asked him, "Who is this noble guest from a distant country?" And Li replied, "I have a sister, and the Prime Minister of the Kingdom of Lu has heard of her reputation and has sent a delegate to ask for her." "May I see her?" asked the Prime Minister. "Ask her to come and meet me at the Li Pavilion." "Yes, sir," replied Li, and he returned and told his sister that the Prime Minister expected to see her the next evening at the Li Pavilion. "You must go there yourself first in order to be there when I arrive," said the girl.

The Prime Minister then arrived at the time and asked to see Nühuan. She was presented and they drank a great deal. Nühuan played on the *ch'in*, and before her song was finished, the Prime Minister was greatly pleased and asked her to stay there for the night. . . .

This, then, was the social background of cultivated ladies and leisurely scholars, which produced for us the first important development of prose in China. There were ladies who could talk and read and write and play on a musical instrument, making for that peculiarly light mixture of social, artistic and literary motives that was always found in a society where men and women mixed together. It was undoubtedly aristocratic in character and atmosphere, for the Prime Minister Ch'unshen was difficult to see, but when he heard of a lady who could play on a musical instrument and had mastered one of the classics, he insisted on seeing her. This was, then, the life of leisure which the early Chinese sophists and philosophers lived. The books of these early Chinese philosophers were nothing but the results of leisurely conversation among these scholars.

It is clear that only in a society with leisure can the art of conversation be produced, and it is equally clear also that only when there is an art of conversation can there be good familiar essays. In general, both the art of conversation and the art of writing good prose came comparatively late in the history of human civilization, because the human mind had to develop a certain subtlety and lightness of touch, and this was possible only in a life of leisure. I am quite aware that to-day, from the point of view of the Communists, to enjoy leisure or to belong to the hated leisured class is already to be counter-revolutionary, but I am quite convinced that the aim of true Communism and Socialism is that all people should be able to enjoy leisure, or that the enjoyment of leisure should become general. Therefore, the enjoyment of leisure cannot be a sin, but on the other hand the progress of culture itself depends on an intelligent use of leisure, of which conversation is only one form. Business men who are busy the whole day and immediately go to bed after supper, snoring like cows, are not likely to contribute anything to culture.

Sometimes this "leisure" is enforced upon one and does not come of one's own seeking. All the same, many good works of literature have been produced in an atmosphere of enforced leisure. When we see a literary genius with great promise, dispersing his energy in futile social parties or writing essays on current politics, the best and kindest thing we can do to him is to shut him up in jail. For we must remember that it was in prison that the King Wen wrote his *Book of Changes,* a classic of philosophy on the changes of human life, and Ssema Ch'ien wrote his masterpiece, *Shihchi* (conventionally spelled *Shiki*), the best history ever written in the Chinese language. Sometimes the authors were defeated in their ambitions for a political career, or the political situation was too discouraging, and great works of literature or of art were produced. That is the reason why we had such great Yüan painters and Yüan dramatists during the Mongol regime and such great painters as Shih T'ao and Pata Shanjen during the beginning of the Manchu conquest of China. Patriotism in the form of a sense of utter humiliation under foreign rule made their whole-hearted devotion to art and learning possible. Shih T'ao is undoubtedly one of the very greatest painters China has ever produced, and the fact that he is not generally known in the West is due to an accident and to the fact that the Manchu emperors were not willing to give credit to these artists not in sympathy with their rule. Other great writers who had failed in the Imperial examination began to sublimate their energy and turn to creation, as in the case of Shih Naian who gave us *All Men are Brothers* and P'u Liuhsien who gave us *Strange Stories from a Chinese Studio*.

We have in the preface to *All Men are Brothers,* attributed to Shih, one of the most delightful descriptions of the pleasure of conversation among friends:

When all my friends come together to my house, there are sixteen persons in all, but it is seldom that they all come. But except for rainy or stormy days, it is also seldom that none of them comes. Most of the days, we have six or seven persons in the house, and when they come, they do not immediately begin to drink; they would take a sip when they feel like it and stop when they feel like it, for they regard the pleasure as consisting in the conversation, and not in the wine. We do not talk about court politics, not only because it lies outside our proper occupation but also because at such a distance most of the news is based upon hearsay; hearsay news is mere rumour, and to discuss rumours would be a waste of our saliva. We also do not talk about people's faults, for people have no faults, and we should not malign them. We do not say things to shock people and no one is shocked; on the other hand, we do wish people to understand what we say, but people still don't understand what we say. For such things as we talk about lie in the depths of the human heart, and the people of the world are too busy to hear them.

It was in this kind of style and with this kind of sentiment that Shih's great work was produced, and this was possible because they enjoyed leisure.

The rise of Greek prose took place clearly in the same kind of a leisurely social background. The lucidity of Greek thought and clearness of the Greek prose style clearly owe their existence to the art of leisurely conversation, as is so clearly revealed in the title of Plato's *Dialogues*. In *The Banquet* we see a group of Greek scholars reclining on the ground and chatting merrily along in an atmosphere of wine and fruit and beautiful boys. It was because these people had cultivated the art of talking that their thought was so lucid and their style so clear, providing a refreshing contrast to the pomposity and pedantry of modern academic writers. These Greeks evidently had learned to handle the topic of philosophy lightly. The charming conversational atmosphere of the Greek philosophers, their desire for talking, the value they placed upon hearing a good talk and the choice of surroundings for conversations were beautifully described in the introduction to *Phaedrus*. This gives us an insight into the rise of Greek prose.

Plato's *Republic* itself does not begin, as some of the modern writers would have it, with some such sentence as, "Human civilization, as seen through its successive stages of development, is a dynamic movement from heterogeneity to homogeneity," or some other equally incomprehensible rot. It begins rather with the genial sentence: "I went down yesterday to the Piraeus, with Glauco, the son of Aristo, to pay my devotion to the goddess; and desirous, at the same time, to observe in what manner they would celebrate the festival, as they were now to do it for the first time." The same atmosphere that we find among the early Chinese philosophers when thinking was most active and virile, we find in the picture of Greek men, gathered to discuss the topic whether a great writer of tragedies should or should not be also a writer of comedies, as described in *The Banquet*. There was an atmosphere of mixed seriousness and gaiety and friendly repartee. People were making fun of Socrates' drinking capacity, but there he sat, drinking or stopping as he liked, pouring a cup for himself when he felt like it, without bothering about others. And thus he talked the whole night out until everybody in the company fell asleep except Aristophanes and Agathon. When he had thus talked everybody to sleep and was thus the only one awake, he left the banquet and went to Lyceum to have a morning bath, and passed the day as fresh as ever. It was in this atmosphere of friendly discourse that Greek philosophy was born.

There is no question but we need the presence of women in a cultured conversation, to give it the necessary frivolity which is the soul of conversation. Without frivolity and gaiety, conversation soon becomes heavy and philosophy itself becomes foolish and a stranger to life. It has been found in all countries and in all ages that, whenever there was a culture interested in the understanding of the art of living, there always developed a fashion of welcoming women in society. This was the case of Athens in the time of Pericles, and it was so in the eighteenth-century French salons. Even in China, where mixed company was tabooed, Chinese men scholars still demanded the presence of women who could join in their conversation. In the three dynasties, Chin, Sung and Ming, when the art of conversation was cultivated and became a fashion, there always appeared accomplished ladies, like Hsieh Taoyün, Ch'aoyün, Liu Jushih and others. For although Chinese men demanded that their wives be virtuous and abstain from seeing men, they did not on that account cease to desire the company of talented women themselves. Chinese literary history, after all, was very much mixed up with the lives of professional courtesans. The demand for a touch of feminine charm in a company during conversation is a universal demand. I have met German ladies who can talk from five o'clock in the afternoon till eleven at night, and I have come across English and American ladies who frighten me by their familiarity with economics, a subject that I despair of ever having the courage to study. But it seems to me, even if there are no ladies around who can debate with me on Karl Marx and Engels, conversation is always pleasantly stimulated when there are a few ladies who know how to listen and look sweetly pensive. I always find it more delightful than talking to stupid-looking men.

IV. ON TEA AND FRIENDSHIP

I do not think that, considered from the point of view of human culture and happiness, there have been more significant inventions in the history of mankind, more vitally important and more directly contributing to our enjoyment of leisure, friendship, sociability and conversation, than the inventions of smoking, drinking and tea. All three have several characteristics in common: first of all, that they contribute toward our sociability; secondly, that they do not fill our stomach as food does, and therefore can be enjoyed between meals; and thirdly, that they are all to be enjoyed through the nostrils by acting on our sense of smell. So great are their influences upon culture that we have smoking cars besides dining cars, and we have wine restaurants or taverns and tea-houses. In China and England at least, drinking tea has become a social institution.

The proper enjoyment of tobacco, drink and tea can only be developed in an atmosphere of leisure, friendship and sociability. For it is only with men gifted with the sense of comradeship, extremely select in the matter of forming friends and endowed with a natural love of the leisurely life, that the full enjoyment of tobacco and drink and tea becomes possible. Take away the element of sociability, and these things have no meaning. The enjoyment of these things, like the enjoyment of the moon, the snow and the flowers, must take place in proper company, for this I regard as the thing that the Chinese artists of life most frequently insist upon: that certain kinds of flowers must be enjoyed with certain types of persons, certain kinds of scenery must be associated with certain kinds of ladies, that the sound of raindrops must be enjoyed, if it is to be enjoyed fully, when lying on a bamboo bed in a temple deep in the mountains on a summer day; that, in short, the mood is the thing, that there is a proper mood for everything, and that wrong company may spoil the mood entirely. Hence the beginning of any artist of life is that he or anyone who wishes to learn to enjoy life must, as the absolutely necessary condition, find friends of the same type of temperament, and take as much trouble to gain and keep their friendship as wives take to keep their husbands, or as a good chess-player takes a journey of a thousand miles to meet a fellow chess-player.

The atmosphere, therefore, is the thing. One must begin with the proper conception of the scholar's studio and the general environment in which life is going to be enjoyed. First of all, there are the friends with whom we are going to share this enjoyment. Different types of friends must be selected for different types of enjoyment. It would be as great a mistake to go horseback-riding with a studious and pensive friend, as it would be to go to a concert with a person who doesn't understand music. Hence as a Chinese writer expresses it:

> For enjoying flowers, one must secure big-hearted friends. For going to sing-song houses to have a look at sing-song girls, one must secure temperate friends. For going up a high mountain, one must secure romantic friends. For boating, one must secure friends with an expansive nature. For facing the moon, one must secure friends with a cool philosophy. For anticipating snow, one must secure beautiful friends. For a wine party, one must secure friends with flavour and charm.

Having selected and formed friends for the proper enjoyment of different occasions, one then looks for the proper surroundings. It is not so important that one's house be richly decorated as that it should be situated in beautiful country, with the possibility of walking about on the rice-fields or lying down under shady trees on a river-bank. The requirements for the house itself are simple enough. One can "have a house with several rooms, grain fields of several *mow*, a pool made from a basin and windows made from broken jars, with the walls coming up to the shoulders and a room the size of a rice bushel, and in the leisure time after enjoying the warmth of cotton beddings and a meal of vegetable soup, one can become so great that his spirit expands and fills the entire universe. For such a quiet studio, one should have *wut'ung* trees in front and some green bamboos behind. On the south of the house the eaves will stretch boldly forward, while on the north side there will be small windows, which can be closed in spring and winter to shelter one from rain and wind, and opened in summer and autumn for ventilation. The beauty of the *wut'ung* tree is that all its leaves fall off in spring and winter, thus admitting us to the full enjoyment of the sun's warmth, while in summer and autumn its shade protects us from the scorching heat." Or as another writer expressed it, one should "build a house of several beams, grow a hedge of *chin* trees and cover a pavilion with a hay-thatch. Three *mow* of land will be devoted to planting bamboos and flowers and fruit trees, while two *mow* will be devoted to planting vegetables. The four walls of a room are bare and the room is empty, with the exception of two or three rough beds placed in the pavilion. A peasant boy will be kept to water the vegetables and clear the weeds. So then one may arm one's self with books and a sword against solitude, and provide a *ch'in* (a stringed instrument) and chess to anticipate the coming of good friends."

An atmosphere of familiarity will then invest the place. "In my studio, all formalities will be abolished, and only the most intimate friends will be admitted. They will be treated with rich or poor fare such as I eat, and we will chat and laugh and forget our own existence. We will not discuss the right and wrong of other people and will be totally indifferent to worldly glory and wealth. In our leisure we will discuss the ancients and the moderns, and in our quiet, we will play with the mountains and rivers. Then we will have thin, clear tea and good wine to fit into the atmosphere of delightful seclusion. That is my conception of the pleasure of friendship."

In such a congenial atmosphere, we are then ready to gratify our senses, the senses of colour and smell and sound. It is then that one should smoke and one should drink. We then transform our bodies into a sensory apparatus for perceiving the wonderful symphony of colours and sounds and smells and tastes provided by Nature and by culture. We feel like good violins about to be played on by master violinists. And thus "we burn incense on a moonlight night and play three stanzas of music from an ancient instrument, and immediately the myriad worries of our breast are banished and all our foolish ambitions or desires are forgotten. We will then inquire, what is the fragrance of this incense, what is the colour of the smoke, what is that shadow that comes through the white papered windows, what is this sound that arises from below my finger-tips, what is this enjoyment which makes us so quietly happy and so forgetful of everything else, and what is the condition of the infinite universe?"

Thus chastened in spirit, quiet in mind and surrounded by proper company, one is fit to enjoy tea. For tea is invented for quiet company as wine is invented for a noisy party. There is something in the nature of tea that leads us into a world of quiet contemplation of life. It would be as disastrous to drink tea with babies crying around, or with loud-voiced women or politics-talking men, as to pick tea on a rainy or a cloudy day. Picked at early dawn on a clear day, when the morning air on mountain top was clear and thin, and the fragrance of dews was still upon the leaves, tea is still associated with the fragrance and refinement of the magic dew in its enjoyment. With the Taoist insistence upon return to nature, and with its conception that the universe is kept alive by the interplay of the male and female forces, the dew actually stands for the "juice of heaven and earth" when the two principles are united at night, and the idea is current that the dew is a magic food, fine and clear and ethereal, and any man or beast who drinks enough of it stands a good chance of being immortal. De Quincey says quite correctly that tea "will always be the favourite beverage of the intellectual," but the Chinese seem to go farther and associate it with the high-minded recluse.

Tea is, then, symbolic of earthly purity, requiring the most fastidious cleanliness in its preparation, from picking, frying and preserving to its final infusion and drinking, easily upset or spoiled by the slightest contamination of oily hands or oily cups. Consequently, its enjoyment is appropriate in an atmosphere where all ostentation or suggestion of luxury is banished from one's eyes and one's thoughts. After all, one enjoys sing-song girls with wine and not with tea, and when sing-song girls are fit to drink tea with, they are already in the class that Chinese poets and scholars favour. Su Tungp'o once compared tea to a sweet maiden, but a later critic, T'ien Yiheng, author of *Chuch'üan Hsiaop'in* (Essay On Boiling Spring Water)[1] immediately qualified it by adding that tea could be compared, if it must be compared to women at all, only to the Fairy Maku, and that, "as for beauties with peach-coloured faces and willow waists, they should be shut up in curtained beds, and not be allowed to contaminate the rocks and springs." For the same author says, "One drinks tea to forget the world's noise; it is not for those who eat rich food and dress in silk pyjamas."

It must be remembered that, according to *Ch'alu,* "the essence of the enjoyment of tea lies in appreciation of its *colour, fragrance and flavour,* and the principles of preparation are *refinement, dryness and cleanliness.*" An element of quiet is therefore necessary for the appreciation of these qualities, an appreciation that comes from a man who can "look at a hot world with a cool head." Since the Sung Dynasty, connoisseurs have generally regarded a cup of *pale* tea as the best, and the delicate flavour of pale tea can easily pass unperceived by one occupied with busy thoughts, or when the neighbourhood is noisy, or servants are quarrelling, or when served by ugly maids. The company, too, must be small. For, "it is important in drinking tea that the guests be few. Many guests would make it noisy, and noisiness takes away from its cultured charm. To drink alone is called *secluded;* to drink between two is called *comfortable;* to drink with three or four is called *charming;* to drink with five or six is called *common;* and to drink with seven or eight is called [contemptuously] *philanthropic.*" As the author of *Ch'asu* said, "to pour tea around again and again from a big pot, and drink it up at a gulp, or to warm it up again after a while, or to ask for extremely strong taste would be like farmers or artisans who drink tea to fill their belly after hard work; it would then be impossible to speak of the distinction and appreciation of flavours."

[1] The classic on tea is *Ch'aching,* by Lu Yü (*d.* A.D. 804); other well-known treatises mentioned below are *Ch'alu,* by Ts'ai Hsiang (1012–1067); *Ch'asu,* by Hsü Ts'eshu; *Chuchüan Hsiaop'in,* by T'ien Yihing (*c.* 1570); *Ch'achieh,* by T'u Lung (*c.* 1592).

For this reason, and out of consideration for the utmost rightness and cleanliness in preparation, Chinese writers on tea have always insisted on personal attention in boiling tea, or since that is necessarily inconvenient, that two boy servants be specially trained to do the job. Tea is usually boiled on a separate small stove in the room or directly outside, away from the kitchen. The servant boys must be trained to make tea in the presence of their master and to observe a routine of cleanliness, washing the cups every morning (never wiping them with a towel), washing their hands often and keeping their finger-nails clean. "When there are three guests, one stove will be enough, but when there are five or six persons, two separate stoves and kettles will be required, one boy attending to each stove, for if one is required to attend to both, there may be delays or mix-ups." True connoisseurs, however, regard the personal preparation of tea as a special pleasure. Without developing into a rigid system as in Japan, the preparation and drinking of tea is always a performance of loving pleasure, importance and distinction. In fact, the preparation is half the fun of the drinking, as cracking melon-seeds between one's teeth is half the pleasure of eating them.

Usually a stove is set before a window, with good hard charcoal burning. A certain sense of importance invests the host, who fans the stove and watches the vapour coming out from the kettle. Methodically he arranges a small pot and four tiny cups, usually smaller than small coffee-cups, in a tray. He sees that they are in order, moves the pewter-foil pot of tea leaves near the tray and keeps it in readiness, chatting along with his guests, but not so much that he forgets his duties. He turns round to look at the stove, and from the time the kettle begins to sing, he never leaves it, but continues to fan the fire harder than before. Perhaps he stops to take the lid off and look at the tiny bubbles, technically called "fish eyes" or "crab froth," appearing on the bottom of the kettle, and puts the lid on again. This is the "first boil." He listens carefully as the gentle singing increases in volume to that of a "gurgle," with small bubbles coming up the sides of the kettle, technically called the "second boil." It is then that he watches most carefully the vapour emitted from the kettle-spout, and just shortly before the "third boil" is reached, when the water is brought up to a full boil, "like billowing waves," he takes the kettle from the fire and scalds the pot inside and out with the boiling water, immediately adds the proper quantity of leaves and makes the infusion. Tea of this kind, like the famous "Iron Goddess of Mercy," drunk in Fukien, is made very thick. The small pot is barely enough to hold four *demi-tasses* and is filled one-third with leaves. As the quantity of leaves is large, the tea is immediately poured into the cups and immediately drunk. This finishes the pot, and the kettle, filled with fresh water, is put on the fire again, getting ready for the second pot. Strictly speaking, the second pot is regarded as the best; the first pot being compared to a girl of thirteen, the second compared to a girl of sweet sixteen, and the third regarded as a woman. Theoretically, the third infusion from the same leaves is disallowed by connoisseurs, but actually one does try to live on with the "woman."

The above is a strict description of preparing a special kind of tea as I have seen it in my native province, an art generally unknown in North China. In China generally, tea-pots used are much larger, and the ideal colour of tea is a clear, pale, golden yellow, never dark red like English tea.

Of course, we are speaking of tea as drunk by connoisseurs and not as generally served among shopkeepers. No such nicety can be expected of general mankind or when tea is consumed by the gallon by all comers. That is why the author of *Ch'asu*, Hsü Ts'eshu, says, "When there is a big party, with visitors coming and going, one can only exchange with them cups of wine, and among strangers who have just met or among common friends, one should serve only tea of the ordinary quality. Only when our intimate friends of the same temperament have arrived, and we are all happy, all brilliant in conversation and all able to lay aside the formalities, then may we ask the boy servant to build a fire and draw water, and decide the number of stoves and cups to be used in accordance with the company present." It is of this state of things that the author of *Ch'achieh* says, "We are sitting at night in a mountain lodge, and are boiling tea with water from a mountain spring. When the fire attacks the water, we begin to hear a sound similar to the singing of the wind among pine trees. We pour the tea into a cup, and the gentle glow of its light plays around the place. The pleasure of such a moment cannot be shared with vulgar people."

In a true tea lover, the pleasure of handling all the paraphernalia is such that it is enjoyed for its own sake, as in the case of Ts'ai Hsiang, who in his old age was not able to drink, but kept on enjoying the preparation of tea as a daily habit. There was also another scholar, by the name of Chou Wenfu, who prepared and drank tea six times daily at definite hours from dawn to evening, and who loved his pot so much that he had it buried with him when he died.

The art and technique of tea enjoyment, then, consist of the following: first, tea, being most susceptible to contamination of flavours, must be handled throughout with the utmost cleanliness and kept apart from wine, incense, and other smelly substances and people handling such substances. Second, it must be kept in a cool, dry place, and during moist seasons, a reasonable quantity for use must be kept in special small pots, best made of pewter-foil, while the reserve in the big pots is not opened except when necessary, and if a collection gets mouldy, it should be submitted to a gentle roasting over a slow fire, uncovered and constantly fanned, so as to prevent the leaves from turning yellow or becoming discoloured. Third, half of the art of making tea lies in getting good water with a keen edge; mountain spring water comes first, river water second, and well water third; water from the tap, if coming from dams, being essentially mountain water and satisfactory. Fourth, for the appreciation of rare cups, one must have quiet friends and not too many of them at one time. Fifth, the proper colour of tea in general is a pale golden yellow, and all dark red tea must be taken with milk or lemon or peppermint, or anything to cover up its awful sharp taste. Sixth, the best tea has a "return flavour" (*hueiwei*), which is felt about half a minute after drinking and after its chemical elements have had time to act on the salivary glands. Seven, tea must be freshly made and drunk immediately, and if good tea is expected, it should not be allowed to stand in the pot for too long, when the infusion has gone too far. Eight, it must be made with water just brought up to a boil. Nine, all adulterants are taboo, although individual differences may be allowed for people who prefer a slight mixture of some foreign flavour (*e.g.*, jasmine or cassia). Eleven, the flavour expected of the best tea is the delicate flavour of "baby's flesh."

In accordance with the Chinese practice of prescribing the proper moment and surrounding for enjoying a thing, *Ch'asu*, an excellent treatise on tea, reads thus:

Proper moments for drinking tea:

When one's heart and hands are idle.
Tired after reading poetry.
When one's thoughts are disturbed.
Listening to songs and ditties.
When a song is completed.
Shut up at one's home on a holiday.
Playing the *ch'in* and looking over paintings.
Engaged in conversation deep at night.
Before a bright window and a clean desk.
With charming friends and slender concubines.
Returning from a visit with friends.
When the day is clear and the breeze is mild.
On a day of light showers.
In a painted boat near a small wooden bridge.
In a forest with tall bamboos.
In a pavilion overlooking lotus flowers on a summer day.
Having lighted incense in a small studio.
After a feast is over and the guests are gone.
When children are at school.
In a quiet, secluded temple.
Near famous springs and quaint rocks.

Moments when one should stop drinking tea:
At work.
Watching a play.
Opening letters.
During big rain and snow.
At a long wine feast with a big party.
Going through documents.
On busy days.
Generally conditions contrary to those enumerated in the
above section.

Things to be avoided:
Bad water.
Bad utensils.
Brass spoons.
Brass kettles.
Wooden pails (for water).
Wood for fuel (on account of smoke).
Soft charcoal.
Coarse servant.
Bad-tempered maid.
Unclean towels.
All varieties of incense and medicine.

Things and places to be kept away from:
Damp rooms.
Kitchens.
Noisy streets.
Crying infants.
Hotheaded persons.
Quarrelling servants.
Hot rooms.

V. ON SMOKE AND INCENSE

The world to-day is divided into smokers and non-smokers. It
is true that the smokers cause some nuisance to the non-smokers,
but this nuisance is physical, while the nuisance that the non-

smokers cause the smokers is spiritual. There are, of course, a lot of non-smokers who don't try to interfere with the smokers, and wives can be trained even to tolerate their husbands smoking in bed. That is the surest sign of a happy and successful marriage. It is sometimes assumed, however, that the non-smokers are morally superior, and that they have something to be proud of, not realizing that they have missed one of the greatest pleasures of mankind. I am willing to allow that smoking is a moral weakness, but on the other hand, we must beware of the man without weaknesses. He is not to be trusted. He is apt to be always sober and he cannot make a single mistake. His habits are likely to be regular, his existence more mechanical and his head always maintains its supremacy over his heart. Much as I like reasonable persons, I hate completely rational beings. For that reason, I am always scared and ill at ease when I enter a house in which there are no ash-trays. The room is apt to be too clean and orderly, the cushions are apt to be in their right places, and the people are apt to be correct and unemotional. And immediately I am put on my best behaviour, which means the same thing as the most uncomfortable behaviour.

Now the moral and spiritual benefits of smoking have never been appreciated by these correct and righteous and unemotional and unpoetic souls. But since we smokers are usually attacked from the moral, and not the artistic side, I must begin by defending the smoker's morality, which is, on the whole, higher than that of the non-smokers. The man with a pipe in his mouth is the man after my heart. He is more genial, more sociable, has more intimate indiscretions to reveal, and sometimes he is quite brilliant in conversation, and in any case, I have a feeling that he likes me as much as I like him. I agree entirely with Thackeray, who wrote: "The pipe draws wisdom from the lips of the philosopher, and shuts up the mouths of the foolish; it generates a style of conversation contemplative, thoughtful, benevolent, and unaffected."

A smoker may have dirtier finger-nails, but that is no matter when his heart is warm, and in any case a style of conversation contemplative, thoughtful, benevolent, and unaffected is such a rare thing that one is willing to pay a high price to enjoy it. And most important of all, a man with a pipe in his mouth is always happy, and after all, happiness is the greatest of all moral virtues. W. Maggin says that "no cigar smoker ever committed suicide," and it is still truer that no pipe smoker ever quarrels with his wife. The reason is perfectly plain: one cannot hold a pipe between one's teeth and at the same time shout at the top of one's voice. No one has ever been seen doing that. For one naturally talks in a low voice when smoking a pipe. What happens when a husband who is a smoker gets angry is that he immediately lights a cigarette, or a pipe, and looks glum. But that will not be for long. For his emotion has already found an outlet, and although he may want to continue to look angry in order to justify his indignation or sense of being insulted, still he cannot keep it up, for the gentle fumes of the pipe are altogether too agreeable and soothing, and as he puffs the smoke out, he also seems to let out, breath by breath, his stored-up anger. That is why, when a wise wife sees her husband about to fly into a fit of rage, she should gently stick a pipe in his mouth and say, "There! forget about it!" This formula always works. A wife may fail, but a pipe never.

The artistic and literary value of smoking can best be appreciated only when we imagine what a smoker misses when he stops smoking for a short period. Every smoker has, in some foolish moment, attempted to abjure his allegiance to Lady Nicotine, and then after some wrestling with his imaginary conscience, come back to his senses again. I was foolish enough once to stop smoking for three weeks, but at the end of that period my conscience irresistibly urged me on to the right road again. I swore I would never relapse, but would keep on being a devotee and a worshipper at her shrine until my second childhood, when I might conceivably fall prey to some Temperance Society wives. When that unhappy old age arrives, one is of course not responsible for one's actions. But so long as I have a modicum of will-power and moral sense left, I shall not attempt it again. As if I had not seen the folly of it all—the utter immorality of trying to deny oneself the spiritual force and sense of moral well-being provided by this useful invention. For according to Haldane, the great English bio-chemist, smoking counts as one of the four human inventions in the history of mankind that have left a deep biologic influence on human culture.

The story of those three weeks, when I played the coward to my own better self and wilfully denied myself something that I knew to be of great soul-uplifting force, was indeed a disgraceful one. Now that I can look back upon it in a matter-of-fact and rational way, I can hardly understand at all how that fit of moral irresponsibility lasted so long. If I were to detail my spiritual Odyssey by day and by night during those three weeks in the Joycean manner, I am sure it would fill three thousand good Homeric lines in verse, or a hundred and fifty closely printed pages in prose. Of course, the object, to begin with, was ridiculous. Why, in the name of the human race and the universe, should one not smoke? I cannot answer now. But such un-reasonable moods do come to a man sometimes, when one, I suppose, wishes to do something against the grain just for the pleasure of overcoming resistance and in this way use up his momentary excess of moral energy. Beyond this, I cannot account for my sudden and unholy resolution to cut out smoking. In other words, I was giving myself a moral test much in the same manner as people undulge in Swedish gymnastics—movement for the sake of movement, without actually accomplishing any work useful to society. It was apparently this kind of moral luxury that I was giving myself, and that was all.

Of course, in the first three days I felt a queer sinking sensation somewhere along the alimentary canal, especially in the upper part of it. To relieve that queer sensation, I took Double-Mint chewing-gun, good Fukien tea, and Montesserat Lime-Fruit Pastilles. I conquered and killed that sensation in exactly three days. This was the physical, and therefore the easiest and, to my mind, the most contemptible part of the battle. People who think that herein lies the whole of the unholy struggle against smoking have no idea of what they are talking about. They forget that smoking is a spiritual act, and those who have no idea of the spiritual significance of smoking ought never to meddle with the affair. After three days I encountered the second stage, when the real spiritual battle began. Scales fell from my eyes and I saw that there were two races of smokers, one of which never deserved the name at all. For these people the second stage never existed. I began to understand why we hear of the "easy conversions" of many smokers who seem to have given up their smoking without any struggle at all. The fact that they could stop such a habit as easily as they could throw away an old toothbrush shows that they have never really learned to smoke at all. People credit them with a "strong will-power," whereas the fact is these people are never true smokers and have never been so in their lives. For them, smoking is a physical act, like the washing of their faces and brushing of their teeth every morning—a mere physical, animal habit without any soul-satisfying qualities. I doubt whether this race of matter-of-fact people would ever be capable of tuning up their souls in ecstatic response to Shelley's "Skylark" or Chopin's "Nocturne." These people miss nothing by giving up their smoke. They are probably happier reading *Æsop's Fables* with their Temperance wives.

For us true smokers, however, a problem existed of which neither the Temperance wives nor their Æsop-reading husbands have even an inkling. For us, the injustice to oneself and the senselessness of it all soon became apparent. Good sense and reason soon began to revolt against it and ask: for what reason, social, political, moral, physiological or financial, should one consciously use one's will-power to prevent oneself from attaining that complete spiritual well-being, that condition of keen, imaginative perception, and full, vibrant creative energy—a condition necessary to our perfect enjoyment of a friend's conversation by the fireside, or to the creating of real warmth in the reading of an ancient book, or to that bringing forth of a perfect cadence of words and thought from the mind that we know as authorship? At such moments, one instinctively feels that reaching out for a cigarette is the only morally right thing to do, and that sticking a piece of chewing-gum in the mouth instead would be criminally wicked. Of such moments, I can tell only a few here.

My friend B—— had arrived from Peiping and called on me. We had not seen each other for three years. At Peiping, then called Peking, we used to chat and smoke the evenings out, discussing politics and philosophy and modern art. And now he had come, and we were engaged in the fascinating task of rambling reminiscences. We discussed the whole bunch of professors, poets and cranks we used to know in Peiping. At every pointed remark, I was mentally reaching out for a cigar, but instead inhibited myself and only rose up and sat down again. My friend, on the other hand, was rattling along amidst his cigar fumes in perfect contentment. I had told him that I had given up smoking, and I had enough self-respect not to break down right in his presence. But down in my heart, I knew I was not at my best, and was only unjustly making myself look coldly rational, when I wished to partake of the full communion of the two souls with a complete surrender of the emotions. The conversation went on, somewhat one-sidedly, with half of myself there, and then my friend left. I had stuck it all out somewhat grimly. By that fiction of "will-power," I had "won," but I knew only that I was unhappy. A few days later, my friend wrote me on his voyage that he had found me not the old, vibrant, ecstatic self, and suggested that perhaps living in Shanghai had something to do with it. To this day, I have not forgiven myself for failing to smoke that night.

Another night, there was a club meeting of certain "intellectuals," which was usually a time for some furious smoking. After the sumptuous repast, some one of us usually read a paper. This time, the speaker was C——, talking on "Religion and Revolution," a paper punctuated with many brilliant remarks. One was that while Feng Yühsiang had joined the *Northern* Methodist Church, Chiang Kai-shek had chosen to join the *Southern* Methodist Church. Someone therefore suggested that it would not be long before Wu Peifu joined the *Western* Methodists. As such remarks passed round, the density of the smoke grew, and it seemed to me the very atmosphere was laden with wicked, fugitive thoughts. The poet H—— was sitting in the middle, and was trying to send successive smoke-rings up the heavy air, very much as a fish would let forth bubbles of air through the water— lost apparently in his own thoughts and happy. I alone did not smoke, and felt like a God-forsaken sinner. The senselessness of it all was growing very apparent to myself. In that moment of clear vision, I saw that I was mad not to smoke. I tried to think up the reasons why I had decided not to smoke, and none could present itself to me with any validity.

After this, my conscience began to gnaw upon my soul. For, I said to myself, what was thought without imagination, and how could imagination soar on the clipped wings of a drab, non-smoking soul? Then one afternoon I visited a lady. I was mentally prepared for the re-conversion. Nobody else was in the room, and we were apparently going to have a real *tête-à-tête*. The young lady was smoking with one arm resting on her crossed knee, slightly inclined forward, and looking wistful and in her best style. I felt the moment had arrived. She offered the tin, and I took one firmly and slowly from it, knowing that by that act I had recovered from my temporary fit of moral degradation.

I came back, and at once sent my boy to buy a tin of Capstan Minum. On the right side of my desk there was a regular mark, burnt in by my habitually placing burning cigarette ends there. I had calculated that it would take somewhere between seven and eight years to burn through the two-inch desk-top, and had regretted to observe that, after my last disgraceful resolution, it was going to remain at about half a centimetre. It was with great delight, therefore, that I had the pleasure of placing my burning cigarette on that old mark again, where it is happily at work now, trying to resume its long journey ahead.

In contrast with wine, there is comparatively little praise of tobacco in Chinese literature, because smoking as a habit was introduced by Portuguese sailors as late as the sixteenth century. I have ransacked the entire Chinese literature after that period, but have found only a few scattered insignificant lines, quite unworthy of the fragrant weed. An ode in praise of tobacco evidently has to come from some undergraduate of Oxford. The Chinese people, however, always had a very high sense of smell, as is evident in their appreciation of tea and wine and food. In the absence of tobacco, they had developed the art of burning incense, which in Chinese literature was always classified in the same category, and mentioned in the same breath, with tea and wine. From the earliest time, as far back as the Han Dynasty when the Chinese Empire extended its rule to Indo-China, incense brought as tribute from the South began to be used at court and in rich men's homes. In books on the art of living, sections have always been devoted to a discussion of the varieties and quality and preparation of incense. In the chapter on incense in the book *K'aop'an Yüshih,* written by T'u Lung, we have the following description of the enjoyment of incense:

The benefits of the use of incense are manifold. High-minded recluse scholars, engaged in their discussion of truth and religion, feel that it clears their mind and pleases their spirit when they burn a stick of incense. At the fourth watch of the night, when the solitary moon is hanging in the sky, and one feels cool and detached toward life, it emancipates his heart and enables him to whistle leisurely. When one is examining old rubbings of calligraphy before a bright window, or leisurely singing some poetry with a fly-whip in his hand, or when one is reading at night in the lamp light, it helps to drive away the Demon of Sleepiness. You may therefore call it "the ancient companion of the moon." When a lady in red pyjamas is standing by your side, and you are holding her hand around the incense-burner and whispering secrets to each other, it warms your heart and intensifies your love. You may therefore call it "the ancient stimulant of passion." Or when one has waked up from his afternoon nap and is sitting before a closed window on a rainy day and practising calligraphy and tasting the mild flavour of tea, the burner is just getting warm and its subtle fragrance floats about and encircles our bodies. Even better still is it when one wakes up from a drinking party and

[243]

a full moon is shining upon the clear night, and he moves his fingers across the strings or makes a whistle in an empty tower, with the green hills in the distance in full sight, and the half-visible smoke from the remaining embers floats about the door screen. It is also useful for warding off evil smells and the malicious atmosphere of a swamp, useful anywhere and everywhere one goes. The best in quality is *chianan*, but this is difficult to obtain, not accessible to a man living in the mountains. The next best is aloeswood or eaglewood, which is of three grades. The highest grade has too strong a smell, tending to be sharp and pungent; the lowest grade is too dry and also too full of smoke; the middle grade, costing about six or seven cents an ounce, is most soothing and fragrant and can be regarded as exquisite. After one has boiled a pot of tea, he can make use of the burning charcoals and put them in the incense container and let the fire heat it up slowly. In such a satisfying moment one feels like being transported to the heavenly abode in the company of the immortals, entirely oblivious of human existence. Ah, indeed great is the pleasure! People nowadays lack the appreciation of true fragrance and go in for strange and exotic names, trying to outdo one another by having a mixture of different kinds, not realizing that the fragrance of aloeswood is entirely natural, and that the best of its kind has an indescribable subtlety and mildness.

Mao Pichiang in his *Reminiscences of My Concubine,* describing the art of life of this rich poet and his accomplished and understanding mistress, gives various descriptions of their enjoyment of incense, of which the following is one:

My concubine often sat quietly with me in her fragrant bedchamber to sample or judge famous incense. The so-called "palace incense" is seductive in quality, while the popular way of preparing aloeswood is vulgar. The ordinary people often set aloeswood right on the fire and its fragrant fume is soon put out by the burning resin. Thus not only has its fragrance failed to be brought out, but it also leaves a smoky, choking odour behind around one's body. The hard quality with horizontal grains called *hengkoch'en,* has a superb fragrance, being one of the four kinds of aloeswood, but distinguished by having horizontal fibres. There is another variety of this wood, known as *p'englaihsiang,* which is the size of a mushroom and conically shaped, being not yet fully grown. We kept all these varieties, and she burned them on top of fine sand over a slow fire so that no actual smoke was visible. Its subtle perfume permeated the chamber like the smell of *chianan* wood wafted by a breeze, or like that of dew-bedecked roses, or of a piece of amber rubbed hot by friction, or of fragrant liquor being poured into a horn cup. When bedding is perfumed by this method, its fragrance blends with that of the woman's flesh, sweet and intoxicating even in one's dreams.

VI. ON DRINK AND WINE GAMES

I am no drinker and am therefore totally unqualified to talk of wines and liquors. My capacity is three cups of *shaohsing* rice wine, and I am even capable of getting tipsy on a mere glass of beer. This is evidently a matter of natural gift, and the gifts of drinking tea and wine and smoking do not seem to go together. I have found among my friends great drinkers who get sick before they go through half a cigar, while I smoke every waking hour of the day without any appreciable effect, but am not very good with liquors. Anyway, Li Liweng has put down on record his sworn opinion that great drinkers of tea are not fond of wine, and *vice versa.* Li himself was a great tea connoisseur, but confessed that he had no pretensions to being a drinker of wine at all. It is therefore my special delight and comfort to discover so many distinguished Chinese authors that I like who had really but a small capacity for wine, and who said so. It has taken me some time to collect these confessions from their letters or other writings. Li was one, Yüan Tsets'ai, Wang Yüyang, and Yüan Chunglang were others. All of them, however, were people who had "the sentiment for wine" without having an actual capacity for it.

In spite of my disqualification, I still cannot ignore this topic, because, more than anything else, it has made an important contribution to literature, and in the same measure as smoking, wherever the custom of smoking was known, it has greatly helped man's creative power, with considerable lasting results. The pleasure of wine-drinking, especially in what the Chinese call "a little drink," so constantly met with in Chinese literature, had always seemed a mystery to me, until a beautiful Shanghai lady, when half-drunk herself, dilated upon its virtues with such convincing power that I finally thought the condition described must be real. "One just babbles along and babbles along in the state of half-drunkenness, which is the best and happiest state," she said. There seems to be a sense of elation, of confidence in one's power to overcome all obstacles and a heightened sensibility, and man's power of creative thinking, which seems to lie in the borderland of fact and fancy, is brought up to a higher pitch than at normal times. There seems to be a force of self-confidence and emancipation, which is so necessary at the creative moment. The importance of this sense of confidence and emancipation from mere rules and technique will be made quite clear when we come to the section on art.

There is a wise thought in the suggestion that the modern dictators of Europe are so dangerous to humanity because they don't drink. In my reading of current literature of the past year, I have come across no better and wiser and wittier writing than an article by Charles W. Ferguson on "Dictators Don't Drink" in *Harper's* for June, 1937. The thought is worth pursuing, and the writing is so good throughout that I feel tempted to quote it in full but have to refrain from doing so. Mr. Ferguson starts out with the thought that: "Stalin, Hitler and Mussolini are models of sobriety. . . . The men who symbolize tyranny in the modern manner, who are up-to-date rulers of men, are fellows worthy of emulation by any ambitious young man who earnestly wants to get ahead. Every one of the lot would make a good son-in-law and husband. They represent an evangelist's ideal of moral rectitude. . . . Hitler eats no meat, does not drink, does not smoke. To these suffocating virtues he adds the further and more notable virtue of continence. . . . Mussolini is more of a horse in his eating, but he abstains with grim fortitude from spirituous liquors, now and then taking only a tantalizing glass of light wine —but nothing which might seriously interfere with such high matters as the subjugation of an inferior people. Stalin lives frugally in a three-room apartment, dresses inconspicuously and in self-effacing taste, eats frightfully simple meals, and sips brandy like a connoisseur." The question is, what do these facts signify for us? "Do they indicate that we are to-day in the grip of a coterie of men essentially smug, disastrously self-righteous, grimly aware of their tremendous rectitude, and hence so dangerous that the world at large would be better off if it could entice them on a roaring drunk?" . . . "No man could be a dangerous dictator with a hang-over. His sense of God-almighty-ness would be wrecked. He would feel himself to have been gross and humiliated in the presence of his subjects. He would have become one of the masses—one of the lowest of them—and the experience would have done something to his insufferable conceit." The writer thinks that should there be an international cocktail party, attended only by these chosen leaders, in which "the main object would merely be to fry the dignitaries as smoothly and as quickly as possible," the next morning, "Far from being the irreproachable supermen of to-day, the world's best would have become ordinary fellows, afflicted like their meanest followers, and perhaps in a frame of mind to grapple with matters as men and not as demi-gods."

The reason I don't like dictators is that they are inhuman, and anything which is inhuman is bad. An inhuman religion is no religion, inhuman politics is foolish politics, inhuman art is just bad art, and the inhuman way of life is the beast's way of life. This test of *humanness* is universal and can be applied to all walks of life and all systems of thought. The greatest ideal that man can aspire to is not to be a show-case of virtue, but just to be a genial, likeable and reasonable *human being*.

While the Chinese can teach the Westerners about tea,

Westerners can teach the Chinese about wine. A Chinese is easily dazzled by the variety of bottles and labels when he enters an American wine-shop for wherever he goes, in his own country, he sees *shaohsing*, again *shaohsing*, and nothing but *shaohsing*. There are six or seven other varieties, and there are distilled liquors from millet, the *kaoliang*, besides the class of medicinal wines, but the list is soon exhausted. The Chinese have not developed the nicety of serving different drinks with different courses of food. On the other hand, the popularity of *shaohsing* is such at the place giving its name to this wine, that there as soon as a girl is born her parents make a jar of wine, so that by the time she marries she is sure to have at least a jar of wine about twenty years old as part of her trousseau. Hence the name *huatiao*, the proper name for this wine, which means "florally decorated," from the jar decoration.

This lack in the variety of wine they make up for by greater insistence on the proper moment and surrounding for drinking. The feeling for wine is essentially correct. The contrast between wine and tea is expressed in the form that "tea resembles the recluse, and wine resembles the cavalier; wine is for good comradeship, and tea is for the man of quiet virtue." Specifying the proper moods and places for drink, a Chinese writer says: "Formal drinking should be slow and leisurely, unrestrained drinking should be elegant and romantic; a sick person should drink a small quantity, and a sad person should drink to get drunk. Drinking in the spring should take place in a court-yard, in summer in the outskirts of a city, in autumn on a boat and in winter in the house, and at night it should be enjoyed in the presence of the moon."

Another writer says: "There is a proper time and place for getting drunk. One should get drunk before flowers in the daytime, in order to assimilate their light and colour; and one should get drunk in snow in the night-time, in order to clear his thoughts. A man getting drunk when happy at success should sing, in order to harmonize his spirit; and a man getting drunk at a farewell party should strike a musical tone, in order to strengthen his spirit. A drunk scholar should be careful in his conduct, in order to avoid humiliations; and a drunk military man should order gallons and put up more flags, in order to increase his military splendour. Drinking in a tower should take place in summer, in order to profit from the cool atmosphere; and drinking on the water should take place in autumn, in order to increase the sense of elated freedom. These are proper ways of drinking in respect of mood and scenery, and to violate these rules is to miss the pleasure of drinking."

The Chinese attitude toward wine and behaviour during a wine feast is partly incomprehensible or reprehensible to me, and partly commendable. The reprehensible part is the custom of getting pleasure out of forcing a man to drink beyond his capacity. I am not aware that such a practice exists or is common in Western society. It is usual among drinkers to place a mystic value upon the mere quantity of drinking, whether by oneself or by those in the company. No doubt there is a certain hilarity connected with it and such urging is done in a playful or friendly spirit, resulting generally in a lot of noise and hubbub and confusion, which adds to the fun of the occasion. It is beautiful to look at when the company reach a state when they all forget themselves and the guests shout for more wine or leave or exchange their seats, and nobody remembers who is the host and who are the guests. It usually degenerates into a drinking match, played with great pride and subtlety and finesse and always with the desire to see the other fellow under the table. One has to be on the look-out for foul play, and guard against the other party's underhanded tactics. Probably the fun lies there, in the spirit of contest.

The commendable side of Chinese drinking lies in the noise. Eating at a Chinese restaurant sometimes makes one imagine one is attending a football match. How is the volume of noise produced and whence come those noises with beautiful rhythm resembling cheers and yells at a football match? The answer lies in the custom of "guessing fingers," in which each party puts up a number of fingers simultaneously with his opponent and shouts the number of the total sum of fingers that he guesses will be put out by both parties. The numbers "one, two, three, four," and so on, are given in poetic, polysyllabic phrases like "seven stars" (*Ch'ich'iao,* the constellation "Dipper"), or "eight horses" or "eight immortals crossing the sea." The necessity for perfectly timed and simultaneous action in putting out the fingers forces the phrases into definite musical beats or bars, into which the varying syllables have to be compressed, and these are accompanied during the interval by a set introductory phrase occupying another musical bar, and the song is carried on without interruption rhythmically until one party makes a correct conjecture and the other party has to drink a full cup, large or small, or two or three, as previously agreed. Guessing at the total is not mere blind conjecture, but is based on observation of the opponent's habit of sequence or alternation of numbers and demands some quick thinking. The fun and swing of the game depend entirely upon the speed and uninterrupted rhythm of the players.

We have come to the real point about the conception of a wine party, for this alone gives a satisfactory explanation of the length of a Chinese feast, its number of courses and its method of service. One does not sit down at a feast to eat, but to have a good time, provided by telling of stories and jokes and all kinds of literary puzzles and poetic games between the serving of different dishes. The party looks more like a time for oral games, punctuated every five or seven or ten minutes with the appearance of a dish on the table and a bite or two by the company. This produces two effects: first, the vociferousness of oral games undoubtedly helps to let the spirituous liquors evaporate from the system, and secondly, by the time one comes to the end of a feast lasting over an hour, some of the food is already digested, so that the more one eats, the more hungry he becomes. Silence, after all, is a vice during eating; it is mmoral because it is unhygienic. Any foreigner in China who has lasting doubts about the Chinese being a gay and happy people with a touch of Latin gaiety, who still clings to the preconceived notion that the Chinese people are silent, sedate and unemotional, should watch them while eating, for then the Chinaman is in his natural element and his moral perfections are complete. If the Chinaman does not have a good time when he is eating, when does he have a good time?

Famous as the Chinese are for their puzzles, their wine games are less well known. With wine as forfeit, a great variety of games have been invented as excuses for drinking. All Chinese novels dutifully record the names of dishes served at a dinner, and equally dutifully describe the contests of poetry which have no difficulty in filling an entire chapter. The feminist novel *Chinghuayüan* describes so many games among the literary girls (including games in phonetics) as to seem to make these the main theme of the story.

The simplest game is *shehfu,* in which a syllable forming the beginning of one word and the end of another is concealed by joining the other syllables into a word, and the player has to guess at the missing syllable. Thus "drum" being the syllable common to "hum*drum*" and "*drum*stick," the puzzle is given in the combination "hum-stick" and the other party is to supply the missing syllable. Or given "a-starch," the other person is to find the missing middle syllable "corn" in "a*corn-corn*starch." Properly played, the person who has guessed at the middle syllable is not to declare it, but to form a counter-puzzle with the syllable "corn" and simply answer "pop-er" ("pop-*corn-corn*er"), or "pop-muffin," from which the original maker of the puzzle is able to tell whether he has got the correct answer, while it remains a mystery to the rest of those present. Sometimes an answer not originally intended, but even better than the one the maker has in mind, has to be accepted. Both parties can set syllable-puzzles for each other to solve at the same time. Some puzzles are simple and some are carefully concealed, as "a-ounce" for the missing syllable "pron," while "cam-ephant" can be easily detected to contain "el" in "cam*el-el*ephant." Rare and difficult words might be used, and in the practice of scholars, rare historical names might be used, taxing one's scholarship: *e.g.,* names from one of Shakespeare's plays or Balzac's novels.

Variations of literary games are infinite. One popular among scholars is for each person in turn to say a doggerel line of seven words for the other person to follow up with another rhymed line, the poem as a whole degenerating into pure nonsense at the end. Lines usually begin with some comment on some object or person in view, or the scenery. Every person is to say two lines, the first one completing a couplet begun by the preceding person, and the second leading off a new couplet for the successor to finish. The first line sets the rhyme, and the third, fifth, seventh (and so on) lines must keep to it. In the *milieu* of scholars, by whom every name and sentence from the *Four Books* or the *Book of Poetry* has been memorized by heart, demands may be made by the toastmaster for apt quotations illustrating a topic (*e.g.,* "Girl shy," "Girl happy," "Girl cries"). Names of popular ditties, and lines from T'ang poems are often included. Or the party may be required to give names of medicines or flowers that answer to the description in a given title of a popular tune, or, to make the matter appear simpler in English, to give names of medicines or flowers that refer to an article pertaining to women; *e.g.,* *Queen Anne's lace, fox-glove,* etc. Possibility of such combinations depends on the beauty of names given to flowers, medicines, trees, etc., in a language. English family names might, for instance, be given to call up names of popular songs (as an instance "Rockefeller" may suggest "Sit Down, You're Rocking the Boat," and "Whitehead" may suggest "Silver Threads Among the Gold"). The aptness of such juxtapositions depends on one's ingenuity, and the fun of such games lies in spontaneity and fanciful, but not necessarily learned, associations. Names like "Tugwell," "Sitwell" and "Frankfurter" can easily be made to serve any humorous purpose (for the last I suggest "Non-cold Not-Pig"). College students can have a good time making wine games out of their professors' names.

More elaborate games require specially designed chips. In the novel *An Orchid's Dream* one finds, for instance, a description of the following game. Three sets of chips (which may be made of paper) contain the following combination of six persons doing six things in six places:

Dandy	goes horse-riding	thoroughfare
Abbot	says prayers	abbot's room
Lady	embroiders	lady's chamber
Butcher	fights	streets
Courtesan	flirts	red-light district
Beggar	sleeps	cemetery

Chips drawn from the three sets by a person may form the weirdest combinations: thus, "Abbot flirts in a lady's room," "Courtesan says prayers in a cemetery," "Beggar sleeps in the red-light district," "Butcher embroiders in a thoroughfare," "Lady fights in an Abbot's room," etc., all of which would make good newspaper headlines. With some such situation as the main theme, each person is to give a five-word line from a poem, followed by the name of a song, and concluded by a line from the *Book of Poetry*, the whole to make an apt description of the situation.

It is no wonder therefore that a wine feast easily lasts two hours. The object of a dinner is not to eat and drink, but to join in merry-making and to make a lot of noise. For that reason, he who drinks half drinks best. Like the poet T'ao Yüanming playing upon a stringless instrument, for the drinker the sentiment is the thing. And one may enjoy the sentiment for wine without the capacity to drink it. "There are people who cannot read a single word, but have the sentiment for poetry; people who cannot repeat a single prayer but have the sentiment for religion; people who cannot touch a drop but have the sentiment for wine; and people who do not understand a thing about rocks, but have the sentiment for painting." It is such people who are fit company for poets, saints, drinkers and painters.

VII. ON FOOD AND MEDICINE

A broader view of food should regard it essentially as including all things that go to nourish us, just as a broader view of house should include everything pertaining to living conditions. As we are all animals, it is but common sense to say that we are what we eat. Our lives are not in the lap of the gods, but in the lap of our cooks. Hence every Chinese gentleman tries to befriend his cook, because so much of the enjoyment of life lies within his power to give or to take away as he sees fit. Chinese, and I suppose Western, parents always try to befriend the wet-nurse and treat her royally, because they realize that the health of their baby depends on the temper and happiness and general living conditions of the wet-nurse. *Pari passu,* we should give our cooks who feed us the same royal treatment, if we care as much for our own health as we care for that of our babies. If a man will be sensible and one fine morning, when he is lying in bed, count at the tips of his fingers how many things in this life truly give him enjoyment, invariably he will find food is the first one. Therefore it is the invariable test of a wise man whether he has good food at home or not.

The tempo of modern city life is such that we are giving less and less time and thought to the matter of cooking and feeding. A housewife who is at the same time a brilliant journalist can hardly be blamed for serving her husband with canned soup and beans. Nevertheless, it is a pretty crazy life when one eats in order to work and does not work in order to eat. We need a certain kindness and generosity to ourselves before we learn kindness and generosity to others. What good does it do a woman to do some muckraking for the city and improve general social conditions, if she herself has to cook on a two-burner range and allow ten minutes for eating her meal? Confucius undoubtedly would divorce her, as he divorced his wife for failure in good cooking.

The story is not exactly clear as to whether Confucius divorced her or she just had to run away in order to flee from the demands of this fastidious artist of life. For him "rice could never be white enough and mince-meat could never be chopped fine enough." He refused to eat "when meat was not served with its proper sauce," "when it was not cut square," "when its colour was not right," and "when its flavour was not right." I am quite sure that even then his wife could have stood it, but when one day, unable to find fresh food, she sent her son Li to buy wine and cold meat from some delicatessen and be through with it, and he announced that he "would not drink wine that was not home-made, nor taste meat that was bought from the shops," what else could she do except pack up and run away? This insight into the psychology of Confucius' wife is mine, but the severe conditions that he imposed upon his poor wife stand there to-day in the Confucian classics.[1]

Taking, then, the broader view of food as nourishment, the Chinese do not draw any distinction between food and medicine. What is good for the body is medicine and at the same time food. Modern science has only in the last century come to realize the importance of diet in curing diseases, and happily to-day all modern hospitals are well equipped with trained dietitians. If modern doctors would carry it a step farther, and send these dietitians to be trained in China, they might have less use for their glass bottles. An early medical writer, Sun Ssemiao (sixth century, A.D.), says: "A true doctor first finds out the cause of the disease, and having found that out, he tries to cure it first by food. When food fails, then he prescribes medicine." Thus we find the earliest existing Chinese book on food, written by an Imperial physician at the Mongol Court in 1330, regards food essentially as a matter of regimen for health, and makes the introductory remarks: "He who would take good care of his health should be sparing in his tastes, banish his worries, temper his desires, restrain his emotions, take good care of his vital force, spare his words, regard lightly success and failure, ignore sorrows and difficulties, drive away foolish ambitions, avoid great likes and dislikes, calm his vision and his hearing, and be faithful in his internal regimen. How can one have sickness if he does not tire his spirits and worry his soul? Therefore he who would nourish his nature should eat only when he is hungry and not fill himself with food, and he should drink only when he is thirsty and not fill himself with too much drink. He should eat little and between long intervals and not too much and too constantly. He should aim at being a little hungry when well-filled, and being a

[1] *Analects,* Chapter X.

[255]

little well-filled when hungry. Being well-filled hurts the lungs and being hungry hurts the flow of vital energy." This cook book, like all Chinese cook books, therefore reads like a pharmacopœia.

Walking down Honan Road in Shanghai and passing through the shops selling Chinese medicine, one might find it hard to decide whether they sell more medicine than food or more food than medicine. For there one finds cinnamon bark standing side by side with ham, tigers' tendons and beaver kidneys along with sea slugs, and horns of young deer along with mushrooms and Peiping dates. All of them are good for the body and all of them nourish us. The distinction between food and medicine is positively impossible in the case of a bottle of "tiger-tendon and quince wine." Happily a Chinese tonic does not consist of three grammes of hypophosphate and .02 grain of arsenic. It consists of a bowl of black-skinned chicken soup, cooked with *rehmannia lutea*. This is due entirely to the practice of Chinese medicine, for while Western medicines are taken in pills or tablets, Chinese medicines are served as stews and literally called "soups." And Chinese medicine is conceived and prepared in the same manner as ordinary soup, with proper regard for mixing of the flavours and ingredients. There are anywhere from seven or eight to twenty ingredients in a Chinese stew, so designed as to nourish and strengthen the body as a whole, and not to attack the disease solely. For Chinese medicine essentially agrees with the most up-to-date Western medicine in thinking that, when a man's liver is sick, it is not his liver alone but the entire body that is sick. After all, all that medicine can do comes down to the essential principle of strengthening our vital energy, through acting on this most highly complicated system of organs and fluids and hormones called the human body, and letting the body cure itself. Instead of giving patients aspirin tablets, Chinese doctors would therefore ask them to take large bowls of medicinal tea to produce perspiration. And instead of taking quinine tablets, the patients of the future world might conceivably be required to drink a bowl of rich turtle soup with mushrooms, cooked with pieces of cinchona bark. The dietetics department of a modern hospital will have to be enlarged, and the future hospital itself will very nearly resemble a sanatorium-restaurant. Eventually we have to come to a conception of health and disease by which the two merge into each other, when men eat in order to prevent disease instead of taking medicine in order to cure it. This point is not stressed enough in the West, for the Westerners go to see a doctor only when they are sick, and do not see him when they are well. Before that time comes, the distinction between medicine which nourishes the body and medicine which cures disease will have to be abolished.

We have, therefore, to congratulate the Chinese people on their happy confusion of medicine and food. This makes their medicine less of a medicine, but makes their food more of a food. There seems to be a symbolic significance in the fact that the God of Gluttony appeared even in our semi-historical period, the God *T'aot'ieh* being found to-day as a favourite motif among our earliest bronze and stone sculptures. The spirit of *T'aot'ieh* is in us. It makes our pharmacopœias resemble our cook books and our cook books resemble a pharmacopœia, and it makes the rise of botany and zoology as branches of the natural science impossible, for the Chinese scientists are thinking all the time of how a snake, a monkey, or a crocodile's flesh or a camel's hump would taste. True scientific curiosity in China is a gastronomic curiosity.

With the confusion of medicine and magic, found in all savage tribes, and with the Chinese Taoists making the "nourishment or life" and the search after immortality or long life their central object, we find that food and medicine often lie in their hands. In the Imperial Cook Book of the Mongol Dynasty referred to above, *Yinshan Chengyao,* there are chapters devoted to preserving long life and warding off disease. With the Taoist passionate devotion to Nature, the tendency is always to emphasize fruits and food of a vegetarian nature. There is a sort of combination of poetry and Taoist detachment from life, regarding the eating of fresh lotus seeds with their delicate flavour born of the dew as the height of a scholar's refined pleasure. He would drink the dew itself, if he could. In this class belong the seeds of pine trees, arrowroot and

Chinaroot, which are all regarded as tending toward long life, because they clarify one's heart and purify one's soul. One is not supposed to have mortal desires, like the desire for women, when eating a lotus seed. More like medicine and constantly taken as part of one's food and highly valued for prolonging life are *asparagus lucidus, rehmannia lutea, lycium chinense, atratylis ovata, polygonatum giganteum,* and particularly *ginseng* and *astragalus hoantely.*

The Chinese pharmacopœia offers an immense field waiting for Western scientific research. Western medicine has only within the past decade discovered the blood-building value of liver, while Chinese have all along regarded it as an important tonic for old people. I have a suspicion that when a Western butcher kills a pig, he throws away all the parts that have the greatest nourishing food value—kidneys, stomachs, intestines (which must be full of gastric juice), blood, bone marrow and brains. It is beginning to be discovered that the bone is the place where the red corpuscles of one's blood are manufactured, and I cannot help thinking the throwing away of mutton bones and pigs' bones and cows' bones without stewing them into a fine soup is a terrific waste of food value.

There are many Western foods that I like, and first of all I must mention the honeydew melon, because its suggestion of dew is so Chinese. Also, if an ancient Chinese Taoist were given a grapefruit, he might imagine that he had discovered the elixir of immortality, for it was the exotic flavour of strange and unknown fruits that the Taoists were looking for. Tomato juice must be ranked as one of the greatest Western discoveries in the twentieth century, for the Chinese, like the Westerners of a century ago, used to consider tomatoes not fit for eating. Next comes the eating of raw celery, which comes nearest to the Chinese idea of eating food for texture, as with bamboo shoots. Asparagus is fine, when it is not green, but it is not unknown in China. Finally I must confess to a great liking for English roast beef, and for all roasts. Every food is good when cooked and tasted in its own country and in its proper season. I have always liked American food when it is served in American homes, but have never yet tasted food that impressed me as good in the best hotels of New York. The fault is not due to hotels or restaurants, for even in Chinese restaurants it is impossible to get good food unless with long notice and unless it is prepared with individual care.

On the other hand, there are glaring deficiencies in American and European cuisine. Far ahead in bakery and the making of sweets and desserts, Western cuisine strikes one as being pretty dull and insipid and extremely limited in variety. After eating in any hotel or boarding house or steamship for three weeks, and after one has had chicken *à la king,* prime ribs of beef and lamb chops and fillet for the thirteenth time, the food begins to pall on one's palate. The most undeveloped branch of Western cooking is that of preparing vegetables. In the first place, vegetables are extremely limited in variety; in the second place, they are merely boiled in water; and in the third place, they are always over-cooked until they lose their colour and look mushy. Spinach, the calamity of all children, is never cooked properly; it is cooked until it becomes mushy, whereas if it is fried on a very hot pan with oil and salt and taken away before it loses its crispness, it is one of the most palatable of foods. Lettuce prepared in the same manner is also delightful, the only consideration being not to allow it to stand in the pan for too long. Chicken liver is con-sidered a delicacy in the West, and even grilled lamb kidneys, but there is a large number of foods of the same class which have not even been experimented upon. This explains the lack of variety in Western food. Fried chicken gizzard, along with fried chicken liver, dipped in salt, is among the commonest dishes in China. Carp's head, with its delicate flesh around the cheeks and jowl, is served as a special dish of great delicacy. Pig's tripe is my favourite food, and for that matter, certain parts of the ox's tripe. It makes a delicious soup with noodles, or it may be thrown into boiling soup over an extremely hot fire and immediately taken out, so that it has a crispness almost like that of raw celery. Large snails (meaning only the thick covering at their mouth) are a delicacy much sought after in France, and they are also a delicacy in China.

In taste and texture and resistance to the teeth, they are practically the same as abalones and scallops.

The lack of variety of soups is due to two causes. First, the lack of experiment on mixtures of vegetables with meat. By combinations and permutations, five or six ingredients, like dried shrimp, mushroom, bamboo-shoot, melon, pork, etc., can give a hundred varieties of different soups. Melon soup is unknown in the West, and yet, made with different varieties and prepared with a dash of dried shrimp, it is one of the most delicious dishes in summer. Secondly, the lack of variety in soup is due to failure to make full use of sea food. Scallops are always fried in the West, but dried scallops are one of the most important elements for making good soup, and so is abalone. As for clam chowder, I never smell the clam in it, and one, of course, never sees turtle flesh in turtle soup. A real turtle soup, cooked until it is sticky on the lips, is one of the favourite Cantonese dishes, sometimes being prepared with the webbed feet of ducks or geese. The Shaohsing people of Chekiang have a favourite dish called "the big corners," consisting of the wings and legs of chicken, because there is a happy combination of skin and tendon and meat in chicken wings and feet. The best soup I have tasted, however, is the soup of bastard carp and small soft-shell clams combined. The test of soup generally made from shell food is that it should not be oily.

As an instance of Chinese feeling about food, I may quote here from Li Liweng's essay on "Crabs" in the section on food in his *Art of Living*.

There is nothing in food and drink whose flavour I cannot describe with the utmost understanding and imagination. But as for crabs, my heart likes them, my mouth relishes them, and I can never forget them for a year and a day, but find it impossible to describe in words why I like them, relish them, and can never forget them. Ah, this thing has indeed become for me a weakness in food, and is in itself a strange phenomenon of the universe. All my days I have been extremely fond of it. Every year before the crab season comes, I set aside some money for the purpose and because my family say that "crab is my life," I call this money "my life ransom." From the day it appears on the market to the end of the season, I have never missed it for a night. My friends who know this weakness of mine always invite me to dinner at this season, and I therefore call October and November "crab autumn." . . . I used to have a maid quite devoted to attending to the care and preparation of crabs and I called her "my crab maid." Now she is gone! O crab! my life shall begin and end with thee!

The reason that Li finally gave for his appreciation of crab was that it was perfect in the three requisites of food—*colour, fragrance* and *flavour*. Li's feeling about crabs is quite generally shared by Chinese of all classes to-day, the kind eaten being from freshwater lakes.

For me, the philosophy of food seems to boil down to three things: freshness, flavour and texture. The best cook in the world cannot make a savoury dish unless he has fresh things to cook with, and any good cook can tell you that half the art of cooking lies in buying. Yüan Tsets'ai, the great epicure and poet of the seventeenth century, wrote beautifully about his cook as a man carrying himself with great dignity who absolutely refused to cook a dish ordered unless the thing was in its best season. The cook had a bad temper, but confessed that he continued to serve the poet because the latter understood flavour. To-day there is a cook over sixty years old in Szechuen who must be courteously invited to prepare a dinner for some special occasion, and who must be given a week's notice to collect and buy things and must be left entirely free to be the sole lord and judge of the menu to be served.

For the common people who cannot afford expensive cooks, there is comfort in the knowledge that anything tastes good in its season, and that it is always better to depend upon nature than upon culture to furnish us with the greatest epicurean delights. For this reason, people who have their own garden or who live in the country may be quite sure that they have the best food, although they may not have the best cook. For the same reason, food ought to be tasted in its place of origin before any judgment can be pronounced upon it. But for a wife who does not know how to buy fresh food or a man who is willing to put up with cold storage foods, any discussion of epicurean values is futile.

The texture of food, as regards tenderness, elasticity, crispness and softness, is largely a matter of timing and adjusting the heat of the fire. Chinese restaurants can produce dishes not possible in the home because they are equipped with a fine oven. As for flavour, there are clearly two classes of food, those that are best served in their own juice, without adulteration except salt or soya bean sauce, and those that taste best when they are combined with the flavour of another food. Thus, in the case of fish, fresh mandarin fish or trout should be prepared in its natural juice to get its full flavour, while more fatty fish like the shad tastes best with Chinese pickled beans. The American succotash is an example of the perfect combination of tastes. There are certain flavours in nature which seem to be made for each other and reach their highest degree of delectability only in combination with each other. Bamboo-shoot and pork seem to make a perfect pair, each borrowing its fragrance from the other and lending it in return its own. Ham somehow combines well with the sweet flavour, and one of the proudest dishes of my cook in Shanghai is ham with rich Peking golden dates, steamed together in a casserole. So does black tree fungus combine perfectly with duck's egg in soup, and Yew York lobster combine with Chinese pickled bean-curd sauce (*nanju*). In fact, there is a large class of eatables whose chief function seems to be to lend their flavour to others— mushroom, bamboo-shoots, Szechuen *tsats'ai,* etc. And there is a large class of food, most valued by the Chinese, which have no flavour of their own, and depend entirely on borrowing from others.

The three necessary characteristics of the most expensive Chinese delicacies are that they must be *colourless, odourless,* and *flavourless.* These articles are shark's fin, birds' nest and the "silver fungus." All of them are gelatinous in quality and all have no colour, taste or smell. The reason why they taste so wonderful is because they are always prepared in the most expensive soup possible.

VIII. SOME CURIOUS WESTERN CUSTOMS

One great difference between Oriental and Occidental civilizations is that the Westerners shake each other's hands, while we shake our own. Of all the ridiculous Western customs, I think that of shaking hands is one of the worst. I may be very progressive and able to appreciate Western art, literature, American silk stockings, Parisian perfumes and even British battleships, but I cannot see how the progressive Europeans could allow this barbarous custom of shaking hands to persist to the present day. I know there are private groups of individuals in the West who protest against this custom, as there are people who protest against the equally ridiculous custom of wearing hats or collars. But these people don't seem to be making any headway, being apparently taken for men who make mountains of molehills and waste their energy on trivialities. I am one of these men who are always interested in trivialities. As a Chinese, I am bound to feel more strongly against this Western custom than the Europeans, and prefer always to shake my own hands when meeting or parting from people, according to the time-honoured etiquette of the Celestial Empire.

Of course, everyone knows this custom is the survival of the barbaric days of Europe, like the other custom of taking off one's hat. These customs originated with the medieval robber barons and chevaliers, who had to lift their visors or take off their steel gauntlets to show that they were friendly or peacefully disposed toward the other fellow. Of course it is ridiculous in modern days to repeat the same gestures when we are no longer wearing helmets or gauntlets, but survivals of barbaric customs will always persist, as witness, for instance, the persistence of duels down to the present day.

I object to this custom for hygienic and many other reasons. Shaking hands is a form of human contact subject to the finest variations and distinctions. An original American graduate student could very well write a doctorate dissertation on a "Time-and-motion Study of the Varieties of Hand-Shaking," reviewing it, in the approved fashion, as regards pressure, duration of time, humidity, emotional response, and so forth, and further studying it under all its possible variations as regards sex, the height of the person concerned (giving us undoubtedly many "types of marginal differences"), the condition of the skin as affected by professional work and social classes, etc. With a few charts and tables of percentages, I am sure a candidate would have no difficulty in getting a Ph.D., provided he made the whole thing sufficiently abstruse and tiresome.

Now consider the hygienic objections. The foreigners in Shanghai, who describe our copper coins as regular reservoirs of bacteria and will not touch them, apparently think nothing of shaking hands with any Tom, Dick, or Harry in the street. This is really highly illogical, for how are you to know that Tom, Dick or Harry has not touched those coppers which you shun like poison? What is worse is, sometimes you may see a consumptive-looking man who hygienically covers his mouth with his hands while coughing and in the next moment stretches his hand to give you a friendly shake. In this respect, our celestial customs are really more scientific, for in China, each of us shakes his own hand. I don't know what was the origin of this Chinese custom, but its advantage from a medical or hygienic point of view cannot be denied.

Then there are æsthetic and romantic objections to handshaking. When you put out your hand, you are at the mercy of the other person, who is at liberty to shake it as hard as he likes and hold it as long as he likes. As the hand is one of the finest and most responsive organs in our body, every possible variety of pressure is possible. First you may have the Y.M.C.A. type of handshaking; the man pats you on the shoulder with one hand and gives you a violent shake with the other until all your joints are ready to burst within you. In the case of a Y.M.C.A. secretary who is at the same time a baseball player with a powerful grip—and the two often go together—his victim often does not know whether to scream or to laugh. Coupled with his straightforward self-assertive manner, this type of handshaking practically seems to say, "Look here, you are now in my power. You must buy a ticket for the next meeting or promise to take back with you a pamphlet by Sherwood Eddy before I'll let your hand go." Under such circumstances I am always very prompt with my pocket-book.

Coming down the scale, we find different varieties of pressure, from the indifferent handshake which has utterly lost all meaning, to that kind of furtive, tremulous, retiring handshake which indicates that the owner is afraid of you, and finally to the elegant society lady who condescends to offer you the very tip of her fingers in a manner that almost suggests that you look at her red-painted finger-nails. All kinds of human relationships, therefore, are reflected in this form of physical contact between two persons. Some novelists profess that you can tell a man's character from his type of handshake, distinguishing between the assertive, the retiring, the dishonest and the weak and clammy hands which instinctively repel one. I wish to be spared the trouble of analysing a person's moral character every time I have to meet him, or reading from the degree of his pressure the increase or decrease of his affection towards me.

More senseless still is the custom of taking off one's hat. Here we find all kinds of nonsensical rules of etiquette. Thus a lady should keep her hat on during church service or during afternoon tea indoors. Whether this custom of wearing hats in church has anything to do with the customs of Asia Minor in the first century A.D. or not, I do not profess to know, but I suspect it comes from a senseless following of St. Paul's injunction that women should have their heads covered in church while men should not, being based thus on an Asiatic philosophy of sexual inequality which the Westerners have so long repudiated. For the men, there is that ridiculous custom of taking off one's hat in a lift when there are ladies in it. There can be absolutely no defence for this meaningless custom. In the first place, the lift is but a continuation of the corridor, and if men are not required to take off their hats in a corridor, why should they be made to do so in a lift? Anyone would see the utter senselessness of it all if he happens to pass from one floor to another in the same building with a hat on. In the second place, the lift cannot by any logical analysis be distinguished from other types of conveyance, the motor-car, for instance. If a man can, with a free conscience, keep his hat on while driving in a motor-car in the company of ladies, why should he be forbidden from doing the same in a lift?

All in all, this is a very crazy world of ours. But I am not surprised. After all, we see human stupidity around us everywhere, from the stupidity of modern international relations to that of the modern educational system. Mankind may be intelligent enough to invent the radio and wireless telephones, but mankind is simply not intelligent enough to stop wars, nor will ever be. So I am willing to let stupidity in the more trivial things go by, and content merely to be amused.

IX. THE INHUMANITY OF WESTERN DRESS

In spite of the popularity of Western dress among the modern Turks, Egyptians, Hindus, Japanese and Chinese, and in spite of its universality as the official diplomatic costume in the entire world, I still cling to the old Chinese dress. Many of my best friends have asked me why I wear Chinese instead of foreign dress. And those people call themselves my friends! They might just as well ask me why I stand on two legs. The two happen to be related, as I shall try to show. Why must I give a reason for wearing the only "human" dress in the world? Need anyone who in his native garb practically goes about the house and outside in his pyjamas and slippers give reasons why he does not like to be encased in a system of suffocating collars, vests, belts, braces and garters? The prestige of the foreign dress rests on no more secure basis than the fact that it is associated with superior gunboats and Diesel engines. It cannot be defended on æsthetic, moral, hygienic or economic grounds. Its superiority is simply and purely political.

Is my attitude merely a pose, or symptomatic of my progress in knowledge of Chinese philosophy? I hardly think so. In taking this attitude, I am supported by all the thinking persons of my generation in China. The Chinese dress is worn by all Chinese gentlemen. Furthermore, all the scholars, thinkers, bankers and people who made good in China either have never worn foreign dress, or have swiftly come back to their native dress the moment they have "arrived" politically, financially or socially. They have swiftly come back because they are sure of themselves and no longer feel the need for a coat of foreign appearance to hide their bad English or their inferior mental outfit. No Shanghai kidnapper would think of kidnapping a Chinese in foreign clothes, for the simple reason that he is not worth the candle. Who are the people wearing foreign clothes to-day in China? The college students, the clerks earning a hundred dollars a month, the political busybodies who are always on the point of landing a job, the *tangpu*[1] young men, the *nouveaux riches*, the nincompoops, the feeble-minded. . . . And then, of course, last but not least, we have Henry P'uyi, who has the incomparably bad taste to adopt a foreign name, foreign dress, and a pair of dark spectacles. That outfit of his alone will kill all his chances of coming back to the Dragon Throne, even if he has all the bayonets of the Mikado behind him. For you may tell any lies to the Chinese people, but you cannot convince them that the fellow who wears a foreign dress and dark spectacles is their "emperor." So long as he wears that foreign dress and so long as he calls himself Henry, Henry will be perfectly at home in the dockyards of Liverpool, but not on a Dragon Throne.

Now the philosophy behind Chinese and Western dress is that the latter tries to reveal the human form, while the former tries to conceal it. But as the human body is essentially like the monkeys', usually the less of it revealed the better. Think of Gandhi in his loin-cloth! Only in a world of people blind in sense of beauty is the foreign dress tolerable. It is a platitude that the perfect human figure rarely exists. Let anyone who

[1] Kuomintang party office.

doubts this go to Coney Island and see how beautiful real human forms are. But the Western dress is so designed that any man in the street can tell whether your waistline is thirty-two or thirty-eight. Why must one proclaim to the world that his waist-line is thirty-two, and if it happens to be above normal, why can he not have the right to make it his private affair?

That is why I also believe in the foreign dress for young women of good figure between twenty and forty and for all children whose natural bodily rhythm has not yet been subjected to our uncivilized form of living. But to demand that all men and women reveal their figure to the eyes of the world is another story. While the graceful woman in foreign evening dress shines and charms in a way not even remotely dreamed of by the Oriental costume-makers, the average over-fed and over-slept lady of forty who finds herself in the golden horseshoe at an opera *première* is also one of the eyesores invented by the West. The Chinese dress is kinder to them. Like death, it levels the great and the small, the beautiful and the ugly. The Chinese dress is therefore more democratic.

So much for the æsthetic considerations. Now for the reasons of hygiene and common sense. No sane-minded man can pretend that the collar, that survival of Cardinal Richelieu's and Sir Walter Raleigh's times, is conducive to health, and all thinking men in the West have repeatedly protested against it. While the Western female dress has achieved a large measure of comfort in this respect formerly denied to the fair sex, the male human neck is still considered by the Western educated public as so ugly and immoral and socially unpresentable that it must be concealed as much as his waist-line must be revealed. That satanic device makes proper ventilation impossible in summer, proper protection against cold impossible in winter and proper thinking impossible at all times.

From the collar downwards, it is a story of continuous and unmitigated outrage of common sense. The clever foreigner who can invent Neon lights and Diesel engines has not enough common sense to see that the only part of his body which is free is his head. But why go into details—the tight-fitting underwear, which interferes with free ventilation, the vest which allows for no bending of the body, and the braces or the belt which allow for no natural difference in different states of nutrition? Of these, the least logical is the vest. Anybody who studies the natural forms of the naked human body knows that, except when in a perfectly straight position, the lines of the back and the front are never equal. Anyone who wears a stiff shirt-front also knows by experience that it bulges every time the body bends forward. But the vest is designed on the assumption that these lines remain always equal, which compels one to keep in a perfectly straight position. As no one actually lives up to this standard, the consequence is that the end of the vest either protrudes or falls into creases pressing on the body at every movement. In the case of a male victim of obesity, the vest describes a protruding arc and invariably ends in the air, from which point the receding arc is taken up by the belt and the pants. Can anything invented by the human mind be more grotesque? Is it any wonder that a nudist movement has sprung up as a protest and a reaction against this grotesque bondage of the human body?

But if mankind were still in the quadruped stage, there could be some justification for the belt, which then could be adjusted as the saddle strap is adjusted on the horse. But while mankind has adopted the erect position, his belt is designed on the assumption that he is still a quadruped, just as anatomy of the peritoneal muscles shows that these are designed for the quadruped position with all weight suspended from the backbone. The disastrous consequence of this erect position is that, while human mothers are liable to miscarriage and abortion, from which animals are exempt, the belt of the male dress also has a tendency to gravitate downwards. The only way to prevent this is to keep the belt so tight that it does not gravitate, but also with the result that it interferes with all natural intestinal movements.

I am quite convinced that when the Westerners have made more progress in the impersonal things, they will one day also come to devote more time to their personal things and exercise more common sense in the matter of dress. Western men are paying a severe penalty for their conservatism in this matter of dress and for their fear of innovation, while Western women long ago achieved simplicity and common sense in their dress. To speak not for the immediate decades but for the distant centuries, I am quite convinced that men will eventually evolve a dress for themselves that is logical and consistent with their biped position, as is already achieved in women's dress. Gradually all cumbersome belts and braces will be eliminated and men's dress will be so designed that it hangs naturally down from the shoulder in a sort of graceful and fitting form. There will be no meaningless padded shoulders and lapels, and in place of the present design there will be a much more comfortable type of dress, more nearly resembling the house jacket. As I see it, the great difference, then, between men's dress and women's dress will be only that men wear pants while women wear skirts. So far as the upper part of the body is concerned, the same essential consideration of ease and comfort will prevail. Men's necks will be just as free as women's, the vest will correspondingly disappear and the jacket will be used exactly to the same extent as women's coats are used to-day. Most of the time men will go about without their jackets as women are doing to-day.

This involves, of course, a revolution in our present conception of the shirt. Instead of being something to be worn inside, it will be made of darker material and worn outside, from the lightest silk to the heaviest woollen material, according to the season, and cut accordingly for better appearance. And then they can slip the jacket on, whenever they want to, but more for consideration of the weather than for formality, for this future apparel will be practically correct and acceptable in any company. In order to destroy the insufferable belts and suspenders, there will be a kind of combination shirt and pants, to be slipped over the head as women's dresses are slipped over now, with certain adjustments, pretended or real, around the waist to bring out the figure better.

Even at present, a reform is possible for the elimination of the belt or suspenders while maintaining the present pattern of men's dress. The whole principle is: weight should be suspended from the shoulders and evenly distributed, and should not be clamped on to the vertical wall of the abdomen by sheer force of adhesion, friction and compression, and the human male waist should be liberated from its duty as a bottle-neck, to the end that a system of loose-fitting undergarments may become possible. If we start on the road of progress *without the vest,* men can just have their shirts buttoned to the pants, as children's dresses are to-day. In time, then, as the shirt becomes outside apparel, it will be made of finer material, probably of the same colour and quality as the pants, or matching them. Or if we start on dress reform with the vest as a necessary part, we should have a combination vest and pants, preserving their present form, but made of one piece, the back of the vest being reduced to two diagonal straps. Even at the present time, belts and suspenders can easily be eliminated by having six little appendages, four in front and two behind, sewed on to the inside of the vest, with buttonholes to fit into the buttons on the pants. As the vest comes outside the pants, there will be no visible difference from vests as they are worn at present. Once the innovations are started and men begin to think that their present dress designs are not co-eternal with the universe, it will be possible to gradually modify and eliminate the vest itself, by having this combination garment so cut as to be better looking than an overall, but still going on the same principle.

It requires no imagination to see that for adjustment to varying climatic conditions, the Chinese dress is also the only logical mode. While the Westerner is compelled to wear underwear, one shirt, perhaps one vest and one coat, whether the weather temperature is below zero or above a hundred, the Chinese dress is infinitely flexible. There is a story told of the fond Chinese mother who puts one gown on her boy when he sneezes once, puts on another when he sneezes twice, and puts on a third when he sneezes thrice. No Western mother can do that; she would be at her wit's end at the third sneeze. All she can do is to call for the doctor. I am led to believe that the only thing which saves the Chinese nation from extermination by tuberculosis and pneumonia is the cotton-padded gown.

X. ON HOUSE AND INTERIORS

The word "house" should include all the living conditions or the physical environment of one's house. For everyone knows it is more important in selecting a house to see what one looks out on from the house than what one sees in it. The location of the country and its surrounding landscape are the thing. I have seen rich men in Shanghai very proud of a tiny plot of land that they own, which includes a fish-pond about ten feet across and an artificial hill that takes ants three minutes to crawl to the top, not knowing that many a poor man lives in a hut on a mountain side and owns the entire view of the hillside, the river and the lake as his private garden. There is absolutely no comparison between the two. There are houses situated in such beautiful scenery up in the mountains that there is no point whatsoever in fencing off a piece of land as one's own, because wherever he wanders, he owns the entire landscape, including the white clouds nestling against the hills, the birds flying in the sky and the natural symphony of falling cataracts and birds' song. That man is rich, rich beyond comparison with any millionaire living in a city. A man living in a city may see sailing clouds, too, but he seldom sees them actually, and when he does, the clouds are not set off against an outline of blue hills, and then, what is the point of seeing clouds? The background is all wrong.

The Chinese conception of house and garden is therefore determined by the central idea that the house itself is only a detail forming a part of the surrounding country, like a jewel in its setting, and harmonizing with it. For this reason, all signs of artificiality must be hidden as much as possible, and the rectilinear lines of the walls must be hidden or broken by overhanging branches. A perfectly square house, shaped like a magnified piece of brick, is justifiable in a factory building, because it is a factory building where efficiency is the first consideration. But a perfectly square house for a home to live in is an atrocity of the first order. The Chinese conception of an ideal home has been succinctly expressed by a writer in the following manner:

Inside the gate there is a footpath and the footpath must be winding. At the turning of the footpath there is an outdoor screen and the screen must be small. Behind the screen there is a terrace and the terrace must be level. On the banks of the terrace there are flowers and the flowers must be fresh. Beyond the flowers is a wall and the wall must be low. By the side of the wall, there is a pine tree and the pine tree must be old. At the foot of the pine tree there are rocks and the rocks must be quaint. Over the rocks there is a pavilion and the pavilion must be simple. Behind the pavilion are bamboos and the bamboos must be thin and sparse. At the end of the bamboos there is a house and the house must be secluded. By the side of the house there is a road and the road must branch off. At the point where several roads come together there is a bridge and the bridge must be tantalizing to cross. At the end of the bridge there are trees and the trees must be tall. In the shade of the trees there is grass and the grass must be green. Above the grass plot there is a ditch and the ditch must be slender. At the top of the ditch there is a spring and the spring must gurgle. Above the spring there is a hill and the hill must be deep. Below the hill there is a hall and the hall must be square. At the corner of the hall there is a vegetable garden and the vegetable garden must be big. In the vegetable garden there is a stork and the stork must dance. The stork announces that there is a guest and the guest must not be vulgar. When the guest arrives there is wine and wine must not be declined. During the service of the wine, there is drunkenness and the drunken guest must not want to go home.

The charm of a house lies in its individuality. Li Liweng has several chapters on houses and interiors in his book on the *Art of Living,* and in the introductory remarks he emphasizes the two points of *familiarity* and *individuality.* Familiarity, I feel, is more important than individuality. For no matter how big and pretentious a house a man may have there is always one particular room that he likes and really *lives* in, and that is invariably a small, unpretentious room, disorderly and familiar and warm. So says Li:

A man cannot live without a house as his body cannot go about without clothing. And as it is true of clothing that it should be cool in summer and warm in winter, the same thing is true of a house. It is all very imposing to live in a hall twenty or thirty feet high with beams several feet across, but such a house is suitable for summer and not for winter. The reason why one shivers when he enters an official's mansion is because of its space. It is like wearing a fur coat too broad for girdling around the waist. On the other hand, a poor man's house with low walls and barely enough space to put one's knees in, while having the virtue of frugality, is suitable for the owner, but not suitable for entertaining guests. That is why we feel cramped and depressed without any reason when we enter a poor scholar's hut. . . . I hope that the dwellings of officials will not be too high and big. For a house and the people living in it must harmonize as in a picture. Painters of landscape have a formula saying, "ten-feet mountains and one-foot trees; one-inch horses and bean-sized human beings." It would be inappropriate to draw trees of two or three feet on a hill of ten feet, or to draw a human being the size of a grain of rice or millet riding on a horse an inch tall. It would be all right for officials to live in halls twenty or thirty feet high if their bodies were nine or ten feet. Otherwise the taller the building the shorter the man appears, and the wider the space the thinner the man seems. Would it not be much better to make his house a little smaller and his body a little stouter? . . .

I have seen high officials or relatives of officials who throw away thousands and ten thousands of dollars to build a garden and who begin by telling the architect, "For the pavilion, you copy the design of So-and-so, and for the covered terrace overlooking a pond, you follow the model of So-and-so, down to its last detail." When the mansion is completed, its owner will proudly tell people that every detail of the house, from its doors and windows to its corridors and towers, has been copied from some famous garden without the slightest deviation. Ah, what vulgarity! . . .

Luxury and expensiveness are the things most to be avoided in architecture. This is so because not only the common people, but also the princes and high officials, should cherish the virtue of simplicity. For the important thing in a living house is not splendour, but refinement; not elaborate decorativeness, but novelty and elegance. People like to show off their rich splendour, not because they love it but because they are lacking in originality, and, besides trying to show off, they are at a total loss to invent something else. That is why they have to put up with mere splendour. Ask two persons to put on two new dresses, one simple and elegant and original, and the other rich and decorative, but common. Will not the eye of spectators be directed to the original dress rather than to the common dress? Who doesn't know the value of silk and brocade and gauze, and who has not seen them? But a simple, plain dress with a novel design will attract the eyes of spectators because they have never seen it before.

There are points about house designs and interiors which Li Liweng goes into fully in his book. The subjects he deals with cover houses, windows, screens, lamps, tables, chairs, curios, cabinets, beds, trunks, and so on. Being an exceptionally original and inventive mind, he has something new to say on every topic, and some of his inventions have become a part of the Chinese tradition to-day. The most outstanding contributions are his letter paper, which were sold in his lifetime as "*Chiehtseyüan letter paper*," and his windows and partition designs. Although his book on the *Art of Living* is not so generally well known, he is always remembered in connection with the *Chiehtseyüan Painting Patterns,* the most generally used beginners' handbook of Chinese painting, and for his *Ten Comedies,* for he was a dramatist, musician, epicure, dress designer, beauty expert and amateur inventor all combined.

Li had new ideas about beds. He said that whenever he moved into a new house, the first thing he looked for and attended to was the bed. The Chinese bed has always been a curtained and framed affair, resembling a large cabinet or a small room in itself, with poles, shelves and drawers built around the pole, for placing books, tea-pots, shoes, stockings and odds and ends. Li conceived the idea that one should have flower-stands as well in the bed. His method was to build a thin, tiny piece of wooden shelf, over a foot wide but only two or three inches deep, and have it fixed to the embroidered curtain. According to him, the wooden shelf should be wrapped up in embroidered silk to resemble a floating cloud, with certain irregularities. There he would put whatever flowers were in season, or burn "Dragon's Saliva" incense, or keep "Buddha's Fingers" or quince for their fragrance. Thus, he says: "My body is no longer a body, but a butterfly flitting about and sleeping and eating[1] among flowers, and the man is no longer a man but a fairy, walking about and sitting and lying in a paradise. I have thus once in my sleep felt in a half-awake state the fragrance of plum flowers so that my throat and teeth and cheeks were permeated with this subtle fragrance, as if it came out from my chest. And I felt my body so light that I almost thought I was not living in a human world. After waking up I told my wife, 'Who are we to enjoy this happiness? Are we not thus "curtailing" the entire lot of happiness allowed

[1] A Chinese rich man having a good time with his concubine at night often has food and wine served in bed by attending maidservants.

[276]

to us?'[1] My wife replied, 'Perhaps that's the reason why we always remain poor and low! The thing is true and not a lie.' "

Li's most outstanding contribution, I believe, is in his ideas about windows. He invented "fan windows" (for pleasure house-boats used on lakes), landscape windows, and plum-flower windows. The idea of having fan-shaped windows on the sides of a houseboat was connected with the Chinese habit of painting and writing on fans and collecting such fan paintings in albums. Li's idea was therefore that with the fan window on a boat as the frame, both the people inside the boat looking out on the scenery on the banks and the people walking on the banks looking at those having a wine or tea party in the boat would see the view like a picture on a Chinese fan. For the significance of the window lies in the fact that it is primarily a place for looking out on a view, as when we say that the eye is the "window" of the soul. It should be so designed as to look out on the best view and also to enable one to see the view in the most favourable manner, in this way introducing the element of nature into house interiors by "borrowing" from the outside landscape, as Li put it. Thus:

When a man is sitting in the boat, the light of the lake and the colour of the hills, the temples, clouds, haze, bamboos, trees on the banks, as well as the woodcutters, shepherd boys, drunken old men and promenading ladies, will all be gathered within the framework of the fan and form a piece of natural painting. Moreover, it is a living and moving picture, changing all the time, not only when the boat is moving, giving us a new sight with every movement of the oar and a new view with every punting of the pole, but even when the boat is lying at anchor, when the wind moves and the water ripples, changing its form at every moment. Thus we are able to enjoy hundreds and thousands of beautiful paintings of hills and water in a day by means of this fan-shaped window. . . .

[1] The Chinese idea is that every man born into this world is predestined with a certain quantity of luck or happiness, which may not be changed, and if one enjoys too much of something, his luck in other respects is curtailed, or he may live a shorter life.

I have also made a window for looking out on hills, called landscape window, otherwise known also as "unintentional painting." I will tell how I came to make one. Behind my studio, the Studio of Frothy White (signifying "drinking"), there is a hill about ten feet high and seven feet wide only, decorated with a miniature scenery of red cliffs and blue water, thick forests and tall bamboos, singing birds and falling cataracts, thatched huts and wooden bridges, complete in all the things that we see in a mountain village. For at first a modeller of clay made a clay figure of myself with a wonderful expression, and furthermore, because my name Liweng meant "an old man with a bamboo hat," also made me into a fisherman, holding a fishing pole and sitting on top of a rock. Then we thought, since there was a rock there must be also water, and since there was water there must be also a hill, and since there were both hill and water there must be a mountain retreat for the old man with a bamboo hat to retire and fish in his old age. That was how we gradually built up the entire scenery. It is clear, therefore, that the artificial hill grew out of a clay statue without any idea of making it serve the purpose of a window view. Later I saw that although the things were in miniature, their suggested universe was great, and it seemed to recall the Buddhist idea that a mustard seed and the Himalayas are equal in size, and therefore I sat there the whole day looking at it, and could not bear to close the window. And one day, inspired, I said to myself, "This hill can be made into a painting, and this painting can be made into a window. All it will cost me will be just one day's drink money to provide the 'mounting' for this painting." I therefore asked a boy servant to cut out several pieces of paper, and paste them above and below the window and at the sides, to serve as the mounting for a real picture. Thus the mounting was complete, and only the space usually occupied by the painting itself was left vacant, with the hill behind my house to take its place. Thus when one sits and looks at it, the window is no more a window but a piece of painting, and the hill is no longer the hill behind my house but a hill in the painting. I could not help laughing out loud, and my wife and children, hearing my laughter, came to see it and joined in laughing at what I had been laughing at. This is the origin of the "unintentional painting" and the "landscape window."

In the matter of tables and chairs and cabinets, Li also had a number of novel ideas. I can only mention here his invention of a heated arm-chair for use in winter. It is quite a practicable and useful invention wherever the rooms are not properly heated. It is a long wooden settee on a raised wooden platform built into the settee itself. The platform is two or three feet deep, with upright wooden panels at the sides about the height of a low desk. The front of the settee is also provided with two wooden door panels,[1] and as one goes up the platform, he closes the door, which together with the upright panels on the side forms a perfect support for a removable desk-top. The sitter is thus encased behind the desk. The platform itself is provided with a drawer containing hot ashes and well-burned and smokeless charcoal. The settee is so made that one can sit and work there, and also lie down when he is tired. Li claimed that the cost of thus providing a perfectly warm and comfortable place to work in was no more than four pieces of charcoal a day, two being added in the morning and two in the afternoon. He claimed further that, when travelling, two strong bamboo poles could be tied to its sides and the settee could be used like a regular sedan-chair, with the certainty of avoiding cold feet, and the added advantage of keeping warm whatever food and drink were taken on the journey. For the summer, he also thought of a bench resembling a bath-tub, with a porcelain tub specially ordered to fit into it. The tub could then be filled with cold water, reaching to the back of the seat and cooling it.

The Western world has invented rotating, collapsable, adjustable, reversible and convertible beds, sofas and barber chairs, but somehow it has not struck upon the idea of detachable and divisible tables and curio-stands. This is a thing that has had a long

[1] It would be more practical to have the door panel at one side, instead of in front.

development in China, showing considerable ingenuity. The principle of divisible tables, known as *yenchi,* originated with a game similar to building blocks for Western children, according to which a collection of blocks of wood forming a perfect square can be made into the most diverse symbolic figures of animals, human figures, utensils and furniture on a flat surface. A *yenchi* table of six pieces could be arranged to form one or several tables of different size, square or rectangular or T-shaped, or with the tops at various angles, making a total of forty ways of arrangement.[1]

Another type, called *tiehchi,* or "butterfly tables," differs from the *yenchi* in having triangular pieces and diagonal lines, and therefore the resulting shapes of pieces put together present a greater diversity of outline. Whereas the first type of *yenchi* tables was largely designed for dinner- or card-tables of different size, sometimes with a vacant space in the centre for candle-stands, this second type is designed for dinner-tables and card-tables and flower- and curio-stands as well, because flower- and curio-stands require a greater diversity of arrangement. This butterfly table consists of thirteen pieces, and together they form square tables, rectangular tables, diamond-shaped tables, with or without varying kinds of holes, the possibility of novel arrangements being limited only by the ingenuity of the housewife.[2]

There is a great desire among housewives both of the East and West to vary their interior arrangements, and divisible flower-stands or tea-tables seem to provide the possibility for infinite variety. The resulting shapes of such tables look strangely modernistic, for modernistic furniture emphasizes the idea of simplicity of line, which is also characteristic of Chinese furniture. The art seems to lie in combining variety in line with simplicity.

[1] The first divisible tables were invented either by the great Yüan painter, Ni Yünlin, who was also a great collector of curios and old furniture, or still further back by certain Huang Posse of the southern Sung Dynasty. A later man, Hsüan Kuch'ing, added one more piece, with the possibility of seventy-six different arrangements, for which pictures of the different arrangements exist. The design is simple enough, consisting of seven pieces all one unit wide, of which three pieces are two units long, two pieces are three units long and two pieces are four units long. The actual dimension given for the unit is one foot and three-quarters, so that the two longest tables of four units are seven feet long.

[2] This was invented by a certain Ko Shan, at the end of the Ming Dynasty, and the book giving sixty-two diagrams of its arrangements has been reprinted in various old Chinese libraries on the art of living.

I have seen, for instance, an old Chinese redwood flower-stand so made that its legs are not perfectly straight, but there is a slight turn in their middle. As for varying arrangements, the simplest way would be not to order a round or square table but to have the round table consist of two semi-circular halves, and the square table consist of two triangular tops, forming a square with the common base of the triangles as its diagonal line. When not wanted for playing cards, such round or square tables can be broken up in two and placed against the wall with the base of the triangle or of the semi-circle against it, and used for flower-pots or books. With the "butterfly tables" one can then have, instead of a triangular table against the wall, one similar to it but with a twin apex to the triangle, like two peaks of a hill. Card-tables can be made larger or smaller in size according to the company present. Tea-tables can be made to look like two squares overlapping one another at one of their corners, or they may resemble a "T" shape or a "U" or an "S" shape. It might be quite interesting to have a small party sitting at dinner around a "U"- or "S"-shaped table in a small apartment.

There exists to-day a perfect copy of a detachable bookcase made of hardwood, found in Ch'angshu, Kiangsu. Sectional bookcases are common in the West, but the new feature about this detachable bookcase is that its sections are so designed that, when taken apart, they can be put one inside another, the whole occupying no more space than a large suitcase. As it stands, it looks like a strangely modernistic bookcase. But it is possible to vary it and modify it so that one can break it up and have two or three small bookcases, perhaps twelve, eighteen, or twenty-four inches long, to be put at the head of sofas and beds, instead of one big bookcase, standing for ever at one point in the room.

The ideal of Chinese interiors seems to consist of the two ideas, simplicity and space. A well-arranged room always has few pieces of furniture, and these are generally of mahogany with extremely polished surface and simple lines, usually curved around the ends. Mahogany is polished by hand, and the difference in polish, entailing enormous labour, accounts for a wide difference in price.

A long board table without drawers generally stands against one wall, supporting one big "liver" vase. At another corner perhaps may be seen one, two or three mahogany flower- or curio-stands, of different height, and perhaps a few stools with gnarled roots as supports. A bookcase or curio cabinet stands on one side, with sections of various heights and levels, giving a strangely modernistic effect. And on the wall are just one or two scrolls, either oɪ calligraphy, showing the sheer joy of brush movement, or of painting, with more empty space than brush-strokes in it. And like the painting itself, the room should be *k'ungling,* or "empty and alive." The most distinctive feature of Chinese home design is the stone-paved courtyard, similar in effect to a Spanish cloister, and symbolizing peace, quiet and repose.

CHAPTER TEN

The Enjoyment Of Nature

I. PARADISE LOST?

IT IS A CURIOUS THING that among the myriad creations on this planet, while the entire plant life is deprived from taking any attitude toward Nature and practically all animals can also have no "attitude" to speak of, there should be a creature called man who is both self-conscious and conscious of his surroundings and who can therefore take an attitude toward it. Man's intelligence begins to question the universe, to explore its secrets and to find out its meaning. There are both a scientific and a moral attitude toward the universe. The scientific man is interested in finding out the chemical composition of the inside and crust of the earth upon which he lives, the thickness of the atmosphere surrounding it, the quantity and nature of cosmic rays dashing about on the top layers of the atmosphere, the formation of its hills and rocks, and the law governing life in general. This scientific interest has a relationship to the moral attitude, but in itself it is a pure desire to know and to explore. The moral attitude, on the other hand, varies a great deal, being sometimes one of harmony with nature, sometimes one of conquest and subjugation, or one of control and utilization, and sometimes one of supercilious contempt. This last attitude of supercilious contempt toward our own planet is a very curious product of civilization and of certain religions in particular. It springs from the fiction of the "Lost Paradise," which, strange to say, is pretty generally accepted as being true to-day, as a result of a primitive religious tradition.

It is amazing that no one ever questions the truth of the story of a lost Paradise. How beautiful, after all, was the Garden of Eden, and how ugly, after all, is the present physical universe? Have flowers ceased to bloom since Eve and Adam sinned? Has God cursed the apple tree and forbidden it to bear fruit because one man sinned, or has He decided that its blossoms should be made of duller or paler colours? Have orioles and nightingales and skylarks ceased to sing? Is there no snow upon the mountain tops and are there no reflections in the lakes? Are there no rosy sunsets to-day and no rainbows and no haze nestling over villages, and are there no falling cataracts and gurgling streams and shady trees? Who, therefore, invented the myth that the "Paradise" was "lost" and that to-day we are living in an ugly universe? We are indeed ungrateful spoiled children of God.

A parable has to be written of this spoiled child. Once upon a time there was a man whose name we will not yet mention. He came to God and complained that this planet was not good enough for him, and said he wanted a Heaven of Pearly Gates. And God first pointed out to the moon in the sky and asked him if it was not a good toy, and he shook his head. He said he didn't want to look at it. Then God pointed out the blue hills in the distance and asked him if the lines were not beautiful, and he said they were common and ordinary. Next God showed him the petals of the orchid and the pansy, and asked him to put out his fingers and touch gently their velvety lining and asked if the colour scheme was not exquisite, and the man said, "No." In His infinite patience, God took him to an aquarium, and showed him the gorgeous colours and shapes of Hawaiian fishes, and the man said he was not interested. God then took him under a shady tree and commanded a cool breeze to blow and asked him if he couldn't enjoy that, and the man replied again that he was not impressed. Next God took him to a mountain lake and showed him the light of the water, the sound of winds whistling through a pine forest, the serenity of the rocks and the beautiful reflections in the lake, and the man said that still he could not get excited over it. Thinking that this creature of His was not mild-tempered and wanted more exciting views, God took him then to the top of the

Rocky Mountains, the Grand Canyon, and caves with stalactites and stalagmites, and geysers, and sand dunes, and the fairy-finger-shaped cactus plants on a desert, and the snow on the Himalayas, and the cliffs of the Yangtse Gorges, and the granite peaks of the Yellow Mountains, and the sweeping cataract of Niagara Falls, and asked him if He had not done everything possible to make this planet beautiful to delight his eyes and his ears and his stomach, and the man still clamoured for a Heaven with Pearly Gates. "This planet," the man said, "is not good enough for me." "You presumptuous, ungrateful rat!" said God. "So this planet is not good enough for you. I will therefore send you to Hell where you shall not see the sailing clouds and the flowering trees, nor hear the gurgling brooks and live there for ever till the end of your days." And God sent him to live in a city apartment. His name was Christian.

It is clear that this man is pretty difficult to satisfy. There is a question as to whether God can create a heaven to satisfy him. I am sure that with his millionaire complex, he will be pretty sick of the Pearly Gates during his second week in Heaven, and God will be at His wits' end to invent something else to please this spoiled child. Now it must be pretty generally accepted that modern astronomy, by exploring the entire visible universe, is forcing us to accept this earth itself as a very heaven, and the Heaven that we dream of must occupy some space, and occupying some space, it must be somewhere among the stars in the firmament, unless it is in the inter-stellar void. And since this Heaven is to be found in some star, with or without moons, my imagination rather fails to conceive of a better planet than our own. Of course there may be a dozen moons instead of one, coloured pink, purple, Prussian blue, cabbage green, orange, lavender, aquamarine, and turquoise, and in addition there may be better and more frequent rainbows. But I suspect that a man who is not satisfied with one moon will also get tired of a dozen moons, and one who is not satisfied with an occasional snow scene or rainbow will be equally tired of better and more frequent rainbows. There may be six seasons in a year instead of four, and there will be the same beautiful alternation of spring and summer and day and night, but I don't see how that will make a difference. If one doesn't enjoy spring and summer on earth, how can he enjoy spring and summer in Heaven? I must seem to be talking either like a great fool or an extremely wise man now, but certainly I don't share the Buddhist or Christian desire to escape from the senses and physical matter by assuming a heaven occupying no space and constructed out of sheer spirit. For myself, I would as soon live on this planet as on any other. Certainly no one can say that life on this planet is stale and monotonous. If a man cannot be satisfied with the variety of weather and the changing colours of the sky, the exquisite flavours of fruits appearing by rotation in the different seasons, and flowers blooming by rotation in the different months, that man had better commit suicide and not try to go on a futile chase after an impossible Heaven that may satisfy God Himself and never satisfy man.

As the facts of the case really stand to-day, there is a perfect, and almost a mystic, co-ordination between the sights, sounds, smells and tastes of nature and our organs of seeing, hearing, smelling and eating. This co-ordination between the sights and sounds and smells of the universe and our own perceptive organs is so perfect that it forms a perfect argument for teleology, so much ridiculed by Voltaire. But we need not all be teleologists. God might have invited us to this feast, or He might not. The Chinese attitude is that we will join in the feast whether we are invited or not. It simply doesn't make sense not to taste the feast when the food looks so tempting and we have such an appetite. Let the philosophers carry on their metaphysical researches and try to find out whether we are among the invited guests, but the sensible man will eat up the food before it gets cold. Hunger always goes with good common sense.

Our planet is a very good planet. In the first place, there is the alternation of night and day, and morning and sunset, and a cool evening following upon a hot day, and a silent and clear dawn presaging a busy morning, and there is nothing better than that. In the second place, there is the alternation of summer and winter, perfect in themselves, but made still more perfect by being gradually ushered in by spring and autumn, and there is nothing better than that. In the third place, there are the silent and dignified trees, giving us shade in summer and not shutting out the warm sunshine in winter, and there is nothing better than that. In the fourth place, there are flowers blooming and fruits ripening by rotation in the different months, and there is nothing better than that. In the fifth place, there are cloudy and misty days alternating with clear and sunny days, and there is nothing better than that. In the sixth place, there are spring showers and summer thunderstorms and the dry crisp wind of autumn and the snow of winter, and there is nothing better than that. In the seventh place, there are peacocks and parrots and skylarks and canaries singing inimitable songs, and there is nothing better than that. In the eighth place, there is the zoo, with monkeys, tigers, bears, camels, elephants, rhinoceros, crocodiles, sea lions, cows, horses, dogs, cats, foxes, squirrels, woodchucks and more variety and ingenuity than we ever thought of, and there is nothing better than that. In the ninth place, there are rainbow fish, sword-fish, electric eels, whales, minnows, clams, abalones, lobsters, shrimps, turtles and more variety and ingenuity than we ever thought of, and there is nothing better than that. In the tenth place, there are magnificent redwood trees, fire-spouting volcanoes, magnificent caves, majestic peaks, undulating hills, placid lakes, winding rivers and shady banks, and there is nothing better than that. The menu is practically endless to suit individual tastes, and the only sensible thing to do is to go and partake of the feast and not complain about the monotony of life.

II. ON BIGNESS

Nature is itself always a sanatorium. If it can cure nothing else, it can cure man of megalomania. Man has to be "put in his place," and he is always put in his place against nature's background. That is why Chinese paintings always paint human figures so small in a landscape. In a Chinese landscape called "Looking at a Mountain After Snow," it is very difficult to find the human figure supposed to be looking at the mountain after snow. After a careful search, he will be discovered perching beneath a pine tree—his squatting body about an inch high in a painting fifteen high, and done in no more than a few rapid strokes. There is another Sung painting of four scholarly figures wandering in an autumn forest and raising their heads to look at the intertwining branches of majestic trees above them. It does one good to feel terribly small at times. Once I was passing a summer in Kuling, and lying there on top of the mountain, I began to see two little creatures, the size of ants, a hundred miles off in Nanking, hating and intriguing against each other for a chance to serve China, and it made the whole thing seem a little comical. That is why a mountain trip is supposed by the Chinese to have a cathartic effect, cleansing one's breast of a lot of foolish ambitions and unnecessary worries.

Man is liable to forget how small and often how futile he is. A man seeing a hundred-storey building often gets conceited, and the best way to cure that insufferable conceit is to transport that skyscraper in one's imagination to a little contemptible hill and learn a truer sense of what may and what may not be called "enormous." What we like about the sea is its infiniteness, and what we like about the mountain is its enormity. There are peaks in Huangshan or the Yellow Mountains which are formed by single pieces of granite a thousand feet high from their visible base on the ground to their tops, and half a mile long. These are what inspire the Chinese artists, and their silence, their rugged enormity and their apparent eternity account partly for the Chinese love of rocks in pictures. It is hard to believe that there are such enormous rocks until one visits Huangshan, and there was a Huangshan School of painters in the seventeenth century, deriving their inspiration from these silent peaks of granite.

On the other hand, by association with nature's enormities, a man's heart may truly grow big also. There is a way of looking upon a landscape as a moving picture and being satisfied with nothing less big as a moving picture, a way of looking upon tropic clouds over the horizon as the backdrop of a stage and being satisfied with nothing less big as a backdrop, a way of looking upon the mountain forests as a private garden and being satisfied with nothing less as a private garden, a way of listening to the roaring waves as a concert and being satisfied with nothing less as a concert, and a way of looking upon the mountain breeze as an air-cooling system and being satisfied with nothing less as an air-cooling system. So do we become *big* even as the earth and firmaments are big. Like the "Big Man" described by Yüan Tsi (A.D. 210–263), one of China's first romanticists, we "live in heaven and earth as our house."

The best "spectacle" I ever saw took place one evening on the Indian Ocean. It was truly immense. The stage was a hundred miles wide and three miles high, and on it nature enacted a drama lasting half an hour, now with giant dragons, dinosaurs and lions moving across the sky—how the lions' heads swelled and their manes spread and how the dragons' backs bent and wriggled and curled!—now showing armies of white-clad and grey-uniformed armies and officers with golden epaulets, marching and counter-marching and united in combat and retreating again. As the battle and the chase were going on, the stage-lights changed, and the soldiers in white uniform burst out in orange and the soldiers in grey uniforms seemed to don purple, while the backdrop was a flaming iridescent gold. Then as nature's stage technicians gradually dimmed the lights, the purple overcame and swallowed up the orange, and changed into deeper and deeper mauve and grey, presenting for the last five minutes a spectacle of unspeakable tragedy and black disaster before the lights went out. And I did not pay a single cent to watch the grandest show of my life.

There is, too, the silence of the mountains, and that silence is therapeutic—the silent peaks, the silent rocks, the silent trees, all silent and all majestic. Every good mountain with an enclosing gesture is a sanatorium. One feels good nestling like a baby on its breast. A disbeliever in Christian Science, I do believe in the spiritual, healing properties of grand, old trees and mountain resorts, not for curing a fractured shoulder-bone or an infected skin, but for curing the ambitions of the flesh and diseases of the soul—kleptomania, megalomania, egocentricity, spiritual halitosis, bonditis, couponitis, managitis (the desire to manage others), war-neurosis, verse-phobia, spitefulness, hatred, social exhibitionism, general muddle-headedness and all forms of moral distemper.

III. TWO CHINESE LADIES

The enjoyment of nature is an art, depending so much on one's mood and personality, and like all art, it is difficult to explain its technique. Everything must be spontaneous and rise spontaneously from an artistic temperament. It is therefore difficult to lay down rules for the enjoyment of this or that tree, this or that rock and this or that landscape in a particular moment, for no landscapes are exactly alike. He who understands will know how to enjoy nature without being told. Havelock Ellis and Van der Velde are wise when they say that what is allowable and what is not allowable, or what is good and what is bad taste in the art of love between husband and wife in the intimacy of their bedroom, is not something that can be prescribed by rules. The same thing is true of the art of enjoying nature. The best approach is probably by studying the lives of such people who have the artistic temperament in them. The feeling for nature, one's dreams of a beautiful landscape seen a year ago, and one's sudden desire to visit a certain place—these things come in at the most unexpected moments. One who has the artistic temperament shows it wherever he goes, and writers who truly enjoy nature will go off in descriptions of a beautiful snow scene or a spring evening, forgetting entirely about the story or the plot. Autobiographies of journalists and statesmen are usually full of reminiscences of past events, while the autobiographies of literary men should mainly concern themselves with reminiscences of a happy night, or a visit with some of their friends to some valley. In this sense I find the autobiographies of Rudyard Kipling and G. K. Chesterton disappointing. Why are the important anecdotes of their lives regarded as so unimportant, and why are the unimportant anecdotes regarded as so important? Men, men, men, everywhere, and no mention of flowers and birds and hills and streams!

The reminiscences of Chinese literary men, and also their letters, differ in this respect. The important thing is to tell a friend in one's letter about a night on the lake, or to record in one's autobiography a perfectly happy day and how it was passed. In particular, Chinese writers, at least a number of them, have gone to the length of writing reminiscences about their married lives. Of these, Mao Pichiang's *Reminiscences of My Concubine,*[1] Shen Sanpo's *Six Chapters of a Floating Life,* and Chiang T'an's *Reminiscences Under the Lamp-light* are the best examples. The first two were written by the husbands after their wives' death, while the last was written in the author's old age during his wife's lifetime.[2] We will begin with certain select passages from the *Reminiscences Under the Lamp-light,* with the author's wife Ch'iufu as the heroine, and follow it with selections from *Six Chapters of a Floating Life,* with Yün as the heroine. Both these women had the right temperament, although they were not particularly educated or good poets. It doesn't matter. No one should aim at writing immortal poetry; one should learn the writing of poems merely as a way to record a meaningful moment, a personal mood, or to help the enjoyment of nature.

A. CH'IUFU

Ch'iufu often said to me: "A man's life lasts only a hundred years, and of this hundred sleep and dream occupy one-half, days of illness and sorrow occupy one-half, and the days of swaddling clothes and senile age again occupy one-half.[3] What we have got left is only a tenth or fifth part. Besides, we who are made of the stuff of willows can hardly expect to live a hundred years."

[1] Quoted in the section on "Smoke and Incense."
[2] There are a number of others; for instance, Li Liweng has also two sketches about his two concubines, who were good singers, personally trained by him.
[3] This is merely Chinese mathematics.

One day when the autumn moon was at its best, Ch'iufu asked a young maid to carry a *ch'in* and accompany her to a boating trip among the lotus flowers of the West Lake. I was then returning from the West River, and when I arrived and found that Ch'iufu had gone boating, I bought some melons and went after her. We met at the Second Bridge of the Su Tungp'o Embankment, when Ch'iufu was playing the sad ditty of "Autumn in Han Palace." Stopping to listen with my gown gathered in my hands, I listened to her music. At this moment, the hills all around were enveloped in the evening haze, and the reflections of the stars and the moon were seen in the water. Different musical sounds came to my ear so that I could not distinguish whether it was the sounds of the wind in the air or the sounds of jingling jade. Before the song was completed, the bow of our boat had already touched the southern bank of the Garden of Swirling Waters. We then knocked at the gate of the White Cloud Convent, for we knew the nuns there. After sitting down for a while, the nuns served us with freshly picked lotus seeds prepared in soup. Their colour and their fragrance were enough to cool one's intestines, a world different from the taste of meats and oily foods. Coming back, we landed at Tuan's Bridge, where we spread a bamboo matting on the ground and sat talking for a long time. The distant rumble of the city rather annoyed our ears like the humming of flies. . . . Then the stars in the sky became fewer and fewer and the lake was blanketed with a stretch of white. We heard the drum on top of the city wall and realized that it was already the fourth watch [about 3 a.m.] and carried the *ch'in* and paddled the boat home.

The banana trees that Ch'iufu planted had already grown big leaves which cast their green shade across the screen. To have heard raindrops beating upon the leaves in autumn when lying inclined on a pillow was enough to break one's heart. So one day I playfully wrote three lines on one of the leaves:

> What busybody planted this sapling?
> Morning tapping,
> Evening rapping!

Next day, I saw another three lines following them, which read:

> It's you who're lonesome, fretting!
> Banana getting,
> Banana regretting!

The characters were delicately formed, and they came from Ch'iufu's playful pen. But I have learnt something from what she wrote.

One night we heard the noise of wind and rain, and the pillows and matting revealed the cooler spirit of autumn. Ch'iufu was just undressing for the night, and I was sitting by her side and had just gone through an album of hundred flowers with inscriptions that I was making. I heard the noise of several yellow leaves falling upon the floor from the window, and Ch'iufu sang the lines:

> Yesterday was better than to-day;
> And this year I'm older than the last.

I consoled her, saying, "One never lives a full hundred years. How can we have time to wipe the tears for others [the falling leaves]?" And with a sigh I laid aside the painting brush. When the night was getting late, and Ch'iufu wanted to have something to drink, I found that the fire in the earthen stove had already died out, and the maidservants were all in dreamland, drooping their heads. I then took the oil lamp on the table and placed it under the little tea stove, and warmed up a cup of lotus seeds for her. Ch'iufu has been suffering from an affection in the lungs for ten years, and always coughs in late autumn and sleeps well only when upholstered on a high pillow. This year, she is feeling stronger, and we often sit face to face with each other deep into the night. Perhaps it is due to proper care and nourishment.

I made a dress with a plum-flower design for Ch'iufu, with

fragrant snow all over her body, and at a distance she looked like a Plum Fairy standing alone in a world of mortal beings. In late spring, when her green sleeves were resting on the balcony, butterflies would flit about her temples, not knowing that the season of the Eastern Wind was already gone.

Last year, the swallows came back later than usual, and when they came, half of the peach blossoms outside the screen had already bloomed. One day, the clay from their nest fell down and a young swallow fell to the ground. Afraid that a wild cat might get it, Ch'iufu immediately took it up, and made a bamboo support for its nest. This year the same swallows have returned and are chirping around the house. Do they perhaps remember the one who protected the young one last year?

Ch'iufu loves to play chess but is not very good at it. Every night, she would force me to play "the conversation of fingers" with her, sometimes till daybreak. I playfully quoted the line of Chu Chuchia: "At tossing coins and matching grass-blades you have both lost. I ask you with what are you going to pay me to-night?" "Are you so sure I cannot win?" she said, evading the question. "I will bet you this jade tiger." We then played and when twenty or thirty stones had been laid, and she was getting into a worse situation, she let the cat upon the chess-board to upset the game. "Are you regarding yourself as Yang Kueifei [who played the same trick upon Emperor T'ang Minghuang]?" I asked. She kept quiet, but the light of silver candles shone upon her peach-coloured cheeks. After that, we did not play any more.

There are several cassia trees at the Hupao Spring, stretching low over some rocks. During blossom, its yellow flowers cover up the stone steps, its perfume making one feel like visiting the Kingdom of Divine Fragrance. I have a weakness for flowers and often boiled tea[1] under them. Ch'iufu plucked the flowers and decorated her hair with them, but sometimes her hair would be caught or upset by the overhanging branches. I arranged it and smoothed it with the spring water. On our departure, we

[1] Hupao Spring water is famous for making tea.

plucked a few twigs and brought them home, putting them on the back of our cart as we went through the city streets, that people might know the latest news of the new autumn.

B. Yün

In the *Six Chapters of a Floating Life* we have the reminiscences of an obscure Chinese painter about his married life with Yün. They were both simple artistic souls, trying to snatch every moment of happiness that came their way, and the story was told in a simple unaffected manner. Somehow Yün has seemed to me the most beautiful woman in Chinese literature. Theirs was a sad life, and yet it was one of the gayest, with a gaiety that came from the soul. It is interesting to see how the enjoyment of nature came in as a vital part of their spiritual experience. Below are three passages describing their enjoyment of the seventh of the seventh moon and the fifteenth of the seventh moon, both festivals, and of how they passed a summer inside the city of Soochow:

On the seventh night of the seventh moon of that year [1780] Yün prepared incense, candles and some melons and fruits, so that we might together worship the Grandson of Heaven[1] in the Hall called "After My Heart." I had carved two seals with the inscription, "That we might remain husband and wife from incarnation to incarnation." I kept the seal with positive characters, while she kept the one with negative characters, to be used in our correspondence. That night, the moon was shining beautifully and when I looked down at the creek, the ripples shone like golden chains. We were wearing light silk dresses and sitting together with a small fan in our hands, before a window overlooking the creek. Looking up at the sky, we saw the clouds sailing through the heavens, changing at every moment into a myriad forms, and Yün said: "This moon is common to the whole universe. I wonder if there is another pair of lovers quite as passionate as ourselves looking at the

[1] The seventh day of the seventh moon is the only day in the year when the pair of heavenly lovers, the Cowherd ("Grandson of Heaven") and the Spinster are allowed to meet each other across the Milky Way.

same moon to-night?" And I said: "Oh, there are plenty of people who will be sitting in the cool evening and looking at the moon, and perhaps also many women criticizing or enjoying the clouds in their chambers; but when a husband and wife are looking at the moon together, I hardly think that the clouds will form the subject of their conversation." By and by, the candle-lights went out, the moon sank in the sky, and we removed the fruits and went to bed.

The fifteenth of the seventh moon was All Souls' Day. Yün prepared a little dinner, so that we could drink together with the moon as our company, but when night came, the sky was suddenly overcast with dark clouds. Yün knitted her brow and said: "If it be the wish of God that we two should live together until there are silver threads in our hair, then the moon must come out again to-night." On my part I felt disheartened also. As we looked across the creek, we saw will-o'-the-wisps flitting in crowds hither and thither like ten thousand candle-lights, threading their way through the willows and smartweeds. And then we began to compose a poem together, each saying two lines at a time, the first completing the couplet which the other had begun, and the second beginning another couplet for the other to finish, and after a few rhymes, the longer we kept on, the more nonsensical it became, until it was a jumble of slap-dash doggerel. By this time, Yün was buried amidst tears and laughter and choking on my breast, while I felt the fragrance of the jasmine in her hair assail my nostrils. I patted her on the shoulder and said jokingly: "I thought that the jasmine was used for decoration in women's hair because it was round like a pearl; I did not know that it is because its fragrance is so much finer when it is mixed with the smell of women's hair and powder. When it smells like that, even the citron cannot remotely compare with it." Then Yün stopped laughing and said: "The citron is the gentleman among the different fragrant plants because its fragrance is so slight that you can hardly detect it; on the other hand, the jasmine is a common fellow because it borrows its fragrance partly from others.

Therefore, the fragrance of the jasmine is like that of a smiling sycophant." "Why, then," I said, "do you keep away from the gentleman and associate with the common fellow?" And Yün replied: "I am amused by the gentleman that loves the common fellow." While we were thus bandying words about, it was already midnight, and we saw the wind had blown away the clouds in the sky and there appeared the full moon, round like a chariot wheel, and we were greatly delighted. And so we began to drink by the side of the window, but before we had tasted three cups, we heard suddenly the noise of a splash under the bridge, as if someone had fallen into the water. We looked out through the window and saw there was not a thing, the water was as smooth as a mirror, except that we heard the noise of a duck scampering in the marshes. I knew that there was a ghost of someone drowned by the side of the Ts'anglang Pavilion, but knowing that Yün was very timid, dared not mention it to her. And Yün sighed and said: "Alas! whence cometh this noise?" and we shuddered all over. Quickly we shut the window and carried the wine-pot back into the room. A lamplight was then burning as small as a pea, and the curtains moved in the dark, and we were shaking all over. We then put out the light and went inside the bed curtain, and Yün already had run up a high fever. Soon I had a high temperature myself, and our illness dragged on for about twenty days. True it is that when the cup of happiness overflows, disaster follows, as the saying goes, and this was also an omen that we should not be able to live together until old age.

The book is strewn literally with passages of such charm and beauty, showing an overflowing love of nature, but the following description of how they spent a summer must suffice:

After we had moved to Ts'angmi Alley, I called our bedroom the "Tower of Guests' Fragrance," with a reference to Yün's name,[1] and to the story of Liang Hung and Meng Kuang who as husband and wife were always courteous to each other

1 "Yün" in Chinese means a certain fragrant weed.

"like guests." We rather disliked the house because the walls were too high and the courtyard was too small. At the back, there was another house, leading to the library. Looking out of the window at the back, one could see the old garden of Mr. Lu, then in a dilapidated condition. Yün's thoughts still hovered about the beautiful scenery of the Ts'anglang Pavilion.

At this time there was an old peasant woman living on the east of Mother Gold's Bridge and the north of Kenghsiang. Her little cottage was surrounded on all sides by vegetable fields and had a wicker gate. Outside the gate there was a pond about thirty yards across, surrounded by a wilderness of trees on all sides. . . . A few paces to the west of the cottage, there was a mound filled with broken bricks, from the top of which one could command a view of the surrounding country, which was an open ground with a stretch of wild vegetation. Once the old woman happened to mention the place, and Yün kept on thinking about it. . . . So the next day I went there and found that the cottage consisted only of two rooms, which could be partitioned into four. With paper windows and bamboo beds, the house would make quite a delightfully cool place to stay in. . . .

Our only neighbours were an old couple who raised vegetables for the market. They knew that we were going to stay there for the summer, and came and called on us, bringing us some fish from the pond and vegetables from their own fields. We offered to pay for them, but as they wouldn't take any money, Yün made a pair of shoes for them, which they were finally persuaded to accept. This was in July when the trees cast a green shade over the place. The summer breeze blew over the water of the pond, and cicadas filled the air with their singing the whole day. Our old neighbour also made a fishing-line for us, and we used to angle together under the shade. Late in the afternoons, we would go up on the mound to look at the evening glow and compose lines of poetry, when we felt so inclined. Two of the lines were:

. Beast-clouds swallow the sinking sun,
And the bow-moon shoots the falling stars.

After a while, the moon cut her image in the water, insects
began to cry all around, and we placed a bamboo bed near
the hedgerow to sit or lie upon. The old woman then would
inform us that wine had been warmed up and dinner prepared,
and we would sit down to have a little drink under the moon.
After we had a bath, we would put on our slippers and carry a
fan, and lie or sit there, listening to old tales of retribution told
by our neighbour. When we came in to sleep about midnight,
we felt our whole bodies nice and cool, almost forgetting that
we were living in a city.

There along the hedgerow, we asked the gardener to plant
chrysanthemums. The flowers bloomed in the ninth moon,
and we continued to stay there for another ten days. My
mother was also quite delighted and came to see us there. So
we ate crabs in the midst of chrysanthemums and whiled away
the whole day. Yün was quite enchanted with all this and said:
"Some day we must build a cottage here. We'll buy ten *mow*
of ground, and around it we'll plant vegetables and melons for
our food. You will paint and I will do embroidery, from which
we could make enough money to buy wine and compose poems
over dinners. Thus, clad in simple gowns and eating simple
meals, we could live a very happy life together without going
anywhere." I fully agreed with her. Now the place is still there
while the one who knows my heart is dead. Alas, such is life!

IV. ON ROCKS AND TREES

I don't know what we are going to do now. We are building
houses square and are building them in a row, and we are having
straight roads without trees. There are no more crooked streets,
no more old houses, no more wells in one's garden, and whatever
private garden there is in the city is usually a caricature. We have
quite successfully shut nature out from our lives, and we are
living in houses without roofs, the roofs being the neglected end

of a building, left in any old shape after the utilitarian purposes have been served and the building contractor is a little tired and in a hurry to get through his job. The average building looks like wooden blocks built by a peevish or fickle child who is tired of the game before he finishes building, and leaves them unfinished and uncrowned. The spirit of nature has left the modern civilized man, and it seems to me we are trying to civilize the trees themselves. If we ever remember to plant them on boulevards, we usually number them serially, disinfect them, cut them and trim them to assume a shape that we humans consider beautiful.

We often plant flowers and lay them out on a plot so that they resemble either a circle, or a star, or different letters of the alphabet, and we are horrified when some of the flowers so planted get out of line as we are horrified when we see a West Point cadet march out of step, and we proceed to cut them down with scissors. And at Versailles, we plant these conically cut trees in pairs and arrange them with perfect symmetry along a perfectly round circle or in perfectly rectilinear rows in army formation. Such is human glory and power and our ability to train and discipline the trees as we train and discipline uniformed soldiers. If one tree of a pair grows taller than the other, our hands itch to cut off its top so as not to let it disturb our sense of symmetry and human power and glory.

There exists, therefore, the great problem of recovering nature and bringing nature back to the home. This is an exasperating problem. What can one do with the best artistic temperament, when one lives in an apartment and away from the soil? How is one going to have a plot of grass or a well or a bamboo grove even if he is rich enough to rent a penthouse? Everything is wrong, utterly and irretrievably wrong. What has one got left to admire except tall skyscrapers and lighted windows in a row at night? Looking at these skyscrapers and these lighted windows in a row at night, one gets more and more conceited about the power of human civilization and forgets what puny little creatures human beings are. I am therefore forced to give up the problem as hopeless of solution.

We must begin, therefore, by giving man land, and plenty of it. No matter what the excuse, a civilization that deprives man of land is wrong. But suppose in a future civilization every man is able to own an acre of land, then he has got something to start with. He can have trees, his own trees, and rocks, his own rocks. He will be careful to choose a site where there are already full-grown trees, and if there are not already full-grown trees, he will plant trees that grow fast enough for him, such as bamboos and willows. Then he will not have to keep birds in cages, for birds will come to him and he will see to it that there are frogs in the neighbourhood, and preferably also some lizards and spiders. His children will then be able to study nature in Nature and not study nature in a glass case. At least his children will be able to watch how chickens hatch from their eggs and they need not be woefully ignorant about sex and reproduction as the children of "good" Boston families often are. And they will have the pleasure of watching a fight between lizards and spiders. And they will have the pleasure also of getting comfortably dirty.

The Chinese sentiment for rocks has already been explained, or hinted at, in a previous section.[1] That explanation sufficiently accounts for the love of rocky peaks in Chinese landscape painting. This explanation is basic, but it does not sufficiently account for Chinese rock gardens and the love of rocks in general. The basic idea is that rocks are enormous, strong and suggest eternity. They are silent, unmovable and have strength of character like great heroes, and they are independent and detached from life like retired scholars. They are invariably old, and the Chinese love whatever is old. Above all, from the artistic point of view they have grandeur, majesty, ruggedness, and quaintness. There is the further sentiment of *wei*, which means "dangerous" but is really untranslatable. A tall cliff that rises abruptly three hundred feet above the ground is always fascinating to look at because of its suggestion of "danger."

But then it is necessary to go further. As one cannot visit the mountains every day, it is necessary to have rocks brought to the

[1] See above, Section II.

home. In the case of rock gardens and artificial rock grottoes—a subject which is difficult for Western travellers in China to understand and appreciate—the idea is still to retain a suggestion of the rugged, "dangerous" and majestic lines of rocky peaks. Western travellers are not to blame because most of the rockeries are done with atrocious taste, and fail to convey the suggestion of natural grandeur and majesty. Artificial grottoes built out of several pieces of rock are usually cemented together, and the cement shows. A really artistic rockery should have the composition and contrast of a painting. There is no question that the artistic appreciation of artificial rock sceneries and that of mountain rocks in landscape painting are closely associated, as we find the Sung painter, Mi Fei, was the author of a book on ink-stones, and there was a book *Shihp'u* on rocks by a Sung author, Tu Kuan, giving detailed descriptions of the quality of over a hundred kinds of rocks produced at different places and used for rockeries showing that rockeries were already a highly developed art in the time of the great Sung painters.

Side by side with this appreciation of the grandeur of rocks on mountain peaks, there developed then a different appreciation of rocks in gardens, emphasizing their colour, texture, surface, grains and sometimes the sounds they produced when struck. The smaller the stones, the more emphasis was laid on quality of texture and colour of grains. The development along this direction was greatly helped by the hobby of collecting the finest ink-stones and seals, two things which the literary man in China daily associated with. Daintiness, texture, light or translucence and shades of colour became then of the first importance, as also in the case of stone, jade and jadeite snuff bottles, which came later. A good stone seal or a good snuff bottle could cost six or seven hundred dollars.

For the fullest appreciation of all uses of stone in the house and gardens, however, one has to go back to Chinese calligraphy. For calligraphy is nothing but a study of rhythm and line and composition in the abstract. While really good pieces of rock should suggest majesty or detachment from life, it is even more important that the lines be correct. By "line" one does not mean a straight line, or a circle or a triangle, but the rugged lines of nature. Laotse, "The Old Boy," always emphasized in his *Taotehching* the *uncarved* rock. Let us not tamper with nature, for the best work of art, like the best poem or literary composition, is one which shows no sign of human effort, as natural as a winding river or a sailing cloud, or as the Chinese literary critics always say, "without axe and chisel marks." This applies to every field of art. The appreciation is of beauty in irregularity, in lines that suggest rhythm and movement and gesture. The appreciation of the gnarled roots of an oak tree, sometimes used as stools in a rich man's studio, is based on the same idea. Consequently most of the rockeries found in Chinese gardens are uncut rocks, which may be the fossilized bark of a tree ten or fifteen feet high standing vertically alone and unmovable like a great man, or of rocks found in lakes and caves, generally bearing perforations and having the utmost irregularity of outline. One writer suggested that if the perforations happen to be perfectly round, some little pebble should be inserted to break up the regularity of the circle. Rockeries near Shanghai and Soochow are mostly built of rocks from the Taihu Lake, bearing marks of former sea-waves. Such rocks were dug out of the bottom of the lake, and sometimes, when something was needed to correct their lines, they would be chiselled until they were perfect and let down into the water again for a year or so, so that the chisel marks might be obliterated by the movement of water.

The feeling for trees is easier to understand, and is, of course, universal. Houses without trees around them are naked, like men and women without clothing. The difference between trees and houses is that houses are built but trees grow, and anything which grows is always more beautiful to look at than anything which is built. There are considerations of practical convenience which force us to build our walls straight and our storeys level, although in the matter of floors, there is absolutely no reason why the floors of different rooms in a house should not be on different levels. Nevertheless, there is an inevitable tendency to go in for straight lines and square shapes, and such straight lines and square shapes can be brought into pleasurable relief only by the company of trees. In the colour scheme, too, we dare not paint our houses green. But nature dares and has painted the trees green.

The wisdom of art consists in concealing art. We are so anxious to show off. In this respect, I must pay my tribute to a great scholar of the Manchu Dynasty, Yüan Yüan, who as governor had an islet built in the water of the West Lake, known to-day as Governor Yüan's Islet, and who refused to put a single human edifice on the place, not a pavilion, not a pillar, not even a monument. He completely obliterated himself as an architect. To-day the Governor Yüan's Islet stands in the middle of the lake, a level piece of land about a hundred yards across, rising barely a foot above the water and planted all around with willow trees. And to-day as you stand looking at it on a misty day, the magic island seems to rise out of the water, and the willow trees cast their reflections in the water, breaking the monotony of the lake's surface and harmonizing with it. Therefore Governor Yüan's Islet is in perfect harmony with nature. It is not obtrusive to the eye, like the lighthouse-shaped monument next to it built by a student returned from America, which gives me inflammation of the eyelids every time I look at it. I have made a public promise that if one day I should emerge as a bandit general and capture Hangchow, my first official act would be to direct a cannon and blow that lighthouse-shaped thing to pieces.

Out of the myriad variety of trees, Chinese critics and poets have come to feel that there are a few which are particularly good for artistic enjoyment, due to their special lines and contours which are æsthetically beautiful from a calligrapher's point of view. The point is, that while all trees are beautiful, certain trees have a particular gesture or strength or gracefulness. These trees are therefore picked out from among the others and associated with definite sentiments. It is clear that an ordinary olive tree has no rugged manner, for which we go to the pine, and while a willow is graceful, it can never be said to be "majestic" or "inspiring." There are then a small number of trees which are more constantly painted in paintings and sung about in poems. Of these the most outstanding are the pine tree, enjoyed for its grand manner, the plum tree, enjoyed for its romantic manner, the bamboo tree, enjoyed for its delicacy of line and the suggestion of the home, and the willow tree, enjoyed for its gracefulness and its suggestion of slender women.

The enjoyment of the pine tree is probably most notable and of the greatest poetic significance. It typifies better than other trees the conception of nobility of manner. For there are trees noble and trees ignoble, trees distinguished for their grand manner and trees of the common manner. The Chinese artists therefore speak of the grand old manner of the pine tree, as Matthew Arnold spoke of the grand manner of Homer. It would be as hopeless to look for this grand manner in willows among the trees as it is to look for the grand manner of poetry in Swinburne among the poets. There are so many kinds of beauty; beauty of tenderness, of gracefulness, of majesty, of austerity, of quaintness, of ruggedness, of sheer strength, and of a suggestion of the antique. It is this antique manner of the pine tree that gives the pine a special position among the trees, as it is the antique manner of a recluse scholar, clad in a loose-fitting gown, holding a bamboo cane and walking on a mountain path, that sets him off as the highest ideal among men. For this reason Li Liweng says that to sit in an orchard full of peach trees and flowers and willows without a pine nearby is like sitting in the company of young children and women without the presence of an austere master or old man, whom we can look up to. It is also for this reason that when Chinese admire pine trees, they go in for the old ones; the older the better, for then they become more majestic. Classed with the pine tree is the cedar cypress which has the same manner, particularly the kind known as *selaginela involvens,* with twisting, encircling and ruggedly downward-pointing branches. While branches that stretch upwards toward heaven seem to symbolize youth and aspiration, downward-pointing branches seem to symbolize the posture of old men bending down toward youth.

I say the enjoyment of pine trees is artistically most significant because it represents silence and majesty and detachment from life which are so similar to the manner of the recluse. This enjoyment is then associated with "stupid" rocks and with figures of old people loitering around underneath its shade, as we so often see in Chinese paintings. As one stands there beneath a pine tree, he looks up to it with a sense of its majesty and its old age, and its strange happiness in its own independence. Laotse says, "Nature does not talk," nor does the old pine tree. There it stands silent and imperturbable; from its height it looks down upon us, thinking it has seen so many children grow up into maturity and so many middle-aged people pass on to old age. Like wise, old men, it understands everything, but it does not talk, and therein lie its mystery and grandeur.

The plum tree is enjoyed partly for its romantic manner in its branches, and partly for the fragrance in its flowers. It is curious that among the trees selected for our poetic enjoyment, the pine tree, the plum tree and the bamboo are associated with winter, being known as the "Three Friends of Winter," for the bamboo tree and the pine tree are evergreens, while the plum tree blossoms at the end of winter and the beginning of spring. The plum tree, therefore, in particular, symbolizes purity of character, the purity that we find in the crisp, cold winter air. Its splendour is a cold splendour, and like the recluse, the cooler the atmosphere it finds itself in, the better it prospers. Like the orchid flower, it typifies the idea of charm in seclusion. A Sung poet and recluse, Lin Hoching, declared that he had married plum trees as his wives, and had a stork for his son. To-day the site of his seclusion on the Kushan in the middle of the West Lake is an object of pilgrimage for poets and scholars, and below his tomb is the tomb of the stork, his "son." Now the appreciation of the plum tree, of its type of fragrance and its outline, is best expressed by this poet in his famous line of seven words:

An hsiang fou tung ying heng sheh

"Its dim fragrance floats around, its shadow leaning across." It is admitted by all poets that the essence of the beauty of the plum is expressed in those seven words and cannot be improved upon.

The bamboo tree is loved for its delicacy of trunk and leaves, and being more delicate, it is more enjoyed in the intimacy of a scholar's home. Its beauty is more a kind of smiling beauty and the happiness it gives us is mild and temperate. Bamboos are best enjoyed when they are thin and slender and sparse, and for this reason two or three trees are as good as a whole bamboo grove, either in life or in painting. The appreciation of its slender outlines makes it possible to paint just two or three twigs of bamboo in a picture, as it is also possible to paint a single twig of plum flowers. Somehow its slender lines go very well with the rugged lines of rocks, and hence one finds always one or two rocks painted along with a few bamboos. Such rocks are invariably painted as having the beauty of *slenderness*.

The willow grows easily anywhere and often on a bank.[1] It is the feminine tree *par excellence*. That is why Chang Ch'ao counts the willow among the four things in the universe which touch man's heart most profoundly, and why he says the willow tree makes a man sentimental. Chinese ladies of slender waist are said to have "willow waists," and Chinese female dancers, with their long sleeves and their flowing robe, try to simulate the movement of willow branches swaying and bowing in the wind. As willows grow most easily, there are places in China where willows are planted for miles around and then when a wind blows over them, the effect of the combination is spoken of as "willow-waves," or *liulang*. Furthermore, as orioles love to perch on their hanging branches, they are associated in pictures or in life with the presence of orioles, or with cicadas which also love to rest there. One of the ten scenic spots of the West Lake is therefore called *Liulang Wen Ying*, or "Listening to Orioles among Willow-Waves."

There are, of course, other trees, and a good number of them admired for other reasons, like the *wut'ung* (*sterculia platanitolia*), admired for the cleanliness of its bark and the possibility of

---

[1] I have translated in *My Country and My People* a passage by Li Liweng on the enjoyment of the willow tree.

carving poems on its smooth surface with a knife. There is also great love of gigantic old creepers, two or three inches across at their roots, encircling old trees or rocks. Their encircling and undulating movement contrasts pleasurably with the straight trunks of erect trees. Sometimes a particularly good creeper suggests a sleeping dragon and is given that name. Old trees that have zigzag and more or less sloping trunks are also greatly loved and valued for this reason. At Mutu, a point on the Taihu Lake near Soochow, there are four such cypress trees which have been given the four respective names "Pure," "Rare," "Antique" and "Quaint." "Pure" goes up by a long, straight trunk, spreading out a foliage on top resembling an umbrella; "Rare" crouches on the ground and rolls along in three zigzag bands like the letter "Z"; "Antique" is bald and bare at the top and broad and stumpy, with its straggling limbs half dried up and resembling a man's fingers; and "Quaint's" trunk twists around in spiral formation all the way up to its highest branches.

Above all, the enjoyment of trees is not only in and for themselves, but in association with other elements of nature, such as rocks, clouds, birds, insects and human beings. Chang Ch'ao says that "planting flowers serves to invite butterflies, piling up rocks serves to invite clouds, planting pine trees serves to invite the wind, . . . planting banana trees serves to invite the rain, and planting willow trees serves to invite the cicada." One enjoys the sounds of birds along with the trees, and enjoys the sounds of crickets along with the rocks, for birds sing where trees are, and crickets sing where rocks are found. The Chinese enjoyment of croaking frogs, chirping crickets and intoning cicadas is immeasurably greater than their love of cats and dogs and other animal pets. Among all the animals, the only one which belongs in the same category with pine trees and plum trees is the stork, because he, too, is the symbol of the recluse. As one sees a stork, or even a heron, standing motionless in the marshes of some secluded pond, dignified, elegant and white and pure, the scholar wishes that he were a stork himself.

The final picture of man harmonizing with nature and happy

because the animals are happy is best expressed by Cheng Panch'iao (1693-1765) in his letter to his younger brother, pointing out his disapproval of keeping birds in cages:

> In regard to what I said about not keeping birds in cages, I wish to add that it isn't that I don't love birds, but there is a proper way of loving them. The best way of keeping birds is to plant hundreds of trees around the house, and let them find in their green shade a bird kingdom and bird homes. So then, at dawn, when we have waked up from sleep and are still tossing about in bed, we hear a chorus of chirping songs like a celestial symphony. When we have got up and put on our gowns and are washing our faces or gargling our mouths or sipping the morning tea, we see their gorgeous plumes flitting to and fro, and before we have time to look at one, our eyes are attracted by another—an enjoyment that is not to be compared with looking at a single bird in a single cage. Generally the enjoyment of life should come from a view regarding the universe as a park and the rivers and lakes as a pond, so that all beings can live according to their nature, and great indeed is such happiness! How does this compare in kindness and cruelty and in the magnitude of enjoyment with the enjoyment of a bird in a cage, or of a fish in a jar!

V. ON FLOWERS AND FLOWER ARRANGEMENTS

There seems to be a certain randomness about the enjoyment of flowers and flower arrangements, as we know it to-day. The enjoyment of flowers, like the enjoyment of trees, must begin with the selection of certain noble varieties, with a sense of grading of their relative standing, and with the association of definite sentiments and surroundings with definite flowers. To begin with, there is the matter of fragrance, from the strong and obvious, like that of jasmine, to the delicate, like that of lilac, and finally to the most refined and subtle kind, like that of the Chinese orchid. The more subtle and less easily perceivable its fragrance, the more noble the flower may be regarded. Then there is the matter of colour and appearance and charm, which again varies a great deal. Some are like buxom lassies and others are like slender, poetic, quiet ladies. Some seem to pander their charms to the crowd, and others are happy in their own fragrant being and seem contented merely to dream their hours away. Some go in for a dash of colour, while others have a milder and more restrained taste. Above all, flowers are always associated with the outward surroundings and seasons of their bloom. The rose is naturally associated in our minds with a bright sunny spring day; the lotus is naturally associated with a cool summer morning on a pond; the cassia is naturally associated with the harvest moon and mid-autumn festivities; the chrysanthemum is associated with the eating of crabs in late autumn; the plum is naturally associated with snow and together with the narcissus it forms a definite part of our enjoyment of the New Year. Each seems perfect in its own natural surroundings, and it is the easiest of all things for lovers of flowers to make them stand in our mind for definite pictures of the different seasons, as the holly stands for Christmas.

Like the pine tree and the bamboo, the orchid, the chrysanthemum and the lotus are selected for certain definite qualities and stand in Chinese literature as symbols for the gentleman, the orchid more particularly for an exotic beauty. The plum flower is probably most beloved by Chinese poets among all flowers, and has been partly dealt with already in the previous section. It is said to be the "first" among the flowers, because it comes with the New Year and therefore stands first in the procession of flowers in the course of the year. Opinions differ, of course, and the peony has been traditionally regarded as the "king of flowers," particularly in the T'ang Dynasty. On the other hand, the peony, being rich in its colours and its petals, is rather regarded as the symbol of the rich and happy man, whereas, the plum flower is the poet's flower, and symbol of the quiet, poor scholar, and therefore the latter is spiritual as the former is materialistic. One scholar voiced his sympathy for the peony only because of the fact that, when Empress Wu of the T'ang Dynasty commanded one day, in one of her megalomaniac whims, that all the flowers in the

Imperial garden should bloom on a certain day in mid-winter, just because she wanted it, the peony was the only one that dared to offend her Imperial Majesty by blooming a few hours late, and consequently, all the thousands of pots of peony flowers were banished by Imperial decree from Sian, the capital, to Loyang. Although falling out of Imperial favour, the cult of the peony was still maintained and Loyang became a centre for peony flowers. I think the reason that the Chinese do not place more importance on the rose is because its colour and shape belong in the same class with the peony, but have been overshadowed by the latter's gorgeousness. According to early Chinese sources, there were ninety varieties of the peony distinguished, and each was given a most poetic name.

Unlike the peony, the orchid stands as the symbol of secluded charm because it is often found in a deserted shady valley. It is said to have the virtue of "enjoying its own lonely charm," not caring whether people look at it or not, and extremely unwilling to be moved into the city. If it consents to be moved, it must be cultivated on its own terms, or it dies. Hence we often speak of a beautiful secluded maiden, or a great scholar living away in the mountains with contempt for power and fame, as "a secluded orchid in a deserted valley." Its fragrance is so subtle that it doesn't seem to make a particular effort to please anybody, but when people do appreciate it, how divine is its fragrance! This makes it a symbol for the gentleman not caring to cater to the public, and also for true friendship, because an ancient book says, "After entering and remaining in a house with orchids for a long time, one ceases to feel the fragrance," when he himself is permeated with it. Li Liweng advised that the best way to enjoy orchids was not to place them in all rooms, but only in one room and then to enjoy the fragrance when passing out and in. American orchids do not seem to have this subtle fragrance, but on the other hand, are bigger and more gorgeous in shape and colour. In my native city and province, we are supposed to have the best orchids in China, known as "Fukien orchids." The flower is pale green with spots of purple and is of a very much smaller size, the petals being slightly over an inch long. The best and most highly valued variety, the Ch'en Mengliang, has such a colour that it is barely visible when immersed in water, being of the same colour as the water itself. Unlike the peony, whose varieties are known after their place of origin, the different famous varieties of the orchid are known, like many American flower varieties, after their owners, as "General P'u," "Quartermaster Shun," "Judge Li," "Eighth Brother Huang," "Ch'en Mengliang," "Hsü Chingch'u."

There is no question that the extreme difficulty of cultivating orchids and the flower's extreme delicacy of health contributed to the idea of its nobility of character. Among all the flowers, the orchid is the one that most easily withers or rots away with the slightest mishandling. Hence an orchid-lover always attends to it with his personal care and does not leave it to the servants, and I have seen people caring for their orchids like their own parents. An extremely valuable plant aroused as much jealousy as a particularly good piece of bronze or vase, and hatred from a friend's refusal to give away its new offshoots could be extremely bitter. Chinese notebooks record the case of a scholar who was refused new offshoots from a plant and was sentenced to jail for stealing it. This sentiment is well expressed by Shen Fu in *Six Chapters of a Floating Life* in the following manner:

> The orchid was prized most among all the flowers because of its subdued fragrance and graceful charm, but it was difficult to obtain really good classic varieties. When Lanp'o died, he presented me with a pot of spring orchids, whose flowers had lotus-shaped petals; the centre of the flowers was broad and white, the petals were very neat and even at the "shoulders," and the stems were very slender. This type was classical, and I prized it like a piece of old jade. When I was working away from home, Yün used to take care of it personally and it grew beautifully. After two years, it died suddenly one day. I dug up its roots and found that they were white like marble, while nothing was wrong with the sprouts, either. At first, I could not understand this, but ascribed it with a sigh merely to my

own bad luck, which might be unworthy to raise such flowers. Later on, I found out that someone had asked for some of the flowers from the same pot, had been refused, and had therefore killed it by pouring boiling water over it. Thenceforth I swore I would never grow orchids again.

The chrysanthemum is the flower of the poet T'ao Yüanming, as the plum flower was the flower of the poet Lin Hoching, and the lotus was the flower of the Confucian doctrinaire, Chou Liench'i. Blooming in late autumn, it shares the idea of "cold fragrance" and "cold splendour." The contrast between the cold splendour of the chrysanthemum and the gorgeous splendour, say, of the peony is easily seen and understood. Hundreds of varieties exist, and so far as I know, a great Sung scholar, Fan Ch'engta, started the fashion of recording its different varieties with the most beautiful names. Variety seems to be the very essence of the chrysanthemum flower, both variety of shape and of colour. The white and the yellow are regarded as the "orthodox" colours of the flower, while purple and red are regarded as deviations and therefore given a low grading. The colours of white and yellow gave rise to the names of the varieties like "Silver Bowl," "Silver Bells," "Golden Bells," "Jade Basin," "Jade Bells," "Jade-embroidered Ball." Some were given the names of famous beauties, like "Yang Kueifei" and "Hsishih." Sometimes their shapes resemble a lady's close-cropped hair and sometimes their quills resemble flowing locks. Some varieties have more fragrance than others, and the best are supposed to have the fragrance of musk, or of an incense called "Dragon's Brains."

The lotus or water-lily is in a class by itself and seems to me personally the most beautiful of all flowers, when we consider the flower, including its stem and its leaves floating on the water, as a whole. It is impossible to enjoy summer without having lotus flowers around, and if one does not have a house near a pond, he can grow them in big earthen jars. In this case, however, we miss much of the beauty of a half a mile's stretch of lotus flowers, their perfume pervading the air, and their white-and-red-tipped blossoms contrasting with their broad green leaves with water running on them like liquid pearls. (The American water-lilies are different from the lotus.) The Sung scholar Chou wrote an essay explaining why he loved the lotus and pointing out that the lotus, like the gentleman, grew out of dirty water but was not contaminated by it. He was talking like a regular Confucian doctrinaire. From the utilitarian point of view, every part of the flower is utilized. The lotus root is used to make a cooling drink, its leaves are used for wrapping fruits or food to be steamed, its flowers are enjoyed for their shape and fragrance, and finally the lotus seed is regarded as the food of the fairies, either eaten raw, fresh from the pod, or dried and sugared.

The *hait'ang* pyrus, resembling apple-blossoms, enjoys as great a popularity among poets as any other flower, although Tu Fu failed to make a single mention of this flower which grew in his native province, Szechuen. Various explanations have been offered, but the most plausible one was that the *hait'ang* was his mother's name and he had avoided it out of deference to his mother. There are only two flowers for whose fragrance I am willing to forgo the orchid, and they are the cassia and the narcissus. The last is also a special product of my native city, Changchow, and its import into the United States in the form of cultivated roots at one time ran to hundreds of thousands of dollars, until the Department of Agriculture saw fit to deprive the American people of this flower with a heavenly fragrance, in order to protect them from possible germs. The notion that the white roots of the narcissus, as clean as a fairy itself, and intended to be planted not in mud but in a glass or china basin of water supported with pebbles, and prepared with the utmost care, could contain germs is most fantastic. The azalea is supposed to be a tragic flower, in spite of its smiling beauty, because it was supposed to spring from the tears of blood of the cuckoo, who was formerly a boy in search of his lost brother persecuted out of home by a stepmother.

Quite as important as the selection and grading of the flowers themselves is their arrangement in vases. This was an art that could be traced back at least as far as the eleventh century. The

author of *Six Chapters of a Floating Life,* written at the beginning
of the nineteenth century, gives a description of the art of
arranging flowers to resemble a picture with good composition in
his chapter on "The Little Pleasures of Life":

> The chrysanthemum, however, was my passion in the autumn
> of every year. I loved to arrange these flowers in vases, but not
> to raise them in pots, not because I did not want to have them
> that way, but because I had no garden in my home and could
> not take care of them myself. Those I bought at the market
> were not properly trained and not to my liking. When arrang-
> ing chrysanthemum flowers in vases, one should take an odd,
> not an even number, and each vase should have flowers of only
> one colour. The mouth of the vase should be broad so that the
> flowers can lie easily together. Whether there be half a dozen
> flowers or even thirty or forty of them in a vase, they should
> be so arranged as to come up together straight from the mouth
> of the vase, neither overcrowded, nor too much spread out, nor
> leaning against the mouth of the vase. This is called "keeping
> the handle firm." Sometimes they can stand gracefully erect,
> and sometimes spread out in different directions. In order to
> avoid a bare monotonous effect, they should be mixed with
> some flower-buds and arranged in a kind of studied disorder-
> liness. The leaves should not be too thick and the stems should
> not be too stiff. In using pins to hold the stems up, one should
> break the long pins off rather than expose them. This is called
> "keeping the mouth of the vase clear." Place from three to
> seven vases on a table, depending on the size of the latter, for if
> there were too many of them, they would be overcrowded,
> looking like chrysanthemum screens at the market. The stands
> for the vases should be of different height, from three or four
> inches to two and a half feet, so that the different vases at
> different heights would balance one another and belong
> intimately to one another as in a picture with unity of com-
> position. To put one vase high in the centre with two low at
> the sides, or to put a low one in front and a tall one behind, or

to arrange them in symmetrical pairs, would be to create what is vulgarly called "a heap of gorgeous refuse." Proper spacing and arrangement must depend on the individual's understanding of pictorial composition.

In the case of flower-bowls or open dishes, the method of making a support for the flowers is to mix refined resin with elm bark, flour and oil, and heat the mixture with hot hay ashes until it becomes a kind of glue, and with it glue some nails upside down on to a piece of copper. This copper plate can then be heated up and glued on to the bottom of the bowl or dish. When it is cold, tie the flowers in groups by means of wire and stick them on those nails. The flowers should be allowed to incline sideways and not shoot up from the centre; it is also important that the stems and leaves should not come too closely together. After this is done, put some water in the bowl and cover up the copper support with some clean sand, so that the flowers will seem to grow directly from the bottom of the bowl.

When picking branches from flower trees for decoration in vases, it is important to know how to trim them before putting them in the vase, for one cannot always go and pick them oneself, and those picked by others are often unsatisfactory. Hold the branch in your hand and turn it back and forth in different ways in order to see how it lies most expressively. After one has made up one's mind about it, lop off the superfluous branches, with the idea of making the twig look thin and sparse and quaintly beautiful. Next think how the stem is going to lie in the vase and with what kind of bend, so that when it is put there, the leaves and flowers can be shown to the best advantage. If one just takes any old branch in hand, chooses a straight section and puts it in the vase, the consequence will be that the stem will be too stiff, the branches will be too close together and the flowers and leaves will be turned in the wrong direction, devoid of all charm and expression. To make a straight twig crooked, cut a mark half-way across the stem and insert a little piece of broken brick or stone at the joint; the straight branch will then become a bent one. In case the stem is too weak, put one or two pins to strengthen it. By means of this method, even maple leaves and bamboo twigs or even ordinary blades of grass and thistles will look very well for decoration. Put a twig of green bamboo side by side with a few berries of Chinese matrimony vine or arrange some fine blades of grass together with some branches of thistle. They will look quite poetic, if the arrangement is correct.

VI. THE "VASE FLOWERS" OF YÜAN CHUNGLANG

Probably the best treatise on the arrangement of flowers was written by Yüan Chunglang, one of my favourite authors in other respects, living at the end of the sixteenth century. His book on the arrangement of flowers in vases, called *P'ingshih,* is highly valued in Japan, and there is known to be a "Yüan School" of flower arrangement. He began in his preface by noting that since hills and water and flowers and bamboos luckily lay outside the scope of the strugglers for fame and power, and furthermore, since such people were so busy with their engrossing pursuits and therefore had no time for the enjoyment of hills and water and flowers and bamboos, the retiring scholar was enabled to snatch this opportunity and monopolize the enjoyment of the latter for himself. He explained, however, that the enjoyment of vase flowers should never be regarded as normal, but at best only as a temporary substitute for people living in cities, and their enjoyment should not cause one to forget the greater happiness of enjoying the hills and lakes themselves.

Proceeding from a consideration that one should be careful in admitting flowers for decoration in his studio, and that it would be better to have no flowers at all than to have promiscuous varieties admitted, he went on to describe the various types of bronze and porcelain vases to be used. Two types are distinguished. Those who are rich and possess antique bronze vessels of Han Dynasty and have big halls should have big flowers and tall branches standing

[317]

in huge vases. On the other hand, scholars should have smaller branches of flowers to go with smaller vases, which should also be carefully selected. The only exceptions allowed are the peony and the lotus, which, being big flowers, should be placed in big vases. In putting flowers in vases:

One should avoid having them too profuse, or too meagre. At most, two or three varieties may be put in a vase, and their relative height and arrangement should aim at the composition of a good picture. In placing flower vases, one should avoid having them in pairs, or uniform, or in a straight row. One should also avoid binding the flowers with string. For the neatness of flowers lies exactly in their irregularity and natural-ness of manner, like the prose of Tu Sungp'o, which flows on or stops as it pleases, and like the poems of Li Po, which do not necessarily go in couplets. This is true neatness. How can it be called neatness when the branches and leaves merely match each other and red is mixed with white? The latter resemble the trees in the courtyard of minor provincial officials or the stone gateways leading to a tomb.

In selecting and breaking off the branches, one should choose the slender and exquisite ones and should not have the branches too thick together. Only one kind of flowers should be used, and at most two, and the two should be so arranged together that they seem to grow out of one branch. . . . Generally the flowers should match with the vases, and they may be four or five inches taller than the height of the vase itself. Suppose the vase is two feet high and its shape is broad in the centre and bottom, the flowers may be two feet and six or seven inches from the mouth of the vase. . . . If the vase is tall and slender, one should have two branches, one long and one short, and perhaps stretching out in curves, and then it is better that the flowers are a few inches shorter than the vase itself. What is most to be avoided is that the flowers be too slender for the vase. Profusion is also to be avoided, as, for instance, when flowers are tied up together like a handle, lacking all charm. In placing flowers in small vases, one should let the flowers come out two inches shorter than the body of the vase. For instance, a narrow vase of eight inches should have flowers of only six or seven inches. But if the vases are stout in shape, flowers may also be two inches longer than the vases.

The room in which flowers are placed should contain a simple table and a cane couch. The table must be broad and thick and should be of fine wood and have a smooth surface. All lacquered tables with decorated margins, golden-painted couches and stands with coloured floral designs should be eliminated.

With regard to the "bathing" of flowers, or watering them, the author shows a loving insight into the moods and sentiments of the flowers themselves:

For flowers have their moods of happiness and sorrow and their time of sleep. If one bathes flowers in their morning and evening, at the proper time, the water is like good rain to them. A day with light clouds and a mild sun and the sunset and beautiful moon are morning to the flowers. A big storm, a pouring rain, a scorching sun and bitter cold are evening to the flowers. When their stands bask in the sunlight and their delicate bodies are protected from wind, that is the happy mood of the flowers. When they seem drunk or quiet and tired and when the day is misty, that is the sorrowful mood of the flowers. When their branches incline and rest sideways as if unable to hold themselves erect, that is when the flowers are dreaming in their sleep. When they seem to smile and look about, with a shining light in their eyes, that is when the flowers have waked up from their sleep. In their "morning" they should be placed in an empty pavilion or a big house; in their "evening" they should be placed in a small room or a secluded chamber; when they are sad they should sit quietly with abated breath, and when they are happy they should smile and shout and tease each other; during their sleep they should let down the curtain, and when they have waked up they should attend to their toilet. All this is done to please their nature and regulate

[319]

their times of getting up and going to bed. To bathe flowers in their "morning" is the best; to bathe them when they are asleep is second; and to bathe them when they are happy is the last. As for bathing them during their "evening," or during their sorrow, it really seems more like a way of punishing the flowers.

The way of bathing flowers is to use fresh and sweet water from a spring and pour it down gently in small quantities, like a small shower awakening a drunken man, or like the gentle dew itself permeating their body. One should avoid touching the flowers with his hands, or picking them with the tips of fingers, and the work cannot be entrusted to stupid manservants or dirty maids. Plum flowers should be bathed by recluse scholars, the *hait'ang* by charming guests, the peony by beautifully dressed young girls, the pomegranate by beautiful slave-girls, the cassia by intelligent children, the lotus by fascinating concubines, the chrysanthemum by remarkable persons who love the ancients, and the winter plum by a slender monk. On the other hand, flowers blooming in the cold season should not be bathed, but should be protected by thin silk gauze.

According to Yüan, certain flowers go with certain other flowers as their minors or "maids" in a vase. As personal maids who attended to a lady for life were an institution in old China, there developed the notion that beautiful ladies looked perfect when they had pretty maids by their side as their necessary adjuncts. Both ladies and maids should be beautiful, but there is a *je ne sais quoi* which stamps one type of beauty as belonging to a maid rather than to a mistress. Maids who were out of harmony with their mistresses were like stables that did not match a manor house. Carrying the notion over to flowers, Yüan found that, for their "maids" in the vase, the plum flower should have camellias, the *hait'ang* should have apple blossoms and lilacs, the peony should have cinnamon roses, the *paeonia albiflora* should have poppies and Szechuen sunflowers, the pomegranate should have crape myrtle and *hibiscus syriacus,* the lotus should have white day

lilies, the cassia should have *hibiscus mutabilis,* the chrysanthemum should have "autumn *hait'ang,*" and the winter plum
should have narcissus. Each maid is exquisite in its own way, and
they differ in their voluptuous or elegant charms like their
mistresses. Not that any slight was intended upon these flower-
maids, for they were comparable to the famous maids of history,
the narcissus ethereal down to her bones like Liang Yüch'ing, the
maid of the Spinster in heaven, the camellia and the rose fresh
and youthful like the maids Hsiangfeng and Chingwan of the Shih
and Yang families (of Chin Dynasty), the *shanfan* flower clean and
"romantic" like the maidservant of the tragic nun-poetess, Yü
Hsüanch'i, while the lilac was slender, the white day lily was cool
and the "autumn *hait'ang*" was coy, but savoured a little of pedantry
like the maid of Cheng K'angch'eng (scholar of Han Dynasty and
profuse commentator on Confucian classics).[1]

Holding to his central idea that anyone who achieves notable
results in any line, even in such matters as playing chess, must
love it to a point of craze, Yüan develops the same idea with
regard to the love of flowers as a hobby:

I have found that all the people in the world who are dull
in their conversation and hateful to look at in their faces are
those who have no hobbies. . . . When the ancient people
who had a weakness for flowers heard there was a remarkable
variety, they would travel across high mountain passes and
deep ravines in search of them, unconscious of bodily fatigue,
bitter cold or scorching heat, and their peeling skins, and
completely oblivious of their bodies soiled with mud. When a
flower was about to bud, they would move their beds and
pillows to sleep under them, watching how the flowers passed
from infancy to maturity and finally dropped off and died.
Or they would plant thousands in their orchards to study how
they varied, or have just a few in their rooms to exhaust their
interest. Some would be able to tell the size of flowers from

[1] Cheng's maid was reputed to talk the classical language with her learned master,
which is somewhat like talking Latin among the medieval scholars.

smelling their leaves, and some were able to tell from the roots the colour of their flowers. These were the people who were true lovers of flowers and who had a true weakness for them.

in regard to the "enjoyment" (or *shang*) of flowers, it is pointed out that:

Enjoying them with tea is the best, enjoying them with conversation second, and enjoying them with wine the third. As for all forms of noisy behaviour and common vulgar prattle, they are an insult to the spirits of flowers. One should rather sit dumb like a fool than offend them. There is a proper place and time for the enjoyment of flowers and to enjoy them without regard to the proper circumstances would be a sacrilege. The flowers in the cold season should be enjoyed at the beginning of snow, or after the sky has cleared after a snowfall, or during crescent moon, or in a warm room. The flowers in the warm [spring] season should be enjoyed on a clear day, or on a slightly chilly day, in a beautiful hall. The flowers of summer should be enjoyed after rain, in a refreshing breeze, in the shade of nice trees, beneath bamboos, or on a water terrace. The flowers of the cool [autumn] season should be enjoyed under a cool moon, at sunset, on the brink of a stone hall pavement, on a mossy garden path, or in the neighbourhood of rugged rocks surrounded by ancient creepers. If one looks at flowers without regard to wind and sun and place, or when one's thoughts are wandering and bear no relation to the flowers, what difference is it from seeing flowers in sing-song houses and wine taverns?

Finally, Yüan lists the following fourteen conditions as "pleasing" to the flowers, and "twenty-three"[1] conditions as being disgraceful or humiliating to them:

[1] Chinese authors are apparently indifferent to arithmetic and figures in general. After comparing the best available editions of Yüan's works, I still cannot find the reputed "twenty-three" conditions. It really doesn't matter whether one's figures are correct. Mathematical exactitude worries only a petty soul.

"VASE FLOWERS"

Conditions that please the flowers:

A clear window

A clean room

Antique tripods

Sung ink-stones

"Pine waves" and river sounds

The owner loving hobbies and poetry

Visiting monk understands tea

A native of Chichow arrives with wine

Guests in the room are exquisite

Many flowers in bloom

A carefree friend has arrived

Copying books on flower cultivation

Kettle sings deep at night

Wife and concubines editing stories of flowers

Conditions humiliating to the flowers:

The owner constantly seeing guests

A stupid servant putting in extra branches, upsetting the arrangement

Common monks talking *zen*

Dogs fighting before the window

Singing boys of Lientse Alley

Yiyang [*Kiangsi*] tunes

Ugly women plucking flowers and decorating their hair with them

Discussing people's official promotion and demotion

False expressions of love

Poems written for courtesy

Flowers in full bloom before one has paid his debts

The family asking for accounts

Writing poems by consulting rhyming dictionaries

Books in bad condition lying about

Fukien agents

Kiangsu spurious paintings

Fæces of mice and rats

Trailing marks of slime left by snails

Servants lying about

Wine runs out after one begins to play wine games

Being neighbour to wine-shops

A piece of writing with phrases like the "purple morning air" [common in imperial eulogies] on the desk

VII. THE EPIGRAMS OF CHANG CH'AO

We have seen that the enjoyment of nature does not lie merely in art and painting. Nature enters into our life as a whole. It is all sound and colour and shape and mood and atmosphere, and man as the perceiving artist of life begins to select the proper moods of nature and harmonize them with his own. This is the attitude of all Chinese writers of poetry or prose, but I think its best expression is found in the epigrams of Chang Ch'ao (mid-seventeenth century), in his book *Yumengying* (or *Sweet Dream Shadows*). This is a book of literary maxims, of which there are many collections, but none comparable to those written by Chang Ch'ao himself. Such literary maxims stand in relation to popular proverbs as the fairy tales of Andersen stand in relation to old English fairy tales, or as Schubert's art songs stand in relation to folk melodies. His book has been so beloved that a group of Chinese scholars have added comments of their own to each of his maxims, in a most delightful chatty vein. I am compelled, however, to translate only some of the best of his maxims about the enjoyment of Nature. A few of his maxims on human life are so good and form such a vital part of the whole that I shall include some of them at the end.

On What is Proper

It is absolutely necessary that flowers should have butterflies, hills should have springs, rocks should have moss, water should have water-cress, tall trees should have entwining creepers, and human beings should have hobbies.

One should enjoy flowers in the company of beauties, get drunk under the moon in the company of charming friends, and enjoy the light of snow in the company of high-minded scholars.

Planting flowers serves to invite butterflies, piling up rocks serves to invite the clouds, planting pine trees serves to invite the wind, keeping a reservoir of water serves to invite duck-weed, building a terrace serves to invite the moon, planting banana trees serves to invite the rain, and planting willow trees serves to invite the cicada.

One always gets a different feeling when looking at hills from the top of a tower, looking at snow from a city wall, looking at the moon in the lamp-light, looking at coloured clouds in a boat, and looking at beautiful women in the room.

Rocks lying near a plum tree should look "antique," those beneath a pine tree should look "stupid," those by the side of bamboo trees should look "slender," and those inside a flower basin should be exquisite.

Blue waters come from green hills, for the water borrows its colour from the hills; good poems come from flavoury wine, for poetry begs its inspiration from the wine.

When the mirror meets with an ugly woman, when a rare ink-stone finds a vulgar owner, and when a good sword is in the hands of a common general, there is utterly nothing to be done about it.

On Flowers and Women

One should not see flowers wither, see the moon decline below the horizon, or see beautiful women die in their youth.

One should see flowers when they are in bloom, after planting the flowers; should see the moon when it is full, after waiting for the moon; should see a book completed, after starting to write it; and should see beautiful women when they are gay and happy. Otherwise our purpose is defeated.

One should look at beautiful ladies in the morning toilet after they have powdered themselves.

There are faces that are ugly but stand looking at, and other faces that do not stand looking at, although not ugly; there are writings which are lovable although ungrammatical, and there are other writings which are extremely grammatical, but are disgusting. This is something that I cannot explain to superficial persons.

If one loves flowers with the same heart that he loves beauties, he feels a special charm in them; if one loves beautiful women with the same heart that he loves flowers, he feels a special tenderness and protective affection.

Beautiful women are better than flowers because they understand human language, and flowers are better than beautiful women because they give off fragrance; but if one cannot have both at the same time, he should forsake the fragrant ones and take the talking ones.

In putting flowers in liver-coloured vases, one should arrange them so that the size and height of the vase match with those of the flowers, while the shade and depth of its colour should contrast with them.

Most of the flowers that are seductive and beautiful are not fragrant, and flowers that have layers upon layers of petals mostly are ill-formed. Alas, rare is a perfect personality! Only the lotus combines both.

The plum flower makes a man feel high-minded, the orchid makes a man feel secluded, the chrysanthemum makes a man simple-hearted, the lotus makes a man contented, the spring *hait'ang*[1] makes a man passionate, the peony makes a man chivalrous, the bamboo and the banana tree make a man charming, the autumn *hait'ang* makes a man graceful, the pine tree makes a man feel like a recluse, the *wut'ung* (*sterculia platanifolia*) makes a man clean-hearted, and the willow makes a man sentimental.

If a beauty should have the face of a flower, the voice of a bird, the soul of the moon, the expression of a willow, the charm of an autumn lake, bones of jade and skin of snow, and a heart of poetry, I should be perfectly satisfied. [I should say so!—Tr.][2]

If there are no books in this world, then nothing need be said, but since there are books, they must be read; if there is no wine, then nothing need be said, but since there is wine, it must be drunk; if there are no famous hills, then nothing need

[1] This is a flowering tree about ten feet high, belonging to the pyrus species, and bearing fruits like crab-apples.
[2] This is in the manner of the Chinese commentators

be said, but since there are, they must be visited; if there are no flowers and no moon, then nothing need be said, but since there are, they must be enjoyed and "played"; if there are no talented men and beautiful women, then nothing need be said, but since there are, they must be loved and protected.

The reason why a looking-glass doesn't become the enemy of ugly-looking women is because it has no feeling; if it had, it certainly would have been smashed to pieces.

One feels tender toward even a good potted flower that he has just bought; how much more should he be tender toward a "talking flower"!

Without wine and poetry, hills and water would exist for no purpose; without the company of beautiful ladies, flowers and the moon would be wasted. Talented men who are at the same time handsome, and beautiful ladies who at the same time can write, can never live a long life. This is not only because the gods are jealous of them, but because this type of person is not only the treasure of one generation, but the treasure of all ages, so that the Creator doesn't want to leave them in this world too long, for fear of sacrilege.

On Hills and Water

Of all the things in the universe, those that touch man most profoundly are: the moon in heaven, the *ch'in* in music, the cuckoo among animals, and the willow tree among plants.

To worry with the moon about clouds, to worry with books about moths, to worry with flowers about storms, and to worry with talented men and beautiful women about a harsh fate is to have the heart of a Buddha.

One dies without regret if there is one in the whole world a "bosom friend," or one who "knows his heart."

An ancient writer said that if there were no flowers and moon and beautiful women, he would not want to be born in this world, and I might add, if there were no pen and ink and chess and wine, there was no purpose in being born a man.

The light of hills, the sound of water, the colour of the moon, the fragrance of flowers, the charm of literary men, and the expression of beautiful women are all elusive and indescribable. They make one lose sleep dreaming about them and lose appetite thinking about them.

The snow reminds one of a high-minded scholar; the flower reminds one of beautiful ladies; wine reminds one of good swordsmen; the moon reminds one of good friends; and hills and water remind one of good verse and good prose that the author himself is pleased with.

There are landscapes on earth, landscapes in painting, landscapes in dreams, and landscapes in one's breast. The beauty of landscapes on earth lies in depth and irregularity of outline; the beauty of landscapes in painting lies in the freedom and luxuriousness of the brush and ink; the beauty of landscapes in dreams lies in their strangely changing views; and the beauty of landscapes in one's breast lies in the fact that everything is in its proper place.

For places that we pass by during our travel, we need not be fastidious in our artistic demands, but for places where we are going to settle down for life we must be fastidious in such demands.

The bamboo-shoot is a phenomenon among the vegetables; the *lich'i* is a phenomenon among fruits; the crab is a phenomenon among aquatic animals; wine is a phenomenon among our foods and drinks; the moon is a phenomenon in the firmament; the West Lake is a phenomenon among hills and waters; and the Sung lyrics (*ts'e*) and Yüan dramatic poems (*ch'ü*) are phenomena in literature.

In order to see famous hills and rivers, one must have also predestined luck; unless the appointed time has come, one has no time to see them even though they are situated within a dozen miles.

The images in a looking-glass are portraits in colour, but the images [shadows] under a moonlight are pen sketches. The images in a looking-glass are paintings with solid outlines, but the images under a moonlight are "paintings without bones."

The images of hills and waters in the moon are geography in heaven, and the images of stars and the moon in water are astronomy on earth.

On Spring and Autumn

Spring is the natural frame of mind of heaven; autumn is one of its changing moods.

The ancient people regarded winter as the "extra" [or resting period] of the other three seasons, but I think we should regard summer as the season of "three extras": getting up at a summer dawn is the extra of the night; sitting at a summer night is the extra of the day; and an afternoon nap is the extra of social intercourse. Indeed, "I love the long summer days," as an ancient poet says.

One should discipline oneself in the spirit of autumn, and deal with others in the spirit of spring.

Good prose and "T'ang poems" should have the spirit of autumn; good Sung lyrics and Yüan dramatic poems should have the spirit of spring.[1]

On Sounds

One should listen to the sounds of birds in spring, to the sounds of cicadas in summer, to the sounds of insects in autumn and the sounds of snowfall in winter; he should listen to the sounds of playing chess in the daytime, the sounds of flute under the moonlight, the sounds of pine trees in the mountains, and the sounds of ripples on the waterside. Then he shall not have lived in vain. But when a young loafer starts a racket in the street or when one's wife is scolding, one might just as well be deaf.

Hearing the sound of geese makes one feel like in Nanking; hearing the sound of oars makes one feel like in Soochow, Ch'angchow and Huchow;[2] hearing the sound of waves on the beach makes one feel like being in Chekiang; and hearing the

---

[1] Both these latter forms are highly sentimental poetry in form and feeling.
[2] The Lake District in Kiangsu.

sound of bells beneath the necks of thin horses makes one feel like being on the road to Sian.

All sounds should be listened to at a distance; only the sounds of the *ch'in* can be listened to both at a distance and nearby.

There is a special flavour about one's ears when listening to *ch'in* music under pine trees, listening to a flute in the moonlight, listening to a waterfall by a brook, and listening to Buddhist chants in the mountains.

There are four kinds of sounds of water: the sounds of cataracts, of gushing springs, of rapids, and of gullets. There are three kinds of sounds of wind: the sounds of "pine waves," of autumn leaves, and of storm upon the water. There are two kinds of sounds of rain: the sounds of raindrops upon the leaves of *wut'ung* and lotus, and the sounds of rain-water coming down from the eaves into bamboo pails.

On Rain

This thing called rain can make the days seem short and the nights seem long.

A spring rain is like an Imperial edict conferring an honour; a summer rain is like a writ of pardon for a condemned criminal; an autumn rain is like a dirge.

A rainy day in spring is suitable for reading; a rainy day in summer is suitable for playing chess; a rainy day in autumn is suitable for going over things in the trunks or in the attic; and a rainy day in winter is suitable for drinking.

I would write a letter to the God of Rain and tell him that rain in spring should come after the fifteenth of the first moon [when the Lantern Festival is over], and continue till ten days before *ch'ingming* [the third day of the third moon, at which time the peach-trees begin to blossom], and come also at *kuyü* [time for planting rice]; that summer rain should come in the first and last ten days of every month [so as not to interfere with our enjoyment of the moon]; that autumn rain should come in the first and last ten days of the seventh and the ninth moon [leaving the eighth moon, or mid-autumn, entirely dry for enjoyment of the harvest moon]; and that as for the three months of winter, no rain is called for at all.

On the Moon, Wind and Water

One is exasperated at the crescent moon for declining so early, and exasperated at the waning moon in its third quarter for coming up so late.

To listen to a Buddhist lesson under the moon makes one's mental mood more detached; to discuss swordsmanship under the moon makes one's courage more inspired; to discuss poetry under the moon makes one's personal flavour more charming in seclusion; and to look at beautiful women under the moon makes one's passion deeper.

The method of "playing" the moon is to look up at it from a low place when it is clear and bright, and to look down at it from a height when it is hazy and unclear.

The spring wind is like wine; the summer wind is like tea; the autumn wind is like smoke; and the winter wind is like ginger.

On Leisure and Friendship

Only those who take leisurely what the people of the world are busy about can be busy about what the people of the world take leisurely.

There is nothing that man enjoys more than leisure, and this does not mean that one simply does nothing during that time. Leisure enables one to read, to travel to famous places, to form beneficial friendships, to drink wine, and to write books. What greater pleasures can there be in the world than these?

When a cloud reflects the sun, it becomes a coloured cloud (*hsia*), and when a spring gullet flows over a cliff, it becomes a waterfall. By a different association, it is given a new name. That is why friendship is so valuable.

When celebrating the Lantern Festival on the fifteenth of

the first moon, one should drink with nonchalant friends; when celebrating the Dragon Boat Festival on the fifth of the fifth moon, one should drink with handsome friends; when celebrating the annual reunion of the Cowherd and the Spinning Maid in Heaven on the seventh day of the seventh moon, one should drink with friends who have charm; when looking at the harvest moon, at the Mid-Autumn Festival, one should drink with quiet or mild-tempered friends; when going up to high mountains on the ninth day of the ninth moon, one should drink with romantic friends.

To talk with learned friends is like reading a rare book; to talk with poetic friends is like reading the poems and prose of distinguished writers; to talk with friends who are careful and proper in their conduct is like reading the classics of the sages; and to talk with witty friends is like reading a novel or romance.

Every quiet scholar is bound to have some bosom friends. By "bosom friends" I do not mean necessarily those who have sworn a life-and-death friendship with us. Generally bosom friends are those who, although separated by hundreds or thousands of miles, still have implicit faith in us and refuse to believe rumours against us; those who on hearing a rumour try every means to explain it away; those who in given moments advise us as to what to do and what not to do; and those who at the critical hour come to our help, and, sometimes without our knowing, undertake of their own accord to settle a financial account, or make a decision, without for a moment questioning whether by doing so they are not making themselves open to criticism of perhaps injuring our interests.

It is easier to find bosom friends ("those who know our hearts") among friends than among one's wife and concubines, and it is still more difficult to find a bosom friend in the relationship between ruler and ministers.

A "remarkable book" is one which says things that have never been said before, and a "bosom friend" is one who unburdens to us his family secrets.

Living in the country is only enjoyable when one has got good friends with him. One soon gets tired of the peasants and woodcutters who know only how to distinguish the different kinds of grains and to forecast the weather. Again, among the different kinds of friends, those who can write poems are the best, those who can talk or hold a conversation come second, those who can paint come next, those who can sing come fourth, and those who understand wine games come last.

On Books and Reading

Reading books in one's youth is like looking at the moon through a crevice; reading books in middle age is like looking at the moon in one's courtyard; and reading books in old age is like looking at the moon on an open terrace. This is because the depth of benefits of reading varies in proportion to the depth of one's own experience.

Only one who can read books without words [*i.e.*, the book of life itself] can say strikingly beautiful things; and only one who understands truth difficult to explain by words can grasp the highest Buddhist wisdom.

All immortal literature of the ancients and the moderns was written with blood and tears.

All Men are Brothers (*Shuihu*) is a book of anger, *The Monkey Epic* (*Hsiyuchi*) is a book of spiritual awakening, and *Gold-Vase Plum* (*Chinp'ingmei*) [a pornographic novel] is a book of sorrow.

Literature is landscape on the desk, and a landscape is literature on the earth.

Reading is the greatest of all joys, but there is more anger than joy in reading history. But, after all, there is pleasure in such anger.[1]

One should read the classics in winter, because then one's mind is more concentrated; read history in summer, because

---

[1] By "anger" is meant one's feeling mad reading in history about a good man being shot or a government falling into the hands of eunuchs and dictators. This feeling mad is æsthetically a beautiful sensation.

one has more time; read the ancient philosophers in autumn, because they have such charming ideas; and read the collected works of later authors in spring, because then Nature is coming back to life.

When literary men talk about military affairs, it is mostly military science in the studio [literally, "discussing soldiers on paper"]; and when military generals discuss literature, it is mostly rumours picked up on hearsay.

A man who knows how to read finds everything becomes a book wherever he goes: hills and waters are also books, and so are chess and wine, and so are the moon and flowers. A good traveller finds that everything becomes a landscape wherever he goes: books and history are landscapes, and so are wine and poetry, and so are the moon and flowers.

An ancient writer said that he would like to have ten years devoted to reading, ten years devoted to travel and ten years devoted to preservation and arrangement of what he had got. I think that preservation should not take ten years and two or three years should be enough. As for reading and travel, I do not think even twice or five times the period suggested would be enough to satisfy my desires. To do so one would have to live three hundred years, as Huang Chiuyen says.

The ancient people said that "poetry becomes good only after one becomes poor or unsuccessful,"[1] for the reason that an unsuccessful man usually has a lot of things to say, and it is thus easy to show himself to advantage. How can the poetry of the rich and successful people be good when they neither sigh over their poverty nor complain about their being unpromoted, and when all they write about are the wind, the clouds, the moon and the dew? The only way for such a person to write poetry is to travel, so that all he sees on his way, the hills and rivers and people's customs and ways of life, and perhaps the sufferings of people during war or famine, may all go into his poems. Thus borrowing from the sorrows of other

[1] The idea is that poetry acquires depth through sorrow.

people, for the purpose of his own songs and sighs, one can write good poetry without waiting to be poor or unsuccessful.

On Living in General

Passion holds up the bottom of the universe and genius paints up its roof.

Better be insulted by common people than be despised by gentlemen; better be flunked by an official examiner than be unknown to a famous scholar.

A man should so live as to be like a poem, and a thing should so look as to be like a picture.

There are scenes which sound very exquisite, but are really sad and forlorn, as, for instance, a scene of mist and rain; there are situations which sound very poetic, but are really hard to bear, as, for instance, sickness and poverty; and there are sounds which seem charming when mentioned, but are really vulgar, as, for instance, the voices of girls selling flowers.

I cannot be a farmer myself, and all I can do is to water the garden; I cannot be a woodcutter myself, and all I can do is to pull out the weeds.

My regrets, or things that exasperate me, are ten: (1) that book bags are easily eaten by moths, (2) that summer nights are spoiled by mosquitoes, (3) that a moon terrace easily leaks, (4) that the leaves of chrysanthemums often wither, (5) that pine trees are full of big ants, (6) that bamboo leaves fall in great quantities upon the ground, (7) that the cassia and lotus flowers easily wither, (8) that the *pilo* plant often conceals snakes, (9) that flowers on a trellis have thorns, and (10) that porcupines are often poisonous to eat.

It is extremely pretty to stand outside a window and see someone writing characters on the window paper from the inside.

One should be the *hsüan* [*hemerocalis flava,* a plant called "Forget-sorrow"] among the flowers, and not be the cuckoo [reputed to shed tears of blood which grow up into azaleas] among the birds.

THE ENJOYMENT OF NATURE

To be born in times of peace in a district with hills and lakes when the magistrate is just and upright, and to live in a family of comfortable means, marry an understanding wife and have intelligent sons—this is what I call a perfect life.

To have hills and valleys in one's breast enables one to live in a city as in a mountain woods, and to be devoted to clouds transforms the Southern Continent into a fairy isle.

To sit alone on a quiet night—to invite the moon and tell her one's sorrow; to keep alone on a good night—and to call the insects and tell them one's regrets.

One living in a city should regard paintings as his landscape, miniature sceneries in a pot as his garden, and books as his friends.

To ask a famous scholar to teach one's children, to go into a famous mountain and learn the art of writing examination essays, and to ask a famous writer to be his literary ghost—all these three things are utterly wrong.

A monk need not abstain from wine, he needs only abstain from vulgarity; a red petticoat need not understand literature, she need only understand what is artistically interesting.

If one is annoyed by the coming of tax-gatherers, he should pay the land taxes early; if one enjoys talking Buddhism with monks, he cannot help making contributions to temples from time to time.

It is easy to forget everything except this one thought of fame; it is easy to grow indifferent to everything except three cups of wine.

Wine can take the place of tea, but tea cannot take the place of wine; poems can take the place of prose, but prose cannot take the place of poems; Yüan dramatic poems can take the place of Sung lyrics, but Sung lyrics cannot take the place of Yüan dramatic poems; the moon can take the place of lamps, but lamps cannot take the place of the moon; the pen can take the place of the mouth, but the mouth cannot take the place of the pen; a maidservant can take the place of a manservant, but a manservant cannot take the place of a maid.

A little injustice in the breast can be drowned by wine; but a great injustice in the world can be drowned only by the sword.

A busy man's private garden must be situated next to his house; while a man of leisure may have his private garden separated from his house at a distance.

There are people who have the pleasures of a mountain recluse lying before them and don't know how to enjoy them—fishermen, woodcutters, farmers, gardeners and monks; there are people who have the pleasures of gardens, pavilions and concubines before them and don't know how to enjoy them—rich merchants and high officials.

It is easy to stand a pain, but difficult to stand an itch; it is easy to bear the bitter taste, but difficult to bear the sour taste.[1]

It is true that the ink-stone of a man of leisure should be exquisite, but a busy man's ink-stone should equally be exquisite; it is true that a concubine for pleasure should be pretty, but a concubine for the continuation of the family line should also be pretty.

The stork gives a man the romantic manner, the horse gives a man the heroic manner, the orchid gives a man the recluse's manner, and the pine gives a man the grand manner of the ancients.

I want one day to give a grand nudist ball, first to propitiate the spirits of the talented men of all ages, and secondly to propitiate the spirits of the beautiful women of all ages. When I have found a really high monk,[2] then I am going to give the ball and ask him to preside at it.

It is against the will of God to eat delicate food hastily, to pass gorgeous views hurriedly, to express deep sentiments superficially, to pass a beautiful day steeped in food and drinks, and to enjoy your wealth steeped in luxuries.

[1] The great idea that it is more difficult to stand an itch than to stand pain is not original with this epigrammatist, but was found in the correspondence between Su Tungp'o and Huang Shanku, so far as I can remember.

[2] A "high monk," *kaoseng*, as distinguished from the common, everyday monks, is a person who returns to the world, eats pork and perhaps dog-meat, and drinks in the company of prostitutes, as Jesus did.

CHAPTER ELEVEN

The Enjoyment Of Travel

I. ON GOING ABOUT AND SEEING THINGS

TRAVEL USED TO BE a pleasure, now it has become an industry. No doubt there are greater facilities for travelling to-day than a hundred years ago, and governments with their official travel bureaux have exploited the tourist trade, with the result that the modern man travels on the whole much more than his grandfather. Nevertheless travel seems to have become a lost art. In order to understand the art of travel, one should first of all beware of the different types of false travel, which is no travel at all.

The first kind of false travel is travel to improve one's mind. This matter of improving one's mind has undoubtedly been overdone. I doubt very much whether one's mind can be so easily improved. Anyway, there is very little evidence of it at clubs and lectures. But if we are usually so serious as to be bent upon improving our minds, we should at least during a vacation let the mind lie fallow, and give it a holiday. This false idea of travel has given rise to the institution of tourist guides, the most intolerable chattering kind of interfering busybodies that I can imagine. One cannot pass a square or a bronze statue without his attention being called to the fact that So-and-so was born on April 23, 1792, and died on December 2, 1852. I have seen convent sisters escorting school-children to a cemetery, and as the group stopped before a tombstone, reading to them from a book the dates of the deceased, the age at which he married, the name and surname of his wife, and such learned nonsense which, I am sure, spoiled the pleasure of the entire trip for the children.

The grown-ups themselves are turned into a group of school-children being vociferously lectured to by the guide, and in the case of travellers of the more studious type, also taking notes very assiduously like good school-children. Chinese tourists suffer like American tourists at Radio City, with the difference that Chinese guides are not professional but are fruit-sellers, donkey-drivers and peasant boys, whose information is less correct, if their personalities are more lively. Visiting Huch'iu Hill at Soochow one day, I came back with a terrible confusion of historical dates and sequence, for the awe-inspiring bridge suspended forty feet over the Sword Pond, with two round holes in the stone slabs of the bridge through which a sword had flown up as a dragon, became, according to my orange-selling boy, the place where the ancient beauty Hsishih attended to her morning toilet! (Hsishih's "dressing-table" was actually about ten miles away from the place.) All he wanted was to sell me some oranges. But then I had a chance of seeing how folklore was changed and modified and "metamorphosed."

The second kind of false travel is travel for conversation, in order that one may talk about it afterwards. I have seen visitors at Hupao of Hangchow, a place famous for its tea and spring water, having their picture taken in the act of lifting tea-cups to their lips. To be sure, it is a highly poetic sentiment to show friends a picture of themselves drinking tea at Hupao. The danger is that one spends less thought on the actual taste of the tea than on the photograph itself. This sort of thing can become an obsession, especially with travellers provided with cameras, as we so often see on sight-seeing buses in Paris and London. The tourists are so busy with their cameras that they have no time to look at the places themselves. Of course they have the privilege of looking at them in the pictures afterwards when they go home, but it is obvious that pictures of Trafalgar Square or the Champs-Elysées can be bought in New York or in Peiping. As these historical places become places to be talked about afterwards instead of places to be looked at, it is natural that the more places one visits, the richer the memory will be, and the more places there will be to talk about. This urge for learning and scholarship therefore impels the tourist to cover as many points as possible in a day. He has in his hand a programme of places to visit, and as he comes to a place, he checks it off with a pencil on the programme. I suspect such travellers are trying to be efficient even on their holiday.

This sort of foolish travel necessarily produces the third type of false travellers, who travel by schedule, knowing beforehand exactly how many hours they are going to spend in Vienna or Budapest. Before such a traveller departs, he makes a perfect schedule for himself and religiously adheres to it. Bound by the clock and run by the calendar as he is at home, he is still bound by the clock and run by the calendar while abroad.

In place of these false types of travel, I propose that the true motives of travel are, or should be, otherwise. In the first place, the true motive of travel should be travel to become lost and unknown. More poetically, we may describe it as travel to forget. Everyone is quite respectable in his home town, no matter what the higher social circles think of him. He is tied by a set of conventions, rules, habits and duties. A banker finds it difficult to be treated just as an ordinary human being at home and to forget that he is a banker, and it seems to me, the real excuse for travel is that he shall be able to find himself in a community in which he is just an ordinary human being. Letters of introduction are all very well for people on business trips, but business trips are by definition outside the category of pure travel. A man stands a poorer chance of discovering himself as a human being if he brings along with him letters of introduction, and of finding out exactly how God made him as a human being, apart from the artificial accidents of social standing. Against the comforts of being well received by friends in a foreign country and guided efficiently through the social strata of one's own class, there is the greater excitement of a boy scout in a forest, left to his own devices. He has the chance to prove for himself that he can order a fried chicken with the language of fingers alone, or find his way about town by communicating with a Tokyo policeman.

[340]

At least, such a traveller can come home with a less tenderfootish dependence upon his chauffeur and butler.

A true traveller is always a vagabond, with the joys, temptations and sense of adventure of the vagabond. Either travel is "vagabonding" or it is no travel at all. The essence of travel is to have no duties, no fixed hours, no mail, no inquisitive neighbours, no receiving delegations, and no destination. A good traveller is one who does not know where he is going to, and a perfect traveller does not know where he came from. He does not even know his own name and surname. This point has been emphasized by T'u Lung in his idealized sketch of the *Travels of Mingliaotse*— which I have translated in the next section. Probably he hasn't got a single friend in a strange land, but as a Chinese nun expressed it, "Not to care for anybody in particular is to care for mankind in general." Having no particular friend is having everybody as one's friend. Loving mankind in general, he mixes with them and goes about observing the charms of people and their customs. This kind of benefit is entirely missed by those travellers on the sight-seeing buses, who stay in the hotel, converse with their fellow-passengers from the home country, and in the case of many American travellers in Paris, make a point of eating at the favourite rendezvous of American tourists, where they can be sure of seeing all their fellow-passengers who came over on the same ship all over again, and can eat American doughnuts which taste exactly as they taste at home. English travellers in Shanghai make sure that they put up at an English hotel where they can have their bacon and eggs and toast with marmalade at breakfast, and hang about the cocktail lounge and fight shy of any inducement to get them to take a rickshaw ride. They are terribly hygienic, to be sure, but why go to Shanghai at all? Such travellers never allow themselves the time and leisure for entering into the spirit of the people and thus forfeit one of the greatest benefits of travelling.

The spirit of vagabondage makes it possible for people taking a vacation to get closer to Nature. Travellers of this kind will therefore insist on going to the summer resorts where there are the fewest people and one can have some sort of real solitude and communion with Nature. Travellers of this sort, therefore, do not in their preparation for journeys go into a department store and take a lot of time to select a pink or a blue bathing suit. Lipstick is still allowable because a vacationist, being a follower of Jean-Jacques Rousseau, wants to be natural, and no lady can be quite natural without a good lipstick. But that is due to the fact that one goes to the summer resorts and beaches where everybody goes, and the entire benefit of a closer association with Nature is lost or forgotten. One goes to a famous spring and says to himself, "Now I am entirely by myself," but after supper at the hotel he takes up a paper in the lounge and discovers that Mrs. B—— came up to the place on Monday. Next morning on his "solitary" walk, he encounters the entire family of the Dudleys, who arrived by train the night before. On Thursday night he finds out, to his great delight, that Mrs. S—— and her husband are also having a vacation in this wonderful secluded valley. Mrs. S—— then invites the Dudleys to tea, and the Dudleys invite Mr. and Mrs. S—— to a bridge party, and you can hear Mrs. S—— exclaim, "Isn't it wonderful? It is just like being in New York, isn't it?"

I may suggest that there is a different kind of travel, travel to see nothing and to see nobody but the squirrels and muskrats and woodchucks and clouds and trees. A friend of mine, an American lady, described for me how she went with some Chinese friends to a hill in the neighbourhood of Hangchow, *in order to see nothing*. It was a misty day in the morning, and as they went up, the mist became heavier and heavier. One could hear the soft beat of drops of moisture on the leaves of grass. There was nothing to be seen but fog. The American lady was discouraged. "But you must come along; there's a wonderful sight on top," insisted her Chinese friends. She went up with them and after a while saw an ugly rock in the distance enveloped by the clouds, which had been heralded as a great sight. "What is there?" she asked. "That is the Inverted Lotus," her friends replied. Somewhat mortified, she was ready to go down. "But there is a still more wonderful

sight on top," they said. Her dress was already half damp with
the moisture, but she had given up the fight already and went on
with them. Finally they reached the summit. All about them
was an expanse of mists and fogs, with the outline of distant hills
barely visible on the horizon. "But there is nothing to see here,"
my American friend protested. "That is exactly the point. We
come up to see nothing," her Chinese friends replied.

There is all the difference between seeing things and seeing
nothing. Many travellers who see things really see nothing, and
many who see nothing see a great deal. I am always amused at
hearing of an author going to a foreign country to "get material for
his new book," as if he had exhausted all there was to see in
humanity in his own town or country and as if the theme could
ever be exhausted. "Thrums" must be unromantic and the Island
of Guernsey too dull to build a great novel upon! We come therefore to the *philosophy of travel as consisting of the capacity to see
things,* which abolishes the distinction between travel to a distant
country and going about the fields of an afternoon.

The two become the same thing, as Chin Shengt'an insisted.
The most necessary outfit a traveller has to carry along with him is
"a special talent in his breast and a special vision below his eyebrows," as the Chinese dramatic critic expressed it in his famous
running comment on the drama *Western Chamber.* The point is
whether one has got the heart to feel and the eyes to see. If he
hasn't, his visits to the mountains are a pure waste of time and
money; on the other hand, if he has got "a special talent in his
breast and a special vision below his eyebrows," he can get the
greatest joy of travel even without going to the mountains, by
staying at home and watching and going about the field to watch
a sailing cloud, or a dog, or a hedge, or a lonely tree. I translate
below Chin's dissertation on the true art of travel:

I have read the travel sketches of people and realize that very
few people understand the art of travelling. Surely the man
who knows how to travel will not be frightened by a long
journey to see all the sights of the land and sea and explore all

their grandeur and mystery. But a certain talent in his breast and a certain vision below his eyebrows tell him that it is not necessary to go to all the famous beauty spots of land and sea in order to explore nature's wonder and mystery. One day he goes to a stone cave after using up a great deal of the energy of his legs, his eyes and his mind, and when he has done that, the next day he goes again to another blessed spot and uses up some more of the energy of his legs, his eyes and his mind. People who do not understand him will say, "What a wonderful time you have been having, visiting places these days! Just after seeing one stone cave, you have gone ahead to visit another blessed spot." They have entirely missed the point. For there is a distance between the two places he visited, perhaps twenty or thirty *li,* or perhaps, eight, seven, six, five, four, three, two *li,* or perhaps even one *li* or just half a *li.* With the special talent in his breast and the special vision beneath his pair of eyebrows, has he not looked at that little distance of a *li* or half a *li* in the same way he looked at the stone cave and the blessed spot?

It is true that there is something which terrifies the eye and surprises the soul to find that Mother Nature, with her great skill and wisdom and energy, has suddenly produced a thing like a stone cave or a blessed spot. But I have often stared casually at little things of this universe—a bird, a fish, a flower, or a small plant, and even at a bird's feather, a fish's scale, a flower petal and a blade of grass—and realized how Mother Nature has also created it with all her great skill and wisdom and energy. As it is said that the lion uses the same energy to attack an elephant as to attack a wild rabbit, so does Mother Nature truly do the same thing. She uses all her energy in producing a stone cave or a blessed spot, but she also uses all her energy in producing a bird, a fish, a flower, a blade of grass, or even a feather, a scale, a petal, a leaf. Therefore, it is not alone the stone cave or the blessed spot that terrifies the eye and surprises the soul in this world.

Furthermore, have we ever thought how the stone cave and

the blessed spot were produced? Chuangtse has wisely said, "To comprehend the different organs of the horse is not to comprehend the horse itself. What we call the horse exists before its different organs." To take another analogy, we see forests growing around the great lakes and timber and rocks spread all over the great mountains. It gives the traveller joy to know that the great forests and timber and rocks are assembled together to form the great lakes and great mountains. But the towering peaks are formed by little rocks and the falling cataracts are formed and nourished by little springs of water. If we examine them one by one, we see that the stones are no bigger than the palm of one's hand, and the springs are no bigger than little rivulets. Laotse has said: "Thirty spokes are grouped around the hub of a wheel, and when they lose their own individuality, we have a functioning cart. We knead clay into a vessel and when the clay loses its own existence we have a usable utensil. We make a hole in the wall to make windows and doors, and when the windows and doors lose their own existence,[1] we have a house to live in." And so when we view a stone cave or a blessed spot and see the vertically uprising peaks, horizontally-stretching mountain passes, those that go up and form a precipice, those that go down and form a river, those that are level and form a plateau, those that are inclined and form a hillside, those that stretch across and become bridges, and those that come together and become ravines, we realize that, however incomparably manifold they are in their greatness and mystery, this mystery and grandeur arises when the parts lose their individual existence. For when they lose their own existence, there are no passes, no precipices, no rivers and no plateaux, hillsides, bridges and ravines. But it is exactly in their non-existence that the special talent in our breast and the special vision below our eyebrows wander and float at ease. And since this special talent in our breast and this special vision below our eyebrows can wander and float at ease only when these things are non-

---

[1] By being blanks in space.

existent, why, then, must we insist on going to the stone cave and to the blessed spot?

If, therefore, with the special talent in my breast and the special vision below my eyebrows, I can still wander and float about at ease only when these things lose their individual existence, isn't it then unnecessary that I visit the stone cave and the blessed spot? For as I have just said, in the distance of twenty or thirty *li*, or even one or half *li*, are there not also everywhere things that lose their existence? A crooked little bridge—a shaggy lonely tree—a glimpse of water—a village—a hedge—a dog—how do I know that the mystery and the grandeur of the stone cave and the blessed spot where I may wander and float about at ease are not even here? . . .

Besides, it is not necessary that we have a special talent in our breast and a special vision below our eyebrows: should one require a special talent in order to float about and require a special vision in order to wander at ease, we might not find a single person in the world who understands the art of travelling. According to Shengt'an [the writer himself], there are no special talents and no special visions: to be willing to float about is already to have the special talent, and to be able to wander about at ease is already to have a special vision. The criteria of Old Mi [Mi Fei] for judging rocks are *hsiou, tsou, t'ou* and *sou* [delicacy, undulation, clarity and slenderness]. Now a little patch of water, a village, a bridge, a tree, a hedge or a dog at the distance of one *li* or half a *li* has each its great delicacy, great undulation, great clarity and great slenderness. If we fail to see this, it is because we do not understand how to look at them as Old Mi looked at the rocks. If we only see their delicacy, their undulation, their clarity and their slenderness, we cannot help but wander and float about at ease among them. What is there in the grandeur and mystery of peaks and mountain passes and precipices and rivers and the plateaux, the slopes, the bridges and the ravines in the stone cave and the blessed spot outside their being delicate, undulated, clear and slender? Those who insist on visiting the stone caves and the blessed spots therefore have left much that they have not visited; in fact, they have not visited any place at all. For those who fail to see the mystery and grandeur of a single hedge or a dog have seen only what is not grand and what is not mysterious in the stone caves and the blessed spots.

Toushan [Chin's friend] said: "The one who understands best the art of travel in all history is Confucius, and the second, Wang Hsichih [acknowledged master of Chinese calligraphy]." On being asked to explain, Toushan said: "I know this of Confucius from the two sentences that for him 'rice could not be white enough, and mincemeat could not be chopped fine enough,' and I know this of Wang from seeing examples of his calligraphy. There are things in it which his son Hsienchih could not even understand." "What you have just said is devastating to the entire mankind," said I. Toushan once told me: "When Wang Hsichih was at home, he often counted the pistils of every flower on every branch in his yard, and he would be thus occupied the whole day without saying a word, while his students stood by with towels at his side." "Where did you find the authority for this statement?" asked Shengt'an. "I found it in my own heart," replied Toushan. Such a marvellous person is Toushan. Alas, that the world has not discovered Toushan and admired his romantic imagination!

II. "THE TRAVELS OF MINGLIAOTSE"[1]

a. *The Reason for the Flight*

Mingliaotse was once an official, and he was tired of the ways of the world, of having to say things against his heart and to perform ceremonies against good form. What is "to say things against one's heart"? A host and his visitor make a low bow to

[1] This is a translation from a Chinese sketch entitled *The Travels of Mingliaotse*, which draws a vivid picture of the glorified, cultured vagabond so much idealized by Chinese scholars, and sets forth a happy, carefree philosophy of living, characterized by love of truth, freedom and vagabondage. It was written by T'u Lung (*alias* T'u Ch'ihshui), a writer who lived toward the end of the sixteenth century and who, together with Hsü Wench'ang, Yüan Chunglang, Li Chowu and others living at the period, have never been given their due by the orthodox Chinese critics.

each other, and after a few casual remarks about the weather, dare not make another comment. People we have met for the first time shake hands with us and insist they are our bosom friends, but after they have parted from us, we are totally indifferent to each other. When we praise a person, we compare him to the saint Poyi, and as soon as he has turned away, we talk behind his back and compare him to the thief Cheh. And when we are sitting at ease enjoying a conversation, we try to preserve a curt dignity, although we have so much we should like to say to each other; and we gabble about noble ideals, while we have immoral conduct. Being afraid that to unbosom our heart would betray the truth and to tell the truth would hurt, we lay these thoughts aside and let the conversation drift aimlessly on trivial topics. Sometimes we even play the actor and sigh or shout to cover up our thoughts, so that our ears, our eyes, our mouth and our nose are no more our own, and our anger, our joy, our laughter and our condemnations are no longer genuine. Such is the established convention of society, and there is no way of rectifying it. And what is "to perform ceremonies against good form"? In dealings with our fellow-men, no matter of what rank, we bow and kow-tow the whole day, although they are our old friends. We dissociate ourselves without reason from some, as if they were our mortal enemies, and equally without reason try to get close to others, although they have no real affinity to us. Hardly has a nobleman opened his mouth when we answer, "Yes, sir!" with a roar, and yet he need only raise an arm and our heads may be chopped off. We see two people calling on each other, and although they hate to see each other's faces, they spend their days busily dismounting from their horses and leaving their cards. Now calling on a friend to inquire after his welfare should not be merely an empty form. Did the ancient kings who established these ceremonies mean it to be this way? We put on our gowns and girdles, feeling like caged monkeys, so that even when a louse bites our body and our skin itches, we cannot scratch it. And when we are walking at leisure in the streets, we are afraid of disobeying the law. Immediately our eyes look at our nose and we dare not look beyond a short distance, and if we look beyond a short distance, other people will look at us and try to detect what we are doing. When we want to ease ourselves and the feeling is intense, we hardly dare to stop without some excuse. The higher officials are ever mindful of the sword in front and other people's criticism behind. The cold and hot seasons disturb their bodies, and the desire of possession and the fear of loss trouble their hearts. Thus they suffer greater loss than comes from the mere fear of being incorrect. Even the noblest and most chivalrous spirits, who have a sense of wise disenchantment and are pleased with their own being, fall into this trap once they have become officials. So, wishing to emancipate his heart and liberate his will, Mingliaotse sets forth to travel in the Country of the Nonchalant.

Someone may say: "I have heard that the follower of Tao lives in quiet and does not feel lonely, and lives in a crowd and does not feel the noise. He lives in the world and yet is out of it, is without bondage and without need for emancipation, and soon a willow tree grows from his left armpit and a bird makes its nest on the top of his head. This is the height of the culture of quietism and emancipation. To be a servant in the kitchen, or to pick up the waste on the ground, is one of the lowest of professions, and yet the saint is not disturbed by it. Are you not making your spirit the servant of your body, when you are afraid of the restrictions of the official life, and desire to travel to unusual places?"

And Mingliaotse replies: "He who has attained the Tao can go into water without becoming wet, jump into fire without being burned, walk upon reality as if it were a void and travel on a void as if it were reality. He can be at home wherever he is and be alone in whatever surroundings. That is natural with him. But I am not one who has attained the Tao, I am merely a lover of Tao. One who has attained the Tao is master of himself, and the universe is dissolved for him. Throw him in the company of the noisy and the dirty, and he will be like a lotus flower growing from muddy water, touched by it, yet unstained. Therefore he does not have to choose where to go. I am yet unqualified for this, for I am like a willow tree following the wind—when the wind is quiet, then I am quiet, and when the wind moves, I move, too. I am like sand in the water—which is clean or muddy as the water is. I have often achieved purity and quiet for a whole day and then lost it in a moment, and have sometimes achieved purity and quiet for a year and then lost it in a day. It has not been possible for me to let everything alone and not be disturbed by material surroundings. If an emperor could follow the Tao, why did Ch'ao Fu and Hsü Yu have to go to the Chi Hill and the Ying River? If a prince could follow the Tao, why did Sakyamuni have to go to the Himalayas? If a duke could follow the Tao, why did Chang Liang have to ask for sick leave? And if a minor official could follow the Tao, why did T'ao Yüanming have to resign from his office? I am going to emancipate my heart and release my spirit and travel in the Country of the Nonchalant."

"Let me hear about your travels," the friend says, and Mingliaotse replies:

"One who travels does so in order to open his ears and eyes and relax his spirit. He explores the Nine States[1] and travels over the Eight Barbarian Countries, in the hope that he may gather the Divine Essence and meet great Taoists, and that he may eat of the plant of eternal life and find the marrow of rocks.[2] Riding upon the wind and sailing upon ether, he goes coolly whithersoever the wind may carry him. After these wanderings, he comes back, shuts himself up and sits looking at the blank wall, and in this way ends his life. I am not one who has attained the Tao. I would like to house my spirit within my body, to nourish my virtue by mildness, and to travel in ether by becoming a void. But I cannot do it yet. I tried to house my spirit within my body, but suddenly it disappeared outside; I tried to nourish my virtue by mildness, but suddenly it shifted to intensity of feeling; and I tried to wander in ether by keeping in the void, but suddenly there sprang up in me a desire. And so, being unable to find peace within myself, I

[1] Ancient nomenclature for parts of North and Central China.
[2] Stalactites and stalagmites.

made use of the external surroundings to calm my spirit, and being unable to find delight within my heart, I borrowed a landscape to please it. Therefore strange were my travels.

b. *The Way of Travelling*

"I go forth with a friend who loves the mountain haze and each of us carries a gourd and wears a cassock, taking with us a hundred cash. We do not want more, but try always to keep it at a hundred to meet emergencies. And we two go begging through cities and through hamlets, at vermilion gates and at white mansions, before Taoist temples and monks' huts. We are careful of what we beg for, asking for rice and not for wine, and for vegetables and not for meat. The tone of our begging is humble, but not tragic. If people give, we then leave them, and if people don't give, we also leave them; the whole object being merely to forestall hunger. If some people are rude, we take it with a bow. Sometimes when there is no place at which to beg and we cannot do otherwise, we spend one or two from the hundred cash we carry along with us, and make it up whenever possible. But we do not spend any cash unless we are actually forced to it.

"We travel without a destination and stop over wherever we find ourselves, and we go very slowly, perhaps ten *li* a day, perhaps twenty, or perhaps thirty, forty or fifty. We do not try to do too much, lest we feel tired. And when we come to mountains and streams, and are enchanted with the springs and white rocks and water fowls and mountain birds, we choose a spot on a river islet and sit on a rock, looking at the distance. And when we meet woodcutters or fishermen or villagers or rustic old men, we do not ask for their names and surnames, nor give ours, nor talk about the weather, but chat briefly on the charms of the country life. After a while we part company with them without regret.

"In times of great cold or great heat, we have to seek shelter, lest we be affected by the weather. On the road, we stand aside and let other people pass, and at a ferry, we wait to let other people get into the boat first. But if there is a storm we do not try to cross the water, or if a storm comes up when we are already half-way across, we calm our spirit, and leaving it to fate with an understanding of life, we say: 'If we should be drowned while crossing, it is Heaven's will. Can we escape by worrying over it?' If we cannot escape, there our journey ends. If fortunately we escape, then we go on as before. If we meet some rough young fellow on the way or accidentally bump into him, and if the young man is rude, we politely apologize to him. If after the apology we still cannot escape a fight, then there our journey ends. But if we escape it, then we go on as before. If one of us falls ill, we stop to attend to the illness, and the other tries to beg a little for some medicine, but he himself takes it calmly. He looks within himself and is not afraid of death. And so a severe illness is changed into a light illness, and a light illness is immediately cured. If it is willed that our days are numbered, then there our journey ends. But if we escape it, then we go on as before. It is natural that during our wanderings, we might arouse the suspicion of detectives or guards and might be arrested as spies. We then try to escape either by our cunning or by our sincerity. If we cannot escape, then there our journey ends. But if we escape, then we go on as before. Of course we stop over for the night at a mat-shed hut or a stone lodge, but if it is impossible to find such a place, we stop for the night lying outside a temple gate, or beneath a rock cave, or outside people's house walls or beneath tall trees. Perhaps the mountain spirits and tigers or wolves may be looking upon us, and what are we to do? The mountain spirits can do us no harm, but we are unable to defend ourselves against the tigers or wolves. But haven't we a fate controlled up in heaven? We therefore leave it to the laws of the universe, and we do not even change the colour of our face. If we are eaten up, that is our fate, and there our journey ends. But if we escape it, then we go on as before. . . .

c. *At Austere Heights*

"As for my destinations, I visit chiefly the Five Sacred Mountains and the Four Sacred Waters and generally the sacred places on mountain tops, and secondarily include also the famous mountains and rivers of the Nine States. But I limit myself to only those parts within the jurisdiction of the Nine States and where human beings have set foot. As for those regions lying outside the Celestial Empire, like the Himalayas and the Ten Small Islands and Three Big Islands of the China Sea, I do not think I should be able to go there, not being provided with a pair of wings. I expect also to meet only travelling scholars of the lakes and rivers or retired men of the mountains; as for the various immortals, I do not think I shall be able to come across them, not being provided with an immortal body myself.

"When I go up to the Five Sacred Mountains, there I stand high above the celestial winds and look beyond the Four Seas, and the myriad mountain peaks appear like little snails, the myriad rivers seem like winding girdles, and the myriad trees appear like kale. The Milky Way seems to graze by my collar, white clouds pass through my sleeves, the eagles of the air seem within my arm's reach, and the sun and the moon brush my temples and pass by. And there I have to speak in a low voice, not only for fear I may frighten away the spirit of the mountain, but also lest it be overheard by God on His throne. Above us there is the pure firmament, without a single speck of dust in that vast expanse of space, while below us rain and thunder and stormy darkness take place without our knowledge, and the rumbling of the thunder is heard only as the gurgling of a baby. At this moment, my eyesight is dazzled by the light, and my spirit seems to fly out of the limitations of space, and I feel as if I were riding upon the far-journeying winds, but do not know where to go. Or when the western sun is about to hide itself and the eastern moon is bursting out from below the horizon, there the light of the clouds shines forth in all directions and the purple and the blue scintillate in the sky and the distant and the nearby peaks change from a deeper into a lighter hue in a short moment. Or again in the middle of the night, I hear the sound of the temple bells and the roar of a tiger, followed by a gust of rustling wind, and the door of the main temple hall being open, I slip on my gown and get up, and lo! there the Spirit of the Rabbit[1] is reclining, and some remains of the last snowfall still cover up the upper slopes, the light of the night lies like a mass of undefined white, and the distant mountains present a hardly visible outline. At such a moment, I feel my body steeped in the cool air and all desires of the flesh have melted away. Or perhaps I see the God of the Sacred Mountain sitting in state, giving audience to the inferior spirits. There is a profusion of banners and canopies, and the air is filled with the music of the flute and the bells, and the palace roofs are clothed in a mantle of clouds and scarfs of haze, seeming to have and yet not to have a visible outline, and giving the illusion of now being so near and now being so far away. Ah, thrice happy is it to hear the music of the gods, and why is it suddenly interrupted by a gust of cold wind?

"Besides these Five Sacred Mountains, there are a number of other famous mountains, like Szeming, T'ient'ai, Chinhua, Kuats'ang, Chint'ing, T'ienmu, Wuyi, Lushan, Omei, Chungnan, Chungt'iao, Wut'ai, T'aiho, Lofu, Kweich'i, Maoshan, Chiuhua, and Linwu, and such sacred places without number, which have been called the dwellings of the fairies or the abodes of the spirits. I go forth in sandals, carrying a bamboo cane, and though I may not be able to visit them all, I wander about as far as my energy permits. I drink the water of the Gods' Faeces, inquire after the name of the Fairy Mouse, chew the rice of sesame and drink the dew of pine trees. When I come to a steep peak or overhanging precipice which rises abruptly into the sky, never scaled by man, I tie myself to a rope and climb up to the top. Coming to a broken stone bridge, or an old gate suddenly discovered open, I walk into it without fear; or coming to a rocky cave so dark that one cannot see its bottom, with but a single ray of light coming in through a crevice in its roof, I light a torch and go in by myself without fear, in the hope of finding some high-minded Taoists, or immortal plants, or perhaps the bodily remains of some Taoists who have gone up to heaven.

"I visit also the famous rivers and lakes, like the Tungt'ing, the

[1] The moon.

[354]

Yünmeng, the Chüt'ang, the Wuhsia,[1] the Chüch'ü, the P'engli, the Yangtse, and the Ch'ient'ang. Such deep expanses of water are the abodes of fish, dragons, and the water spirits. When the air is calm and the water smooth like a mirror, we know that then the Divine Dragon is peacefully asleep, holding a pearl in its breast. When the lights of the water merge with the colour of the sky under a clear moon, we know then it is the Princess of the Dragon King and the Mistress of the River coming out in a canopied procession, flute in hand and clad in their new scarfs of light gauze, treading in embroidered shoes upon the rippling waves. This procession continues for some time and then disappears. Ah, how cool it is then! Or a furious wind lashes upon the water and gigantic waves rise, and we know then it is the spirit of Ch'ihyi[2] in anger, assisted by T'ienwu.[3] Then the great earth churns about like a mill and our earthly abode shakes and rolls like a sifter, and we seem to see Old Dragon Chang breaking his way into heaven, carrying his nine sons in his arms. Ah, how magnificent it is then! Or if we go in for the gentle beauty of well-dressed women, there is no better place than the West Lake of Hangchow, where the willows line the banks and the peach flowers look at their own image in the water, and we know then it is the Imperial Consort Lihua opening her vanity box in the morning. When the water-caltrops are in bloom and the lotus flowers look fresh and gay on a bright morning and the place is filled with a subtle fragrance, we know then that the beauties Yichu and Hoteh are coming out of their bath. When the sky is clear and the sun is shining and the things of the place have a bright charm, and people are leaning upon their balconies in the vermilion towers in the morning, or boating on the lake with painted oars in the evening, we know then it is the Queen Yang Kweifei in her smiling mood. When a mist and rain hang over the lake and the many hills are enveloped in grey, changing into the most unexpected colours, it is also a source of great delight, for we know then it is Hsishih, Queen of the Wu kingdom, knitting her eyebrows."

[1] The Yangtse Gorges.
[2] A mythical bird.
[3] The Spirit of the Sea, with eight heads, eight legs and eight tails.

d. *Back to Humanity*

Then Mingliaotse walks leisurely past the Six Bridges of Hsiling and goes up to T'ienchu and Lingch'iao, where, after visiting some ancient scholars, he comes out and looks for Wild Stork Ting in some stone cave amidst the clouds. Then there is Ch'aoyin (Poo-too) which is the monastic home of Mingliaotse, and where the temple in honour of the Goddess of Mercy is situated. Mingliaotse goes there to pick lotus flowers and look at the great sea. Ah, is this not a great delight!

And so wandering farther and farther, happy of heart, Mingliaotse proceeds leisurely, covering a distance of ten thousand *li* on foot. And when he is pleased with what he sees or hears, he stays at a place for ten days.

[At a temple] he sits still with crossed legs to master the Three Precious Spirits. The five thousand words of *Taotehching*—is not the philosophy subtle and fine? The Golden Casket of Taoist books—is it already lost or still to be found? The *Jade Book* of Fusang—shall he not ask his neighbours concerning its whereabouts? The Two Books of *Yinfu*—does their secret lie right before his eyes? The Supreme Ruler guides his perceptive mind, and the Ancient Buddha directs his spiritual wisdom. And so trying to understand the law of the changing universe, he is not lonely during his contemplation.

In the temple of Buddha, there is the gracious appearance of his golden body, irradiating a glorious halo. The candles have been lighted and the incense smoke fills the air with a light fragrance, and there the Taoists or monks are seated in order on their straw cushions, drinking tea and eating fruit and perusing the classics. After a while, when they are tired, they control their respiration and enter the stage of quietude. After a long time, they get up, and see the moon shining from behind the wistarias, while the universe lies hushed in silence. An acolyte is kowtowing with his head against the ground, and a boy servant is taking a nap near the stove where the medicine of fairies is being stewed. At this moment how can an earthly thought enter our minds, even if it is there?

[356]

When out in the open country, he sees low walls enclosing mud huts thatched with straw. A piercing wind is blowing through the door and a mild sun is shining upon the forests. The cattle and sheep are returning home to the hillside, and hungry birds are making a noisy sound in the fields on the plain. An old farmer in ragged clothes and dishevelled hair is sunning himself beneath a small mulberry tree, and an old woman is holding an earthen vessel filled with water and serving a wheat meal. When the landscape and the mood of the moment are so sad, one feels too that it is as beautiful as a picture. If a Taoist on travel should regard such views as too ordinary, he might just as well not travel at all.

On entering a big city, where crowds jostle and the traffic or carts and horses fills the streets, Mingliaotse goes along singing and observing the people—storekeepers, butchers, minstrel singers, fortune-tellers, people occupied in a dispute, jugglers, animal trainers, gamblers and sportsmen. Mingliaotse looks at them all. And when the spirit moves him, he enters a wine shop and orders some strong wine with dried fish and green vegetables, and the two men drink across a table. Thus getting warmed up, they sing the ditty *Gathering the Immortal Plant,* and look about, supremely satisfied with themselves. The people of the street wonder at the sight of these two ragged souls carrying themselves with such an air of charm and happiness, and suspect that they are perhaps fairies incarnated. After a short while, they suddenly disappear altogether.

In the great mansions behind tall gates, dukes and princes or officials of high ranks are having a wine feast. Food is being served on jade plates, and beauties are sitting around the table. An orchestra is playing in the hall and the sound of song pierces the clouds. An old servant with a cane in hand is watching the door. Mingliaotse goes right in to beg for food. With his bright, wide-open eyes and a dignified air, he shouts to the company, "Stop all this noise and listen to a Taoist singing the song of 'Dew Drops on Flowers'":

Dew drops on flowers,
    Oh, how gay!
Fear not the cutting wind,
    But dread the coming day!
Eastward flows the River,
    Westward the Milky Way.
Farmers till the field where
    Once the Bronze Tower lay.
Better to have got
A day with this all-precious pot
Than future names remembered not.
    Oh, make merry while ye may!

Dew drops on flowers,
    Oh, how bright!
So long they last, they shine
    Like pearls in morning light,
Where grave mounds dot the wilds,
    And winds whine through the night;
Foxes' howls and screech-owls
    On poplars ghastly white.
See where red leaves blow,
Down on the Fragrant Gullet flow,
And mosses over Ch'inien Palace grow.
    Oh, make merry while ye might!

After Mingliaotse has finished his song, one of the guests seems to be angry and says: "Who is this Taoist to spoil our enjoyment in the midst of our wine feast? Give him a piece of sesame cake and send him away!" Mingliaotse receives the cake and leaves. Then another guest speaks to his attendant, saying, "Quick! Ask that Taoist to come back!" "But we were just enjoying our wine," says the former, "and he came to spoil our pleasure. That was why I sent him away with a piece of sesame cake. It's just fine. Why do you want him to come back?" "It seems to me," replies the latter, "there's something unusual about this Taoist, and I want to ask him to return to have a good look at him." "Why, he is only a beggar!" replies the former. "What is unusual about him? All he wants is a cold dish of left-overs." Then another guest joins in and says, "It doesn't seem from the song he sang that he is just a beggar."

At this moment, a sing-song girl in red gauze rises up from her seat and says, "According to my humble opinion, this Taoist is a fallen fairy from heaven. His eyes and forehead are delicately formed and his voice is strong and clear. He is disguised as a beggar, but something in his behaviour betrays his noble breeding. The song he sang is graceful and deep in meaning, more like the song of fairies in heaven than the song of men on earth. What beggar could have sung such a song. He is a fairy travelling among mortals in disguise. Please ask him to come back, for we must not lose him."

"What has all this to do with him?" says the last one. "All he wants is perhaps a drink of wine. You ask him to come back and we'll find out that he is a common fellow after all."

The girl in red gauze is still unconvinced and remarks, "Well, all I can say is, we haven't the luck to meet with immortals."

Then another girl in green gauze rises up from her seat and says, "Will the gentlemen make a bet with me? Ask the Taoist to return, and if he is an extraordinary person[1] then those who say he is extraordinary win the bet, and if we find that he is a common fellow, then those who say he is a common fellow win." "Good!" shout the gentlemen together. They then send a servant to go after Mingliaotse, but he has completely disappeared, and the servant returns with the news. "I knew that he was no common fellow!" says the former. "Alas, we have just lost an immortal!" says the girl in red gauze. "Why, he just went out of the door and has completely disappeared!"

Mingliaotse then proceeds with his cane and leisurely passes out of the outer city gate. He passes by a dozen big cities without entering one of them, until he comes to a place where he sees a

---

[1] "Extraordinary person" is the regular phrase for some saint or Taoist or fairy, gifted with magic powers.

city wall nestling against a mountain range. There are fine, tall towers and spacious, magnificent temples, whose roofs overlap one another in irregular formations, overlooking a clear pond below. It is a beautiful spring day, birds are singing on splendid trees and all the flowers are in their full glory. The men and women of the city, clad in their new clothes and riding in carved carriages or sitting on embroidered saddles, have come out of the city to "pace the spring." Some are drinking in the shade of tall trees, and some have spread a mat on the fragrant grass, and others have climbed up to a high vermilion tower, or are rowing on "green sparrow" boats; again others are riding shoulder to shoulder to visit the flowers, or are walking hand in hand and singing folk songs. Mingliaotse feels extremely happy and hangs about for a long time.

By and by a scholar with a clean face and nice complexion appears, coming along gracefully in his long gown. Making a low bow to Mingliaotse, he says, "Do Taoists come out to pace the spring, too? I have a few friends having a picnic over there, beneath the cherry trees in front of the little tower across the river. It is a jolly company and I shall be much pleased if you can join us. Can you come along?"

Mingliaotse gladly follows the young man, and when he arrives, he sees six or seven scholars, all handsome and young. The first young man introduces him to the company with a smile. "My friends, this is just a spring party among ourselves. I just met this Taoist gentleman on the road and saw he was not at all vulgar, and I therefore propose that we share our cups with him. What do you think?" "Good!" they all reply.

So then they all take their seats in order and Mingliaotse sits at the end of the table. When sufficient wine has been served and everybody is tipsy and happy, the conversation waxes more and more brilliant, and they pass witty remarks about the different people and the gentry. Some declaim poems celebrating the spring, some sing the song of gathering flowers, some discuss the policies of the court, and some tell of the secluded charm of hills and woods. There is then an exciting conversation going on, with each trying to outdo the others, while the Taoist merely occupies himself by chewing his rice. The first young man looks several times at Mingliaotse amidst his busy conversation, and says, "We must hear something from this Taoist teacher, too." And Mingliaotse replies, "Why, I am just enjoying the many fine and wise things you gentlemen have been saying, and have not been able to understand them all. How can I contribute anything to your conversation?"

After a while, the company rise up to take a walk in the rice fields, some plucking flowers and others pulling willow branches on the way. The place is full of beauties, and everywhere one's eyes turn, one sees beautiful peonies and *miwu*.[1] But Mingliaotse wanders alone into a hill path, and comes out again after a long while. "Why did you go alone?" the gentleman asks. "I was going with two oranges and a gallon of wine to listen to the orioles," replies Mingliaotse. "Why, this is a most extraordinary man, by the way he talks," says one scholar, and Mingliaotse replies by a courteous remark concerning his unworthiness.

So then the company sit down again, and one man says, "It won't do to go home from such an outing without writing some poems," and another expresses his approval.

Soon one person has completed his poem first, which reads:

> The willows drunk with 'circling haze,
> And rain-bathed peach flowers brightly gleam.
> Fear not thy fragrant cup be empty;
> A tavern lies across the stream.

Another finishes his poem, which reads:

> My kitchen shares the mountain green;
> My tower is sprinkled wet with spray.
> If ye drink not when spring is here,
> Soon comes the windy, wintry day.

After three other persons have contributed their quatrains, Mingliaotse is invited to make his contribution. He rises to

---

[1] A short flowering plant.

his feet, and after some expressions of his diffidence and the friends' insistence, he sings:

> I tread along the sandy bank,
> Where clouds are golden, water clear;
> The startled fairy hounds go barking—
> Into the peach grove[1] disappear.

Amazed by this poem, the company rise from their seats and make a low bow to Mingliaotse. "Tut! Tut! To hear such celestial words from a monk! We knew that you were an extraordinary person." And they all come round to ask for his name and surname, but Mingliaotse only smiles without giving reply. As they still insist, Mingliaotse says, "What do you want to know my name for? I am merely a rustic person wandering among clouds and waters, and we've met with a smile. You can just call me 'The Rustic Fellow of Clouds and Waters.'" This intrigues the company still more, and they express their desire to invite him to go into the city with them. "I am merely a poor monk enjoying a vagabond's travel, and all the world is my home," replies Mingliaotse with a smile. "But since you are so kind, I will come along."

They then go back to the city together, and Mingliaotse stays at their homes by turn. During the days that follow, he finds himself now in a rich man's hall, and now in a well-hidden small studio, now enjoying a literary wine dinner and now watching performances of dance and song, and Mingliaotse goes to all the places to which he is invited. The people of the city hear of the Rustic Fellow of Clouds and Waters, and the socially active people shower him with invitations, and he visits them all. When people give him drink, he drinks; when people discuss poetry and literature, he discusses poetry and literature with them; when people take him out for an excursion, he goes with them; but when they ask for his name and surname, he merely smiles without reply. In his discussion of poetry and literature, he makes very apt remarks about the ancient and modern writers

---

[1] The "peach grove" stands in Chinese literature for a fairies' retreat.

and gives a penetrating analysis of their styles and forms. Sometimes he discusses the political order of the ancient kings and makes passing comments on current affairs and enchants the people still more by his witty remarks.

Especially well-versed is he in the teaching of Taoism regarding "nourishing the spirit." Sometimes, when he is watching dancing or singing which borders on the bawdy and people make ribald jokes to find out his attitude toward these things, he seems to be enjoying himself, like the romantic scholars. But when it comes to extinguishing the candle and the host asks him to stay with some girl entertainer, and when the party becomes really rowdy, he sits upright with an austere appearance, and nobody can make anything of him. When he takes a nap during the night, he asks for a straw cushion from the host and sits with crossed legs on it, and merely dozes off when he is tired. For this reason, admiration and wonder grow about him.

After more than a month's stay, he takes leave suddenly one day, against the persistent entreaty of the people. His friends give him money and cloth for presents, and write poems of farewell to him. At the farewell party, the gentlemen all come to give him a send-off; sadly they hold his hands and some shed tears. Mingliaotse arrives at the outer city gate, and after having reserved a hundred cash for himself, he distributes the gentlemen's presents to the poor and goes away. When his friends hear of this, they sigh and marvel still more, knowing not what to make of him.

e. *Philosophy of the Flight*

Mingliaotse then follows a mountain path, and finds himself in deep, rugged mountains. Thousands of old trees, with creepers growing on them, spread their deep shade so that one walking underneath cannot see the sky. There is not a trace of human habitation, and not even a woodcutter or a cowherd is in sight. He hears only the cries of birds and monkeys around him, and a gust of infernally cold wind makes him shiver. Mingliaotse proceeds with his friend for a long while, when they suddenly

[363]

see an old man with a majestic forehead and a delicate face and green veins showing on his eyeballs. His hair falls down to the shoulders, and he is sitting on a rock, hugging his knees. Mingliaotse goes forward and makes a bow. The old man rises to his feet and looks at him steadily for a long time, but does not say a word. Going down on his knees, Mingliaotse speaks to him, "Is Father an extraordinary person who has attained the Tao? How otherwise can I find the sound of footsteps in this deep mountain solitude? Your disciple has always loved the Tao and in his middle age has not yet found it. I feel sad at the vanity of this life which rapidly burns out like a flash from a flint, or like oil in a pan. Will you please take pity on me and disperse my ignorance?" The old man pretends not to hear him. But after Mingliaotse insists upon his request, he merely teaches him a few words about being carefree and quiet and the idea of inaction, and after a little while, goes his way. Mingliaotse's eyes follow him for a long while until he altogether disappears. How does one explain the existence of such an old man in this deep mountain solitude?

Then wandering farther on, he chances to come upon an old friend of his. Sometimes when he thinks of those people with whom he had formed a friendship on the basis of love of prose and poetry, or of respect for each other's character, or of business relations, or of personal intimacy and mutual understanding of one another's hearts, or of a mutual confidence in one another's future, he begins to desire to see them again. Then he goes straight to the home of his friend, without concealing his identity. The friend bows to greet him, and seeing that Mingliaotse is clad in such a strange dress, is surprised and asks him some questions. "I have already retired from the world, and Chichen of T'ungming is my master," explains Mingliaotse. "Are your sons and daughters all married?" the friend asks. "No, not yet," replies Mingliaotse. "When they are all married, then I shall be free of all cares, like the clearing up of the water of the Yellow River. Tsep'ing[1] went away and never returned home, but I

---

[1] An ancient Taoist who went up to heaven.

am still looking forward to returning to the hills of my homeland, in order to live in harmony with my original nature." The host then gives him vegetarian food, and they begin to talk of the days twenty or thirty years ago, and surveying the past with a laugh, feel that everything has passed like a dream. The friend then bows his head and sighs, expressing his envy of the carefree life that Mingliaotse is leading.

"Are you not indeed a carefree man!" his friend says. "Now wealth and power and the glories of this world are things in which people easily get drowned. I sometimes see an old man with white hair on his head marching slowly with a stoop in an official procession, still clinging to these things and unwilling to let them go. If one day he quits office, he looks about with knitted eyebrows. Inquiring if the carriage is ready, he is still slow to depart, and passing out of the city gate of the capital, he still looks back. When back at his farm, he still disdains to occupy himself with planting rice and hemp and beans, and morning and night he will be asking for news from the capital. Or he will still be writing letters to his friends at the court, and such thoughts flit back and forth in his breast ceaselessly until he draws his last breath. Sometimes an Imperial order for his recall to office arrives at the moment when he is breathing his last, and sometimes the official messenger arrives with the news just a few hours after he closes his eyes. Isn't this ridiculous? How have you trained yourself that you are able to emancipate yourself from such things in good time?"

"I have looked at life in my leisure," replies Mingliaotse. "It seems that I have come to an awakening through a sense of life's tragedy. I have looked at the skies, and wondered how the sun and the moon and the stars and the Milky Way rush westward day and night like busy people. To-day passes and never returns, and although to-morrow comes, it is no longer to-day. This year passes and never returns, and although there is next year, it is no longer this year. And so the days of Nature are steadily lengthened or unrolled, while the days of my life are daily shortened, and outside the thirty-six thousand mornings, time

[365]

does not belong to me. The years of Nature are steadily unrolled, while the years of my life become steadily shortened, and beyond a hundred, they do not belong to me. Furthermore, the so-called 'hundred' and the so-called 'thirty-six thousand' in life are not always as we wish them to be, and among the days and years, most are passed in bad weather and sorrow and worry and running about. How many moments are there when the day is beautiful and the company enjoyable, when the moon and the wind are good and our heart is at ease and our spirit happy, when there is music and song and wine and we can enjoy ourselves and while away the hours!

"The sun and the moon pursue their courses, as fast as the bullet, and when their wheels are about to go behind the Western Precipices, the arms of the strongest man on earth cannot hold them and make them travel eastward, even the eloquence of Su Ch'in and Chang Yi cannot persuade them to travel eastward, even the wit and the strategy of Ch'ulitse and Yen Ying cannot change their minds and make them travel eastward, even the sincerity of Chingwei who knocked herself against the Rainbow and was transformed into a bird, trying to fill the sea of her regrets with pebbles, cannot touch their hearts and make them travel eastward. Writers throughout the ages who discussed this point have always held it as a matter of eternal regret.

"And I have looked at the earth, where high banks have been levelled into valleys and deep valleys have been heaved up into mountains, and the water of the rivers and lakes flows night and day eternally eastward into the sea. Fang P'ing[1] has said, 'Since I took over my duty, I have seen the sea three times changed into a mulberry field, and *vice versa*.'

"Again I have looked at the living things of this world, how they are born and grow old and fall ill and die, being ground thus in the mill of *yin* and *yang*, like oil in a frying-pan which, being heated by fire from below, dries up in a short while; or like a candle which flickers in the wind and soon goes out, its tears being dried up and its soot fallen to the table; or like a boat cut adrift

[1] A Taoist fairy.

[366]

on a big sea, washed forward by successive waves and floating it
knows not whither. Besides, the seven desires of man continue
to burn him up and the pleasures of the flesh pare him down;
he is sometimes too much disappointed and sometimes too much
elated, and usually too much worried. Without more than a
hundred years at his disposal, he plans to live for a thousand years,
and while sitting like oil on fire, his ambitions stretch beyond the
universe. Why wonder, therefore, that his being quickly
deteriorates when old age comes along and his vital energy is used
up and his spirit wanders away from its abode?

"I have seen princes and dukes and generals and premiers whose
crowded roofs form a skyline like the clouds. When the dinner-
bell sounds, a thousand people are seen eating together, and
when their gates are opened in the morning, crowds of visitors
rush in. Day and night they give feasts and their halls are full of
painted women. When a monk passes by, they shout at him with
a thundering voice and he dares not even to look at the house. But
after twenty or thirty years, the monk passes by again, and he
sees a stretch of wild grass and broken tiles covered by dew and
frost, and a cold sun is shining upon the place and a moaning wind
passes by, with not a roof left standing. What was once the scene
of song and dance and merry-making is to-day the pasture ground
of a few cowherd boys. Did they ever realize, when they were
at the height of their prosperity and laughing and merry-making,
that this day would come? And why did the great glories of this
world pass away in the twinkling of an eye? Was it alone, the
Garden of Chinku,[1] the Tower of T'ungt'ai,[2] the Hall of
P'ihsiang[3] and the Pool of T'aiyi[4] that gradually became ruins
after the passage of hundreds or thousands of years? On my
leisure days, I have passed out of the city and gone up on hills
where I saw a stretch of grave mounds. Do these belong to
Yen or Han or Chin or Wei? Or were these people princes
and dukes, or were they pages and servants? Or were they

[1] Garden of the fabulously wealthy Shih Ts'ung.
[2] Tower of Ts'ao Ts'ao.
[3] Hall of the pampered Queen Feiyen.
[4] Pool of Emperor Han Wuti.

heroes or were they fools? How can I know from this stretch of yellow soil? I thought how they, when they were living, clung to glory and wealth, vied with one another in their ambitions and struggled for fame, how they planned what they could never achieve and acquired what they could never use. Which one of them did not worry and plan and strive? One morning their eyes closed for the eternal sleep, and they left all their worries behind.

"I have stopped over at the residences of officials and wondered how many had taken another's place as the host of the house. I have looked at the records of the personnel at court and wondered how many times old names had been struck off and new names put in. I have been at mountain passes and at ferries, and have gone up a high hill to look down upon the plain, and I have seen continuous processions of boats and carriages and wondered how many travellers they have carried away. And so I sighed in silence, and sometimes my tears dropped and my heart's desires were turned cold like ashes."

"I have heard it said by Yentse," replies his friend, "that Sangch'iu was happy over the fact that there was no death, and that the King Ching of Ch'i shed tears and was grieved on account of death, and wise people criticized him for not understanding life. Are you not also lacking in the wisdom of those who understand life, when you feel sad and even shed tears because of the swift passing of time and the instability of life?"

"No," replies Mingliaotse. "I have felt sad from the sense of the instability of life, and I have come to an awakening from this feeling of sadness. King Ching of Ch'i feared that his power and glory were temporary and wanted to enjoy them for ever and exhaust the happiness of human life. On the contrary, I feel the instability of wealth and power and wish to keep them at a distance, in order to run my normal course of life. Our aims are different."

"Have you already attained the Tao, then?"

"No, I have not attained the Tao. I am only one who loves it," replies Mingliaotse.

"Why do you wander about, if you love the Tao?"

"Oh, no, do not confuse my wanderings with the Tao," replies Mingliaotse. "I was merely tired of the restrictions of the official life and the bother of worldly affairs, and I am travelling merely to free myself from them. As for winding up the 'great business of life,'[1] I shall have to wait until I return and shut myself up."

"Are you happy, going about with a gourd and a cassock and begging and singing for your living?"

"I have heard from my teacher," replies Mingliaotse, "that the art of attaining happiness consists in keeping your pleasures mild. When people come to a feast where lambs and cows are killed and all the delicacies that come from land and sea are laid out on the table, they all enjoy them at first, but when they come to the point of satiety, they begin to feel a sense of repulsion. Much better are meals of plain rice and green vegetables, which are mild and simple and good for one's health and which will be found to have a lasting flavour, after one gets used to them. People also enjoy themselves at first in parties where there are beautiful women and boys, where some beat the drum and others play the *sheng* and a lot of things are going on in the hall. But after the mood is past, one gets, on the contrary, a sense of sadness. It is much better to light incense and open your book and sit quietly and leisurely, maintaining a calm of spirit, and the charm deepens as you go along. Although I was at one time of my life an official, I had no property or wealth outside a few books. At first I travelled with these books, but fearing that they might be the cause of envy on the part of the water spirits, I threw them into the water. And now I haven't got a thing outside this body. Does not, then, the charm of life remain for me long and lasting, when my burdens are gone, my surroundings are quiet, my body is free and my heart is leisurely? With a cassock and a gourd, I go wherever I like, stay wherever I choose and take whatever I get. Staying at a place, I do not inquire after its owner, and going away, I do not leave my name. I do not feel ill at ease when

[1] Death.

I am left in the cold, and do not become contaminated when I am in noisy company. Therefore, the purpose of my wanderings is also to learn the Tao."

Having heard this, his friend says with a happy smile, "Your words make me feel like having taken a dose of cooling medicine. The disturbing fever has left my body without my knowing it."

[Here follows a discussion on the identity of the Three Religions and the existence of God and Buddha and fairies and ghosts.]

After a while a young man comes along and, pointing his finger at Mingliaotse, shouts, "Get away from here, you beggar! A monk ought to go away quietly when he receives his food. If you keep on babbling nonsense, I must regard you as a sorcerer and prosecute you at court." The young man rolls up his sleeve as if to strike at Mingliaotse, but the latter merely smiles without making a reply. The quarrel is settled by some passer-by.

Mingliaotse goes away singing his songs. At night he stops at an inn, and there is a very well-dressed woman peeping in at the door. Gradually she approaches and begins slyly to tease him. Mingliaotse thinks to himself that she must be an evil spirit, and remains sitting alone. "I am a fairy," says the woman, "and I have come to save you because I know that you have been trying very hard to learn the Tao. Besides, I had an appointment with you in the previous incarnation. Please don't doubt me. I will accompany you to the Enchanted Land." Mingliaotse remembers that when Lü Ch'engtse was learning the Tao at Chingshan, he was once thus deceived by a temptress and finally enslaved by an evil spirit. He lost his left eye, and died without being able to attain the Tao. Even the Classics regard the failure of Lü Ch'engtse as due to his lack of complete control of his mind and to the existence of evil desires. It is natural that, when ghosts and fox spirits tempt people, they destroy their life, and they should therefore be avoided. But even if sages and saints should make a mistake and be thus deceived, it would be a wrong way to control their mind and preserve their spirit. So he sits austerely as before and the woman all of a sudden disappears. Who can know whether she was a ghost or a fox spirit or a temptress?

[370]

Thus for three years Mingliaotse continues in his travels, wandering almost over the entire world. Everything that he sees with his eyes or hears with his ears, or touches with his body, and all the different situations and meetings, are thus used for the benefit of training his mind. And so such vagabond travel is not entirely without its benefits.

He then returns and builds himself a hut in the hills of Szeming and never leaves it again.

CHAPTER TWELVE

The Enjoyment Of Culture

I. GOOD TASTE IN KNOWLEDGE

THE AIM OF EDUCATION or culture is merely the development of good taste in knowledge and good form in conduct. The cultured man or the ideal educated man is not necessarily one who is well-read or learned, but one who likes and dislikes the right things. To know what to love and what to hate is to have taste in knowledge. Nothing is more exasperating than to meet a person at a party whose mind is crammed full with historical dates and figures and who is extremely well posted on current affairs in Russia or Czechoslovakia, but whose attitude or point of view is all wrong. I have met such persons, and found that there was no topic that might come up in the course of the conversation concerning which they did not have some facts or figures to produce, but whose points of view were deplorable. Such persons have erudition, but no discernment, or taste. Erudition is a mere matter of cramming of facts or information, while taste or discernment is a matter of artistic judgment. In speaking of a scholar, the Chinese generally distinguish between a man's scholarship, conduct, and taste or discernment.[1] This is particularly so with regard to historians; a book of history may be written with the most fastidious scholarship, yet be totally lacking in insight or discernment, and in the judgment or interpretation of persons and events in history, the author may show no originality or depth of understanding. Such a person, we say,

[1] *Hsüeh* (scholarship); *hsing* (conduct); *shih* or *shihchien* (discernment, or real insight). Thus one's *shih*, or power of insight into history or contemporary events, may be "higher" than another's. This is what we call "power of interpretation," or interpretative insight.

has no taste in knowledge. To be well-informed, or to accumulate facts and details, is the easiest of all things. There are many facts in a given historical period that can be easily crammed into our mind, but discernment in the selection of significant facts is a vastly more difficult thing and depends upon one's point of view.

An educated man, therefore, is one who has the right loves and hatreds. This we call taste, and with taste comes charm. Now to have taste or discernment requires a capacity for thinking things through to the bottom, an independence of judgment, and an unwillingness to be bulldozed by any form of humbug, social, political, literary, artistic, or academic. There is no doubt that we are surrounded in our adult life with a wealth of humbugs: fame humbugs, wealth humbugs, patriotic humbugs, political humbugs, religious humbugs and humbug poets, humbug artists, humbug dictators and humbug psychologists. When a psychoanalyst tells us that the performing of the functions of the bowels during childhood has a definite connection with ambition and aggressiveness and sense of duty in one's later life, or that constipation leads to stinginess of character, all that a man with taste can do is to feel amused. When a man is wrong, he is wrong, and there is no need for one to be impressed and overawed by a great name or by the number of books that he has read and we haven't.

Taste, then, is closely associated with courage, as the Chinese always associate *shih* with *tan*, and courage or independence of judgment, as we know, is such a rare virtue among mankind. We see this intellectual courage or independence during the childhood of all thinkers and writers who in later life amount to anything. Such a person refuses to like a certain poet even if he has the greatest vogue during his time; then when he truly likes a poet, he is able to say why he likes him, and it is an appeal to his inner judgment. This is what we call taste in literature. He also refuses to give his approval to the current school of painting, if it jars upon his artistic instinct. This is taste in art. He also refuses to be impressed by a philosophic vogue or a fashionable theory, even though it were backed by the greatest name. He is unwilling to be convinced by any author until he is convinced at heart; if the author convinces him, then the author is right, but if the author cannot convince him, then he is right and the author wrong. This is taste in knowledge. No doubt such intellectual courage or independence of judgment requires a certain childish, naïve confidence in oneself, but this self is the only thing that one can cling to, and the moment a student gives up his right of personal judgment, he is in for accepting all the humbugs of life.

Confucius seemed to have felt that scholarship without thinking was more dangerous than thinking unbacked by scholarship; he said, "Thinking without learning makes one flighty, and learning without thinking is a disaster." He must have seen enough students of the latter type in his days for him to utter this warning, a warning very much needed in the modern schools. It is well known that modern education and the modern school system in general tend to encourage scholarship at the expense of discernment and look upon the cramming of information as an end in itself, as if a great amount of scholarship could already make an educated man. But why is thought discouraged at school? Why has the educational system twisted and distorted the pleasant pursuit of knowledge into a mechanical, measured, uniform and passive cramming of information? Why do we place more importance on knowledge than on thought? How do we come to call a college graduate an educated man simply because he has made up the necessary units or week-hours of psychology, medieval history, logic, and "religion"? Why are there school marks and diplomas, and how did it come about that the mark and the diploma have, in the student's mind, come to take the place of the true aim of education?

The reason is simple. We have this system because we are educating people in masses, as if in a factory, and anything which happens inside a factory must go by a dead and mechanical system. In order to protect its name and standardize its products, a school must certify them with diplomas. With diplomas, then, comes the necessity of grading, and with the necessity of grading come school marks, and in order to have school marks, there must be recitations, examinations, and tests. The whole thing forms an entirely logical sequence and there is no escape from it. But the consequences of having mechanical examinations and tests are more fatal than we imagine. For it immediately throws the emphasis on memorization of facts rather than on the development of taste or judgment. I have been a teacher myself and know that it is easier to make a set of questions on historical dates than on vague opinions on vague questions. It is also easier to mark the papers.

The danger is that after having instituted this system, we are liable to forget that we have already wavered, or are apt to waver from the true ideal of education, which as I say is the development of good taste in knowledge. It is still useful to remember what Confucius said: "That scholarship which consists in the memorization of facts does not qualify one to be a teacher." There are no such things as compulsory subjects, no books, even Shakespeare's, that one *must* read. The school seems to proceed on the foolish idea that we can delimit a minimum stock of learning in history or geography which we can consider the absolute requisite of an educated man. I am pretty well educated, although I am in utter confusion about the capital of Spain, and at one time thought that Havana was the name of an island next to Cuba. The danger of prescribing a course of compulsory studies is that it implies that a man who has gone through the prescribed course *ipso facto* knows all there is to know for an educated man. It is therefore entirely logical that a graduate ceases to learn anything or to read books after he leaves school, because he has already learned all there is to know.

We must give up the idea that a man's knowledge can be tested or measured in any form whatsoever. Chuangtse has well said, "Alas, my life is limited, while knowledge is limitless!" The pursuit of knowledge is, after all, only like the exploration of a new continent, or "an adventure of the soul," as Anatole France says, and it will remain a pleasure, instead of becoming a torture, if the spirit of exploration with an open, questioning, curious and adventurous mind is maintained. Instead of the measured, uniform and passive cramming of information, we have to place this ideal of a positive, growing individual pleasure. Once the diploma and the marks are abolished, or treated for what they are worth, the pursuit of knowledge becomes positive, for the student is at least forced to ask himself why he studies at all. At present, the question is already answered for the student, for there is no question in his mind that he studies as a freshman in order to become a sophomore, and studies as a sophomore in order to become a junior. All such extraneous considerations should be brushed aside, for the acquisition of knowledge is nobody else's business but one's own. At present, all students study for the registrar, and many of the good students study for their parents or teachers or their future wives, that they may not seem ungrateful to their parents who are spending so much money for their support at college, or because they wish to appear nice to a teacher who is nice and conscientious to them, or that they may go out of school and earn a higher salary to feed their families. I suggest that all such thoughts are immoral. The pursuit of knowledge should remain nobody else's business but one's own, and only then can education become a pleasure and become positive.

II. ART AS PLAY AND PERSONALITY

Art is both creation and recreation. Of the two ideas, I think art as recreation or as sheer play of the human spirit is more important. Much as I appreciate all forms of immortal creative work, whether in painting, architecture or literature, I think the spirit of true art can become more general and permeate society only when a lot of people are enjoying art as a pastime, without any hope of achieving immortality. As it is more important that all college students should play tennis or football with indifferent skill than that a college should produce a few champion athletes or football players for the national contests, so it is also more important that all children and all grown-ups should be able to create something of their own as their pastime than that the nation should produce a Rodin. I would rather have all school-children taught to model clay and all bank presidents and economic experts able to make their own Christmas cards, however ridiculous the attempt may be, than to have only a few artists who work at art as a profession. That is to say, I am for amateurism in all fields. I like amateur philosophers, amateur poets, amateur photographers, amateur magicians, amateur architects who build their own houses, amateur musicians, amateur botanists and amateur aviators. I get as much pleasure out of listening to a friend playing a sonatina of an evening in an indifferent manner as out of listening to a first-class professional concert. And everyone enjoys an amateur parlour magician, who is one of his friends, more than he enjoys a professional magician on the stage, and every parent enjoys the amateur dramatics of his own children much more heartily than he enjoys a Shakespearean play. We know that it is spontaneous, and in spontaneity alone lies the true spirit of art. That is why I regard it as so important that in China painting is essentially the pastime of a scholar and not of a professional artist. It is only when the spirit of play is kept that art can escape being commercialized.

Now it is characteristic of play that one plays without reason and there must be no reason for it. Play is its own good reason. This view is borne out by the history of evolution. Beauty is something that cannot be accounted for by the struggle for existence, and there are forms of beauty that are destructive even to the animal, like the over-developed horns of a deer. Darwin saw that he could never account for the beauties of plant and animal life by natural selection, and he had to introduce the great secondary principle of sexual selection. We fail to understand art and the essence of art if we do not recognize it as merely an overflow of physical and mental energy, free and unhampered and existing for its own sake. This is the much decried formula of "art for art's sake." I regard this not as question upon which the politicians have the right to say anything, but merely as an incontrovertible fact regarding the psychological origin of all artistic creation. Hitler has denounced many forms of modern art as immoral, but I consider that those painters who paint portraits of Hitler, to be shown at the new Art Museum in order to please the powerful ruler, are the most immoral of all. That is not art, but prostitution. If commercial art often injures the spirit of artistic creation, political art is sure to kill it. For freedom is the very soul of art. Modern dictators are attempting the impossible when they try to produce a political art. They don't seem to realize that you cannot produce art by the force of the bayonet any more than you can buy real love from a prostitute.

In order to understand the essence of art at all, we have to go back to the physical basis of art as an overflow of energy. This is known as an artistic or creative impulse. The use of the very word "inspiration" shows that the artist himself hardly knows where the impulse comes from. It is merely a matter of inner urge, like the scientist's impulse for the discovery of truth, or the explorer's impulse for discovering a new island. There is no accounting for it. We are beginning to see to-day, with the help of biological knowledge, that the whole organization of our mental life is regulated by the increase or decrease and distribution of hormones in the blood, acting on the various organs and the nervous system controlling these organs. Even anger or fear is merely a matter of the supply of adrenalin. Genius itself, it seems to me, is but an over-supply of glandular secretions. An obscure Chinese novelist, without the modern knowledge of hormones, made a correct guess about the origin of all activity as due to "worms" in our body. Adultery is a matter of worms gnawing our intestines and impelling the man to satisfy his desire. Ambition and aggressiveness and love of fame or power are also due to certain other worms giving the person no rest until he has achieved the object of his ambition. The writing of a book, say a novel, is again due to a species of worms which impel and urge the author to create for no reason whatsoever. Between hormones and worms, I prefer to believe in the latter. The term is more vivid.

Given an over-supply or even a normal supply of worms, a man is bound to create something or other, because he cannot help himself. When a child has an over-supply of energy, his normal walking is transformed into hopping or skipping. When a man has an over-supply of energy, his walking becomes transformed into prancing or dancing. So, then, dancing is nothing but inefficient walking, inefficient in the sense that there is a waste of energy from an utilitarian, not an æsthetic, point of view. Instead of going straight to a point, which is the quickest road, a dancer waltzes and goes in a circle. No one really tries to be patriotic when he is dancing, and to command a man to dance according to the capitalist or fascist or proletarian ideology is to destroy the spirit of play and glorious inefficiency in dancing. If a Communist is trying to attain a political objective, or trying to be a loyal comrade, he should just walk, and not dance. The Communists seem to know the sacredness of labour, and not the sacredness of play. As if man in civilization didn't work too much already, in comparison with every other species and variety of the animal kingdom, so that even the little leisure he has, the little time for play and art, must too be invaded by the claims of that monster, the State!

This understanding of the true nature of art as consisting in mere play may help to clarify the problem of the relationship of art and morality. Beauty is merely good form, and there is good form in conduct as well as in good painting or a beautiful bridge. Art is very much broader than painting and music and dancing, because there is good form in everything. There is good form in an athlete at a race; there is good form in a man leading a beautiful life from childhood and youth to maturity and old age, each appropriate in its own time; there is good form in a presidential campaign well directed, well manœuvred and leading gradually to a finale of victory, and there is good form, too, in one's laughter or spitting, as so carefully practised by the old Mandarins in China. Every human activity has a form and expression, and all forms of expressions lie within the definition of art. It is therefore impossible to relegate the art of expression to the few fields of music and dancing and painting.

With this broader interpretation of art, therefore, good form in conduct and good personality in art are closely related and are equally important. There can be a luxury in our bodily movements, as in the movement of a symphonic poem. Given that oversupply of energy, there is an ease and gracefulness and attendance to form in whatever we do. Now ease and gracefulness come from a feeling of physical competence, a feeling of ability to do a thing more than well—to do it *beautifully*. In the more abstract realms, we see this beauty in anybody doing a nice job. The impulse to do a nice job or a neat job is essentially an æsthetic impulse. Even a neat murder, a neat conspiracy neatly carried out, is beautiful to look at, however condemnable the act may be. In the more concrete details of our life, there is, or there can be, ease and gracefulness and competence, too. All the things we call "the amenities of life" belong in this category. Paying a compliment well and appropriately is called a beautiful compliment, and, on the other hand, paying a compliment with bad taste is called an awkward compliment.

The development of the amenities of speech and life and personal habits reached a high point at the end of the Chin Dynasty (third and fourth centuries, A.D.) in China. That was the time when "leisurely conversations" were in vogue. The greatest sophistication was seen in women's dress, and there were a great number of men noted for their handsomeness. There was a fashion for growing "beautiful beards," and men learned to wobble about clad in extremely loose gowns. The dress was so designed that there was no part of one's body unreachable in case one wanted to scratch an itch. Everything was gracefully done. The *chu,* a bundle of hair from the horse's tail tied together around a handle for driving away mosquitoes or flies, became an important accessory of conversation, and to-day such leisurely conversations are still known in literary works as *chut'an* or "*chu* conversations." The idea was that one was to hold the *chu* in his hand and wave it gracefully about in the air during conversation. The fan came in also as a beautiful adjunct to conversation, the conversationalist opening, waving and closing it, as an American old man would take off his spectacles and put them on again during a speech, and was just as beautiful to look at.

In point of utility, the *chu* or the fan was only slightly more useful than an Englishman's monocle, but they were all parts of the style of conversation, as a cane is a part of the style of walking. Among the most beautiful amenities of life I have seen in the West are the clicking of heels of Prussian gentlemen bowing to a lady in a parlour and the curtsying of German girls, with one leg crossed behind the other. That I consider a supremely beautiful gesture, and it is a pity that this custom has gone out of vogue.

Many are the social amenities practised in China. The gestures of one's fingers, hands and arms are carefully cultivated. The method of greeting among the Manchus, known as *tach'ien*, is also a beautiful thing to look at. The person comes into the room, and letting one arm fall straight down at the side, he bends one of his legs and makes a graceful dip. In case there is company sitting around the room, he makes a graceful turn around the axis of his unbent leg while in that position, thus making a general greeting to the entire company. One should also watch a culti-vated chess-player put his stones on the chessboard. Holding one of those tiny white or black stones carefully balanced on his forefinger, he gently pushes it from behind by an outward move-ment of his thumb and an inward movement of the forefinger, and lands it beautifully on the board. A cultured Mandarin made extremely beautiful gestures when he was angry. He wore a gown with the sleeves tucked up at the lower ends showing the silk lining, known as "horse-hoof sleeves," and when he was greatly displeased, he would brandish his right arm or both arms downwards and with an audible jerk bring the tucked-up "horse-hoof" down, and gracefully wobble out of the room. This is known as *fohsiu,* or to "brush one's sleeves and leave."

The speech of a cultured Mandarin official is also a beautiful thing to hear. His words come out with a beautiful cadence, and the musical tones of the Peking accent have a graceful musical rise and fall. His syllables are pronounced gracefully and slowly, and in the case of real scholars, his language is set up with jewels from the Chinese literary language. And then one should hear how the Mandarin laughs or spits. It is positively delightful. The spitting is done generally in three musical beats, the first two being sounds of drawing in and clearing the throat in preparation for the final beat of spitting out, which is executed with a quick forcefulness: *staccato* after *legato*. I really don't mind the germs thus let out into the air, if the spitting is æsthetically done, for I have survived the germs without any appreciable effect on my health. His laughter is an equally regulated and artistically rhythmical affair, slightly artificial and stylized, and finishing off in an increasing generous volume, pleasantly softened by a white beard when there is one.

Such laughter is a carefully cultivated art with an actor as part of his technique of acting, and theatre-goers always enjoy and applaud a perfectly executed laugh. This is, of course, a very difficult thing, because there are so many kinds of laughter: the laughter of happiness, the laughter at someone falling into one's trap, the laughter of sneer or contempt, and most difficult of all, the laughter of despair, of a man caught and defeated by the force of overwhelming circumstances. Chinese theatre-goers watch for these things and for the hand gestures and steps of an actor, the latter being known as *t'aipu,* or "stage steps." Every movement of the arm, every inclination of the head, every twist of the neck, every bend of the back, every waving movement of the flowing sleeve, and of course every step of the foot, is a carefully practised gesture. The Chinese classify acting into the two classes of singing and acting, and there are plays with emphasis on singing, and other dramas with emphasis on acting. By "acting" is meant these gestures of the body, the hands and the face, as much as the more general acting of emotions and expressions. Chinese actors have to learn how to shake their heads in disapproval, how to lift their eyebrows in suspicion, and how to gently stroke their beard in peace and satisfaction.

Now we are ready to discuss the problem of morality and art. The utter confusion of art and propaganda in fascist and communist countries and its naïve acceptance by so many intellectuals in a democracy make it necessary for every intelligent person to come to a clear understanding of the problem. The Communists and Fascists make a false start at the very beginning by ignoring the role of the individual, both as the creating personality and the object of the creation, and placing in its stead the superior claims of either the state or the social class. While literature and art must both be built on personal, individual emotions, the Communists and Fascists emphasize only group or class emotions, without postulating the reality of emotions in varying individuals. With individual personality pushed out of court, one cannot even begin to discuss the problem of art and morality sanely.

Art has a relationship to morals only in so far as the peculiar quality of a work of art is an expression of the artist's personality. An artist with a grand personality produces grand art, an artist with a trivial personality produces trivial art, a sentimental artist produces sentimental art, a voluptuous artist produces voluptuous art, a tender artist produces tender art, and an artist of delicacy produces delicate art. There we have the relationship of art and morality in a nutshell. Morality, therefore, is not a thing that can be superimposed from the outside, according to the changing whims of a dictator or the changing ethical code of the Chief of the Propaganda Department. It must grow from the inside as the natural expression of the artist's soul. And it is not a question of choice but an inescapable fact. The mean-hearted artist cannot produce a great painting, and a big-hearted artist cannot produce a mean picture, even if his life were at stake.

The Chinese notion of *p'in* in art is extremely interesting, sometimes spoken of as *jenp'in* ("personality of the man") or *p'inkeh* ("personality of character"). There is also an idea of grading, as we speak of artists or poets of "the first *p'in*" or "second *p'in*," and we also speak of tasting or sampling good tea as "to *p'in* tea." There are then a whole category of expressions in connection with the personality of a person as shown in a particular action. In the first place, a bad gambler, or a gambler who shows bad temper or bad taste, is said to have a bad *tup'in* or a bad "gambling personality." A drinker who is apt to behave disgracefully after a hard drink is said to have a bad *chiup'in* or bad "wine

[383]

personality." A good or bad chess-player is said to have a good or bad *ch'ip'in* or "chess personality." The earliest Chinese book of poetic criticism is known as *Shihp'in*[1] (*Personalities of Poetry*), with a grading of the different poets, and of course there are books of art criticism known as *huap'in* or "Personalities in Painting."

Connected with this idea of *p'in,* therefore, there is the generally accepted belief that an artist's work is strictly determined by his personality. This "personality" is both moral and artistic. It tends to emphasize the notion of human understanding, high-mindedness, detachment from life, absence of pettiness or triviality or vulgarity. In this sense it is akin to English "manner" or "style." A wayward or unconventional artist will show a wayward or unconventional style and a person of charm will naturally show charm and delicacy in his style, and a great artist with good taste will not stoop to "mannerisms." In this sense, personality is the very soul of art. The Chinese have always accepted implicitly the belief that no painter can be great unless his own moral and æsthetic personality is great, and in judging calligraphy and painting, the highest criterion is not whether the artist shows good technique but whether he has or has not a high personality. A work showing perfect technique may nevertheless show a "low" personality, and then, as we would say in English, that work lacks "character."

We have come thus to the central problem of all art. The great Chinese general and premier, Tseng Kuofan, said in one of his family letters that the only two living principles of art in calligraphy are form and expression, and that one of the greatest calligraphists of the time, Ho Shaochi, approved of his formula and appreciated his insight. Since all art is concrete, there is always a mechanical problem, the problem of technique, which has to be mastered, but as art is also spirit, the vital element in all forms of creation is the personal expression. It is the artist's individuality, over against his mere technique, that is the only significant thing in a work of art. In writing, the only important thing in a book is the author's personal style and feeling, as shown in

[1] By Chung Yung, who lived about A.D. 500.

[384]

his judgment and likes and dislikes. There is a constant danger of this personality or personal expression being submerged by the technique, and the greatest difficulty of all beginners, whether in painting or writing or acting, is to *let oneself go.* The reason is, of course, that the beginner is scared by the form or technique. But no form without this personal element can be good form at all. All good form has a swing, and it is the swing that is beautiful to look at, whether it is the swing of a champion golf-player's club, or of a man rocketing to success, or of a football player carrying the ball down the field. There must be a flow of expression, and that power of expression must not be hampered by the technique, but must be able to move freely and happily in it. There is that swing—so beautiful to look at—in a train going around a curve, or a yacht going at full speed with straight sails. There is that swing in the flight of a swallow, or of a hawk dashing down on its prey, or of a champion horse racing to the finish "in good form," as we say.

We require that all art must have *character,* and character is nothing but what the work of art suggests or reveals concerning the artist's personality or soul or heart or, as the Chinese put it, "breast." Without that character or personality, a work of art is dead, and no amount of virtuosity or mere perfection of technique can save it from lifelessness or lack of vitality. Without that highly individual thing called personality, beauty itself becomes banal. So many girls aspiring to be Hollywood stars do not know this, and content themselves with imitating Marlene Dietrich or Jean Harlow, thus exasperating a movie director looking for talent. There are so many banally pretty faces, and so little fresh, individual beauty. Why don't they study the acting of Marie Dressler? All art is one and based on the same principle of expression or personality, whether it is acting in a movie picture or painting or literary authorship. Really, by looking at the acting of Marie Dressler or Lionel Barrymore, one can learn the secret of style in writing. To cultivate the charm of that personality is the important basis for all art, for no matter what an artist does, his character shows in his work.

The cultivation of personality is both moral and æsthetic, and it requires both scholarship and refinement. Refinement is something nearer to taste and may be just born in an artist, but the highest pleasure of looking at a book of art is felt only when it is supported by scholarship. This is particularly clear in painting and calligraphy. One can tell from a piece of calligraphy whether the writer has or has not seen a great number of Wei rubbings. If he has, this scholarship gives him a certain antique manner, but in addition to that, he must put into it his own soul or personality, which varies, of course. If he is a delicate and sentimental soul, he will show a delicate and sentimental style, but if he loves strength or massive power, he will also adopt a style that goes in for strength and massive power. Thus in painting and calligraphy, particularly the latter, we are able to see a whole category of æsthetic qualities or different types of beauty, and no one will be able to separate the beauty of the finished product and the beauty of the artist's own soul. There may be beauty of whimsicality and waywardness, beauty of rugged strength, beauty of massive power, beauty of spiritual freedom, beauty of courage and dash, beauty of romantic charm, beauty of restraint, beauty of soft gracefulness, beauty of austerity, beauty of simplicity and "stupidity," beauty of mere regularity, beauty of swiftness, and sometimes even beauty of affected ugliness. There is only one form of beauty that is impossible because it does not exist, and that is the beauty of strenuousness or of the strenuous life.

III. THE ART OF READING

Reading or the enjoyment of books has always been regarded among the charms of a cultured life and is respected and envied by those who rarely give themselves that privilege. This is easy to understand when we compare the difference between the life of a man who does no reading and that of a man who does. The man who has not the habit of reading is imprisoned in his immediate world, in respect to time and space. His life falls into a set routine; he is limited to contact and conversation with a few friends and acquaintances, and he sees only what happens in his immediate neighbourhood. From this prison there is no escape. But the moment he takes up a book, he immediately enters a different world, and if it is a good book, he is immediately put in touch with one of the best talkers of the world. This talker leads him on and carries him into a different country or a different age, or unburdens to him some of his personal regrets, or discusses with him some special line or aspect of life that the reader knows nothing about. An ancient author puts him in communion with a dead spirit of long ago, and as he reads along, he begins to imagine what that ancient author looked like and what type of person he was. Both Mencius and Ssema Ch'ien, China's greatest historian, have expressed the same idea. Now to be able to live two hours out of twelve in a different world and take one's thoughts off the claims of the immediate present is, of course, a privilege to be envied by people shut up in their bodily prison. Such a change of environment is really similar to travel in its psychological effect.

But there is more to it than this. The reader is always carried away into a world of thought and reflection. Even if it is a book about physical events, there is a difference between seeing such events in person or living through them, and reading about them in books, for then the events always assume the quality of a spectacle and the reader becomes a detached spectator. The best reading is therefore that which leads us into this contemplative mood, and not that which is merely occupied with the report of events. The tremendous amount of time spent on newspapers I regard as not reading at all, for the average readers of papers are mainly concerned with getting reports about events and happenings without contemplative value.

The best formula for the object of reading, in my opinion, was stated by Huang Shanku, a Sung poet and friend of Su Tungp'o. He said, "A scholar who hasn't read anything for three days feels that *his talk has no flavour* (becomes insipid), *and his own face becomes hateful to look at* (in the mirror)." What he means, of course, is that reading gives a man a certain charm and flavour, which is the entire object of reading, and only reading with this object can be called an art. One doesn't read to "improve one's mind," because when one begins to think of improving his mind, all the pleasure of reading is gone. He is the type of person who says to himself: "I must read Shakespeare, and I must read Sophocles, and I must read the entire Five Foot Shelf of Dr. Eliot, so I can become an educated man." I'm sure that man will never become educated. He will force himself one evening to read Shakespeare's *Hamlet* and come away, as if from a bad dream, with no greater benefit than that he is able to say that he has "read" *Hamlet*. Anyone who reads a book with a sense of obligation does not understand the art of reading. This type of reading with a business purpose is in no way different from a senator's reading up of files and reports before he makes a speech. It is asking for business advice and information, and not reading at all.

Reading for the cultivation of personal charm of appearance and flavour in speech is, then, according to Huang, the only admissible kind of reading. This charm of appearance must evidently be interpreted as something other than physical beauty. What Huang means by "hateful to look at" is not physical ugliness. There are ugly faces that have a fascinating charm and beautiful faces that are insipid to look at. I have among my Chinese friends one whose head is shaped like a bomb and yet who is nevertheless always a pleasure to see. The most beautiful face among Western authors, so far as I have seen them in pictures, was that of G. K. Chesterton. There was such a diabolical conglomeration of moustache, glasses, fairly bushy eyebrows and knitted lines where the eyebrows met! One felt there were a vast number of ideas playing about inside that forehead, ready at any time to burst out from those quizzically penetrating eyes. That is what Huang would call a beautiful face, a face not made up by powder and rouge, but by the sheer force of thinking. As for flavour of speech, it all depends on one's way of reading. Whether one has "flavour" or not in his talk, depends on his method of reading. If a reader gets the flavour of books, he will show that flavour in his conversations, and if he has flavour in his conversations, he cannot help also having a flavour in his writing.

Hence I consider flavour or taste as the key to all reading. It necessarily follows that taste is selective and individual, like the taste for food. The most hygienic way of eating is, after all, eating what one likes, for then one is sure of his digestion. In reading, as in eating, what is one man's meat may be another's poison. A teacher cannot force his pupils to like what he likes in reading, and a parent cannot expect his children to have the same tastes as himself. And if the reader has no taste for what he reads, all the time is wasted. As Yüan Chunglang says, "You can leave the books that you don't like alone, *and let other people read them.*"

There can be, therefore, no books that one absolutely must read. For our intellectual interests grow like a tree or flow like a river. So long as there is proper sap, the tree will grow anyhow, and so long as there is fresh current from the spring, the water will flow. When water strikes a granite cliff, it just goes around it; when it finds itself in a pleasant low valley, it stops and meanders there a while; when it finds itself in a deep mountain pond, it is content to stay there; when it finds itself travelling over rapids, it hurries forward. Thus, without any effort or determined aim, it is sure of reaching the sea some day. There are no books in this world that everybody must read, but only books that a person must read at a certain time in a given place under given circumstances and at a given period of his life. I rather think that reading, like matrimony, is determined by fate or *yinyüan*. Even if there is a certain book that every one must read, like the Bible, there is a time for it. When one's thoughts and experience have not reached a certain point for reading a masterpiece, the masterpiece will leave only a bad flavour on his palate. Confucius said, "When one is fifty, one may read the *Book of Changes*," which means that one should not read it at forty-five. The extremely mild flavour of Confucius' own sayings in the *Analects* and his mature wisdom cannot be appreciated until one becomes mature himself.

Furthermore, the same reader reading the same book at different periods gets a different flavour out of it. For instance, we enjoy a book more after we have had a personal talk with the author himself, or even after having seen a picture of his face, and one gets again a different flavour sometimes after one has broken off friendship with the author. A person gets a kind of flavour from reading the *Book of Changes* at forty, and gets another kind of flavour reading it at fifty, after he has seen more changes in life. Therefore, all good books can be read with profit and renewed pleasure a second time. I was made to read *Westward Ho!* and *Henry Esmond* in my college days, but while I was capable of appreciating *Westward Ho!* in my teens, the real flavour of *Henry Esmond* escaped me entirely until I reflected about it later on, and suspected there was vastly more charm in that book than I had then been capable of appreciating.

Reading, therefore, is an act consisting of two sides, the author and the reader. The net gain comes as much from the reader's contribution through his own insight and experience as from the author's own. In speaking about the Confucian *Analects,* the Sung Confucianist Ch'eng Yich'uan said: "There are readers *and* readers. Some read the *Analects* and feel that nothing has happened, some are pleased with one or two lines in it, and some begin to wave their hands and dance on their legs unconsciously."

I regard the discovery of one's favourite author as the most critical event in one's intellectual development. There is such a thing as the affinity of spirits, and among the authors of ancient and modern times one must try to find an author whose spirit is akin with his own. Only in this way can one get any real good out of reading. One has to be independent and search out his masters. Who is one's favourite author, no one can tell, probably not even the man himself. It is like love at first sight. The reader cannot be told to love this one or that one, but when he has found the author he loves, he knows it himself by a kind of instinct. We have such famous cases of discoveries of authors. Scholars seem to have lived in different ages, separated by centuries, and yet their modes of thinking and feeling were so akin that their coming together across the pages of a book was like a person finding his own image. In Chinese phraseology, we speak of these kindred spirits as re-incarnations of the same soul, as

Su Tungp'o was said to be a re-incarnation of Chuangtse or T'ao Yüanming,[1] and Yüan Chunglang was said to be the re-incarnation of Su Tungp'o. Su Tungp'o said that when he first read Chuangtse, he felt as if all the time since his childhood he had been thinking the same things and taking the same views himself. When Yüan Chunglang discovered one night Hsü Wench'ang, a contemporary unknown to him, in a small book of poems, he jumped out of bed and shouted to his friend, and his friend began to read it and shout in turn, and then they both read and shouted again until their servant was completely puzzled. George Eliot described her first reading of Rousseau as an electric shock. Nietzsche felt the same thing about Schopenhauer, but Schopenhauer was a peevish master and Nietzsche was a violent-tempered pupil, and it was natural that the pupil later rebelled against the teacher.

It is only this kind of reading, this discovery of one's favourite author, that will do one any good at all. Like a man falling in love with his sweetheart at first sight, everything is right. She is of the right height, has the right face, the right colour of hair, the right quality of voice and the right way of speaking and smiling. This author is not something that a young man need be told about by his teacher. The author is just right for him; his style, his taste, his point of view, his mode of thinking, are all right. And then the reader proceeds to devour every word and every line that the author writes, and because there is a spiritual affinity, he absorbs and readily digests everything. The author has cast a spell over him, and he is glad to be under the spell, and in time his own voice and manner and way of smiling and way of talking become like the author's own. Thus he truly steeps himself in his literary lover and derives from these books sustenance for his soul. After a few years, the spell is over and he grows a little tired of this lover and seeks new literary lovers, and after he has had three or four lovers and completely eaten them up, he emerges as an

---

[1] Su Tungp'o performed the unique feat of writing a complete set of poems on the rhymes used by the complete poems of T'ao, and at the end of the collection of *Su's Poems on T'ao's Rhymes*, he said of himself that he was the re-incarnation of T'ao, whom he admired desperately above all other predecessors.

author himself. There are many readers who never fall in love, like many young men and women who flirt around and are incapable of forming a deep attachment to a particular person. They can read any and all authors, and they never amount to anything.

Such a conception of the art of reading completely precludes the idea of reading as a duty or as an obligation. In China, one often encourages students to "study bitterly." There was a famous scholar who studied bitterly and who stuck an awl in his calf when he fell asleep while studying at night. There was another scholar who had a maid stand by his side as he was studying at night, to wake him up every time he fell asleep. This was nonsensical. If one has a book lying before him and falls asleep while some wise ancient author is talking to him, he should just go to bed. No amount of sticking an awl in his calf or of shaking him up by a maid will do him any good. Such a man has lost all sense of the pleasure of reading. Scholars who are worth anything at all never know what is called "a hard grind" or what "bitter study" means. They merely love books and read on because they cannot help themselves.

With this question solved, the question of time and place for reading is also provided with an answer. There is no proper time and place for reading. When the mood for reading comes, one can read anywhere. If one knows the enjoyment of reading, he will read in school or out of school, and in spite of all schools. He can study even in the best schools. Tseng Kuofan, in one of his family letters concerning the expressed desire of one of his younger brothers to come to the capital and study at a better school, replied that: "If one has the desire to study, he can study at a country school, or even on a desert or in busy streets, and even as a wood-cutter or a swineherd. But if one has no desire to study, then not only is the country school not proper for study, but even a quiet country home or a fairy island is not a proper place for study." There are people who adopt a self-important posture at the desk when they are about to do some reading, and then complain they are unable to read because the room is too cold, or the chair is too hard, or the light is too strong. And there are writers who complain that they cannot write because there are too many mosquitoes, or the writing paper is too shiny, or the noise from the street is too great. The great Sung scholar, Ouyang Hsiu, confessed to "three ons" for doing his best writing: on the pillow, on horseback and on the toilet. Another famous Ch'ing scholar, Ku Ch'ienli, was known for his habit of "reading Confucian classics naked" in summer. On the other hand, there is a good reason for not doing any reading in any of the seasons of the year, if one does not like reading:

> To study in spring is treason;
> And summer is sleep's best reason;
> If winter hurries the fall,
> Then stop till next spring season.

What, then, is the true art of reading? The simple answer is to just take up a book and read when the mood comes. To be thoroughly enjoyed, reading must be entirely spontaneous. One takes a limp volume of *Lisao,* or of Omar Khayyám, and goes away hand in hand with his love to read on a river bank. If there are good clouds over one's head, let them read the clouds and forget the books, or read the books and the clouds at the same time. Between times, a good pipe or a good cup of tea makes it still more perfect. Or perhaps on a snowy night, when one is sitting before the fireside, and there is a kettle singing on the hearth and a good pouch of tobacco at the side, one gathers ten or a dozen books on philosophy, economics, poetry, biography and piles them up on the couch, and then leisurely turns over a few of them and gently lights on the one which strikes his fancy at the moment. Chin Shengt'an regards reading a banned book behind closed doors on a snowy night as one of the greatest pleasures of life. The mood for reading is perfectly described by Ch'en Chiju (Meikung): "The ancient people called books and paintings 'limp volumes' and 'soft volumes'; therefore the best style of reading a book or opening an album is the leisurely style." In this mood, one develops patience for everything. As the same author says,

"The real master tolerates misprints when reading history, as a good traveller tolerates bad roads when climbing a mountain, one going to watch a snow scene tolerates a flimsy bridge, one choosing to live in the country tolerates vulgar people, and one bent on looking at flowers tolerates bad wine."

The best description of the pleasure of reading I found in the autobiography of China's greatest poetess, Li Ch'ingchao (Yi-an, 1081-1141). She and her husband would go to the temple, where secondhand books and rubbings from stone inscriptions were sold, on the day he got his monthly stipend as a student at the Imperial Academy. Then they would buy some fruit on the way back, and coming home, they began to pare the fruit and examine the newly bought rubbings together, or drink tea and compare the variants in different editions. As described in her autobiographical sketch known as *Postscript to Chinshihlu* (a book on bronze and stone inscriptions):

> I have a power for memory, and sitting quietly after supper in the Homecoming Hall, we would boil a pot of tea and, pointing to the piles of books on the shelves, make a guess as to on what line of what page in what volume of a certain book a passage occurred and see who was right, the one making the correct guess having the privilege of drinking his cup of tea first. When a guess was correct, we would lift the cup high and break out into a loud laughter, so much so that sometimes the tea was spilled on our dress and we were not able to drink. We were then content to live and grow old in such a world! Therefore we held our heads high, although we were living in poverty and sorrow . . . In time our collection grew bigger and bigger and the books and art objects were piled up on tables and desks and beds, and we enjoyed them with our eyes and our minds and planned and discussed over them, tasting a happiness above those enjoying dogs and horses and music and dance. . . .

This sketch was written in her old age after her husband had died, when she was a lonely old woman fleeing from place to place during the invasion of North China by the Chin tribes.

IV. THE ART OF WRITING

The art of writing is very much broader than the art of writing itself, or of the writing technique. In fact, it would be helpful to a beginner who aspires to be a writer first to dispel in him any over-concern with the technique of writing, and tell him to stop trifling with such superficial matters and get down to the depths of his soul, to the end of developing a genuine literary personality as the foundation of all authorship. When the foundation is properly laid and a genuine literary personality is cultivated, style follows as a natural consequence and the little points of technique will take care of themselves. It really does not matter if he is a little confused about points of rhetoric and grammar, provided he can turn out good stuff. There are always professional readers with publishing houses whose business it is to attend to the commas, semi-colons, and split infinitives. On the other hand, no amount of grammatical or literary polish can make a writer if he neglects the cultivation of a literary personality. As Buffon says, "The style is the man." Style is not a method, a system or even a decoration for one's writing; it is but the total impression that the reader gets of the quality of the writer's mind, his depth or superficiality, his insight or lack of insight and other qualities like wit, humour, biting sarcasm, genial understanding, tenderness, delicacy of understanding, kindly cynicism or cynical kindliness, hard-headedness, practical common sense, and general attitude toward things. It is clear that there can be no handbook for developing a "humorous technique" or a "three-hour course in cynical kindliness," or "fifteen rules for practical common sense" and "eleven rules for delicacy of feeling."

We have to go deeper than the surface of the art of writing, and the moment we do that, we find that the question of the art of writing involves the whole question of literature, of thought, point of view, sentiment and reading and writing. In my literary campaign in China for restoring the School of Self-expression (*hsingling*) and for the development of a more lively and personal style in prose, I have been forced to write essay after essay giving my views on literature in general and on the art of writing in particular. I have attempted also to write a series of literary epigrams under the general title "Cigar Ashes." Here are some of the cigar ashes:

(a) Technique and Personality

Professors of composition talk about literature as carpenters talk about art. Critics analyse a literary composition by the technique of writing, as engineers measure the height and structure of Taishan by compasses.

There is no such thing as the technique of writing. All good Chinese writers who to my mind are worth anything have repudiated it.

The technique of writing is to literature as dogmas are to the church—the occupation with trivial things by trivial minds.

A beginner is generally dazzled by the discussion of technique —the technique of the novel, of the drama, of music and of acting on the stage. He doesn't realize that the technique of writing has nothing to do with the birth of an author, and the technique of acting has nothing to do with the birth of a great actor. He doesn't even suspect that there is such a thing as personality, which is the foundation of all success in art and literature.

(b) The Appreciation of Literature

When one reads a number of good authors and feels that one author describes things very vividly, that another shows great tenderness or delicacy, a third expresses things exquisitely, a fourth has an indescribable charm, a fifth one's writing is like good whisky, a sixth one's is like mellow wine, he should not be afraid to say that he likes them and appreciates them, if only his appreciation is genuine. After such a wide experience in reading, he has the proper experiential basis for knowing what are mildness, mellowness, strength, power, brilliance, pungency, delicacy, and charm. When he has tasted all these

[396]

flavours, then he knows what is good literature without reading a single handbook.

The first rule of a student of literature is to learn to sample different flavours. The best flavour is mildness and mellowness, but is most difficult for a writer to attain. Between mildness and mere flatness there is only a very thin margin.

A writer whose thoughts lack depth and originality may try to write a simple style and end up by being insipid. Only fresh fish may be cooked in its own juice; stale fish must be flavoured with anchovy sauce and pepper and mustard—the more the better.

A good writer is like the sister of Yang Kueifei, who could go to see the Emperor himself without powder and rouge. All the other beauties in the palace required them. This is the reason why there are so few writers who dare to write in simple English.

(c) Style and Thought

Writing is good or bad, depending on its charm and flavour, or lack of them. For this charm there can be no rules. Charm rises from one's writing as smoke rises from a pipe-bowl, or a cloud rises from a hill-top, not knowing whither it is going. The best style is that of "sailing clouds and flowing water," like the prose of Su Tungp'o.

Style is a compound of language, thought and personality. Some styles are made exclusively of language.

Very rarely does one find clear thoughts clothed in unclear language. Much more often does one find unclear thoughts expressed clearly. Such a style is clearly unclear.

Clear thoughts expressed in unclear language is the style of a confirmed bachelor. He never has to explain anything to a wife. *E.g.*, Immanuel Kant. Even Samuel Butler often gets so quizzical.

A man's style is always coloured by his "literary lover." He grows to be like him more and more in ways of thinking and methods of expression. That is the only way a style can be cultivated by a beginner. In later life, one finds one's own style by finding one's own self.

One never learns anything from a book when he hates the author. Would that school-teachers would bear this fact in mind!

A man's character is partly born, and so is his style. The other part is just contamination.

A man without a favourite author is a lost soul. He remains an unimpregnated ovum, an unfertilized pistil. One's favourite author or literary lover is pollen for his soul.

A favourite author exists in the world for every man, only he hasn't taken the trouble to find him.

A book is like a picture of life or of a city. There are readers who look at pictures of New York or Paris, but never see New York or Paris itself. The wise man reads both books and life itself. The universe is one big book, and life is one big school.

A good reader turns an author inside out, like a beggar turning his coat inside out in search of fleas.

Some authors provoke their readers constantly and pleasantly like a beggar's coat full of fleas. An itch is a great thing.

The best way of studying any subject is to begin by reading books, taking an unfavourable point of view with regard to it. In that way one is sure of accepting no humbug. After having read an author unfavourable to the subject, he is better prepared to read more favourable authors. That is how a critical mind can be developed.

A writer always has an instinctive interest in words as such. Every word has a life and a personality, usually not recorded by a dictionary, except one like the *Concise* or *Pocket Oxford Dictionary*.

A good dictionary is always readable, like the *P.O.D.*

There are two mines of language, a new one and an old one. The old mine is in the books, and the new one is in the language of common people. Second-rate artists will dig in the old mines, but only first-rate artists can get something out of the new mine. Ores from the old mine are already smelted, but those from the new mine are not.

[398]

Wang Ch'ung (A.D. 27 – c. 100) distinguished between "specialists" and "scholars," and again between "writers" and "thinkers." I think a specialist graduates into a scholar when his knowledge broadens, and a writer graduates into a thinker when his wisdom deepens.

A "scholar's" writing consists of borrowings from other scholars, and the more authorities and sources he quotes, the more of a "scholar" he appears. A thinker's writing consists of borrowings from ideas in his own intestines, and the greater thinker a man is, the more he depends on his own intestinal juice.

A scholar is like a raven feeding its young that spits out what it has eaten from the mouth. A thinker is like a silkworm which gives us, not mulberry leaves but silk.

There is a period of gestation of ideas before writing, like the period of gestation of an embryo in its mother's womb before birth. When one's favourite author has kindled the spark in one's soul, and set up a current of live ideas in him, that is the "impregnation." When a man rushes into print before his ideas go through this period of gestation, that is diarrhœa, mistaken for birth-pains. When a writer sells his conscience and writes things against his convictions, that is artificial abortion, and the embryo is always stillborn. When a writer feels violent convulsions like an electric storm in his head, and he doesn't feel happy until he gets the ideas out of his system and puts them down on paper and feels an immense relief, that is literary birth. Hence a writer feels a maternal affection toward his literary product as a mother feels toward her baby. Hence a writing is always better when it is one's own, and a woman is always lovelier when she is somebody else's wife.

The pen grows sharper with practice like a cobbler's awl, gradually acquiring the sharpness of an embroidery needle. But one's ideas grow more and more rounded, like the views one sees when mounting from a lower to a higher peak.

When a writer hates a person and is thinking of taking up his pen to write a bitter invective against him, but has not yet seen his good side, he should lay down the pen again, because he is not yet qualified to write a bitter invective against the person.

(d) The School of Self-expression

The so-called "School of *Hsingling*" started by the three Yüan brothers[1] at the end of the sixteenth century, or the so-called "Kungan School" (Kungan being the native district of the brothers) is a school of self-expression. *Hsing* means one's "personal nature," and *ling* means one's "soul" or "vital spirit."

Writing is but the expression of one's own nature or character and the play of his vital spirit. The so-called "divine afflatus" is but the flow of this vital spirit, and is actually caused by an overflow of hormones in the blood.

In looking at an old master or reading an ancient author, we are but watching the flow of his vital spirit. Sometimes when this flow of energy runs dry or one's spirits are low, even the writing of the best calligraphist or writer lacks spirit or vitality.

This "divine afflatus" comes in the morning when one has had a good sleep with sweet dreams and wakes up by himself. Then after his cup of morning tea, he reads the papers and finds no disturbing news and slowly walks into his study and sits before a bright window and a clean desk, while outside there is a pleasant sun and a gentle breeze. At this moment, he can write good essays, good poems, good letters, paint good paintings and write good inscriptions on them.

The thing called "self" or "personality" consists of a bundle of limbs, muscles, nerves, reason, sentiments, culture, understanding, experience, and prejudices. It is partly nature and partly culture, partly born and partly cultivated. One's nature is determined at the time of his birth, or even before it. Some are naturally hard-hearted and mean; others are naturally frank and straightforward and chivalrous and big-hearted; and again others are naturally soft and weak in

---

[1] Yüan Hungtao (usually known as Yüan Chunglang), the second brother, is considered the leader of the school.

character, or given over to worries. Such things are in one's "marrow-bones" and the best teacher or wisest parent cannot change one's type of personality. Again other qualities are acquired after birth through education and experience, but in so far as one's thoughts and ideas and impressions come from the most diverse sources and different streams of influence at different periods of his life, his ideas, prejudices and points of view present a most bewildering inconsistency. One loves dogs and is afraid of cats, while another loves cats and is afraid of dogs. Hence the study of types of human personality is the most complicated of all sciences.

The School of Self-expression demands that we express in writing only our own thoughts and feelings, our genuine loves, genuine hatreds, genuine fears and genuine hobbies. These will be expressed without any attempt to hide the bad from the good, without fear of being ridiculed by the world, and without fear of contradicting the ancient sages or contemporary authorities.

Writers of the School of Self-expression like a writer's most characteristic paragraph in an essay, his most characteristic sentence in a paragraph, and his most characteristic expression in a sentence. In describing or narrating a scene, a sentiment or an event, he deals with the scene that he himself sees, the sentiment that he himself feels and the event as he himself understands it. What conforms to this rule is literature and what does not conform to it is not literature.

The girl Lin Taiyü in *Red Chamber Dream* belonged also to the School of Self-expression when she said, "When a poet has a good line, never mind whether the musical tones of words fall in with the established pattern or not."

In its love for genuine feelings, the School of Self-expression has a natural contempt for decorativeness of style. Hence it always stands for the pure and mild flavour in writing. It accepts the dictum of Mencius that "the sole goal of writing is expressiveness."

Literary beauty is only expressiveness.

The dangers of this school are that a writer's style may degenerate into plainness (Yüan Chunglang), or he may develop eccentricity of ideas (Chin Shengt'an), or his ideas may differ violently from those of established authorities (Li Chowu). That is why the School of Self-expression was so hated by the Confucian critics. But, as a matter of fact, it is these original writers who saved Chinese thought and literature from absolute uniformity and death. They are bound to come into their own in the next few decades.

Chinese orthodox literature expressly aimed at expressing the minds of the sages and not the minds of the authors and was therefore dead; the *hsingling* school of literature aims at expressing the minds of the authors and not the minds of the sages, and is therefore alive.

There is a sense of dignity and independence in writers of this school which prevents them from going out of their way to say things to shock people. If Confucius and Mencius happen to agree with them and their conscience approves, they will not go out of their way to disagree with the Sages; but if their conscience disapproves, they will not give Confucius and Mencius the right of way. They can be neither bribed with gold nor threatened with ostracism.

Genuine literature is but a sense of wonder at the universe and at human life.

He who keeps his vision sane and clear will have always this sense of wonder, and therefore has no need to distort the truth in order to make it seem wonderful. The ideas and points of view of writers of this school always seem so new and strange only because readers are so used to the distorted vision.

A writer's weaknesses are what endear him to a *hsingling* critic. All writers of the *hsingling* school are against imitation of the ancients or the moderns and against a literary technique of rules. The Yüan brothers believed in "letting one's mouth and wrist go, resulting naturally in good form," and held that "the important thing in literature is genuineness." Li Liweng believed that "the important thing in literature is charm and interest." Yüan Tsets'ai believed that "there is no technique in writing." An early Sung writer, Huang Shanku, believed that "the lines and form of writing come quite accidentally, like the holes in wood eaten by insects."

(e) The Familiar Style

A writer in the familiar style speaks in an unbuttoned mood. He completely exposes his weaknesses, and is therefore disarming.

The relationship between writer and reader should not be one between an austere schoolmaster and his pupils, but one between familiar friends. Only in this way can warmth be generated.

He who is afraid to use an "I" in his writing will never make a good writer.

I love a liar more than a speaker of truth, and an indiscreet liar more than a discreet one. His indiscretions are a sign of his love for his readers.

I trust an indiscreet fool and suspect a lawyer.

The indiscreet fool is a nation's best diplomat. He wins people's hearts.

My idea of a good magazine is a fortnightly, where we bring a group of good talkers together in a small room once in a fortnight and let them chat together. The readers listen to their chats, which last just about two hours. It is like having a good evening chat, and after that the reader goes to bed, and next morning when he gets up to attend to his duties as a bank clerk or accountant or a school principal posting notices to the students, he feels that the flavour of last night's chat still lingers around his cheeks.

There are restaurants for giving grand dinners in a hall with gold-framed mirrors, and there are small restaurants designed for a little drink. All I want is to bring together two or three intimate friends and have a little drink, and not go to the dinners of rich and important people. But the pleasure we have in a small restaurant, eating and drinking and chatting

[403]

and teasing each other and overturning cups and spilling wine on dresses is something which people at the grand dinners don't understand and cannot even "miss."

There are rich men's gardens and mansions, but there are also little lodges in the mountains. Although sometimes these mountain lodges are furnished with taste and refinement, the atmosphere is quite different from the rich men's mansions with vermilion gates and green windows and a platoon of servants and maids standing around. When one enters the door, he does not hear the barking of faithful dogs and he does not see the face of snobbish butlers and gatekeepers, and when he leaves, he doesn't see a pair of "unchaste stone lions" outside its gate. The situation is perfectly described by a writer of the seventeenth century: "It is as if Chou, Ch'eng, Chang and Chu[1] are sitting together and bowing to each other in the Hall of Fuhsi, and suddenly there come Su Tungp'o and Tungfang Su who break into the room half naked and without shoes, and they begin to clap their hands and joke with one another. The onlookers will probably stare in amazement, but these gentlemen look at each other in silent understanding."

(f) What is Beauty?

The thing called beauty in literature and beauty in things depends so much on change and movement and is based on life. What lives always has change and movement, and what has change and movement naturally has beauty. How can there be set rules for literature or writing, when we see that mountain cliffs and ravines and streams possess a beauty of waywardness and ruggedness far above that of canals, and yet they were formed without the calculations of an architect? The constellations of stars are the *wen* or literature of the skies, and the famous mountains and great rivers are the *wen* or literature of the earth. The wind blows and the clouds change and we have the pattern of a brocade; the frost comes and leaves fall and we have the colour of autumn. Now, do the stars moving

[1] Sung doctrinaires.

around their orbits in the firmament ever think of their appreciation by men on earth? And yet the Heavenly Dog and the Cowherd are perceived by us by an accident. The crust of the earth shrinks and stretches and throws up mountains and forms deep seas. Did the earth consciously create the Five Sacred Mountains for us to worship? And yet the T'aihua and the K'uenluen Mountains dash along with their magnificent rhythm and the Jade Maiden and the Fairy Boy stand around us on awe-inspiring peaks, apparently for our enjoyment. These are but free-and-easy strokes of the Creator, the great art master. Can clouds, which sail forth from the hill-tops and meet the lashing of furious mountain winds, have time to think of their petticoats and scarves for us to look at? And yet they arrange themselves, now like the scales of fish, now like the pattern of brocade, and now like racing dogs and roaring lions and dancing phœnixes and gambolling unicorns, like a literary masterpeice. Can autumn trees that are feeling the pinch of heat and cold and the devastation of frost, and that are busily occupied in slowing down their breath and conserving their energy, have time to paint and powder themselves for the traveller on the ancient highway to look at? And yet they seem so cool and pure and sad and forlorn, and far superior to the paintings of Wang Wei and Mi Fei.

And so every living thing in the universe has its literary beauty. The beauty of a dried-up vine is greater than the calligraphy of Wang Hsichih, and the austerity of an over-hanging cliff is more imposing than the stone inscriptions on Chang Menglung's tomb. Therefore we know that the *wen* or literary beauty of things arises from their nature, and those that fulfil their nature clothe themselves in *wen* or beautiful lines. Therefore *wen*, or beauty of line and form, is intrinsic and not extrinsic. The horse's hoofs are designed for a quick gallop; the tiger's claws are designed for pouncing on its prey; the stork's legs are designed for wading across swamps, and the bear's paws are designed for walking on ice. Does the horse, the tiger, the stork or the bear ever think of its beauty of form and proportions? All it tries to do is function in life and adopt a proper posture for movement. But from our point of view, we see the horse's hoofs, the tiger's claws, the stork's legs and the bear's paws have a striking beauty, either in their fullness of contour and suggestion of power, or in their slenderness and strength of line, or in their clearness of outline, or in the ruggedness of their joints. Again the elephant's paws are like the *lishu* style of writing, the lion's mane is like the *feipo*, fighting snakes write wonderful wriggling *ts'aoshu* ("grass script"), and floating dragons write *chuanshu* ("seal characters"), the cow's legs resemble *pafen* (comparatively stout and symmetrical writing), and the deer resembles *hsiaok'ai* (elegant "small script"). Their beauty comes from their posture or movement, and their bodily shapes are the result of their bodily functions, and this is also the secret of beauty in writing. When the *shih* or posture of movement requires it, it may not be repressed, and when the posture or movement does not require it, it must stop. Hence a literary masterpiece is like a stretch of nature itself, well-formed in its formlessness, and its charm and beauty come by accident. For this thing we call *shih* is the beauty of movement, and not the beauty of static proportions. Everything that lives and moves has its *shih* and therefore has its beauty, force, and *wen*, or beauty of form and line.

CHAPTER THIRTEEN

Relationship To God

I. THE RESTORATION OF RELIGION

SO many people presume to know God and what God approves and God disapproves that it is impossible to take up this subject without opening oneself to attack as sacrilegious by some and as a prophet by others. We human creatures who individually are less than a billionth part of the earth's crust, which is less than a billionth part of the great universe, presume to know God!

Yet no philosophy of life is complete, no conception of man's spiritual life is adequate, unless we bring ourselves into a satisfactory and harmonious relation with the life of the universe around us. Man is important enough; he is the most important topic of our studies: that is the essence of humanism. Yet man lives in a magnificent universe, quite as wonderful as the man himself, and he who ignores the greater world around him, its origin and its destiny, cannot be said to have a truly satisfying life.

The trouble with orthodox religion is that, in its process of historical development, it got mixed up with a number of things strictly outside religion's moral realm—physics, geology, astronomy, criminology, the conception of sex and woman. If it had confined itself to the realm of the moral conscience, the work of re-orientation would not be so enormous to-day. It is easier to destroy a pet notion of "Heaven" and "Hell" than to destroy the notion of God.

On the other hand, science opens up to the modern Christian a newer and deeper sense of the mystery of the universe and a new conception of matter as a convertible term with energy, and as for God Himself, in the words of Sir James Jeans, "The universe seems to be nearer to a great thought than to a great machine." Mathematical calculation itself proves the existence of the mathematically incalculable. Religion will have to retreat and instead of saying so many things in the realm of natural sciences as it used to do, simply acknowledge that they are none of religion's business; much less should it allow the validity of spiritual experience to depend on totally irrelevant topics, like whether the age of man is 4,000-odd years or a million, or whether the earth is flat, or round, or shaped like a collapsible tea-table, or borne aloft by Hindu elephants or Chinese turtles. Religion should, and will, confine itself to the moral realm, the realm of the moral conscience, which has a dignity of its own comparable in every sense to the study of flowers, the fishes and the stars. St. Paul performed the first surgical operation upon Judaism and, by separating cuisine (eating hoofed animals) from religion, immensely benefited it. Religion stands to gain immensely by being separated not only from cuisine but also from geology and comparative anatomy. Religion must cease to be a dabbler in astronomy and geology and a preserver of ancient folkways. Let religion respectfully keep its mouth shut when teachers of biology are talking, and it will seem infinitely less silly and gain immeasurably in the respect of mankind.

Such religion as there can be in modern life, every individual will have to salvage from the churches for himself. There is always a possibility of surrendering ourselves to the Great Spirit in an atmosphere of ritual and worship as one kneels praying without words and looking at the stained-glass windows, in spite of all that one may think of the theological dogmas. In this sense, worship becomes a true æsthetic experience, an æsthetic experience that is one's own, very similar, in fact, to the experience of viewing a sun setting behind an outline of trees on hills. For that man, religion is a final fact of consciousness, for it will be an æsthetic experience very much akin to poetry.

But what contempt he must have for the churches, as they are at present! For the God that he worships will not be one that can be beseeched for daily small presents. He will not command the wind to blow north when he sails north, and command the wind to blow south when he sails south. To thank God for a good wind is sheer impudence, and selfishness also, for it implies that God does not love the people sailing south when HE, the important individual, is sailing north. It will be a communion of spirits without one party trying to beg a favour of the other. He will not be able to comprehend the meaning of the churches as they are. He will wonder at the strange metamorphosis that religion has gone through. He will be puzzled when he tries to define religions in their present forms. Is religion a glorification of the *status quo* with mystic emotion? Or is it certain moral truths so mystified and decorated and camouflaged as to make it possible for a priestcraft to make a living? Doesn't revelation stand in the same relation to religion as "a secret patented process" stands in relation to certain advertised nostrums? Or is religion a juggling with the invisible and the unknowable because the invisible and the unknowable lend themselves so conveniently to juggling? Is faith to be based on knowledge, or does faith only begin where knowledge ends? Or is religion a baseball that Sister Aimée McPherson can hit with a baseball bat right into an audience— something that Joe can catch and "get" in the way that he catches a baseball? Or is religion the preservation of Aryan, Nordic blood, or is it merely opposition to divorce and birth control and calling every social reformer a "Red" and a "Communist"? Did Christ really have to receive Tolstoy in His arms in a blazing snowstorm after he was excommunicated from the Greek Orthodox Church? Or is Jesus going to stand outside Bishop Manning's cathedral window and beckon to the rich men's children in their pews and repeat His gentle request, "Suffer little children to come unto me"?

So we are left with the uncomfortable and yet, for me, strangely satisfying feeling that what religion is left in our lives will be a very much more simplified feeling of reverence for the beauty and grandeur and mystery of life, with its responsibilities, but will be deprived of the good old, glad certainties and accretions which theology has accumulated and laid over its surface. Religion in this form is simple and, for many modern men, sufficient. The spiritual theocracy of the Middle Ages is definitely receding and as for personal immortality, which is the second greatest reason for the appeal of religion, many men to-day are quite content to be just dead when they die.

Our preoccupation with immortality has something pathological about it. That man desires immortality is understandable, but were it not for the influence of the Christian religion, it should never have assumed such a disproportionately large share of our attention. Instead of being a fine reflection, a noble fancy, lying in the poetic realm between fiction and fact, it has become a deadly earnest matter, and in the case of monks, the thought of death, or life after it, has become the main occupation of this life. As a matter of fact, most people on the other side of fifty, whether pagans or Christians, are not afraid of death, which is the reason why they can't be scared by, and are thinking less of, Heaven and Hell. We find them very often chattering glibly about their epitaphs and tomb designs and the comparative merits of cremation. By that I do not mean only those who are sure that they are going to heaven, but also many who take the realistic view of the situation that when they die, life is extinguished like light from a candle. Many of the finest minds of to-day have expressed their disbelief in personal immortality and are quite unconcerned about it—H. G. Wells, Albert Einstein, Sir Arthur Keith and a host of others—but I do not think it requires first-class minds to conquer this fear of death.

Many people have substituted for this personal immortality, immortality of other kinds, much more convincing—the immortality of the race, and the immortality of work and influence. It is sufficient that when we die, the work we leave behind us continues to influence others and play a part, however small, in the life of the community in which we live. We can pluck the flower and throw its petals to the ground, and yet its subtle fragrance remains in the air. It is a better, more reasonable and more unselfish kind of immortality. In this very real sense, we may say that Louis Pasteur, Luther Burbank and Thomas Edison are still living among us. What if their bodies are dead, since "body" is nothing but an abstract generalization for a constantly changing combination of chemical constituents! Man begins to see his own life as a drop in an ever-flowing river and is glad to contribute his part to the great stream of life. If he were only a little less selfish, he should be quite contented with that.

II. WHY I AM A PAGAN

Religion is always an individual, personal thing. Every person must work out his own views of religion, and if he is sincere, God will not blame him, however it turns out. Every man's religious experience is valid for himself, for, as I have said, it is not something that can be argued about. But the story of an honest soul struggling with religious problems, told in a sincere manner, will always be of benefit to other people. That is why, in speaking about religion, I must get away from generalities, and tell my personal story.

I am a pagan. The statement may be taken to imply a revolt against Christianity; and yet "revolt" seems a harsh word and does not correctly describe the state of mind of a man who has passed through a very gradual evolution, step by step, away from Christianity, during which he clung desperately, with love and piety, to a series of tenets which, against his will, were slipping away from him. Because there was never any hatred, therefore, it is impossible to speak of a rebellion.

As I was born in a pastor's family and at one time prepared for the Christian ministry, my natural emotions were on the side of religion during the entire struggle rather than against it. In this conflict of emotions and understanding, I gradually arrived at a position where I had, for instance, definitely renounced the doctrine of redemption, a position which could most simply be described as that of a pagan. It was, and still is, a condition of belief concerning life and the universe in which I feel natural and at ease, without having to be at war with myself. The process came as naturally as the weaning of a child or the dropping of a ripe apple on the ground; and when the time came for the apple to drop, I would not interfere with its dropping. In Taoistic phraseology, this is but to live in the Tao, and in Western phraseology it is but being sincere with oneself and with the universe, according to one's lights. I believe no one can be natural and happy unless he is intellectually sincere with himself, and to be natural is to be in heaven. To me, being a pagan is just being natural.

"To be a pagan" is no more than a phrase, like "to be a Christian." It is no more than a negative statement, for to the average reader, to be a pagan means only that one is not a Christian; and, since "being a Christian" is a very broad and ambiguous term, the meaning of "not being a Christian" is equally ill-defined. It is all the worse when one defines a pagan as one who does not believe in religion or in God, for we have yet to define what is meant by "God" or by the "religious attitude toward life." Great pagans have always had a deeply reverent attitude toward nature. We shall therefore have to take the word in its conventional sense and mean by it simply a man who does not go to church (except for an æsthetic inspiration, of which I am still capable), does not belong to the Christian fold, and does not accept its usual, orthodox tenets.

On the positive side, a Chinese pagan, the only kind of which I can speak with any feeling of intimacy, is one who starts out with this earthly life as all we can or need to bother about, wishes to live intently and happily as long as his life lasts, often has a sense of the poignant sadness of this life and faces it cheerily, has a keen appreciation of the beautiful and the good in human life wherever he finds them, and regards doing good as its own satisfactory reward. I admit, however, he feels a slight pity or contempt for the "religious" man who does good in order to get to heaven and who, by implication, would not do good if he were not lured by heaven or threatened with hell. If this statement is correct, I believe there are a great many more pagans in this country than are themselves aware of it. The modern liberal Christian and the pagan are really close, differing only when they start out to *talk* about God.

I think I know the depths of religious experience, for I believe one can have this experience without being a great theologian like Cardinal Newman—otherwise Christianity would not be worth having or must already have been horribly misinterpreted. As I look at it at present, the difference in spiritual life between a Christian believer and a pagan is simply this: the Christian believer lives in a world governed and watched over by God, to whom he has a constant personal relationship, and therefore in a world presided over by a kindly father; his conduct is also often uplifted to a level consonant with this consciousness of being a child of God, no doubt a level which is difficult for a human mortal to maintain consistently at all periods of his life or of the week or even of the day; his actual life varies between living on the human and the truly religious levels.

On the other hand, the pagan lives in this world like an orphan, without the benefit of that consoling feeling that there is always someone in heaven who cares and who will, when that spiritual relationship called prayer is established, attend to his private personal welfare. It is no doubt a less cheery world; but there is the benefit and dignity of being an orphan who by necessity has learned to be independent, to take care of himself, and to be more mature, as all orphans are. It was this feeling rather than any intellectual belief—this feeling of dropping into a world without the love of God—that really scared me till the very last moment of my conversion to paganism; I felt, like many born Christians, that if a personal God did not exist the bottom would be knocked out of this universe.

And yet a pagan can come to the point where he looks on that perhaps warmer and cheerier world as at the same time a more childish, I am tempted to say a more adolescent, world; useful and workable, if one keep the illusion unspoiled, but no more and no less justifiable than a truly Buddhist way of life; also a more beautifully coloured world but consequently less solidly true and therefore of less worth. For me personally, the suspicion that anything is coloured or not solidly true is fatal. There is a price one must be willing to pay for truth; whatever the consequences, let us have it. This position is comparable to and psychologically the same as that of a murderer: if one has committed a murder, the best thing he can do next is to confess it. That is why I say it takes a little courage to become a pagan. But, after one has accepted the worst, one is also without fear. Peace of mind is that mental condition in which you have accepted the worst. (Here I see for myself the influence of Buddhist or Taoist thought.)

Or I might put the difference between a Christian and a pagan world like this: the pagan in me renounced Christianity out of both pride and humility, emotional pride and intellectual humility, but perhaps on the whole less out of pride than of humility. Out of emotional pride because I hated the idea that there should be any other reason for our behaving as nice, decent men and women than the simple fact that we are human beings; theoretically and if you want to go in for classifications, classify this as a typically humanist thought. But more out of humility, of intellectual humility, simply because I can no longer, with our astronomical knowledge, believe that an individual human being is so terribly important in the eyes of that Great Creator, living as the individual does, an infinitesimal speck on this earth, which is an infinitesimal speck of the solar system, which is again an infinitesimal speck of the universe of solar systems. The audacity of man and his presumptuous arrogance are what stagger me. What right have we to conceive of the character of a Supreme Being, of whose work we can see only a millionth part, and to postulate about His attributes?

The importance of the human individual is undoubtedly one of the basic tenets of Christianity. But let us see what ridiculous arrogance that leads to in the usual practice of Christian daily life.

Four days before my mother's funeral there was a pouring rain, and if it continued, as was usual in July in Changchow, the city would be flooded, and there could be no funeral. As most of us came from Shanghai, the delay would have meant some inconvenience. One of my relatives—a rather extreme but not an unusual example of a Christian believer in China—told me that she had faith in God, Who would always provide for His children. She prayed, and the rain stopped, apparently in order that a tiny family of Christians might have their funeral without delay. But the implied idea that, but for us, God would willingly subject the tens of thousands of Changchow inhabitants to a devastating flood, as was often the case, or that He did not stop the rain because of them but because of us who wanted to have a conveniently dry funeral, struck me as an unbelievable type of selfishness. I cannot imagine God providing for such selfish children.

There was also a Christian pastor who wrote the story of his life, attesting to many evidences of the hand of God in his life, for the purpose of glorifying God. One of the evidences adduced was that, when he had got together 600 silver dollars to buy his passage to America, God lowered the rate of exchange on the day this so very important individual was to buy his passage. The difference in the rate of exchange for 600 silver dollars could have been at most ten or twenty dollars, and God was willing to rock the bourses in Paris, London, and New York in order that this curious child of His might save ten or twenty dollars. Let us remind ourselves that this way of glorifying God is not at all unusual in any part of Christendom.

Oh, the impudence and conceit of man, whose span of life is but three-score and ten! Mankind as an aggregate may have a significant history, but man as an individual, in the words of Su Tungp'o, is no more than a grain of millet in an ocean or an insect *fuyu* born in the morning and dying at eve, as compared with the universe. The Christian will not be humble. He will not be satisfied with the aggregate immortality of his great stream of life, of which he is already a part, flowing on to eternity, like a mighty stream which empties into the great sea and changes and yet does not change. The clay vessel will ask of the potter, "Why hast thou cast me into this shape and why hast thou made me so brittle?" The clay vessel is not satisfied that it can leave little vessels of its own kind when it cracks up. Man is not satisfied that he has received this marvellous body, this almost divine body. He wants to live for ever! And he will not let God alone. He must say his prayers and he must pray daily for small personal gifts from the Source of All Things. Why can't he let God alone?

There was once a Chinese scholar who did not believe in Buddhism, and his mother who did. She was devout and would acquire merit for herself by mumbling, "*Namu omitabha!*" a thousand times day and night. But every time she started to call Buddha's name, her son would call, "Mamma!" The mother became annoyed. "Well," said the son, "don't you think Buddha would be equally annoyed, if he could hear you?"[1]

My father and mother were devout Christians. To hear my father conduct the evening family prayers was enough. And I was a sensitively religious child. As a pastor's son I received the facilities of missionary education, profited from its benefits, and suffered from its weaknesses. For its benefits I was always grateful and its weaknesses I turned into my strength. For according to Chinese philosophy there are no such things in life as good and bad luck.

I was forbidden to attend Chinese theatres, never allowed to listen to Chinese minstrel singers, and entirely cut apart from the great Chinese folk tradition and mythology. When I entered a missionary college, the little foundation in classical Chinese given me by my father was completely neglected. Perhaps it was just as well—so that later, after a completely Westernized education, I could go back to it with the freshness and vigorous delight of a child of the West in an Eastern wonderland. The complete substitution of the fountain pen for the writing brush during my college and adolescent period was the greatest luck I ever had and preserved for me the freshness of the Oriental mental world unspoiled, until I should become ready for it. If Vesuvius had

---

[1] In the prayer for sickness, it is evidently unreasonable to pray a dozen or a hundred times, as unreasonable as for a child to beg a dozen or a hundred times to be taken to a movie theatre. To ask once is enough, and a promise is a promise, if the father is a good father. The repetitious requests are a botheration.

not covered up Pompeii, Pompeii would not be so well preserved, and the imprints of carriage-wheels on her stone pavements would not be so clearly marked to-day. The missionary college education was my Vesuvius.

Thinking was always dangerous. More than that, thinking was always allied with the devil. The conflict during the collegiate--adolescent period, which, as usual, was my most religious period, between a heart which felt the beauty of the Christian life and a head which had a tendency to reason everything away, was taking place. Curiously enough, I can remember no moments of torment or despair, of the kind that drove Tolstoy almost to suicide. At every stage I felt myself a unified Christian, harmonious in my belief, only a little more liberal than the last, and accepting some fewer Christian doctrines. Anyway, I could always go back to the Sermon on the Mount. The poetry of a saying like "Consider the lilies of the field" was too good to be untrue. It was that and the consciousness of the inner Christian life that gave me strength.

But the doctrines were slipping away terribly. Superficial things first began to annoy me. The "resurrection of the flesh," long disproved when the expected second coming of Christ in the first century did not come off and the Apostles did not rise bodily from their graves, was still there in the Apostles' Creed. This was one of those things.

Then, enrolling in a theological class and initiated into the holy of holies, I learned that another article in the creed, the virgin birth, was open to question, different deans in American theological seminaries holding different views. It enraged me that Chinese believers should be required to believe categorically in this article before they could be baptized, while the theologians of the same church regarded it as an open question. It did not seem sincere and somehow it did not seem right.

Further schooling in meaningless commentary scholarship as to the whereabouts of the "water gate" and such minutiæ completely relieved me of responsibility to take such theological studies seriously, and I made a poor showing in my grades. My professors considered that I was not cut out for the Christian ministry, and the bishop thought I might as well leave. They would not waste their instruction on me. Again this seems to me now a blessing in disguise. I doubt, if I had gone on with it and put on the clerical garb, whether it would have been so easy for me to be honest with myself later on. But this feeling of rebellion against the discrepancy of the beliefs required of the theologian and of the average convert was the nearest kind of feeling to what I may call a "revolt."

By this time I had already arrived at the position that the Christian theologians were the greatest enemies of the Christian religion. I could never get over two great contradictions. The first was that the theologians had made the entire structure of the Christian belief hang upon the existence of an apple. If Adam had not eaten an apple, there would be no original sin, and if there were no original sin, there would be no need of redemption. That was plain to me, whatever the symbolic value of the apple might be. This seemed to me preposterously unfair to the teachings of Christ, who never said a word about the original sin or the redemption. Anyway, from pursuing literary studies, I feel, like all modern Americans, no consciousness of sin and simply do not believe in it. All I know is that if God loves me only half as much as my mother does, He will not send me to Hell. That is a final fact of my inner consciousness, and for no religion could I deny its truth.

Still more preposterous another proposition seemed to me. This was the argument that, when Adam and Eve ate an apple during their honeymoon, God was so angry that He condemned their posterity to suffer from generation to generation for that little offence but that, when the same posterity murdered the same God's only Son, God was so delighted that He forgave them all. No matter how people explain and argue, I cannot get over this simple untruth. This was the last of the things that troubled me.

Still, even after my graduation, I was a zealous Christian and voluntarily conducted a Sunday school at Tsing Hua, a non-Christian college at Peking, to the dismay of many faculty members. The Christmas meeting of the Sunday school was a torture to me, for here I was passing on to the Chinese children the tale of herald angels singing upon a midnight clear when I did not believe it myself. Everything had been reasoned away, and only love and fear remained: a kind of clinging love for an all-wise God which made me feel happy and peaceful and suspect that I should not have been so happy and peaceful without that reassuring love—and fear of entering into a world of orphans.

Finally my salvation came. "Why," I reasoned with a colleague, "if there were no God, people would not do good and the world would go topsy-turvy."

"Why?" replied my Confucian colleague. "We should lead a decent human life simply because we are decent human beings," he said.

This appeal to the dignity of human life cut off my last tie to Christianity, and from then on I was a pagan.

It is all so clear to me now. The world of pagan belief is a simpler belief. It postulates nothing, and is obliged to postulate nothing. It seems to make the good life more immediately appealing by appealing to the good life alone. It better justifies doing good by making it unnecessary for doing good to justify itself. It does not encourage men to do, for instance, a simple act of charity by dragging in a series of hypothetical postulates— sin, redemption, the cross, laying up treasure in heaven, mutual obligation among men on account of a third-party relationship in heaven—all so unnecessarily complicated and roundabout, and none capable of direct proof. If one accepts the statement that doing good is its own justification, one cannot help regarding all theological baits to right living as redundant and tending to cloud the lustre of a moral truth. Love among men should be a final, absolute fact. We should be able just to look at each other and love each other without being reminded of a third party in heaven. Christianity seems to me to make morality appear unnecessarily difficult and complicated and sin appear tempting, natural, and desirable. Paganism, on the other hand, seems alone to be able to rescue religion from theology and restore it to its beautiful simplicity of belief and dignity of feeling.

In fact, I seem to be able to see how many theological complications arose in the first, second, and third centuries and turned the simple truths of the Sermon on the Mount into a rigid, self-contained structure to support a priestcraft as an endowed institution. The reason was contained in the word *revelation*—the revelation of a special mystery or divine scheme given to a prophet and kept by an apostolic succession, which was found necessary in all religions, from Mohammedanism and Mormonism to the Living Buddha's Lamaism and Mrs. Eddy's Christian Science, in order for each of them to handle exclusively a special, patented monopoly of salvation. All priestcraft lives on the common staple food of revelation. The simple truths of Christ's teaching on the Mount must be adorned, and the lily He so marvelled at must be gilded. Hence we have the "first Adam" and the "second Adam," and so on and so forth.

But Pauline logic, which seemed so convincing and unanswerable in the early days of the Christian era, seems weak and unconvincing to the more subtle modern critical consciousness; and in this discrepancy between the rigorous Asiatic deductive logic and the more pliable, more subtle appreciation of truth of the modern man, lies the weakness of the appeal to the Christian revelation or any revelation for the modern man. Therefore only by a return to paganism and renouncing the revelation can one return to primitive (and for me more satisfying) Christianity.

It is wrong, therefore, to speak of a pagan as an irreligious man: irreligious he is only as one who refuses to believe in any special variety of revelation. A pagan always believes in God but would not like to say so, for fear of being misunderstood. All Chinese pagans believe in God, the most commonly met with designation in Chinese literature being the term *chaowu*, or the Creator of Things. The only difference is that the Chinese pagan is honest enough to leave the Creator of Things in a halo of mystery, toward whom he feels a kind of awed piety and reverence. What is more, that feeling suffices for him. Of the beauty of this universe, the clever artistry of the myriad things of this creation, the mystery of the stars, the grandeur of heaven, and the dignity of the human soul he is equally aware. But that again suffices for him. He accepts death as he accepts pain and suffering and weighs them against the gift of life and the fresh country breeze and the clear mountain moon and he does not complain. He regards bending to the will of Heaven as the truly religious and pious attitude and calls it "living in the Tao." If the Creator of Things wants him to die at seventy, he gladly dies at seventy. He also believes that "heaven's way always goes round" and that there is no permanent injustice in this world. He does not ask for more.

CHAPTER FOURTEEN

The Art Of Thinking

I. THE NEED OF HUMANIZED THINKING

THINKING is an art, and not a science. One of the greatest contrasts between Chinese and Western scholarship is the fact that in the West there is so much specialized knowledge, and so little humanized knowledge, while in China there is so much more concern with the problems of living, while there are no specialized sciences. We see an invasion of scientific thinking into the proper realm of humanized knowledge in the West, characterized by high specialization and its profuse use of scientific or semi-scientific terminology. I am speaking of "scientific" thinking in itseveryday sense, and not of true scientific thinking, which cannot be divorced from common sense on the one hand, and imagination on the other. In its everyday sense, this "scientific" thinking is strictly logical, objective, highly specialized and "atomic" in its method and vision. The contrast in the two types of scholarship, Oriental and Occidental, ultimately goes back to the opposition between logic and common sense. Logic, deprived of common sense, becomes inhuman, and common sense, deprived of logic, is incapable of penetrating into nature's mysteries.

What does one find as he goes through the field of Chinese literature and philosophy? One finds there are no sciences, no extreme theories, no dogmas, and really no great divergent schools of philosophy. Common sense and the reasonable spirit have crushed out all theories and all dogmas. Like the poet Po Chuyi, the Chinese scholar "utilized Confucianism to order his conduct, utilized Buddhism to cleanse his mind, and then

[422]

utilized history, paintings, mountains, rivers, wine, music and song to soothe his spirit."[1] He lived in the world and yet was out of it.

China, therefore, becomes a land where no one is trying very hard to think and everyone is trying very hard to live. It becomes a land where philosophy itself is a pretty simple and common-sense affair that can be as conveniently put in two lines of verse as in a heavy volume. It becomes a land where there is no system of philosophy, broadly speaking, no logic, no metaphysics, no academic jargon; where there is much less academic dogmatism, less intellectual or practical fanaticism, and fewer abstract terms and long words. No sort of mechanistic rationalism is ever possible and there is a strong hatred of the idea of logical necessity. It becomes also a land where there are no lawyers in business life, as there are no logicians in philosophy. In place of well-thought-out systems of philosophy, they have only an intimate feeling of life, and instead of a Kant or a Hegel, they have only essayists, epigram-writers and propounders of Buddhist conundrums and Taoist parables.

The literature of China as a whole presents us with a desert of short poems and short essays, seemingly interminable for one who does not appreciate them, and yet as full of variety and inexhaustible beauty as a wild landscape itself. We have only essayists and letter-writers who try to put their feeling of life in a short note or an essay of three or five hundred words, usually much shorter than the school composition of an American schoolboy. In these casual writings, letters, diaries, literary notes and regular essays, one finds here a brief comment on the vicissitudes of fortune, there a record of some woman who committed suicide in a neighbouring village, or of an enjoyable spring party, or a feast in snow, or boating on a moonlight night, or an evening spent in a temple with a thunderstorm raging outside, generally including the remarks made during the conversation that made the occasion memorable. We find a host of essayists who are at the same time poets, and poets who are at the same

[1] From Po Chüyi's composition for his own tomb inscription.

time essayists, writing never more than five or seven hundred words, in which a whole philosophy of life is really expressed by a single line. We find writers of parables and epigrams and family letters who make no attempt to co-ordinate their thoughts into a rigid system. This has prevented the rise of schools and systems. The intellect is always held in abeyance by the spirit of reasonableness, and still more by the writer's artistic sensibility. Actually the intellect is distrusted.

It is hardly necessary to point out that the logical faculty is a very powerful weapon of the human mind, making the conquests of science possible. I am also aware that human progress in the West is still essentially controlled by common sense and by the critical spirit, which is greater than the logical spirit and which I think represents the highest form of thinking in the West. It is unnecessary for me to admit that there is a very much better developed critical spirit in the West than in China. In pointing out the weaknesses of logical thinking, I am only referring to a particular deficiency in Western thought, and sometimes in Western politics also, *e.g.*, the *Machtpolitik* of the Germans and the Japanese. Logic has its charm also, and I regard the development of the detective story as a most interesting product of the logical mind, a form of literature which failed entirely to develop in China. But sheer preoccupation with logical thinking has also its drawbacks.

The outstanding characteristic of Western scholarship is its specialization and cutting up of knowledge into different departments. The over-development of logical thinking and specialization, with its technical phraseology, has brought about the curious fact of modern civilization, that philosophy has been so far relegated to the background, far behind politics and economics, that the average man can pass it by without a twinge of conscience. The feeling of the average man, even of the educated person, is that philosophy is a "subject" which he can best afford to go without. This is certainly a strange anomaly of modern culture, for philosophy, which should lie closest to men's bosom and business, has become most remote from life. It was not so in the classical civilization of the Greeks and Romans, and it was not so in China, where the study of the wisdom of life formed the scholars' chief occupation. Either the modern man is not interested in the problems of living, which are the proper subject of philosophy, or we have gone a long way from the original conception of philosophy. The scope of our knowledge has been so widened, and we have so many "departments" of knowledge zealously guarded over by their respective specialists, that philosophy, instead of being the first of man's studies, has left for it only the field no one is willing to specialize in. Typical of the state of modern education is the announcement of an American university that "the Department of Psychology has kindly thrown open the doors of Psychology 4 to the students of Economics 3." The professor of Economics 3 therefore commits the care of his students to the professor of Psychology 4 with his love and blessings, while as an exchange of courtesy, he allows the students of Psychology 4 to tread in the sacred precincts of Economics 3 with a gesture of friendly hospitality. Meanwhile, Philosophy, the King of Knowledge, is like the Chinese Emperor in the times of the Warring Kingdoms, who instead of drawing tribute from the vassal states, found his authority and domain daily diminishing, and retained the allegiance of only a small population of very fine and loyal but poorly fed subjects.

For we have now come to a stage of human culture in which we have compartments of knowledge but not knowledge itself; specialization but no integration; specialists but no philosophers of human wisdom. This over-specialization of knowledge is not very different from the over-specialization in a Chinese Imperial kitchen. Once during the collapse of a dynasty, a rich Chinese official was able to secure as his cook a maid who had escaped from the palace kitchen. Proud of her, he issued invitations for his friends to come and taste a dinner prepared by one he thought an Imperial cook. As the day was approaching, he asked the maid to prepare a royal dinner. The maid replied that she couldn't prepare a dinner.

"What did you do, then?" asked the official.

"Oh, I helped make the patties for the dinner," she replied.

"Well, then, go ahead and make some nice patties for my guests."

To his consternation the maid announced: Oh, no, I can't make patties. I specialized in chopping up the onions for the stuffing of the patties of the Imperial dinner."

Some such condition obtains to-day in the field of human knowledge and academic scholarship. We have a biologist who knows a bit of life and human nature; a psychiatrist who knows another bit of it; a geologist who knows mankind's early history; an anthropologist who knows the mind of the savage man; an historian who, if he happens to be a genial mind, can teach us something of human wisdom and human folly as reflected in mankind's past history; a psychologist who often can help us to understand our behaviour, but who as often as not tells us a piece of academic imbecility, such as that Lewis Carroll was a sadist, or emerges from his laboratory experiments on chickens and announces that the effect of a loud noise on chickens is that it makes their hearts jump. Some educational psychologists always seem to me stupefying when they are wrong, and still more stupefying when they are right. But along with the process of specialization, there has not been the urgently needed process of integration, the effort to integrate all these aspects of knowledge and make them serve the supreme end, which is the wisdom of life. Perhaps we are ready for some integration of knowledge to-day, as is evidenced by the Institute of Human Relations at Yale University and in the addresses at the Harvard Tercentenary. Unless, however, the Western scientists proceed about this task by a simpler and less logical way of thinking, that integration cannot be achieved. Human wisdom cannot be merely the *adding up* of specialized knowledge or obtained by a study of statistical averages; it can be achieved only by insight, by the general prevalence of more common sense, more wit and more plain, but subtle, intuition.

There is clearly a distinction between logical thinking and reasonable thinking, which may be also expressed as the difference between academic thinking and poetic thinking. Of academic thinking we have a great deal, but of poetic thinking we find very little evidence in the modern world. Aristotle and Plato are strikingly modern, and that is so, perhaps not because the Greeks resembled the moderns, but because they were strictly the ancestors of modern thought. In spite of his humanistic point of view and his Doctrine of the Golden Mean, Aristotle was strictly the grandfather of the modern textbook-writers, being the first man to cut up knowledge into separate compartments—from physics and botany to ethics and politics. As was quite inevitable, he was the first man also to start the impertinent academic jargon incomprehensible to the common man, which is being outdone by the American sociologists and psychologists of to-day. And while Plato had real human insight, yet in a sense he was responsible for the worship of ideas and abstractions as such among the Neo-Platonists, a tradition which, instead of being tempered with more insight, is so familiar among us to-day in writers who talk about ideas and ideologies as if they had an independent existence. Only modern psychology in very recent days is depriving us of the watertight compartments of "reason," "will" and "emotion" and helping to kill the "soul" which was such a real entity with the medieval theologians. We have killed the "soul," but we have created for ourselves a thousand-odd social and political slogans ("revolutionary," "counter-revolutionary," "bourgeois," "capitalist-imperialist," "escapist") which tyrannize over our thoughts, and have created similar beings like the "class," the "destiny" and the "state," and we proceed logically to transform the state into a monster to swallow up the individual.

It seems that a regenerated form of thinking, a more poetic thinking, which can see life steadily and see it whole, is eminently desirable. As the late James Harvey Robinson warns us: "Some careful observers express the quite honest conviction that unless thought be raised to a far higher plane than hitherto, some great set-back to civilization is inevitable." Professor Robinson wisely pointed out that, "Conscientiousness and Insight seem suspicious of one another, and yet they might be friends." Modern economists and psychologists seem to me to have an overdose of conscientiousness and not enough of insight. This is a point which perhaps cannot be over-emphasized, the danger of applying logic to human affairs. But the force and prestige of scientific thinking have been so great in the modern age that, in spite of all warnings, this species of academic thinking constantly encroaches upon the realm of philosophy, with the jejune belief that the human mind can be studied like a sewerage system and the waves of human thought measured like the waves of radio. The consequences are mildly disturbing in our everyday thinking, but disastrous in practical politics.

II. THE RETURN TO COMMON SENSE

The Chinese hate the phrase "logical necessity" because there is no logical necessity in human affairs. The Chinese distrust of logic begins with the distrust of words, proceeds with the abhorrence of definitions and ends with instinctive hatred for all systems and theories. For only words, definitions and systems have made schools of philosophy possible. The degeneration of philosophy began with the preoccupation with words. A Chinese writer, Kung Tingan, said: "The Sage does not talk, the Talented Ones talk, and the stupid ones argue"—this in spite of the fact that Kung himself loved very much to argue!

For this is the sad story of philosophy: that philosophers belonged to the genus of the Talkers and not the Silent Ones. All philosophers love to hear their own voice. Even Laotse himself, who first taught us that the Creator (the Great Silent One) does not talk, nevertheless was persuaded to leave five thousand words to posterity before he retired outside the Hankukuan Pass to pass the remainder of his life in wise solitude and oblivion. More typical of the philosopher-talker genius was Confucius, who visited "seventy-two kingdoms" in order to get a hearing from their kings, or, better still, Socrates, who went about the streets of Athens and stopped passers-by to ask them questions for the purpose of hearing himself give wise answers. The statement that the "Sage does not talk" is therefore only a relative one. But still, the difference exists between the Sage and the Talented Ones, because the Sage talks about life, as he is directly aware of it; the Talented Ones talk about the Sage's words and the stupid ones argue about the words of the Talented Ones. In the Greek Sophists we have the pure type of Talkers who are interested in the play and interplay of words as such. Philosophy, which was the love of wisdom, became the love of words, and in proportion as this Sophist trend grew, the divorce between philosophy and life became more and more complete. As time went on, the philosophers began to use more and more words and longer and longer sentences; epigrams of life gave place to sentences, sentences to arguments, arguments to treatises, treatises to commentaries, and commentaries to philological research; more and more words were needed to define and classify the words they used and more and more schools were needed to differ and secede from the schools already established; the process continued until the immediate, intimate feeling or the awareness of living has been entirely lost sight of, and the layman has the perfect right to ask, "What are you talking about?" Meanwhile, throughout the subsequent history of thought, the few independent thinkers who have felt the direct impact of life itself—a Goethe, a Samuel Johnson, an Emerson, a William James—have refused to speak in the jargon of the Talkers and always been intractably opposed to the spirit of classification. For they are the wise ones, who have kept for us the true meaning of philosophy, which is the wisdom of life. In most cases, they have forsaken arguments and reverted to the epigram. When man has lost the ability to speak in epigrams, he writes paragraphs; when he is unable to express himself clearly in paragraphs, he develops an argument; and when he still fails to make his meaning clear in an argument, he writes a treatise.

Man's love for words is his first step toward ignorance, and his love for definitions the second. The more he analyses, the more he has need to define, and the more he defines, the more he aims at an impossible logical perfection, for the effort of aiming at logical perfection is only a sign of ignorance. Since words are the material of our thought, the effort at definition is entirely laudable, and Socrates started the mania for definitions in Europe. The danger is that, after being conscious of the words we define, we are further forced to define the defining words, so that in the end, besides the words which define or express life itself, we have a class of words which define other words, which then become the main preoccupation of our philosophers. There is evidently a distinction between busy words and idle words, words that do duty in our workaday life and words that exist only in the philosophers' seminars, and also a distinction between the definitions of Socrates and Francis Bacon, and the definitions of our modern professors. Shakespeare, who had the most intimate feeling of life, certainly got along without trying to define anything, or rather because he did not try to define anything, and for that reason, his words had a "body" which the other writers lacked, and his language was infused with that sense of human tragedy and grandeur that is often missing to-day. We can no more hold his words down to any one particular function than we can hold him down to any particular conception of woman. For it is in the nature of definitions that they tend to stifle our thought and deprive it of that glowing, imaginative colour-characteristic of life itself.

But if words, by necessity, cut up our thoughts in the process of expression, the love of system is even more fatal to a keen awareness of life. A system is but a squint at truth, and the more logically that system is developed, the more horrible that mental squint becomes. The human desire to see only one phase of truth which we happen to perceive, and to develop and elevate it into a perfect logical system, is one reason why our philosophy is bound to grow stranger to life. He who talks about truth injures it thereby; he who tries to prove it thereby maims and distorts it; he who gives it a label and a school of thought kills it; and he who declares himself a believer buries it. Therefore any truth which has been erected into a system is thrice dead and buried.

The dirge that they all sing at truth's funeral is, "I am entirely right and you are entirely wrong." It is entirely immaterial what truth they bury, but it is essential that they do the burying. For so truth suffers at the hands of its defenders, and all factions and all schools of philosophy, ancient and modern, are occupied only in proving one point, that "I am entirely right and you are entirely wrong." The Germans, with their *Gründlichkeit,* writing a heavy volume to prove a limited truth until they have turned it into an absurdity,[1] are perhaps the worst offenders, but the same disease of thinking may be seen or noted more or less in most Western thinkers, becoming worse and worse as more and more abstract they become.

As a result of this dehumanized logic we have dehumanized truth. We have to-day a philosophy that has become stranger to life itself, that has almost half disclaimed any intention to teach us the meaning of life and the wisdom of living, a philosophy that has lost that intimate feeling of life or awareness of living which we spoke of as the very essence of philosophy. It is that *intimate feeling of life* which William James has called "the stuff of experience." As time goes on, I feel that the philosophy and logic of William James will become more and more devastating to the modern Western way of thinking. Before we can humanize Western philosophy, we must first humanize Western logic. We have to get back to a way of thinking which is more impatient to be in touch with reality, with life, and above all with human nature, than to be merely correct, logical and consistent. For the disease of thinking typified by Descartes' famous discovery: "*I think, therefore I exist,*" we have to substitute the more human and more sensible statement of Walt Whitman's: "*I am sufficient as I am.*" Life or existence does not have to go down on its knees and beg logic to prove that it exists or that it is there.

William James spent his life trying to prove and defend the Chinese way of thinking, without knowing it. Only there is this difference, that if William James had been a Chinese, he

---

[1] A German writer devoted a whole thesis to proving that genius is due to eye strain. Spengler's show of erudition is splendid, but his reasoning childish and naïve.

would not have written so many words to argue it out, but would have merely stated in an essay of three or five hundred words, or in one of his leisurely diary notes, that he believed it because it is so. He would be shy of the words themselves, for fear that the more words he used, the greater the chances for misunderstanding. But William James was a Chinese in his keen awareness of life and the varieties of human experience, in his rebellion against mechanistic rationalism, his anxiety to keep thought constantly fluid, and his impatience with people who think they have discovered the one all-important, "absolute" and universal truth and have enclosed it in a self-sufficient system. He was Chinese, too, in his insistence on the importance of the artist's sense of perceptual reality over and against conceptual reality. The philosopher is a man who holds his sensibilities at the highest point of focus and watches the flux of life, ready to be for ever surprised by newer and stranger paradoxes, inconsistencies, and inexplicable exceptions to the rule. In his refusal to accept a system, not because it is incorrect but because it is a system, he plays havoc with all the Western schools of philosophy. Truly, as he says, the difference between the monistic conception and the pluralistic conception of the universe is a most pregnant distinction in the history of philosophy. He has made it possible for philosophy to forget its beautiful air-castles and return to life itself.

Confucius said, "Truth may not depart from human nature; if what is regarded as truth departs from human nature, it may not be regarded as truth." Again he says, in a witty line that might have dropped from James's lips, "It is not truth that can make men great, but men that can make truth great." No, the world is not a syllogism or an argument, it is a being; the universe does not talk, it lives; it does not argue, it merely gets there. In the words of a gifted English writer: "Reason is but an item in the mystery; and behind the proudest consciousness that ever reigned, reason and wonder blushed face to face. The inevitable stales, while doubt and hope are sisters. Not unfortunately, the universe is wild, game-flavoured as a hawk's wing. Nature is miracle all: the same returns not save to be different."

It seems what the Western logicians need is just a little humility; their salvation lies in someone curing them of their Hegelian swelled-heads.

III. BE REASONABLE

In contrast to logic, there is common sense, or still better, the Spirit of Reasonableness. I think of the Spirit of Reasonableness as the highest and sanest ideal of human culture, and the reasonable man as the highest type of cultivated human being. No one can be perfect; he can only aim at being a likeable, reasonable being. In fact, I look forward to the time when the people of the world will be informed with this reasonable spirit, both in their personal and their national affairs. Reasonable nations live in peace and reasonable husbands and wives live in happiness. In the selection of husbands for my daughters, I shall have only one standard: is he a reasonable person? We cannot imagine perfect husbands and wives who never quarrel; we can only conceive of reasonable husbands and wives who quarrel reasonably and then patch up reasonably. Only in a world of reasonable beings can we have peace and happiness. The Reasonable Age, if that should ever come about, will be the Age of Peace. It will be the age in which the Spirit of Reasonableness prevails.

The Spirit of Reasonableness is the best thing that China has to offer to the West. I do not mean that Chinese war-lords are reasonable when they tax the people fifty years ahead; I mean only that the Spirit of Reasonableness is the essence and best side of Chinese civilization. I had this discovery of mine accidentally confirmed by two Americans who had lived a long time in China. One, who had lived in China for thirty years, said that the foundation of all Chinese social life is based on the word *chiangli,* or "talk reason." In a Chinese quarrel, the final clinching argument is, "Now, is this reasonable?" and the worst and commonest condemnation is that a man "*pu chiangli*" or "does not talk reason. The man who admits being "unreasonable" is already defeated in the dispute.

I have said in *My Country and My People* that: "For a Westerner, it is usually sufficient for a proposition to be logically sound. For a Chinese it is not sufficient that a proposition be logically correct, but it must be at the same time in accord with human nature. In fact, to be 'in accord with human nature,' to be *chinch'ing* (*i.e.*, to be human), is a greater consideration than to be logical." "The Chinese word for 'reasonableness' is *ch'ingli*, which is composed of two elements, *ch'ing* (*jench'ing*)[1] or human nature, and *li* (*t'ienli*) or eternal reason. *Ch'ing* represents the flexible, human element, while *li* represents the immutable law of the universe." A cultured man is one who understands thoroughly the human heart and the laws of things. By living in harmony with the natural ways of the human heart and of nature, the Confucianist claims that he can become a sage. But then the sage is no more than a reasonable person, like Confucius, who is chiefly admired for his plain common sense and his natural human qualities, *i.e.*, for his great *humanness*.

Humanized thinking is just reasonable thinking. The logical man is always self-righteous and therefore inhuman and therefore wrong, while the reasonable man suspects that perhaps he is wrong and is therefore always right. The contrast between the reasonable man and the logical man is often shown in the postscripts to letters. I always love the postscripts in my friends' letters, especially those that entirely contradict what has been said in the body of the letter. They contain all the reasonable afterthoughts, the hesitancies, and the flashes of wit and common sense. The genial thinker is one who, after proceeding doggedly to *prove* a proposition by long-winded arguments, suddenly arrives at intuition, and by a flash of common sense annihilates his preceding arguments and admits he is wrong. That is what I call humanized thinking.

We can imagine a letter in which the logical man speaks in

[1] *Jench'ing* is really an untranslatable word. Anything which helps to cement social affection or lubricate social friction is called *jench'ing*. Sending flowers and birthday gifts is "to make *jench'ing*" and giving a friend's nephew a job, or saving him from the usual punishment for an offence, is to "present *jench'ing*" to the offender's uncle. Anything which is normal in human passion, *e.g.*, the desire for revenge, is defended by saying that it is *jench'ing* or "merely human."

the body of the letter and the reasonable man, the truly human spirit, speaks in the postscript. A father may be writing to his daughter, who has been begging him for a chance to go to college, and in the letter he proceeds to outline the various perfectly sound reasons, "firstly," "secondly," "thirdly," why he cannot send her to college with a kind of consistent, cumulative, unanswerable logic, those reasons being that he has already three sons to support at college, that her sick mother needs someone to keep her company at home, and so on. After signing his name he adds a little line: "Hang it, Julie, prepare to go to college in the autumn. Somehow I will do it."

Or let us imagine a husband writing to his wife, announcing his decision to arrange for a divorce and giving an unimpeachable array of reasons for it: firstly, that his wife has been unfaithful, secondly, that he can never get a hot meal when he comes home, and so on. They are perfectly valid reasons, even righteous reasons, and if he engages a lawyer to do the job, the logic will be still more perfect and the tone more righteous still. But after writing the letter, something happens in his mind, and he scrawls a barely legible note: "Damn it, darling Sophie, I'm a rotten dog myself. I'm coming home with a bunch of flowers."

While the arguments in both letters are perfectly sound and valid, it is the logical man who speaks there, while in the postscripts there speaks a truly human spirit—a human father and a human husband. For such is the duty of the human mind that it is not called upon to make a stupidly logical argument, but should try to maintain a sane balance in an ever-changing sea of conflicting impulses, feelings, and desires. And such is truth in human affairs that that is true which we will to make so. The unanswerable argument can always be answered with some compassion, and validity itself invalidated by love. In human affairs it is often the illogical course of conduct that is the most convincing. Law itself admits the incompleteness of its claim to absolute justice when it often has to fall back on "a reasonable interpretation" of a clause, or when it allows the chief executive the power of pardon, so well exercised by Abraham Lincoln to a mother's son.

The reasonable spirit humanizes all our thinking, and makes us less sure of our own correctness. Its tendency is to round out our ideas and tone down the angularities of our conduct. The opposite of the reasonable spirit is fanaticism and dogmatism of all sorts in thought and behaviour, in our individual life, national life, marriage, religion and politics. I claim that we have less intellectual fanaticism and dogmatism in China. While a Chinese mob is quite excitable (witness the Boxers of 1900), the Spirit of Reasonableness has humanized to a large extent our monarchical autocracy, our religion, and the so-called "suppression of women." All this must be taken with certain qualifications, but is nevertheless true. It makes our emperors, our gods, and our husbands merely human beings. The Chinese emperor was not a semi-divine being like the Japanese ruler, and Chinese historians have evolved the theory that the emperor rules by a mandate from Heaven, and when he misrules, he forfeits that "heavenly mandate." When he misrules, we just chop off his head, and we have chopped off the heads of too many kings and emperors in the many rising and falling dynasties for us to believe they are "divine" or "semi-divine." Our sages are not canonized as gods but always regarded merely as teachers of wisdom, and our gods are not models of perfection but venal and corrupt and open to cajolement and bribery like our officials. Anything which goes beyond reasonableness is immediately condemned as *puchi'n jench'ing* ("moving far away from human nature"), and a man who is too saintly or too perfect can be a traitor[1] because he is psychologically abnormal.

In the sphere of politics there is something terribly inhuman in the logic of the minds of men and conduct of affairs in certain states of Europe. And I am less terrified by the theories of Fascism and Communism than by the fanatical spirit which infuses them and the method by which men push their theories

---

[1] A thought expressed in an essay directed against the social-reformer Premier Wang Anshih, said to be written by Su Tungp'o's father.

doggedly to logical absurdities. The result is a confusion of values, a weird mixing-up of politics with anthropology, art with propaganda, patriotism with science, government with religion, and, above all, an entire upset of the proper relationship between the claims of the state and the claims of the individual. Only an insane type of mind can erect the state into a god and make of it a fetish to swallow up the individual's right of thinking, feeling and the pursuit of happiness.

Communism and Fascism are both products of the same mind. As Albert Pauphilet says, "No type of mind is so like the extreme right as the extreme left." Characteristic of both regimes and ideologies are, firstly, the sheer belief in force and power, which I regard as the most stupid and shallow manifestation of the Western mind, and secondly, the belief in logical necessity, for, after all, Fascism, as much as Communism, is based on the Marxian dialectic, which ultimately is based on the logic of Hegel. Would that someone realized how man in the second quarter of the twentieth century is suffering for the sins in logic of his fathers, committed some hundred years ago!

In a sense we may say that to-day Europe is not ruled by the reasonable spirit, nor even by the spirit of reason, but rather by the spirit of fanaticism. Looking at the picture of Europe to-day gives one a feeling of nervousness, a nervousness which comes not so much from the mere presence of conflicts of national aims and state boundaries and colonial claims, which the spirit of reason should be amply able to deal with, but rather from the condition of mind of the men who are the rulers of Europe. It is like getting into a taxicab in a strange city and being suddenly overcome by a distrust of the driver. It is not so bad that the driver doesn't seem to be acquainted with the map of the city and cannot take one to his destination by the proper route; it is more alarming when the passenger in the back seat hears the driver talk incoherently and begins to suspect his sobriety. That nervousness is decidedly heightened when the inebriate driver is armed with a gun and the passenger has no chance of getting out. One has reason to believe that this caricature of the human mind is not the human mind itself, that these are mere aberrations, mere stages of temporary insanity, which will burn themselves out like all waves of pestilence. One has reason to express a reassurance in the capacities of the human mind, to believe that the human mortal mind, limited as it is, is something infinitely higher than the intellect of the reckless drivers of Europe, and that eventually we shall be able to live peaceably because we shall have learned to think reasonably.

APPENDIX A

CERTAIN CHINESE NAMES

Chinese scholars always have several names: a personal name (*ming*), a literary name or courtesy name (*tse*), and a fancy name (*hao*), given by themselves or by others. In the course of life, as their taste develops and their wisdom deepens, they often take a fancy to a certain word or phrase fraught with meaning, and give themselves another name to indicate their spiritual progress or a particular meaningful experience: hence a person may have several *hao,* or fancy names. In addition to this, an illustrious person is often addressed by his birthplace, and the great have posthumous titles conferred upon them. Hence the bewildering confusion of names for students of Chinese history and literature. It is impossible to stick consistently to either the personal name or the literary name in this book, because it is neither natural nor advisable. Some are better known by their fancy names, and others by their first names; these things simply happen, and the natural thing to do is to use that particular name which is the most common form of reference in Chinese. If one refers to Mi Fei as Mi Fei, he will have to, for consistency's sake, refer to Su Tungp'o as Su Shih, or Li Chowu as Li Chih, which is simply not being done. And no one, of course, can consistently refer to Confucius as K'ung Ch'iu and Laotse as Li Erh.

Hence the following table for reference, which is not meant to be complete, but gives only the more important historical persons referred to in this book. I have thought it convenient to give their dates also. Surnames are in capitals. (*) indicates the name commonly used in the book.

In Chinese usage, the surname stands before the personal name.

Name and Surname	Literary Name	Fancy Name, etc.	Dates
CHANG Tai*	Tsungtse	T'ao-an	Ca. 1600
CHANG Ch'ao*	Shanlai	Hsintsai	Ca. 1676
CH'EN Chiju*	Chunghsün	Meikung*	1558-1639
CH'EN Yün*	Suchen		1763-1803
CHENG Hsieh	K'ehjou	Panch'iao* ("Wooden Bridge")	1693-1765
CHENG Hsüan	K'angch'eng*		127-200
CHIANG T'an*	Aich'ing		1st half XIX cen.
CHIN Wei	Jenjui	Shengt'an* ("The Sigh of the Sages")	d. 1661
CHUANG Chou		Chuangtse*, Ch'iyüan	d. ca. 275 B.C.
HSIEH Lingyün*		K'anglo	385-433?
HSÜ Wei	Wench'ang*		1521-1593
HUANG T'ingchien	Luchih	Ch'ingt'en ("Green-Vine Mountain Man")	1045-1105
KUAN Ing	Ch'iufu*	Shanku* ("Recluse of the Valley")	1st half XIX cen.
K'UNG Chi	Tsesse*		492-431 B.C.
K'UNG Ch'iu	Chungni	K'ungfutse, Confucius* ("Master K'ung")	551-479 B.C.
LI Chih	Chowu*	Wenling	Ca. 1567
LI Ch'ingchao*		Yi-an* ("Ease and Peace Recluse")	1081-after 1141
LI Erh	Jan	Laotse*, Laojan	571?-? B.C.
LI Yü	Chünfu	Liweng* ("Old Man with Bamboo Hat")	1611-1679
LIN Pu	T'aipo	Hoching* ("Peace and Quiet"—posthumous)	967-1028
LI Po*		Ch'inglien ("Green Lotus")	701-762

LIU Tsungyüan*	Tsehou	Liuchou (official post)	773-819
MAO Hsiang	Pichiang*	Ch'aomin ("Cave-dweller")	1611-1693
MI Fei*	Yüanchang	Mi Tien ("Mi the Crazy One"—nickname)	1051-1107
MENG K'o	Tseyü	Mengtse, Mencius*	372-289 B.C.
PO (PAI) Chüyi*	Lot'ien	Hsiangshan	772-846
SHEN Fu	Sanpo*		1763-after 1808
SU Shih	Tsechan	Tungp'o* ("Recluse of Eastern Hillside")	1036-1101
SSEMA Ch'ien*	Tsech'ang	T'aishihkung ("Great Historian")	145 B.C.-after 85 B.C.
T'AO Chi'en	Yüanming*	Liangchieh ("Brilliant Integrity"—posthumous)	372-427
TU Fu*	Tsemei	Kungpu (official rank)	712-770
T'U Lung*	Ch'angch'ing		Ca. 1592
WANG Anshih*	Chiehfu	Ch'ihshui	1021-1086
WANG Ch'ung*	Chungjen	Chingkung	27-after 107
WANG Hsichih*	Yishao	Yuchün (official rank)	321-379
YEN Huei*	Tseyen	Hsitsai	521-490 B.C.
YEN Yüan*	Yishih		1635-1704
YÜAN Hungtao*	Chunglang*	Shihkung ("Master Rock")	Ca. 1600
YÜAN Mei	Tsets'ai*	Suiyüan ("Let-It-Be Garden")	1716-1797
YÜAN Tsi*	Ts'etsung	Puping (military rank)	210-263

APPENDIX B

A CHINESE CRITICAL VOCABULARY

In my efforts at translation of Chinese literature, for instance in the translation of *The Epigrams of Chang Ch'ao,* I have constantly run across phrases or terms that are extremely difficult to render into English. This has made me think that perhaps a list of Chinese critical terms with explanatory comments will be both useful and enlightening. It will also be enlightening because the Chinese critics seem to have evolved a technique for the enjoyment of nature and art and literature, and an examination of their critical vocabulary will reveal this technique and their æsthetic feelings about things. One is often forced to write bad English in trying to express such Chinese æsthetic ideas or notions, as for instance when one speaks of "enjoying the snow," "singing the wind," "awaiting the moon," "playing water," "facing wine," "sleeping flowers," "pacing the moonlight," "pacing spring," "pillowing water," "lying down travelling," and so on. One needs to explain that "awaiting the moon" means that one goes out to the courtyard after supper to look at the crescent moon, but it has not yet come up and so one has to wait for it, or that "lying down travelling" means mentally travelling while lying in bed. And when one speaks of "the moon being suspended at the roof-corner" or "over the tree-tops," of course the phrase is figurative. But there are more abstract and elusive ideas that are more difficult to paraphrase, as for instance when a Chinese artist speaks of the "five grades of *ch'ing*" ("purity"): "pure and inspired," as when one looks at the moon over the hills and is disgusted with the busy life and thinks of going away to be a recluse; "pure and charming," as when one has books in one's study and has flowers

[442]

well arranged in his vase; "pure and poor," as when one is somewhat sad and forlorn living out in a dreary valley and forsaken
by his relatives; "pure and crazy," as when one loves secluded
spots and rare persons and books; and "pure and rare," as when one
has read the classics of the ages and finds himself at home among
rocks and springs, and "his writing smells of haze and coloured
clouds, and his conduct is far removed from the dusts of the busy
world."

I am trying in the following to interpret briefly some of these
æsthetic notions under seven heads. First, the emotions and
personality of the man; second, æsthetic notions borrowed from
physical objects in general; third, types of beauty characteristic
of spring; fourth, types of beauty characteristic of summer;
fifth, types of beauty characteristic of autumn; sixth, types of
beauty characteristic of winter; seventh, the beauty of perfect
naturalness, which is the highest form of beauty attainable by
human artists. The list is, of course, far from complete and deals
chiefly with the most characteristic æsthetic ideas. But while an
intensive study of this critical vocabulary will increase one's
understanding and enjoyment of Chinese paintings, a great
majority of the terms have moral connotations also. All human
personalities can be described in æsthetic terms, and they usually
are in the Chinese language.[1]

1. *The Perceiving Artist*

All painting, all poetry and all art are based upon two elements,
which are called, in Chinese, *ching* (No. 31) or the scene, the
picture; the *ch'ing* (No. 16), or the sentiment or mood of man.

A. *Expressions concerning man's style and specific charms of culture:*

1. 韻   *yün*: originally meaning "rhyme," now meaning "charm."
   A man without charm is said to be without *yün*. It is
   used in connection with word No. 2 in the phrase
   fengyün, or "wind charm," meaning "charm of atmosphere"

[1] I have not indicated the tone marks, as this book is for the general reader.

or "style." In combination with *ch'i* in the phrase *ch'iyün* (*ch'i*, No. 40, meaning "atmosphere"), it expresses the highest aim of Chinese painters, "rhythmic vitality."

2. 風 *feng*: wind or style. *Fengtiao* means "the style" of a person or of a work of art. *Fengyüeh* ("wind and moon") means "sentimental subjects." *Fengkeh* means "style and character."

3. 調 *tiao*: tune or style, as explained under *fengtiao* (No. 2).

4. 態 *t'ai*: expression of a man or a woman, particularly in the phrase *tset'ai* or *t'aitu,* which means "attitude," physical or spiritual.

5. 姿 *tse*: charm of expression, especially of a winning woman, but also of graceful writing.

6. 致 *chih*: really impossible to translate, originally meaning "fine and delicate lines," now meaning "the quality of being interesting to look at," also "beauty," "flavour," "whimsical charm," "delicate charm." When a man or a writing has delicate charm, we say that he or it has *chih,* or *fengchih.* Quite close to No. 19.

7. 雅 *ya*: refined, elegant, not vulgar, exquisite. *Yajen* means "a charming or cultured scholar." In general, *ya* is contrasted with *shu* or "vulgar." When one drinks tea at a famous spring sitting on a rock with bare feet, it is said to be *ya.* This elegance is always genteel: *wenya, erhya,* both mean "genteel elegance."

8. 騷 *sao*: poetic, sentimental. A poet is called *saojen,* or "sentimental person." *Fengsao* means "amorous."

9. 逸 *yi*: romantic, detached from life, fugitive, leisurely. One can be *ch'ingyi* or "pure and romantic," *kaoyi* or "high and romantic," *k'uangyi* or "expansive and romantic." This is the quality of people who have seen through life and begin to take it easy and leisurely. It is also an important quality of painting. It is understood that all these words in this list can be used indifferently as nouns or adjectives, and sometimes as verbs. *Ch'aoyi* is "to be superior" or "to soar above the common man" or "to be eminent."

10. 達 *ta*: the quality of understanding and consequent ability to take things lightly. A man who takes anything too seriously, or is too deeply involved in business, is "not *ta*" or "*puta*." *Takuan* means "to have seen through life," which enables a man to be less ambitious and put up with temporary disadvantages or obscurity and poverty. But *ta* doesn't necessarily mean "escape"; it simply means "understanding." One can "*ta* the human heart" or "the ways of the world." Again *tach'ing* represents the highest ideal of Confucian moral and political philosophy and means "to enable men and women to satisfy their emotions or sentiments."

11. 通 *t'ung*: similar in meaning to *ta*, with specific variations. *T'ungta* means "to have understanding" of the human heart, or of any particular subject. A man who has understanding is called either *t'ungjen* or *tajen*; *t'ungjen* also specifically refers to a man who has read a great deal and thought things through. Originally *t'ung* meant "to go through" or "have a clear passage." A stupid man is said to have "an unclear passage in his stomach or intestines." It is interesting to note that to be *t'ung* is regarded generally as the criterion and real aim of education. We usually ask, "Has So-and-so read his books *t'ung*?", "Is his writing already *t'ung*?" meaning thereby whether he has reached a point where he has got his ideas in order and adopted an intelligent attitude toward things. Hence a piece of writing which shows muddled thoughts or superficial or involved ideas or is unidiomatic in language, is said to be "not *t'ung*" or "*put'ung*." This is the quality of muddle-headedness. On the other hand, a man who has thought things through and is able therefore to take things lightly or who shows quick comprehension is said to be *t'ungt'uo* (*t'uo* meaning "casting off").

APPENDIX B

B. *Concerning one's talent or character or spirit:*

12　才　*ts'ai*: talent, inborn capacity. The notion is originally
derived from "timber," from which wooden vessels are
made. There are different kinds of talent, *e.g.*, poetic
talent (*shihts'ai*), talent for painting (*huats'ai*). *Ch'ingts'ai*
or "pure talent" corresponds to the English word "talent"
and *ch'its'ai* or "rare talent" corresponds nearly to the
English word "genius," which is also expressed by
tients'ai or "heavenly talent." *Ts'aitse,* "a talented man," is
an important notion going with *chiajen* or "a beautiful
woman." The notion is that a talented scholar must go
with a beautiful woman. Talented girls or women are
known as *ts'ainü*. *Ts'aitiao* means "talent and style."
Ts'aich'i (*ch'i*: vessel) means "talent with regard to its
competence" for big or small jobs. A man whose
ts'aich'i is small is not qualified for big jobs, and will not
be able to get or hold them simply because of deficiencies
in his own character.

13.　品　*p'in*: character, personality, grade, quality. A painter
must have good *jenp'in,* or "human personality." *P'inkeh*
means "moral character." *P'in* is also a verb; "to *p'in*
tea" is to sample its flavour, or merely to drink in a quiet
and leisurely manner. More fully explained in the
section, "Art as Play and Personality."

14.　神　*shen*: spirit. When a man or a piece of writing lacks
spirit or expression, he or it is said to lack *shents'ai*
("spirit and colour"). *Shench'i* means "spirit and force"
or "forceful expression" or "dignity." There was a
school of Chinese poetry, called "the school of *shenyün*,"
with emphasis on the elusive qualities of charm and
spirit. A man or woman with a charming spirit is said
to have *shenyün*.

C. *Concerning human emotions and feelings:*

15.　意　*yi*: mood, inclination, intention. The intention of a painter or calligraphist, or his general conception preceding his brushwork, is spoken of as *piyi* or "intention of the brush." This "intention" is often attributed to nature, as when we say that "the skies have *yüyi*" or "intention to rain"; or that "there is a *ch'iuyi* or intention or spirit of autumn," when at the end of summer we feel there is a chill in the air and leaves are beginning to turn golden. Similarly there is *ch'unyi* or "intention of spring," when the ice begins to melt and the flowers are getting ready to put forth buds.

16. 情 *ch'ing*: sentiment, passion, love, sympathy, friendly feeling. To be able to understand people or the human heart is "to know *jench'ing* or human sentiments." Any man who is inhuman, who is over-austere, or who is an ascetic is said to be *puchin jench'ing*, or "to have departed from human nature or human sentiments." Any philosophy which has departed from human sentiments is a false philosophy, and any political regime which goes against one's natural human instincts, religious, sexual, or social, is doomed to fall. A piece of writing must have both beauty of language and beauty of sentiment (*wen ch'ing ping mou*). A man who is cold or hard-hearted or disloyal is said to be *wuch'ing*, or "to have no heart." He is a worm, or "he has a heart and intestines made of iron and stone."

17. 腸 *ch'ang*: intestines, feelings, emotions. One who is very sad is said to have "his intestines broken," or "tied up into a hundred knots." These intestines are broad or narrow, depending on whether a man is generous or mean. A man whose ideas run dry and who constantly stops during writing is said to have "dried-up intestines."

18. 興 *hsing*: inspiration, happy mood, enthusiasm to do something. One can have *shih-hsing*, or "mood for poetry," or *chiuhsing*, or "mood for drinking." This mood is either deep or shallow. It is an important element of poetry.

19. 趣 *ch'ü*: interesting, having flavour, the quality of being

[447]

interesting to look at. A scene or a man possesses or lacks this *ch'ü*. In particular, *ch'ü* denotes an artistic pleasure, like drinking tea, or watching clouds. A vulgar person is not supposed to "understand *ch'ü*."

20. 思 *sse*: thought, longing, idea. In judging a piece of writing, we say the author's *wensse*, or "the flow of his thoughts" or "literary ideas," is good or bad. One can have "spring thoughts or sentiments" (*ch'unsse*), or "autumn thoughts or sentiments" (*ch'iusse*).

21. 慕 *mu*: ⎫ closely related to this notion of *sse* are different
22. 怨 *yüan*: ⎟ peculiar sentiments. *Mu*, loving admiration,
23. 憐 *lien*: ⎬ longing from a distance; *yüan*, fretting, com-
24. 恨 *hen*: ⎟ plaining, hating; and particuarly three charming
25. 惜 *hsi*: ⎭ words, *lien*, pity, tender love, love for what is small and beautiful; *hen*, regret, exasperation, hating the beloved; *hsi*, be tender, be careful in spending, be worried lest something is spoiled or gone. All these verbs can be used with reference to women, children, flowers or spring. Thus one can "hate the spring" for being so short, "regret spring" for arriving so late, "be sparing of spring," lest it be spoiled, or "mourn the spring," which means to be caught with "spring fever," or feel lonely and sad, or to long for the absent lover.

D. *Some general ideas about culture:*

26. 福 *fu*: luck, predestined happiness. A man born into this world is supposed to have a definite quantity of luck awarded to him for his enjoyment, and some people have more than others. A man whose children die young, or a man who has a beautiful country home but is unable to live in it, is said to have "no luck to enjoy them." On the other hand, a man who enjoys too much, or who enjoys inordinately, or enjoys what is not appropriate, as, for instance, receiving a kowtow from an elderly gentleman older than himself, is said thus to *chehfu*, or "curtail his luck," or shorten his life.

27. 緣 *yüan*: a happy predestination, predestined matrimony between two persons. A man may desire to marry a girl, but unless he has *yüan* or *yinyüan,* he can never succeed. Other people who have this *yinyüan* will fall in love at first sight and get married in spite of all obstacles. A *yüanchia* (*yüan* written with another character) means "predestined enemy," *i.e.,* lover.

28. 識 *shih*: judgment, insight, taste. This is contrasted with mere scholarship or learning: *hsüeh*. A man who is learned and has erudition but lacks insight or judgment or good taste in knowledge is an inferior kind of a scholar, as explained in the section "Good Taste in Knowledge." It comes also in the phrase *shihchien,* or *chienshih,* which means still the same thing.

29. 道 *Tao*: the Way, truth, religion—really untranslatable. This is the *Tao* of Taoism, generally signifying the ways or laws of nature itself, and the object of human wisdom is to fall in line with *Tao* or the ways and laws of Nature and live in harmony with them. A man who achieves this happy state is said "to have attained the Tao," or *tehtao*. Closely related to *tehtao* is *tseteh,* or "to have found oneself." One who has found *Tao* thereby finds himself also. *Tseteh,* or "to have found oneself," means "to be happy."

In contrast to these approved cultured qualities, there are a few expressing disapproval worthy of mention. Some of these are: *fu* (rotten, musty), *yü* (strait-jacket), *suan* (sour) all refer to the doctrinaire and slavish follower of rules and conventions; *suan,* or "sour," in particular refers to "pedantry." *Pan* (wooden), *chih* (straight) and *tai* (stagnant) refer to "stiffness" of style or conduct. *Lu* (colloquially pronounced *lou* at Peking, meaning "exposed") refers to "inartistic plainness" in writing, or painting, or diplomacy. A good boxer is said to be "not *lou*" or *pulou, i.e.,* he never lets people know how good he is until the occasion comes for putting his skill into use. The first condition in the training of a boxer is "never to swagger." *Fou,* from the idea "floating on water," means superficiality plus instability, lack of depth and lack of seriousness. *Lou, shu, p'i* are common terms for "vulgarity" in contrast to *ya*, "refinement" or "elegance." This seems especially to refer to the uncultured state, like unweeded ground, as in the saying of a Chin scholar that "after having not seen a certain cultured friend for three days, one's *p'ilou*, or vulgarity, sprouts up again."

II. *Æsthetic notions borrowed from physical objects in general:*

30. 文 *wen:* originally "grains of pebbles, ripples on water, waving lines of objects (*e.g.*, brocade)," now meaning "literature." The fundamental idea is the natural lines of movement or beauty of lines and form, and when applied to writing, it refers to the movement of one's thoughts and language. We speak also of the "whirls" or "eddies" of one's literary composition (*wenchang p'olan*), describing the curious overlapping and back-and-forth twists and turns of the author's thoughts. In addition, there is the idea of decoration or refinement, as contained in the idea of "dress," and particularly of brocade or embroidery. In connection with *wen*, the idea of *tsao* "water-cress" refers to the "embellishments" or "intrinsic beauties" of a writer's language.

31. 景 *ching:* a picture, a scene, particularly a beautiful scene, as of summer clouds or stars at night. This idea of "picture" is highly subjective, and borrows its charm from human thoughts and sentiments. If one determines to see a thing as a picture, then it becomes a picture. A story of convalescence or of a night on the desert or storm at sea is often more beautiful than the experience itself.

32. 光 *kuang:* light. This is an elusive quality, *e.g.*, "the light of water," or "light of spring." Connected with the following.

33. 彩 *ts'ai:* colour, a group of bright colours, brilliance. A piece of writing may be lacking in brilliance or *kuangts'ai*. One can have, of course, "literary brilliance," "moral

brilliance" ("shining virtue") and brilliance in the quality of ink and pigment in a painting.

34. 味　*wei*: flavour, smell. Good flavour is what is good to "ruminate on"; it is "deep and long"; and it is usually mild. A superficial book or saying is therefore lacking in *wei,* because it does not stand "ruminating." *Hueiwei,* or "back flavour" or "return flavour," is felt a while after eating olives or tasting tea. A man may lack "flavour" (or be uninteresting) and friendship can smell sweet.

35. 影　*ying*: shadow, image in a mirror, reflection in water; that which suggests the original. In the novel *Red Chamber Dream,* certain maids are the shadows, *yingtse,* of certain higher-class girls, being alike in quality, like minor flowers besides the chief flowers in a vase. A character in a novel is also said to be the "shadow" of a real person, its original.

36. 境　*ching*: a state, a condition, particularly of living, and as felt by the person; atmosphere created in a painting or a poem; often *chingchieh.* *Yiching* (*yi,* No. 15), literally "condition of mind," is a mood or atmosphere created by art, which is very important in poetry; otherwise also expressed as *shenching*, or literally "spiritual atmosphere."

37. 理　*li*: reason, inner order, inner form, inner nature of things. Subjective painters (particularly of Sung Dynasty) would emphasize this *li.* Closely related to *wen* (No. 30), especially in the phrase *wenli* (also name of the classical language), *wen* denoting the form and *li* denoting the substance of thought, or its movement.

38. 體　*t'i*: body, literally and figuratively, general shape, framework, structure.

39. 骨　*ku*: bone, skeleton, inner being, as contrasted with temporary appearances. The important thing is what a man has got "in his bones," *e.g.,* as a democrat or aristocrat, or hedonist. The underlying philosophy or attitude of a writer provides "the bones" for his writings, and a superficial writer touching on trivial topics may

have no "bones" at all. In calligraphy, *ku,* or *kuchia,* means the basic framework or pattern of a character, as contained in a few main supporting strokes.

40. 氣 *ch'i*: spirit, force, ether, gas, general atmosphere. There are *ch'unch'i* (spirit or atmosphere of spring), *ch'iuch'i* (spirit or atmosphere of autumn), and an old man may have *laoch'i* if he tries too often to remind people of his age and authority. Like the spirit of the seasons, the *ch'i* of a ruling dynasty may wax and wane; when this *ch'i* is on the decline, everything goes wrong, *e.g.,* there may be no heirs. *Yüanch'i* means "vital force" in the universe and in an individual, and one should do well to nourish or cherish it. A literary or artistic masterpiece is supposed to have stolen the secrets of nature, thus "leaking out the *yüanch'i,*" and it is a thing not to be attempted too often. In connection with *yün* (fate), *ch'iyün,* or the dominant fate of a person or house, is something which "goes round," precipitating different happenings at different appointed times (see also under No. 1). Thus a man may have *ts'aich'i* (money *ch'i*) which is good or bad for a certain year, determining whether he is going to make or lose money. It is an important teaching both of Confucianism and Taoism to *yangch'i* or "nourish this *ch'i,*" by being kind, or generous, or not overworking oneself, or not talking too much.

41. 力 *li*: energy, force. A writing or painting may or may not have energy, shown as force, expressed as *ch'ili.*

42. 勢 *shih*: gesture, posture, social position, battle formation, that which gives advantage of position in any struggle. This notion is extremely important and is connected with every form of dynamic beauty, as against mere beauty of static balance. Thus a rock may have a "rock posture," an outstretching branch has its own branch posture (which may be good or bad, elegant or ordinary); and there are "stroke posture," "character posture," and

"brush posture" in writing and painting and "posture of a hill," "posture of a cloud," etc. A hill which has an embracing or encircling gesture (*huanpao*) is said to be elegant. A situation is conceived as static, while a *shih* denotes that which the situation is going to become, or "the way it looks": one speaks of the *shih* of wind, rain, flood, or battle, as the way the wind, rain, flood or battle looks for the future, whether increasing or decreasing in force, stopping soon or continuing indefinitely, gaining or losing, in what direction, with what force, etc.

III. *Types of beauty characteristic of spring:*

Of the types of beauty modally associated with the different seasons, those of spring and summer are comparatively less striking and peculiar as æsthetic notions than those of autumn and winter. Most of these words are used indifferently as adjectives and nouns.

43. 明 *ming*: bright (a bright moon, a brightly dressed woman). We speak of "bright hills and graceful waters," *shan ming shui hsiu*. Cf. *mei* below.

44. 媚 *mei*: seductive, enticing, beauty of softness. This quality is frequently applied to women, the moon and flowers, and even rivers. "When the rocks contain jade, the hill becomes *hui* (shining); and when the water contains pearls, the river becomes *mei* (enticing)," according to Lu Chi.

45. 嬌 *chiao*: beautiful and helpless, enticing—rather similar to the above word *mei*.

46. 秀 *hsiu*: delicate, graceful, slender and beautiful. A type of beauty symbolized by the bamboo. A girl or woman must, above all, have "an air of delicacy," or *hsiuch'i*. For a woman without this air of delicacy (*e.g.*, one who talks in a loud voice), time spent in beauty parlours is wasted. Nothing can be done about a loud-voiced woman. Certain kinds of trees and rivers also have this delicate beauty.

47. 妍 *yen*: smilingly or elegantly pretty—mostly of flowers, also of women and water or hills.

48. 豔 *yen*: voluptuous, gorgeously beautiful, dazzlingly beautiful, passionate. *E.g.*, the peony, Mae West.

49. 潤 *lun*: lustrous, smooth to the touch, kind to the throat, nourishing as of liquids, not harsh. Thus the colour or light of good jade is said to be *lun,* or lustrous. As a verb, the rain *lun,* or nourishes, the fields, and almond soup nourishes the throat. A forest newly bathed in rain is then spoken of as *kuanglun,* bright and lustrous. This is an atmospheric quality.

50. 靈 *ling (huo, shengch'i, shengtung)*: vitality characteristic of
  （活, spring. A picture is *linghuo* when it is vitally alive.
  生氣, "Stuffiness" of composition prevents this. Hence the
  生動） important notion *k'ungling,* "empty and alive," a quality aimed at in good paintings and rockeries by the generous use of space.

IV. *Types of beauty characteristic of summer:*

In general, summer suggests luxuriance and full power. Some of the notions classified under summer, like *ch'i, ts'iao* (Nos. 57, 59), can just as well belong to autumn.

51. 華 *hua*: flowery, floral splendour. The "Flowery Kingdom." A pretty composition without substance is said to be "flowery without seeds," "seeds" being associated with the autumn harvest (see No. 72).

52. 茂 *mou*: rich, luxuriant—of trees, forests and sentiments.

53. 暢 *ch'ang*: luxuriant, forceful in expression, thoroughly enjoyable. Originally of plants, now of literary compositions. Such *ch'ang* compositions can cure one's headache, as was said of Ch'en Lin's philippic. One feels a pleasure of relief when our instincts are satisified and feelings well expressed.

54. 偉 *wei*: great, grand. In the usual English sense. This and the following four words are usually used together in varying combinations.

[454]

55. 渾 *hun*: whole, strong, massive—of writing which is deep and mature and brushwork which is massive.

56. 雄 *hsiung*: heroic, powerful, majestic.

57. 奇 *ch'i*: rare—really an untranslatable word. Literally, it means "remarkable," "strange," "extraordinary," but it has definite associations not fully expressed by the word "remarkable." There must go with it a subjective love of the unusual, the unconventional and the unattainable by common men. A *ch'ishu* is more than a "remarkable book": it is one of the few world masterpieces not to be duplicated. "Rare" comes nearest to it. Tired of the humdrum world and the common run of men and things, one is on the look-out for *ch'i* or "rare" books, rocks, peaks, flowers, perfumes, delicacies, jewels, curios, etc.

58. 壯 *chuang*: strong, powerful. The combination *peichuang,* "sad and strong," denotes the tragic mood.

59. 峭 *ts'iao*: steep, rugged, abrupt—of landscapes and literary manner.

60. 危 *wei*: literally "dangerous," but really "awe-inspiring." Thus a flimsy wooden bridge across a deep ravine or an overhanging precipice is *wei* or delicious to look at.

61. 豪 *hao* (*fang*): the chivalrous mood, free and nonchalant, (放) unrestrained. Two types of poetic manner are distinguished, the *haofang* or the romantic, expansive style of Li Po, and *wanyüeh,* or the quiet, restrained style of Tu Fu. In this connection there are a number of expressions rather often used in Chinese biographies in praise of romantic persons: *t'it'ang,* ("unconventional"), *t'ungt'uo* ("emancipated"), *puchi* ("unbridled"), etc. A poet or writer writing with the full sweep and mastery of his powers is compared to "a celestial horse galloping in the sky."

V. *Types of beauty characteristic of autumn:*

In general, the autumn season stands for simplicity, maturity and conservation; in contrast to summer luxuriance, an autumn scene suggests ethereal thinness, crispness and the penetrating, yet exhilarating, coolness of the autumn wind. Here the image of a clear autumn moon and an enticing autumn lake undoubtedly plays an important role. Autumn also suggests the tragic mood. In autumn, one is also supposed to have outgrown the luxuriance of summer and begun to love simplicity, peace and contentment. Like the farmer, one no longer tills and no longer runs about in the scorching sun, but begins to *gather in and take stock of what he has got*. If we could only learn to live our life in harmony with the rhythm of nature! But we will not. We want to run for ever in the scorching sun.

The feeling for the dreary beauty of autumn was perfectly expressed by one of the great Yüan dramatists:

> Dry vines, old trees, evening crows—
> Small bridge, flat banks, water flows—
> Old road, slim horse, west wind blows—
> And as the sun westward sets,
> Forlorn love, far away, no one knows!

62. 淡 *tan*: mild, pale in colour, as of a misty lake. Probably the quality in a painting or writing that gives the greatest pleasure to a man of mature taste is *ch'ingtan* (lucid and mild), *p'ingtan* ("even and mild," the natural aroma of simple writing), or *tanyüan* (*yüan*, No. 65; mild-toned and "distant" in perspective, either in painting or in style of thought). A man of a retiring mild temperament is *t'ientan* (quiet and easily contented, or loving simple joys); he adopts an attitude toward money and fame described as *tanpo* (mild and thin).

63. 樸 *p'u*: simple in taste, unadorned, unsophisticated, close to nature. *Shunp'u* (unspoiled and simple) describes the simple character and ways of living of the ancient people, characterized by natural hospitality and kindness, being yet unspoiled by civilization. Its importance has been indicated throughout this book.

64. 高 *kao* (*shen*): high, ethereal, fine (*kao*), and deep (*shen*).

(深) One speaks of "high autumn," which in sentiment is akin to high-mindedness (*kaoyi*, "high and romantic"). A man's ambition or interest is said to be *kaoyüan*, "high and distant," if he aims at the superior things of the spirit. Or it is *kaok'uang* (see No. 65), which can be used of an autumn landscape and a high- and broad-minded person.

65. 曠 *k'uang* (*yüan*): broad-minded, emancipated, expansive in
   (遠) nature (of person) or in view (of landscape). *Yüan* means distant, having a distant perspective. *K'uanghuai* is to have an "expansive breast" or to take a detached view of life.

66. 蕭 *hsiao* (*su*): thin and sparse, like an autumn forest, dreary.
   (疏) Closely connected with the idea of *tan* or "mildness," as in the phrase *sutan*, "sparse and mild-toned," as autumn trees ought to be painted. Often an autumn landscape must be appreciated for its dreariness, as in the poem of Ma Chihyüan quoted above. What is often described as *ch'iuyi*, or "intention or spirit of autumn," is just this quality.

67. 瘦 *sou*: thin, slender. This is a strangely beautiful word in the Chinese language. Slender rocks and bamboos are always painted together. It expresses non-sensuous beauty.

68. 簡 *chien*: simple, few in words or strokes. The ideal political condition is described as a state when the "administration is simple (*chien*) and punishments are light." The opposite conception is *fan*, or complicated, *e.g.*, the income tax. *Chientan* again means "simple and mild." A writer who does not use too many words is said to have the *chientan* (terse and mild) quality.

69. 清 *ch'ing*: clear, lucid, pure, clean, not profuse, not obstructed, not burdened with details, like an autumn landscape. *Ch'ingliang* (clear and cool), *ch'ingtan* (lucid and mild), *ch'ingp'in* (pure and poor), are common combinations. *Ch'inghsin* (clean and novel) expresses the quality of "originality" or "freshness" in thought or expression.

70. 閒 *hsien*: leisure, leisurely. A very much used word. Thus one's "hands" and "mind" can both be "leisurely," or the hands may be leisurely while the mind is busy, or the mind may be leisurely while one's hands are busy. Directions are given by Ch'en Meikung's son on what scholars should do in the different situations. Other expressions are: "leisurely affairs" (*hsienshih*), "leisurely conversation" (*hsient'an*), "leisurely sentiments" (*hsiench'ing*), "leisurely gossip" (*hsienhua*), "luck of leisure" (*hsienfu*), "leisurely pleasures" (*hsiench'ü*). *Ch'inghsien* means both to "enjoy the luck of leisure" and (euphemistically) "to be unemployed." Li Liweng's book on the art of living is called *Hsiench'ing Ouchi* (*Casual Occupations of Leisurely Sentiments*). "To kill time" is expressed by *hsiaohsien*, or to "consume" leisure.

71. 涼 *liang* (*shuang*): nice and cool, mainly associated with the
(爽) disappearance of heat or any sort of oppressiveness. A philosophy of detachment is compared to a "dose of cooling medicine." A man who readily complies with a request for help, or signs a contract without too much negotiation over terms, is said to be *shuangli*, "direct and pleasantly sharp," like the autumn wind.

72. 實 *shih*: substance, having substance; originally "seeds," characteristic of autumn. Floral language without thought is "*hua* and not *shih*"—flowers without seeds.

VI. *Types of beauty characteristic of winter*:

The beauty of winter is chiefly that of old age, of cold splendour, of quiet and seclusion.

73. 寒 *han* (*leng*): cold, poor. Opposed to heat and excitement.
(冷) *Lengyen* means "cold splendour," characteristic of the chrysanthemum and the plum flower. The white pear flowers, although appearing in spring, are said to have this quality also. *Hanching* is a comfortable state known as "cold and quiet." In the sense of winter rigour, *han* also means "poverty."

74. 靜 *ching*: quiet or quietness, solitude, serenity, a quality as much appreciated as the notion of "leisure," and often used as part of a name for a girl or a private garden. *Ch'ingching* is to have quiet and privacy, or not to have too many callers.

75. 古 *ku*: ancient, antique, of ancient times, of ancient manner, mature. Almost anything which is *ku* is good in China. An old, rugged pine tree or a simple, kind old peasant is said to have the "manner of the ancients" (*kuyi*). The notion "ancient" is also associated with "simplicity" (*kup'u*), with "elegance" (*kuya*), and with "eccentricity" (*kukuai*).

76. 老 (遒) *lao* (*mai*): old, mature, experienced. *Laolien* means "to be experienced." A mature style is said to be *laotao* ("old and having arrived"), and what seems ancient and precious is said to be *kulao*. There is a fascination about what is old, expressed by the phrase *ts'anglao,* as speaking of a big old tree.

77. 枯 *ku*: dried-up, beautifully desolate or desolately beautiful, associated with the idea of *ku* (No. 75).

78. 幽 *vu*: secluded, charming in seclusion, having the manner of a recluse, content with oneself. A charming secluded scholar is a *yujen,* and his charm is known as *yuyün*. "Secluded elegance" is expressed by *yuya*. Typical of this quality is the "secluded orchid" growing in a deserted valley, "content to smell its own lonely fragrance."

79. 隱 (含蓄) *wen* (*hanhsü*): recluse, hidden from the world, hidden in meaning, not exposed to the public. True wisdom is that which conceals wisdom; as Laotse expressed it, "Great wisdom is like stupidity." True art conceals art. Good writing leaves something unsaid for the reader to think about. The opposite quality, *lou,* or "exposed," is a sign of immaturity, or of downright vulgarity.

80. 拙 (愚) *chüeh* (*yü*): the beauty of stupidity as typified by rocks and tree-roots, often selected for enjoyment. Rocks seem to typify an absolute return to nature. This is but

an extreme formulation of the worship of non-sensuous beauty, as a reaction to the worship of sensuous beauty, *e.g.*, the beauty of flowers. There are types of calligraphy which purposely aim at being *chüeh* (stupid), or *kuchüeh* (ancient and stupid), which shows really a greater refinement of spirit than the love of sensuous calligraphy. This type of calligraphy would imitate the lines of rocks, gnarled roots and dried-up vines.

VII. *The beauty of complete naturalness*:

The highest art is like nature. Hence all traces of "axe- and chisel-marks" must be obliterated. Such works can only be done by a master, with complete seeming artlessness and absence of effort, as in a poem where we feel there is no labour at embellishments, because the simple beauty of the sentiments is absolutely adequate.

81. 化 *hua*: changed, transformed, with all artificiality obliterated. This is the highest praise that can be given a poem or a painting. Sometimes *shenhua* is used, meaning "divinely transformed." This is far higher praise than other epithets like *miao* (exquisite), *neng* (clever). In grading different masters or works of art, the *huap'in* or *shenp'in* grade always tops the list. One speaks of such work as done by "ghost's axe and god's craft." The best prose, like that of Su Tungp'o, is compared to "sailing clouds and flowing water," going or stopping according to their inner law.

INDEX

INDEX

[463]

INDEX

INDEX

INDEX

INDEX

INDEX

INDEX

INDEX